LENIN

COLLECTED WORKS

34

ИНСТИТУТ МАРКСИЗМА-ЛЕНИНИЗМА при ЦК КПСС

В. И. ЛЕНИН

СОЧИНЕНИЯ

Издание четвертое

ГОСУДАРСТВЕННОЕ ИЗДАТЕЛЬСТВО
ПОЛИТИЧЕСКОЙ ЛИТЕРАТУРЫ
МОСКВА

V. I. LENIN

COLLECTED WORKS

VOLUME
34

LETTERS
November 1895 – November 1911

PROGRESS PUBLISHERS
MOSCOW

TRANSLATED FROM THE RUSSIAN
BY CLEMENS DUTT
EDITED BY BERNARD ISAACS

PUBLISHERS' NOTE

Translated from the fourth Russian
edition of V. I. Lenin's *Collected Works*.
Corrections have been made in some
of the letters and notes in accordance
with the fifth Russian edition.

First printing 1966
Second printing 1974

Printed in the Union of Soviet Socialist Republics

CONTENTS

1903

1904

1905

1907

PREFACE

The thirty-fourth and thirty-fifth volumes contain Lenin's correspondence with organisations and persons—letters, telegrams and notes—during the period from 1895 to 1922.

The documents in these volumes comprise a considerable part of Lenin's correspondence and form a valuable supplement to his writings published in the preceding volumes of the *Collected Works*. These documents reflect the immense and varied activity of Lenin in building up the Bolshevik Party, a party of a new type, his irreconcilable struggle against opportunists of all shades, his struggle for the proletarian revolution, for the dictatorship of the proletariat, his leadership of the world's first Soviet socialist state.

Volume 34 includes letters of Lenin written in the period from November 1895 to November 1911.

The letters of 1895-1901 reflect Lenin's activities in building up the Social-Democratic Labour Party in Russia, his struggle against Narodism, "legal Marxism" and Economism. The letters addressed to G. V. Plekhanov, Lydia Knipovich, N. E. Bauman and others show how Lenin's plan for the creation of the first all-Russia newspaper of the revolutionary Marxists—*Iskra*—was carried out; they reveal Lenin's leading role in *Iskra*, and his struggle within the editorial board of the newspaper.

A considerable part of the volume consists of the letters of 1901-04. A group of letters of this period, addressed to G. V. Plekhanov, deal with questions concerning the drafting of the revolutionary programme of the proletarian party. In his correspondence with local committees—those of Kharkov and Nizhni-Novgorod, the St. Petersburg organisation (letters to I. V. Babushkin and others), and the

Organising Committee for convening the Second Party Congress—Lenin calls on the Social-Democratic organisations in Russia to unite on the basis of the programmatic and organisational principles of *Iskra*, and gives precise directives for developing Party work and preparing for the Party Congress. In a number of letters written after the Second Congress Lenin exposes the splitting activities of the Mensheviks, wages a relentless struggle against certain demoralised Bolsheviks (Krasin, Noskov, Galperin) who had gone over to the Mensheviks and helped them gain a majority in the Central Committee. These are his letters to the Central Committee, to the Siberian Committee, to N. Y. Vilonov, A. M. Stopani, Rozalia Zemlyachka and others.

The letters to the Caucasian Union Committee reflect Lenin's leadership of the Bolshevik organisations in the Caucasus.

The letters of the period of the first Russian revolution (1905-07) reflect Lenin's struggle for the convocation of the Third Party Congress, for the implementation of its decisions, and for the tactical principles of Bolshevism. Included here are letters to the Central Committee, S. I. Gusev, Rozalia Zemlyachka and others.

The letters of the period of Stolypin reaction reveal Lenin's struggle against liquidationism, Trotskyism, otzovism and ultimatumism, conciliation, and distortions of the theoretical principles of the revolutionary Marxist Party. This volume includes a letter to G. Y. Zinoviev in which Lenin brands Trotsky as a despicable careerist and factionalist. A number of letters published in this volume expose the international revisionists who supported the Russian Menshevik opportunists.

An important place in Lenin's correspondence of 1908-11 is occupied by his letters to Maxim Gorky.

The letters in this volume depict Lenin's struggle to create a Marxist revolutionary party, to rally the Party's forces and make the Bolsheviks an independent party, a party of a new type, a party of Leninism, a Bolshevik party.

The following letters, which have previously appeared in various publications, are included in Lenin's *Collected*

Works for the first time: to the Editorial Board of *Iskra*,
February 26, 1904; to M. K. Vladimirov, August 15, 1904;
to the Caucasian Union Committee, December 20, 1904;
to the St. Petersburg organisation of the R.S.D.L.P., October-December 1904; Letter to a Comrade in Russia, January
6, 1905; five letters to A. V. Lunacharsky, 1905, 1907 and
1908; to Maxim Gorky, February 7, 1908; to P. Yushkevich,
November 10, 1908; two letters to A. I. Lyubimov, August
and September 1909; a letter to G. Y. Zinoviev, August 24,
1909; draft of a letter to the "Trustees", February-March
1910; to N. G. Poletayev, December 7, 1910; to A. Rykov,
February 25, 1911.

Published for the first time is the letter in this volume
to G. D. Leiteisen, July 24, 1902, in which Lenin notes
the union of Russian Social-Democratic organisations
around *Iskra*.

* * *

The letters in volumes 34 and 35 are arranged in chrono-
logical order; those sent from Russia are dated according
to the old style, those sent from abroad are dated according
to the new style. Where Lenin's manuscript is undated, the
editors have given the date at the end of the letter. Each
letter has a serial number and it is stated to whom and
where it was sent, the date of writing and the address of
the sender.

Besides brief notes, each volume of the letters is provided
with an index of deciphered pseudonyms, nicknames and
initials.

1895

1
TO P. B. AXELROD[1]

You are probably cursing me for this delay. There were some good reasons for it.

I will recount them in order. First of all, I was in Vilna.* I had talks with our people about the Miscellany.[3] Most of them are agreed on the need for such a publication and promise support and supply of material. Their mood is in general sceptical (I recalled your expression about the pal.** provinces), as much as to say—we shall see whether it will correspond to agitational tactics, to the tactics of the economic struggle. I stressed that this would largely depend on us.

Further, I was in Moscow. I saw no one, for there was no trace of the "Teacher of Life". Is he all right? If you know anything about him and have an address, write to him to send it to us, otherwise we cannot find any contacts there. Great havoc has been played there,[4] but it seems that some people have survived and the work did not cease. We have material from there—a description of some strikes. If you have not had it, write and we shall send it to you.

After that I was in Orekhovo-Zuyevo. Places like this, frequently to be met with in the central industrial area, are extremely peculiar: a purely manufacturing town with tens of thousands of inhabitants, whose only means of livelihood is the mills. The mill management is the sole authority. The mill office "runs" the town. There is the sharpest division of the people into workers and bourgeois. Hence

---

* The key is the same as the one we have been using.[2]
** The word "pal." has not been deciphered.—*Ed*.

the workers' frame of mind is rather oppositional, but, after the recent smash-up there, so few of our people are left and all of them so closely watched that contacts are very difficult. However, we shall be able to deliver the literature.

Further, the delay has been due to local trouble. This also accounts for the meagreness of the material sent.

I don't like the address in Zurich. Can't you find another— not in Switzerland, but in Germany? That would be much better and safer.

Further, in sending your reply—*a book on technology*, address: Mr. Luchinsky, Alexandrovsky Iron Works, Chemical Laboratory, St. Petersburg—add, if there is room, other material: pamphlets issued in Geneva, interesting cuttings from *Vorwärts*,[5] etc. Write in detail about the Miscellany: what material there is already, what is planned, when the first issue will appear, and what exactly is lacking for the second. We shall probably send money, but later on. Reply *as quickly as possible* so that we may know whether this method is suitable.

Send the Pole a rendezvous address as quickly as possible, since we need delivery facilities. The address is: student Mikhail Leontievich Zakladny, Technological Institute, the same town, ask for Ivanov. The money for the publication in Russian of his *Geschichte*, etc., has been promised.*

Another request: we are badly in need of ink; as to what kind, you can find out from Mögli, who has it. Could you send it somehow? Is there no opportunity? Please think it over or ask your "practical men" to do so. By the way, you asked us to approach them directly. In that case, tell us: 1) do they know our method and key? 2) do they know who these letters come from?

You are now being sent: 1) information about the expulsion of the Dukhobors; 2) an account about rural workers in the south; and 3) a description of the Thornton mills— for the time being, only the beginning, about a quarter, of this is being sent.

---

* The publication and its author have not been ascertained.—*Ed.*

It is necessary to write with *Chinese ink*. Better still, add a small crystal of *potassium dïchromate* ($K_2Cr_2O_7$): then it won't wash off. Use the *thinnest paper possible*. All the best. Yours....

Regards to the comrade.

Written at the beginning of
November 1895
Sent from St. Petersburg to Zurich

First published in part in 1923
First published in full in 1924

Printed from
the original

2
TO P. B. AXELROD

We have received the Breslau report.[6] We unstuck it with great difficulty, in the course of which a large part was torn (the letter, thanks to the good paper, remained intact). Evidently you have not yet received the second letter. You must use very thin paste—not more than a teaspoonful of starch (and it must be potato starch, not wheat starch, which is too strong) to a glass of water. Ordinary (good) paste is needed only for the top sheet and coloured paper, and the paper holds well, under the action of a press, even with the thinnest paste. At any rate, the method is suitable and it should be used.

I am sending you the end of Thornton. We have material on the strike 1) at Thornton's, 2) at Laferm's, 3) on the Ivanovo-Voznesensk strike, 4) on the Yaroslavl strike (a worker's letter, very interesting), and on the St. Petersburg Boot Manufacturing Factory. I am not sending it, as we have had no time yet to copy it and because I do not count on being in time for the first issue of the Miscellany. We have established contacts with the Narodnaya Volya printing-press,[7] which has already put out three things (not ours) and has taken one of ours.* We are planning to publish a newspaper,[8] in which this material will be printed. This will be definitely settled in about $1\frac{1}{2}$ to 2 months' time. If you think the material will arrive in time for the first issue, let us know at once.

Yours,
Ilyin

Have you any difficulty in handling our parcels? We must jointly improve the method.

Written mid-November 1895
Sent from St. Petersburg to Zurich
First published in 1923

Printed from
the original

---

* Send us material, if you have any, for workers' pamphlets. They will gladly print it.

1897

3

TO P. B. AXELROD

Dear Pavel Borisovich,

I am very, very glad to have succeeded after all in getting a letter from you (I received it yesterday, i.e., August 15) and news of you and of G. V. Your and his opinions on my literary efforts* (for the workers) have been extremely encouraging. There is nothing I have wanted so much, or dreamed of so much, as an opportunity of writing for workers. But how to do this from here? It is very, very difficult, but not impossible, I think. How is the health of V. Iv.?

I know only one method—the one by which I am writing these lines.[9] The question is whether it is possible to find a copyist, who will have no easy task. You, apparently, consider it impossible and this method, in general, unsuitable. But I do not know any other.... It is a pity, but I do not despair: if one does not succeed now—one can succeed later on. Meanwhile, it would be good if you were to write occasionally by the method which you use with your "old friend".[10] That will enable us to keep in touch, which is the most important thing.

You, of course, have been told enough about me, so there is nothing to add. I live here all alone. I am quite well and occupy myself both with the journal[11] and with my big job.**

All the very best. Kind regards to V. Iv. and G. V. I have not seen Raichin for over a month. I hope to go to Minusinsk soon to see him.

Yours,

V. U.

August 16

Written August 16, 1897

Sent from the village of Shushenskoye to Zurich

First published in 1924

Printed from the copy written by A. I. Ulyanova-Yelizarova

---

* See "Explanation of the Law on Fines Imposed on Factory Workers" (present edition, Vol. 2).—*Ed.*
** Lenin was working at that time on his book *The Development of Capitalism in Russia* (see present edition, Vol. 3).—*Ed.*

1898

4

TO A. N. POTRESOV[12]

September 2, 1898

Yesterday I received your letter of August 11 with the list of books and the printed matter—the *Archiv*.[13] The article of the "eminent political economist" is highly interesting and excellently composed. The author evidently disposed of very rich material, which had luckily fallen into his hands. Generally speaking, in the journalistic field, he appears to be even a better writer than in the purely economic field. *Archiv*, in general, is an interesting journal and I shall certainly subscribe to it for next year. I should like also to subscribe to some English periodical or newspaper (weekly); can you advise me which to select? I have no idea what there is in the English publicistic field that is most interesting and is available in Russia.

As regards Struve's article,[14] on which we hold different opinions, it has to be said, of course, that it is impossible to judge accurately of the author's views from it alone. It seemed to me, for instance, and still seems to me, that he definitely set himself "general classificatory tasks" (the title itself indicates this), whereas you consider that he set himself "no such tasks".... That "it is necessary to win our handicraft workers away from so-called people's industry" is something with which, of course, I am wholly and definitely in agreement, and I think that this still confronts our "disciples"[15] as an unsolved problem. It was in Struve's article that I saw a *plan* for solving this problem.

Have you paid attention to *N. G.*'s articles in *Russkoye Bogatstvo*[16] (in the two last issues) against "materialism and dialectical logic". They are highly interesting—from the negative aspect. I must admit that I am not competent

to deal with the questions raised by the author, and I am
extremely surprised that the author of *Beiträge zur Geschichte
des Materialismus** has not expressed his opinion in the
Russian literature and does not vigorously oppose neo-
Kantianism, letting Struve and Bulgakov[17] polemise on
specific questions of this philosophy, as if it had already
become part of the views of Russian disciples.[18] Space
would surely be found for philosophical articles in more
than one of our periodicals; moreover, a book could get
through easily. His polemic with Bernstein and Conrad
Schmidt interests me greatly, and I very much regret that
I am quite unable to obtain *Zeit*.[19] I should be greatly obliged to you if you could help me in this. It would be quite
sufficient, of course, to receive this journal even for a short
period. Do you have the issue of *Die Neue Zeit* (of a few
years ago) which carried an article by the same author
on Hegel (the 30th anniversary of his death—something
of that kind)?[20] Neither I nor any of the comrades here get
Die Neue Zeit, although they promised to send it from St.
Petersburg! The devil take all those people who make promises and do not keep them!

Another interesting article is that of Ratner's on *Capital*
in *Russkoye Bogatstvo* (for July). I cannot stand such lovers
of the golden mean, who do not dare to come out openly
against doctrines with which they have no sympathy, but
wriggle, make "amendments", evade the main issues (such
as the theory of the class struggle) and beat about the bush
of particulars.

The articles by another author in *Die Neue Zeit* on social
trends in Russia also sound very interesting[21]: your mentioning them is extremely tantalising. If I have understood
you rightly, this author expresses an idea already expounded by him elsewhere (on the danger of *einer politischen
Isolierung des russischen Proletariats***). It seems to me that
"alienation from society" does not necessarily signify "isolation",*** for there is society and society: in fighting Na-

---

* The author of this book was G. V. Plekhanov.—*Ed.*
** Political isolation of the Russian proletariat.—*Ed.*
*** That we must by no means allow such "isolation"—in this
I believe the author to be wholly and a thousand times right, espe-
cially against narrow adherents of "economics"[22]. — *Ed.*

rodism[23] and all its offshoots, the disciples thereby come closer to those *gauches** who tend to break *decisively* with Narodism and adhere *consistently* to their views. From *such* people the disciples would hardly begin dissociating themselves unreservedly. Rather the contrary. A "conciliatory" (or, rather, alliancist) attitude towards such people is wholly compatible, in my opinion, with the fight against Narodism and all its manifestations.

Please write. All the best.

V. Ulyanov

Well, well, you have already come to blows—and how!—with sticks and what not! Fortunately, Eastern Siberia seems to be lagging somewhat behind the Vyatka Gubernia in bellicosity.[24]

Sent from Shushenskoye village
  to Orlov, Vyatka Gubernia

First published in 1925   Printed from
                                                    the original

---

* Lefts.—*Ed.*

1899

5

TO A. N. POTRESOV

January 26, 1899

I have received your letter of December 24. I am very glad that you have at last got rid of your illness, of which rumours had even reached us. I heard of it during the holidays while I was in Minusinsk, and kept thinking where and how I could obtain news of you. (I thought it inconvenient to write to you directly, as you were said to be seriously ill.) Well, you have now revived just in time for a literary undertaking which is also being revived. Of course, you know already about *Nachalo*,[25] which is to be started in the middle of February. I hope you have now fully recovered—it is already a month since you wrote the last letter—and that you will be able to work. You are probably fairly well provided for in the matter of books and order the chief new ones? If you are not too short of funds for ordering books, I think you can work even in the backwoods—at least I judge by myself, comparing my life in Samara seven years ago, when I was reading almost exclusively other people's books, and now, when I have begun to acquire the habit of ordering books.

In regard to the *Heritage* I have had to agree with your opinion that to consider it as something of an integral nature is a bad tradition of the bad years (the eighties). Perhaps I really ought not to tackle historico-literary themes.... My justification is that nowhere do I propose acceptance of Skaldin's heritage.[26] That one must take over the heritage from other people is indisputable. It seems to me that my defence (from possible attacks of opponents) will be the note on p. 237, where it was precisely Chernyshevsky[27] I had in mind and where I gave reasons why it was inconvenient to take him as a parallel.* It is admitted there that Skaldin is a *Liberalkonservativ*, that he is "not typical"

---

* "The Heritage We Renounce" (see present edition, Vol. 2, pp. 491-534, footnote on p. 505).—*Ed.*

of the sixties, that it is "inconvenient" to take "typical" writers; I did not have Chernyshevsky's articles and do not have them, moreover the chief ones have still not been republished, and I should hardly be able to avoid snags here. Furthermore, I would begin defending myself by pointing to the fact that I gave an exact definition of what I understand by the "heritage" of which I am speaking. Of course, if the article nevertheless gives the impression that the author proposes to accept precisely Skaldin's heritage, this is a fault that cannot be remedied. I forgot what is perhaps my chief "defence", namely, that if Skaldin is a "rarity", then bourgeois liberalism, more or less consistent and free from Narodism, is by no means a rarity, but a very broad trend of the sixties and seventies. You retort: "Coincidence and continuity are poles apart". But the crux of the matter is that the article says it is necessary to purge bourgeois liberalism of Narodism. If this is true and *if it is feasible* (a particularly important condition!), then the result of the purge, the residue after it, will be bourgeois liberalism that not only coincides with Skaldin's but is its successor. Thus, if I am accused of accepting Skaldin's heritage, I shall be entitled to answer that I am merely undertaking to *purge* it of admixtures, but that I myself have nothing to do with it and, in addition to cleaning various Augean stables, have more congenial and more positive occupations.... Well, I'm afraid I have let myself be carried away and really imagine myself a "defendant"!

We have not corresponded for such a long time that to tell you the truth I have forgotten when I last wrote you about the articles *"Die historische Berechtigung"*. I believe I wrote before I received them?* Now I have read them and have found that the author's main idea is fully acceptable (especially at the end concerning the two extremes or snags that have to be avoided). In giving the reasons, however, one should really bring out more sharply the *Klassencharakter* of the *Bewegung*** of which the author speaks (he mentioned it, but only in passing and very briefly), and furthermore not to regard the Fronde-like

---

* See p. 26 of this volume.—*Ed.*
** Movement.—*Ed.*

agrarians with such favour; in their liberalism there is more of the Fronde and of a sense of grievance on account of *einundsechzig** than of a desire for "the most rapid industrialisation" of the country. It is worth while recalling their attitudes towards seasonal work, migration, etc. The author should have formulated the task more accurately: to free all *fortschrittliche Strömungen*** from the rubbish of Narodism and agrarianism and to utilise all of them in this purified form. In my opinion, "utilise" is a much more exact and suitable word than *Unterstützung und Bundesgenossenschaft*.*** The latter indicates the equality of these *Bundesgenossen*,**** yet they must (in this I fully agree with you) follow in the wake, sometimes even "with clenched teeth"; they have absolutely not grown so far as to reach equality and will never grow to reach it, owing to their cowardice, disunity, etc. *Unterstützung*, however, will come by no means from the *Intelligenz und fortschrittliche Grundbesitzer*[5] alone, but also from many others, both from Semites and from *fortschrittliche Kaufleute und Industrielle*[6] (the author has quite wrongly passed them over: it is still a question whether they constitute a smaller percentage in their milieu than in that of the *Grundbesitzer*[7]) and those *Bauern*[8] who tend to represent *Urteil* and not *Vorurteil*, *Zukunft* and not *Vergangenheit*[9] of their class, and very many others. In two respects the author has tipped the scales in the other direction: firstly, in combating the Economists he has left aside *praktische*, immediate *Forderungen*,[10] which are important not only for *industriellen Arbeiter*, but also for *Hausindustrielle* and *Landarbeiter*,[11] etc. Secondly, he has fought against an abstract,

---

* Sixty-one (1861).—*Ed.*
** Progressive trends.—*Ed.*
*** Support and alliance.—*Ed.*
**** Allies.—*Ed.*
   [5] Intelligentsia and progressive landowners.—*Ed.*
   [6] Progressive tradesmen and industrialists.—*Ed.*
   [7] Landowners.—*Ed.*
   [8] Peasants.—*Ed.*
   [9] Reason and not prejudice, the future and not the past.—*Ed.*
   [10] Demands.—*Ed.*
   [11] Not only for industrial workers, but also for handicraftsmen and agricultural workers.—*Ed.*

neglectful attitude to *gemässigten fortschritt'lichen** elements (it is fair to say that they should by no means be entirely neglected, they should be utilised) and thereby, as it
were, obscured the independent and more resolute position
adopted by the *Bewegung* he represents. In the historico-
philosophical sense the proposition which he advances (and
which was earlier advanced by Inorodzew in *Soziale Praxis*[28]) is indisputable, viz., that among óur present *Genossen*** there are no few *verkleideten Liberalen.**** To a
certain extent this can also be said of *Deutschland versus
England.* That is, so to speak, our good fortune; it enables
us to count on an easier and swifter beginning; it compels
us to utilise all these *verkleideten.* But the author's formulation can, perhaps, give rise to some misinterpretation (one
Old-Believer told me: but this is belittling and depersonalis-
ing...), on the one hand, and a certain feeling of distrust
and embarrassment among *Genossen.* In this respect Inorodzew's formulation, too, in my opinion, was unfortunate.

As regards the heart of the matter, however, I think there
are no differences of opinion with the author.

About Parvus, I haven't the slightest notion of his personal character and do not at all deny his great talent.
Unfortunately, I have read very few of his works.

Do you expect to obtain Kautsky's *Die Agrarfrage,*****
which has recently come out?

Regarding Wert, Yevg. Solovyov and M. Filippov, I
must say that the first-named I do not know at all, and I
have read very little of the other two. That there is and will
be "weathering", I have not an iota of doubt. Hence it is especially necessary to have not only *verkleidete Literatur.*****

All the best.

V. U.

Sent from Shushenskoye village
    to Orlov, Vyatka Gubernia

    First published in 1925   Printed from
                                                        the original

---

    * Moderately progressive.—*Ed.*
   ** Comrades.—*Ed.*
  *** Disguised liberals.—*Ed.*
 **** *The Agrarian Question.—Ed.*
***** Disguised literature.—*Ed.*

6

TO A. N. POTRESOV

April 27, 1899

I was very glad, A. N., to receive your letter of March 27, which at last broke your long and persistent silence. A heap of questions to be discussed has indeed accumulated but there is no opportunity of having any detailed conversation here on subjects that are mainly of a literary nature. And now there is the journal[29]: without talks with one's colleagues one feels too cut off for writing. There is only Julius, who takes all this quite closely and *actively* to heart, but the accursed "long distances" prevent sufficiently detailed conversation with him.

I shall begin with what interests and agitates me now most of all—Bulgakov's article in issues 1-2 and 3 of *Nachalo*. On reading your opinion of him, I was exceedingly pleased to meet with sympathy on the most essential point— the more so because, apparently, one cannot count very much on sympathy from the editorial board.... If Bulgakov's article made a "repellent" and "pitiful" impression on you, it absolutely infuriated me. Up till now, though I have read and re-read Bulgakov, I simply cannot understand how he could write an article so completely nonsensical and in such an extremely unbecoming tone, and how the editors found it possible not to dissociate themselves by at least a single comment from such a slashing attack on Kautsky. Like you, I am "convinced that our people are utterly [just so!] confused and puzzled". And who wouldn't be puzzled when told—in the name of "modern science" (No. 3, p. 34)—that Kautsky is all wrong, arbitrary, socially incredible, "with equally little of both real agronomics and real economics" (No. 1-2) and so forth? Moreover, Kautsky is not expounded, *but simply distorted*, while Bulgakov's own views as part of any coherent system are entirely lacking. No man with any sense of party spirit or sense of responsibility to all the *Genossen* and their whole programme and practical activity would dare to take such "side kicks" (to use your apt expression) at Kautsky, without giving anything himself, but merely promising ... a learned work on "Ost-Elbe"! Apparently, he feels himself free from all comradely obligations and responsibility, a "free" and individual spokesman of professorial science. I do not forget, of course, that under Russian conditions it is impossible to demand of a journal that it admit some *Genossen* and exclude others—but a journal like *Nachalo* is not an almanac, allowing Marxism just because it is the mode (*à la Mir Bozhy*,[30] *Nauchnoye Obozreniye*,[31] etc.), but an organ of a definite trend. It is incumbent on such a journal, therefore, to put a certain restraint on learned "kickers" and on all "outsiders" in general. It is to the fact that its editors have run it as an organ of a definite trend and not as an almanac that *Novoye Slovo*[32] owes its great success.

I read through Kautsky's book before Bulgakov's article appeared and I did not find in the latter a *single* at all intelligent argument against Kautsky. What I did find was a heap of *distortions* of Kautsky's ideas and theses. What sheer nonsense Bulgakov talks when he asserts, for example, that Kautsky confuses technics and economics, that he tries to prove the "ruin of agriculture" (No. 3, p. 31. Kautsky says *just* the opposite: S. 289), that he denies agriculture any tendency to develop (No. 3, p. 34), and so on!

I have already written, and sent to the editorial board a fortnight ago, a first article on "Capitalism in Agriculture (Kautsky's Book and Mr. Bulgakov's Article)" and am now starting on a second dealing with the end of Bulgakov's article.* I greatly fear that P.B. will reject it, either on account of its considerable length (it turns out to be larger than Bulgakov's article, firstly, because I have to give reasons for refuting such unsupported and carelessly pronounced verdicts as, for example, that Marx was wrong in teaching that the ratio $\frac{v}{c}$ decreases in agriculture; secondly, because

---

* See present edition, Vol. 4, pp. 105-59.—*Ed.*

it is essential to expound Kautsky), or because a polemic
is considered undesirable (of course, I have not used in the
article a single abusive expression, like those above, and
in general I have tried to avoid anything personal against
Bulgakov. The tone in general is in no way sharper than in
my article against Tugan-Baranovsky[33] on the theory of
the market*). I should be very glad to hear your opinion,
when you have read Kautsky's book and finished reading
Bulgakov: what exactly do you find "true" in Bulgakov?
And do you think it possible to let Bulgakov's article in
the journal go unanswered?

In general, all this "new critical trend" in Marxism,
espoused by Struve and Bulgakov (P. B. is apparently *in
favour of* Bulgakov), looks highly suspicious to me: resounding phrases about "criticism" against "dogma" and so forth—
and absolutely no positive results of the criticism. Moreover,
compiling an article *à la* Bulgakov required, besides "criticism" and sympathy for professorial "modern science",
tactlessness *nec plus ultra*.

I sent Struve a reply to his article on the market.** My
sister[34] writes to me that this reply will be published in
Nauchnoye Obozreniye and that P. B. intends to answer it
in the same journal. I cannot agree with you that "the crux
of the question lies in the concrete impossibility of an ab-
stractly conceivable proposition" and my main argument
against P. B. is precisely that he mixes up abstract-theoreti-
cal and concrete-historical questions. "Concretely impossible" is not only realisation as put forward by Marx, but
also land rent as put forward by him, and average profit,
and the equality between wages and the value of labour-
power, and much more besides. But the impossibility of
something being realised in a *pure* form is not a refutation.
I am quite unable to see any contradiction between my
assertions in the *Studies*[35] and in *Nauchnoye Obozreniye*,
nor do I see the "bourgeois apologetics" with which Struve
has been trying to frighten readers. What I find most objec-

* "A Note on the Question of the Market Theory (Apropos of
the Polemic of Messrs. Tugan-Baranovsky and Bulgakov)" (see present
edition, Vol. 4).—*Ed.*

** "Once More on the Theory of Realisation" (see present edition,
Vol. 4).—*Ed.*

tionable in his article is the fact that he drags in critical
philosophy and that he makes remarks such as that Marx's
theory of value and profit *"indisputably* suffers from a contradiction". P. B. is perfectly well aware that this is *dis-
putable*—why then sow confusion in the minds of our people, who so far *have received no* systematic proof of this contradiction and its correction from any single spokesman of
the "new critical trend"?

And Bulgakov's sally (No. 3, p. 34, note) against the theory
of *Zusammenbruch**!—without any mention of Bernstein
and with the irrevocable authority of a "learned" decree!
I know about the publication of Bernstein's new book and
I have ordered it but it is hardly likely to be sent. The
article about it in the *Frankfurter Zeitung*[36] and in *Zhizn*[37]
(not a bad journal! Its literary section is really good, even
better than any others!) has quite convinced me that I did
not rightly understand Bernstein's disjointed articles and
that he has got himself so tangled up in lies that he really
deserves to be *begraben*,** as the author of *Beiträge zur Geschichte des Materialismus**** expressed it in an open letter
to Kautsky. Bernstein's arguments, which are new to me,
against the materialist conception of history,**** etc., are
(according to *Zhizn*) astonishingly feeble. If P. B. is such
an ardent defender of Bernstein that he is all but prepared
to "quarrel" over him, it is very, very sad, because his
"theory" against *Zusammenbruch*—excessively narrow for
Western Europe—is altogether unsuitable and *dangerous* for
Russia. Do you know that it is already being made use of
by our "young" people (ultra-Economists), who in one
publication gave an account of the Stuttgart debates *in
such a way* that for them Bernstein, Peus, and others were
defenders of "economics, not politics"? What does P. B.

---

* Collapse (of capitalism).—*Ed.*
** Buried.—*Ed.*
*** *Contributions to the History of Materialism.—Ed.*
**** Incidentally, do you remember how one of our common friends[38]
in the "beautiful faraway" maliciously ridiculed and soundly scolded me for having called the materialist conception of history a
"method"? And behold, it turns out that Kautsky, too, in using the
same word: "method", is guilty of the same grievous sin. (*Zhizn*,
January, Book II, p. 53.) Have you any news of this friend? Is his
health better? Is there any hope that he will write?

think of such "allies"? If by the successes of the ultra-Economists you mean the resignation of Volgin and his closest
comrades, I know about it[39]; it was a great shock to me and
I am now puzzled as to how matters stand and what the
future has in store. I think it terribly harmful that this
dispute with the ultra-Economists was not *fully and completely* ventilated in the press: it would have been the only
serious way of clearing things up and establishing certain
precise theoretical propositions. Instead, there is now complete chaos!

My book has come out* and I have asked that it should
be sent to you (I have not yet received it myself). I have
heard that the P.S. to the preface was late, came under
the preliminary censorship and, it seems, "got into trouble".
I shall await your comments with interest.

I ordered Karelin's book and read it before I received
it from you. I liked it very much; it is devilishly annoying
that it was pared down! Aren't you going to write a review
of it?

An acquaintance of mine has sent me *A. P.*'s "Magazine
Notes" (on the "heritage" and the "inheritors"). I wonder
whether the continuation intended to carry on a further
polemic with me or not? I liked A. P.'s article very much;
the issue was much the worse for the cuts in the article.
Truth to tell, I see no differences of opinion between us:
you deal with a *different* question—not what the attitude of
the disciples is to Russian democracy in general and whether they reject it (I wrote *exclusively* about this),** but
what the relations were between democrats of various types
in the good old days. I was concerned only with Mikhailovsky's[40] mistake in supposing that we reject democracy altogether—whereas you fasten on *his other mistake*, the "slurring over" of substantially important distinctions in the
"heritage". I saw Maslov's note in No. 3 of *Nauchnoye
Obozreniye* directed against me, but to tell you the truth
I was not interested in it. By the way, the cuts in A. P.'s
article confirmed my opinion that it is "inconvenient" to

---

* *The Development of Capitalism in Russia* (see present edition,
Vol. 3).—*Ed.*
** "The Heritage We Renounce" (see present edition, Vol. 2).—*Ed.*

take a more striking testator than Skaldin (a sad confirmation!). In general, I find the tone of the journal that of a dying body. If that is so, the end and death is only a question of time. It is simply speculation on *Ratlosigkeit** and bureaucracy in the department which, etc. One could hold one's tongue without any harm and not without advantage to the cause. As a matter of fact, compared with the modern tone, our *Materials* could be a model of "moderation" and "solidity"....[41]

All the best.

V. U.

Write more often, if it's not too much bother, otherwise I am quite unable to get press news from anyone.

I am sending the *Historische Berechtigung*** by registered post. Please don't think me careless about returning books: you did not mention any time limit and so I did not refuse comrades who asked to be allowed to read it. I shall be very grateful for the end of Karelin.

Do you have any German reviews of Kautsky? I have read only that in the *Frankfurter Zeitung*—irate and empty *à la* Bulgakov.

I am very pleased on the whole with the issues of the journal.[42] It is splendidly edited. Have you read Gvozdyov's book[43] and what do you think of it?

Sent from Shushenskoye village
  to Orlov, Vyatka Gubernia

First published in 1925

Printed from
the original

---

* Perplexity.—*Ed.*
** *Historical Justification.*—*Ed.*

7

TO A. N. POTRESOV

June 27, 1899

Last Friday, the 18th, I received your letter of June 2, but *I have not received* either Mehring or Karelin, about which you write. I waited a little at first, thinking there was a delay in the post, but now I am forced to believe that either the parcel has been lost or you put off sending it. If the former is the case, lodge a complaint at once.

Your comments on my book* gave me great joy. All the same, I think you are exaggerating in speaking about a translation of it: I doubt whether the Germans would want to read a thing so crammed with facts of purely local and minor significance. True, they translated N.—on[44] (but then he already had a great reputation and the recommendation, probably, of Engels, although the latter had intended to make hay of it, according to Monist). Have you come across reviews of it in the German literature? If I am not mistaken, they have translated him into French too. I was somewhat surprised at your statement that you "at last succeeded in obtaining" my book.... Didn't you receive it from Moscow or St. Petersburg? I asked that it should be sent to you, as to all the rest of my friends, and they all got it. If you have not received it, let me know and I shall write again to Moscow. So far I have not seen any reviews of it in the press, but I don't expect to find any before the autumn—but then the only newspaper I read is *Russkiye Vedomosti*,[45] which continues to maintain a "tactful silence"....

---

* *The Development of Capitalism in Russia* (see present edition, Vol. 3).—*Ed.*

I have read Bulgakov's article in *Archiv*. I do not intend to write a reply to him for the German public too:
for one thing, I couldn't do it in German; secondly—and
this is the chief thing, for it would be possible, perhaps,
to find a translator from Russian—an article of the kind
that I wrote for the Russian public, i.e., with a detailed
exposition of Kautsky's book, would be quite unsuitable
for the German public. I cannot answer Bulgakov's special
references (from German statistical data) for I have no material. Nor would I undertake to write *for the Germans*
about his general standpoint (Kantian and ... Bernsteinian,
if one can use the term). I think it really is necessary to
correct the Germans' idea of the Russian disciples, but
for this (unless someone would undertake to write a special
article) a simple paragraph about my article against Bulgakov, when this article is published in a Russian journal,
would suffice.* But if it is not published at all—owing to
the demise of *Nachalo* and the refusal of *Zhizn*, or the censorship—then the matter will take quite a different turn.

Regarding the "sensational discoveries" of the Russian
disciples and their neo-Kantianism, I am becoming more
and more indignant. I have read Tugan-Baranovsky's article in No. 5 of *Nauchnoye Obozreniye*.... What utterly
stupid and pretentious nonsense! Without any historical
study of Marx's doctrine, without any new researches, on
the basis of schematic errors (arbitrary alteration of the
norm of surplus-value), on the basis of elevating to a general rule an exceptional case (raising the productiv-
ity of labour *without* decreasing the value of the
product: an absurdity if this is taken as a general phenomenon)—on the basis of this to talk about a "new
theory", about Marx's mistake, about reconstruc-
tion.... No, I cannot believe your statement that Tugan-
Baranovsky is becoming more and more a *Genosse*. Mikhailovsky was right in calling him an "echo man": his article
in *Mir Bozhy* ("according to Beltov", you remember? in

---

* Lenin refers to the article "Capitalism in Agriculture (Kaut-
sky's Book and Mr. Bulgakov's Article)" (see present edition, Vol. 4).
The article was published in the journal *Zhizn* in Jan.-Feb. 1900.—
Ed.

1895) and this article confirm the severe judgement of the prejudiced critic. It is confirmed also by what I have heard about his personal qualities from you and from Nadya. Of course, all this is not enough to draw a final conclusion, and I am quite likely to be mistaken. It would be interesting to know your opinion of his article.

And then there's this idea of distinguishing between "sociological" and "economic" categories, set going by Struve (in No. 1 of *Nauchnoye Obozreniye*) and repeated both by P. Berlin (in *Zhizn*) and by Tugan-Baranovsky. In my view it promises nothing but an utterly meaningless and scholastic play at definitions, to which the Kantians give the resounding name of "critique of concepts" or even "gnosiology". I simply cannot understand what *sense* there is in such a distinction. How can there be something economic apart from social?

Incidentally, concerning neo-Kantianism. What stand do you take? I have read and re-read with great pleasure *Beiträge zur Geschichte des Materialismus*, I have read the articles of the same author in *Neue Zeit* against Bernstein and Conrad Schmidt (*Neue Zeit*, No. 5, 1898-99; the later issues I have not seen),[46] I have read Stammler ("*Wirtschaft und Recht*")* whom our Kantians (P. Struve and Bulgakov) have so highly praised, and I definitely side with Monist. Stammler especially rouses my indignation; I fail to see in him even a hint of anything fresh and significant.... Sheer *erkenntnistheoretische Scholastik***! Stupid "definitions" of a mediocre lawyer, in the worst sense of this last word, and no less stupid "conclusions" drawn from them. After Stammler, I re-read the articles of Struve and Bulgakov in *Novoye Slovo* and found that neo-Kantianism was a thing to be seriously reckoned with. I could no longer restrain myself and stuck in my comments and attacks against it, both in reply to Struve (on his article in *Nauchnoye Obozreniye*.*** Why and by whom the publication of this reply is being held up—I fail to understand. It was to have ap-

---

    * "Economy and Law".—*Ed.*
   ** Epistemological scholasticism. —*Ed.*
  *** "Once More on the Theory of Realisation" (see present edition, Vol. 4).—*Ed.*

peared in No. 6 of *Nauchnoye Obozreniye*. But it is not there.
Meanwhile, my silence is beginning to make things awkward
for me: for example, Nezhdanov's article in *Zhizn* No. 4 [47])
and in reply to Bulgakov. I say, "I could no longer restrain myself" for I am only too well aware of my lack of
philosophical education and I do not intend to write on these
subjects until I have learned more. That is just what I am
now doing—I have started with Holbach and Helvètius,
and am now taking up Kant. I have got hold of the chief
works of the chief classical philosophers, but I do not have
the neo-Kantian books (I have only ordered Lange). Tell
me, please, whether you or your comrades have them and
whether you could not share them with me.

On the same subject I have been greatly interested by
the review in No. 5 of *Nachalo* (May issue, which is in
the last stages of consumption) on Bogdanov's book. I
don't understand how I could have missed the notice of
this book's publication. I have only now ordered it. Already from Bogdanov's first book I suspected Monist, and
the title and contents of the second book strengthen my
suspicions. And how disgustingly pointless and disgustingly supercilious this review is! Not a word on the real
issue and ... a reprimand for ignoring Kantianism, although
it is evident from the reviewer's own words that Bogdanov
does not *ignore* Kantianism, but *refutes* it, having a different
standpoint in philosophy.... I think (if I am not mistaken
about Bogdanov) it is impossible to let this review go unanswered.[48] The only thing I can't understand is how Kamensky could have left unanswered the articles of Struve
and Bulgakov in *Novoye Slovo* against Engels! Could you
explain this for me?

Your information about the reaction against Marxism
which has begun in St. Petersburg was news to me. I am
puzzled. "Reaction"—does that mean among the Marxists?
And which ones? P. B. again? Is it he and his Co. who are
developing a tendency to unite with the liberals? I am
looking forward to your explanations with great impatience.
I fully agree that the "critics" are only confusing our people,
while giving absolutely nothing, and that a serious fight with
them (especially over Bernstein) will be necessary (only
will there be somewhere to fight...?). If P. B. "absolutely

ceases to be a *Genosse*"—so much the worse for him. It will
be a great loss, of course, for all *Genossen*, for he is very tal-
ented and knowledgeable, but, of course, "friendship is
friendship, but service is service", and this does not do
away with the need to fight. I fully understand and share
your "fury" (caused by the epithet "loathsome" [sic!] in
regard to Monist—because of what? because of the article
in *Neue Zeit*? because of the open letter to Kautsky about
who will *begraben* whom?) and I am eager to know about
his answer to your letter giving vent to this fury. (I have
not yet seen Bernstein's book). *Gründliche Auseinanderset-
zung* is necessary, of course, but it will not and cannot
appear in *Nachalo* or *Zhizn*: only specific articles against the
"critics" of Marxism will be published. What is required
for it is a third kind of literature* and *Platform* (if I
have understood you rightly). Only then, at last, the *Genossen*
will be dissociated from "outsiders" and "kickers", and
only then will no kind of personal whimsies or theoretical
"sensational discoveries" be able to produce confusion and
anarchy. The accursed Russian disorganisation is wholly
to blame here!

It is not clear to me in what way your article on the her-
itage (I have read only the first one) was aimed at the St.
Petersburgers. I have not seen the article "Out of Turn".
Send it to me.

I should very much like to have a more detailed and
circumstantial talk about the *Blitzableiter*.** But this, evidently, will have to be left for another time. My term of
exile ends on January 29, 1900. I hope they don't extend
it—a calamity that not infrequently strikes exiles in Eastern
Siberia. I am dreaming of Pskov. And you?

Nadya sends her regards.

All the very best.

V. U.

P.S. I have just re-read the end of my article against
Bulgakov in the rough copy ... and I have noticed that my
tone there is conciliatory; implying, as it were: I am an

---

* Illegal Marxist literature.—*Ed.*
** Lightning conductor.—*Ed.*

"orthodox" and vigorous opponent of the "critics" (that I said plainly), *but* we must not exaggerate these disagreements [as Mr. Bulgakov does] in the face of common enemies. It is quite possible that this "conciliatory" tone [I have tried my hardest to be mild and polemise as a *Genosse*] will prove inappropriate or even ridiculous if expressions like "loathsome" are employed, and if the "critics" cause a definitive cleavage. In that case I should find myself "guilty though guiltless"; not having seen Bernstein's book, not knowing *all* the views of the "critics", and being at a "respectable distance", my view [when I wrote that article] was quite an "old one", simply that of a contributor to *Nachalo*.... It looks as if my statement about the theory of the class struggle not having been touched on by the "critics" is incorrect?[49]

Sent from Shushenskoye village
   to Orlov, Vyatka Gubernia

First published in 1925   Printed from
                                                          the original

1900

8

TO NADEZHDA KRUPSKAYA[50]

I have long been intending to write to you about affairs, but various circumstances have always interfered. My life here is all bustle, even painfully so—and this (N.B.) despite the extraordinary precautions taken against it! I live almost, one might say, in solitude—and yet there is this bustle. But then I suppose it's unavoidable in every new situation, and it would be a sin to complain, seeing that I am not half as nervy as our dear bookseller[51] who succumbs to black melancholy and momentary prostration under the influence of this bustle. But there is much that is good besides the bustle. Well, I shall now tell you something about the affairs of the Union of Russian Social-Democrats Abroad, and I shall do so on the basis of facts and accounts of the *other* side....

In the first place, a completely wrong idea of *Vademecum* prevails in Russia as a result of the cock-and-bull stories of the *Rabocheye Dyelo* supporters. To hear them—it is nothing but indulgence in personalities, and so forth, nothing but acting general and making mountains out of molehills for the sake of denigrating individuals, nothing but the use of "impermissible" methods, etc. Actually, this thing is a *major issue of principle*, and the attacks on individuals are merely an appendage, an appendage that is inevitable in view of the confused relations which the "young" have tried to create and aggravate to the utmost. *Vademecum* is an outcry, a forthright outcry against banal Economism, against the "shame and disgrace" of Social-Democracy. "I never thought I would have to experience such shame," exclaims Plekhanov at the end of the preface to the documents he has published. "We must get out of this chaotic and disgraceful situation at all costs. Woe to the party that patiently tolerates such confusion!" And against all the various accusations levelled at Plekhanov we must first of all categorically establish that the *whole essence* of his pamphlet is precisely a declaration of war against the "disgraceful" principles of "Credoism" and "Kuskova-ism", precisely a split over principles, and the split and "fracas" in the Union are merely a *side* effect of this dissension over principles.

If the split over principles has been combined with this "fracas" (at the Congress of the Union of Russian Social-Democrats Abroad in April 1900, things *literally* came to the pitch of brawling, hysteria, and so on and so forth, which led to Plekhanov's resignation), if things took this turn, the blame for it rests with the *young*. It was from the standpoint of Economism that the young waged a systematic, stubborn and dishonest struggle against the Emancipation of Labour group during 1898—"dishonest" because they did not show their colours *openly*, because they baselessly put all the blame on "Russia" (keeping silent about the anti-"Economist" Social-Democrats of Russia), and because they have used their connections and practical resources to push aside the Emancipation of Labour group in order to declare the latter's unwillingness to let in "disgraceful" ideas and disgraceful stupidity to be an unwillingness to let in all "young forces" in general. This struggle against the Emancipation of Labour group, this pushing it aside, was carried out on the sly, in a "private" fashion, by means of "private" correspondence and "private" conversations— plainly and bluntly speaking, by means of *intrigue*, because the role of the Emancipation of Labour group in the Russian Social-Democratic movement never was, never will be and never can be a *private* matter. The *young* proclaimed "new" views against the old, but concealed those views so artfully and diplomatically (thereby showing that for them the very question of views was a *private* matter) that it was left for the *old* to *set forth* the gist of the disputes. "We sent to St. Petersburg an account of our disputes with the young ones" writes Plekhanov (p. XLVII of *Vademecum*). Thus, as early as 1898 the Emancipation of Labour group *proved* that for it the whole question lay in the vacillation

over principles on the part of the young, who were capable
of sinking as low as complete denial of socialism. As early
as 1898 the Emancipation of Labour group came out with
an *appeal* to Russian Social-Democrats against ideological
waverings,[52] but this appeal proved to be the voice in the
wilderness, since after the arrests in the summer of 1898
all outstanding leaders of the Party were swept from the
battlefield and only the voice of the *Economists* responded
to the appeal.

It is not surprising that after this the Emancipation of
Labour group resigned from the editorial board, it is not
surprising that open war against Economism became more
and more urgent and inevitable. But here, to the aid of the
Economic trend, came people who were united to these
Economists by long-standing hostility towards the Emancipation of Labour group and these people did not shrink
from the attempt to abet Economism, without washing
dirty linen in public, and to enable the Economists to continue, with greater convenience than ever before, the tactics
of "private" propaganda of their views under the flag of
Social-Democracy and under cover of ambiguous statements
by the new editorial board, which wanted to imitate that
dear little calf who sucked two mothers at once.

In the very first issue of *Rabocheye Dyelo* the new editors
declared that they "do not know what young comrades
P. B. Axelrod is talking about" in attacking the Economists. They declared this despite the fact that the whole
history of the Union in recent years was a history of its
struggle with the "young"; they declared this despite the
fact that one of the members of the editorial board of *Rabocheye Dyelo* was *himself an adherent* of the Economic trend
(Mr. V. I—n).[53] To an outsider, to one who has not pon-
dered over the history of Russian Social-Democracy and
the Social-Democratic Union Abroad during the last few
years, it may seem quite incomprehensible and strange
that such a slight and *(apparently)* casual remark dropped
by the editors of *Rabocheye Dyelo* ("we do not know what
young comrades P. B. Axelrod is talking about") could
spark off the most passionate polemics, ending in the split
of the Union and its disintegration. Yet there is nothing
strange about this seemingly strange phenomenon. The

slight remark of *Rabocheye Dyelo*'s editors in connection with their publication of Mr. V. I—n's articles fully and clearly revealed *the cardinal distinction between two conceptions of the immediate tasks and most urgent demands of Russian Social-Democracy*. The first conception can be expressed in the words *laissez faire, laissez passer* in relation to Economism. These are tactics of a conciliatory attitude to Economism, the tactics of concealing the "extremes" of Economism, of defending Economism against open struggle against it, the tactics of "free criticism", i.e., free criticism of Marxism on the part of all overt and covert ideologists of the bourgeoisie. The other conception required a resolute struggle against Economism, an open protest against the threatening vulgarisation and narrowing of Marxism, an irrevocable break with bourgeois "criticism".

Written in August,
prior to 24th, 1900
Sent from Switzerland to Ufa

First published in 1924

Printed from
the original

9

ADDRESSEE UNIDENTIFIED

September 5, 1900
Nuremberg

Comrade,

It looks as if we shall not be able to meet—we are not going to either Mainz or Paris and leave here tomorrow.[54] It is a great pity, but we must accept the situation and confine ourselves to conversing by post.

Firstly, I hasten to correct a remark in your first letter, a correction I would ask you to convey *also to the person* who told you of my "promise to meet". *That is not true.* I did not promise to meet, but said that we would *officially* (i.e., on behalf of our group[55]) get in touch with the Union[56] when we were abroad, *if this appeared to be necessary*. It was wrong of G.[57] to forget about this condition, and to forget besides to tell you that I spoke with him in a personal capacity and, consequently, *could not* have promised anything definite in anticipation of our group's decision. When we heard out the other side here[58] and learned about the congress and the split, we saw that there was now no need for an official contact. That's all. Consequently, the Union has *no right whatever* to "lay claim" to me, whereas I claim that G. told certain other persons of our conversation, although he had *formally* promised me that, prior to our group making contact with the Union, he would inform *no one except the arrested person*. Since you have informed me of his claim, I hope you will not refuse, being in Paris, to inform him likewise of this claim of mine. If "the rumour is heavy on the ground",[59] it is G. who is to blame for it.*

---

* Secondly, yet another little departure: I heard out both G., *whom I met in the course of several days*, and the other side. You, on the other hand, heard out only the Unionists; but no more or less influential and authoritative representatives of the other side. Hence it seems to me that it is you, if anybody, who has violated the rule of *"audiatur et altera pars"* ("hear the other side as well"—*Ed.*).

Now passing to the heart of the matter. Amalgamation is *impossible*. So is federation, if the word is understood in its real sense, i.e., a certain agreement, a treaty, mutual obligations, etc. "The endeavour to afford each other as much help as possible"—is, I think, not bound up with federation, but is possible also without it, and is possible in general, although I do not know whether it is easily practicable. If the Union sincerely desired this, it would hardly have started with ultimatums and the threat of a boycott (that was precisely the meaning of the words used by the person who delivered your letter); that cannot serve to improve relations.

We are an independent literary group. We want to remain independent. We do not consider it possible to carry on without such forces as Plekhanov and the Emancipation of Labour group, but *no one is entitled to conclude* from this that *we shall forego even a particle of our independence*. That is *all* we can say *at the moment* to people who want to know above all what our attitude is to the Emancipation of Labour group. To anyone who is not satisfied with this, we have nothing to say except: judge us by our deeds if you do not believe our words. If, however, it is a question not of the *present moment*, but of the more or less near *future*, then, of course, we shall not refuse to impart to people with whom we shall have close relations more detailed information on the *form* of the relations between us and the Emancipation of Labour group.

You will ask: what kind of relations will you have with the Union? *For the time being none*, because it is our *unalterable* decision to remain an independent group and enjoy the closest co-operation of the Emancipation of Labour group. This decision, however, is distrusted by the Union, which fears that we will not be capable of sustaining our complete independence, that we will fall into an "impossible" (your expression) polemical tone. If our activity dispels this distrust on the part of the Union, good relations can be established between us, otherwise they cannot. *Voilà tout*. You write: "The Union is looking to you"; but obviously we can only help the Union with writings, and it is no less obvious that at the present time, when all our vital juices must go to nourish our coming offspring,[60] we cannot afford to feed other people's children.

You write that 1) there are no disagreements in principle, and that 2) the Union is ready to prove in practice its determination to fight the "Economic trend". We are *certain* that on both these points *you are mistaken*. Our conviction is based on such *writings* as the *postscript* to the Anti-Credo,[61] the *reply* to *Vademecum*,[62] *No. 6* of *Rabocheye Dyelo*,[63] the *preface* to the pamphlet *A Turning Point in the Jewish Labour Movement*, and others. We intend *to come out in writing* with a refutation of the opinion that there are no disagreements in principle (so that we shall have *some* relations with the Union: relations between parties engaged in a polemic).

Now for the last *and main* point: are we right or not in regarding you as having had "a very, very sharp change of views"? Let us recall how things stood in Russia: you *knew* that we wanted to found an *independent* literary enterprise, you *knew* that we were for Plekhanov. Consequently, you knew *everything*, and not only did not refuse to participate, but, on the contrary, yourself used such an expression as *"our"* enterprise (do you remember our last talk in your flat *en trois?*), thus giving us grounds for expecting the *closest* participation from you. Now, however, it turns out that you are *silent* on the question of your participation, that you set us the "task" of "settling the conflict abroad at all costs", that is to say, a task which we have not undertaken and *are not undertaking*—without, of course, giving up the hope that our foundation of an *independent* enterprise with the co-operation of the Emancipation of Labour group may create a basis for settling the conflict. Now, apparently, you doubt the expediency of our group establishing an *independent enterprise*, for you write that the existence of two organisations with "each leaving the other to act as the spirit moves it" will be bad for the cause. It seems indubitable to us that your views have undergone a sharp change. We have now set before you with complete frankness how matters stand with us, and we should be very glad if our exchange of views on the question of "impending tasks" were not limited to this.

Address: Nürnberg, Ph. Roegner.

First published in 1924   Printed from
                                          the original

10

TO APOLLINARIA YAKUBOVA[64]

October 26

I received your letter of October 24 yesterday and am replying at once as requested.

I cannot forward the letter just now, as I am not sending any pasted-in things to the address I have, and only use the chemical method. I have no time to copy the letter by this means. I wrote to the addressee[65] yesterday giving the substance of the letter, and I hope in the near future to communicate the whole letter to him. But if you can copy it into an unbound book by the chemical method, then I will send it at once.

I will give my sister the address: she was not in Paris in September, so you could hardly have been there at the same time. I hope you dropped her a few lines at the address I gave you.

Now, to business.

Your letter to me creates a strange impression. Apart from information concerning addresses and forwarding, it contains nothing but reproaches—bare reproaches without any explanations. You even go to the extent of attempting caustic remarks ("are you sure that you have done this for the benefit of the Russian workers' movement and not for the benefit of Plekhanov?")—but, of course, I am not going to exchange caustic remarks with you.

You reproach me for having "advised against".[66] You quote me very inaccurately. I remember very well that I did not express myself categorically, absolutely. I wrote: "We find it hard at the moment to advise anything"; that is to say, I made our decision depend directly on a preliminary elucidation of the matter. What this elucidation should have been is clear from my letter: it was essential for us to be perfectly sure whether there had really been a "turn" in *Rabochaya Mysl*[67] (as we had been told and as we were entitled to conclude from the fact that you proposed to Plekhanov that he should participate) and what kind of turn.

On this basic and main question you do not say a word.

That we regard *Rabochaya Mysl* as an organ of a special trend with which we differ in the most serious way is something of which you have long been aware. Some months ago both the addressee of your long letter and I flatly refused to take part in an organ of that trend, and obviously, in doing so ourselves, we could not but advise others to do the same.

The news of a "turn" in *Rabochaya Mysl*, however, put us in a "difficulty". A *real* turn could substantially alter the situation. It is natural therefore that in my letter I expressed *above all* the desire to learn all the details of the *turn*—but you have not said a word in reply to this.

Perhaps, however, you consider that the answer to my question about the turn is contained in your letter to my friend[68]? Perhaps, if you approached Plekhanov on behalf of the editorial board of *Rabochaya Mysl*, your letter to my friend could be regarded as an authentic expression of the board's views? If *so*, then I am inclined to draw the conclusion that there has been no turn. If I am mistaken, please explain my mistake to me. The other day, another close supporter of Plekhanov wrote to me about the turn in *Rabochaya Mysl*. But, being in correspondence with you, I cannot, of course, believe these "rumours" of a turn which are not in any way confirmed by you.

Again, I had better say openly and straightaway (even at the risk of incurring further reproaches) that, being in complete solidarity with my friend (to whom you write), I subscribe to his words: "We shall have to fight you"—if there is no turn. But if there is—you must explain in full detail exactly what this turn is.

You write to my friend: "fight us, if you are not ashamed to do so". He will answer you himself, of course, but I for my part beg leave to reply to this. I am not in the least ashamed to fight—seeing that things have gone so far that the disagreements have concerned fundamental issues, that an atmosphere has been created of mutual non-comprehension, mutual distrust and complete discordance of views (I am not speaking of *Rabochaya Mysl alone*; I am speaking about everything I have seen and heard, and *not so much* here as at home), inasmuch as a number of "splits" *has already arisen* on this basis. To get rid of this oppressive atmosphere, even a furious thunderstorm, and not merely a literary polemic, can (and should) be welcomed.

And there is no reason to be so much afraid of a struggle: a struggle may cause annoyance to some *individuals*, but it will clear the air, define attitudes in a precise and straightforward manner, define which differences are important and which unimportant, define where people stand—those who are taking a completely different path and those Party comrades who differ only on minor points.

You write that there have been mistakes in *Rabochaya Mysl*. Of course, we all make mistakes. Without a struggle, however, how is one to distinguish these minor mistakes from the *trend* which stands clearly revealed in *Rabochaya Mysl* and attains its culmination in the "Credo".* Without struggle there cannot be a sorting out, and without a sorting out there cannot be any successful advance, nor can there be any *lasting unity*. And those who are beginning the struggle at the present time are by no means *destroying*

---

* *Note.* In your letter to my friend, for example, there is both misunderstanding and the Economic trend. You are right in stressing that an economic struggle is necessary, that one must know how to make use of legal societies, that all kinds of responses and so forth are necessary, that one should not turn one's back on society. All that is legitimate and true. And if you think that revolutionaries have a different view, that is a misunderstanding. Revolutionaries say merely that every effort must be made to ensure that legal societies and so forth do not *separate* the workers' movement from Social-Democracy and the revolutionary political struggle but, on the contrary, unite them as closely and indissolubly as possible. In your letter, however, there is no effort to combine, but there is an effort to separate, that is, there is Economism or "Bernsteinism",[69] for example, in the statement: "The labour question in Russia, as it stands in reality, was first raised by *Rabochaya Mysl*"—in its arguments about the judicial struggle and so forth.

I apologise if my reference to your letter to my friend offends you; I wanted only to illustrate my thought.

unity. There is no longer any unity, it has already been destroyed all along the line. Russian Marxism and Russian Social-Democracy are already a house divided against itself, and an open, frank struggle is one of the essential conditions for *restoring* unity.

Yes, *restoring*! The kind of "unity" that makes us conceal "Economic" documents from our comrades like a secret disease, that makes us resent the publication of statements revealing what views are being propagated under the guise of Social-Democratic views—such "unity" is not worth a brass farthing, such "unity" is sheer cant, it only aggravates the disease and makes it assume a chronic, malignant form. That an open, frank and honest struggle will cure this disease and create a really united, vigorous and strong Social-Democratic movement—I do not for a moment doubt.

Perhaps it is very inappropriate that in a letter *to you* of all people I have to speak so often of a struggle (literary struggle). But I think that our old friendship most of all makes *complete frankness* obligatory.

All the best.

Petroff

P.S. In a week or two I shall have another address: Herr Philipp Roegner, Cigarrenhandlung, Neue Gasse, Nürnberg (only for letters and in two envelopes). [Please do not write any initials in the letters—heaven knows whether the post here is quite reliable.]

Written October 26, 1900
Sent from Munich to London

First published in 1930   Printed from
                                            the original

1901

11
TO G. V. PLEKHANOV[70]

January 30, 1901

I have received your letter just now, dear G. V., immediately on my return from a "final" talk with Judas.[71] The matter has been settled and I am terribly displeased with the way in which it has been settled. I hasten to write to you while my impressions are still fresh.

Judas did not argue about the "democratic opposition"; he is no romantic and not one to be frightened with words. But, as far as "item 7" is concerned (the utilisation of material for *Iskra*, material reaching *Sovremennoye Obozreniye*), he outsmarted our people, all of whom, P.B. *y compris*, stood up for him, against me. He, Judas—you see—expected that *Iskra* would be more popular, more "working-class"; he finds that our free use of material received by *Sovremennoye Obozreniye* could create competition.... He demands that material for *Iskra* should be used only *by agreement* with the representative of *Sovremennoye Obozreniye*—agreement ceases to be necessary only if it is impossible to communicate with this representative, a condition that, obviously, will rarely operate, for Judas says frankly that he proposes either the existence of a representative *im Auslande** ("not more than 12 hours from Munich") or very punctual correspondence. He would like to publish *each month five* sheets—that is to say, about 200,000 characters—just as much as in two sheets of *Iskra*. That he will be able to *supply* so much material is hardly to be doubted, for he is well-to-do, writes a great deal and has good connections. The thing is clear: the competition is

---

* Abroad.—*Ed.*

aimed not so much against *Zarya*[72] as against *Iskra*; the same preponderance of political material, the same newspaper character—*review* of current events, short articles (Judas with very true intuition attaches very great importance to the frequent publication of booklets with smallish articles). We shall be swamped with material of this kind, we shall be running around carrying out errands for Judas, who by his control of *Sovremennoye Obozreniye* (it is obvious that he will be master and complete master there for he has the money and 99 per cent of the materials—it is rarely, if ever, that we shall be in a position to give them even a very little) will make a magnificent liberal career and try to shoulder aside not only the heavyish *Zarya*, but *Iskra* as well. We shall be running around, keeping ourselves busy with proof-reading and transportation, while His Highness Mr. Judas will be *rédacteur-en-chef* of the most influential (in broad circles of *so genannten** public opinion) little journal. But "romantic" comfort can be offered these *rechtgläubigen*: let it be called "Supplement to the Social-Democratic journal *Zarya*", let them console themselves with catchwords, but meanwhile I shall take the whole affair into my hands. One is entitled to ask—will not the famous "hegemony" of Social-Democracy prove under the circumstances to be mere cant? In what will it find expression other than in the catchword "Supplement to the Social-Democratic journal"? That he will overwhelm us with material is indubitable, for we can't manage as it is to write enough both for *Zarya* and *Iskra*.

Either the one or the other: either *Sovremennoye Obozreniye* is a supplement to the journal *Zarya* (as arranged) and then it should appear not more frequently than *Zarya*, with *complete* freedom to use material for *Iskra*. Or we sell our birthright for a mess of pottage and prove *genasführt*** by Judas, who feeds us with catchwords.

If it is our destiny and if it is possible for us to achieve real hegemony, it will be exclusively by means of a political newspaper (reinforced by a scientific organ), and when we are told with infuriating insolence that the political

---

* So-called.—*Ed.*
** Led by the nose.—*Ed.*

section of our newspaper must not compete with the political enterprise of the liberal gentlemen, our pitiful role
becomes as clear as daylight.

I have made a copy of this letter, and am appending
it to the Minutes of today's meeting as a statement of my
protest and of my "dissenting opinion", and I invite you
too to raise the banner of revolt. Better a break than this
factual subordination to the Credo programme alongside
loud phrases against Credo-ism.

If the majority expresses itself in favour—I shall, of
course, submit, but only after having washed my hands
of it beforehand.

Sent from Munich to Geneva
  First published in 1925

                        Printed from the typewritten
                          copy with insertions
                        in Lenin's handwriting

12

TO P. B. AXELROD

March 20, 1901

Dear P. B.,

I have received all your letters and have given Auntie news of her old friend.[73] There was no need for you to worry about addresses and to think that there had been any change. I am still living at the same place and you should write to me at the old address:

Herrn Georg Rittmeyer, Kaiserstrasse 53/0, München. Inside: *für Meyer.*

I am not expecting my wife for some time yet: her term of exile only ends on Sunday, and she has to make some calls on the way, so she can hardly be here before the second half of April. Even when she does come you can still write to Rittmeyer,[74] for he will always forward everything to me, and I in turn will let you know in good time of any change of address.

We are having trouble with *Zarya*. That capricious gentleman Dietz[75] definitely rejected your editorial article; he was frightened by the references to *Iskra*, scented a whiff of "groups", etc., and referred to the fact that both Bebel and Singer (shareholders in his *G.m.b.H.*) are rather afraid,[76] and so on. To our very great regret, we had to give up your article, replacing it by a few words "to the readers". This new censorship is horribly unpleasant! The cover, too, has suffered: they deleted even "several Russian Social-Democrats". When shall we get rid of the "tutelage" of these *Dreck-Genossen*?!

We are having unpleasantness with that Calf (Judas) too. A very angry letter has come from his friend (=the proposed source of money=*goldene Wanze*[77]), saying: I am sending 200 (two hundred!) rubles *for Sovremennoye Obozreniye*, and bear in mind, he says, that it is for this enterprise and *not* for yours. We are all indignant, and it has been decided: 1) not to publish the statement about the coalition, 2) to send the Calf and his "friend" an *ultimatum*: either firm financing of *our* enterprise or we refuse, 3) to finish the Witte memorandum.[78]

Well, haven't we been fooled again by Judas?

There is one consolation: No. 2 of *Iskra* has reached Russia safely. It is a success and letters are pouring in. The devil knows what is happening in Russia: demonstrations in St. Petersburg, Moscow, Kharkov, Kazan; martial law in Moscow (by the way, they arrested my youngest sister there and even my brother-in-law,[79] who had never taken part in anything!); bloody battles; prisons crammed full, and so on.

In a few days we are expecting Brother[80] and our common friend—Feld[81]—who have already left (at last!); the latter (*so far*) has safely fulfilled everything required of him.

We are publishing a May-Day leaflet,[82] and then we shall start on No. 3 of *Iskra*, and perhaps also No. 4 at the same time—there is a lot of material.

Zarya will come out on Saturday, they say, and will be sent to you directly from Stuttgart.

Our finances are in a *very* bad way. Hence *for the time being* we must definitely refrain from all expenditure on inviting a man out (proposed by you as a carrier).

All the very best.

Yours,

Meyer

Sent from Munich to Zurich
First published in 1925

Printed from
the original

13

TO P. B. AXELROD

April 25, 1901

Dear P. B.,

I haven't had a talk with you for a long time, I could not get down to it and, besides, Alexei has written to you about all business matters,* but the need of a talk has become too great for me to put it off any longer. I should like to consult you about both the Parisians and Zurichers,[83] as well as about matters in general.

Do you know that the Parisians (long ago, about two or three weeks) have "dissolved the *Iskra* promotion group" and have refused (for the second time) to co-operate, on the grounds of our having "violated organisational neutrality" (sic! that we were unfair to the Union[84] and wrongly attacked it in *Zarya*). This was written by the author of "Comments on the Programme of *Rabocheye Dyelo*",[85] who hinted most unambiguously that *Rabocheye Dyelo* was on the mend (in *Listok* No. 6[86] it has even over-mended itself, in our opinion!) and consequently... consequently ... *Vivrons verrons***—this "dear comrade" concluded. Obviously (like certain "young forces" about whom G. V. wrote), he is aiming at a better position in *Rabocheye Dyelo*. The sheer scoundrelism of it made us so indignant that we did not even answer them. In *Iskra* No. 4 (we have been promised that No. 3 will be ready by May 1 and intend to start on No. 4 immediately) we are going to flay *Rabocheye Dyelo* for its shilly-shallying.

I really don't know whether to give these intrigants up as a bad job or to make yet another attempt. They are,

---

* I have been ill here for a week with influenza.
** We shall wait and see.—*Ed.*

undoubtedly, capable people, they have written, they have (both of them) supplied material (Danevich as well), they have collected money skilfully (as much as 350 frs—nowhere yet has so much been collected abroad for *Iskra*). As a matter of fact, we are not blameless either in regard to them: we have not paid them sufficient attention, we have not sent a single article for examination and "comradely advice", we have not offered any "section" (if only a foreign review in *Iskra* or comments in a social chronicle on certain issues). Apparently, under the conditions obtaining abroad, it is impossible, quite *impossible*, not to have something of the sort. Now take the Berliners[87] (Arsenyev was there recently)—they too want a definite position; simply to help *Iskra*, they say, can satisfy a student, but *we* or *Dvinskaya* (she and her husband are withdrawing from the Union, in which, when the members were questioned, only three—*Grishin*[88] *y compris!*—expressed themselves in favour of the conference. *Vive camarade G.!*) require, they say, something of the sort, you know....

I just don't know what to do! It is necessary to "invent" an organisation—without that *es geht nicht.** *

It has occurred to me that the following plan of organisation could be tried: the *Sotsial-Demokrat* organisation,[89] the editorial board of *Zarya* and various groups (the Berliners, for example, the Parisians, *perhaps*, etc.), or various persons, unite in a *League*,[90] let us say. Literary activity to be handled in three ways: the Emancipation of Labour group has its print-shop, *Zarya* has its own, with an *elected* Literary Committee as closest collaborator, taking part in periodic joint editorial sessions and publishing (over the signature of the Literary Committee) pamphlets, etc., in the print-shops of *Sotsial-Demokrat* and *Zarya—eventuell* also in a third print-shop should the *League* set one up (there is such a prospect). The *supreme decision* on literary questions in the League will belong to a *conference of three members*: from the Emancipation of Labour group, from *Zarya*, and from the Literary Committee. There will be a joint, elected management.

---

* There is nothing doing.—*Ed.*

Such, in substance, is my plan (of course, *Iskra*, being a Russian publication, *does not* formally *come into* the League). In principle this plan is approved here—by Elder Sister too. I believe that such a "constitution" ("Austrian" Alexei jokingly calls it) holds no dangers for us, and something of the kind is absolutely necessary, otherwise there will be general dissatisfaction and we may lose all our people. In this way we shall be fully guaranteed against dissensions and squabbles, keeping full control of our print-shops and editorial boards, while giving people the requisite scope without which they will not agree to co-operate.

Please write what you think of this idea, and talk it over with G. V. (to whom I am not writing, for he should soon be here and will, of course, call on you on the way). I am not going into details; they can be easily settled. If we all (i.e., the whole *Sotsial-Demokrat*) agree on this, the chances are that the Berliners (who have a print-shop and are eager to "work" from a definite "position") will join us, and then we shall be able to counterpose to the Union a united "League" developing extensive activities.

There is no need to fear an elected management, for it will only control transport and the collection of money abroad, divided in a definite proportion between *Sotsial-Demokrat*, *Zarya*, etc., but it will not have anything to do with *Iskra*, which informally will be behind *Zarya* and together with *Zarya*. Formally the League can be declared the ally abroad of the *Iskra organisation in Russia*, which we are already establishing.

Nor is there any need to fear literary stupidities, for (1) the Literary Committee can be bound by its Rules as far as independent publishing is concerned; (2) it will publish over its own signature: the Emancipation of Labour group and *Zarya* will not be confused with it; (3) our people as well can be in it; (4) it will be subordinated to the conference, in which we have a majority.

I don't know, of course, whether this will satisfy the Parisians—they are so proud. We feel awkward about approaching them. If you approve of the plan, would you care to write to them and throw out a feeler, seeing that they spoke to you earlier in Paris about their sad situation; you could now suggest this way out to them. If you approve of the idea, we shall get in touch with Koltsov and ask him to draft Rules for the League.*

Now about the Lettish Zurichers. I don't know whether you have heard that the transport arranged with their help *came to grief*: 3,000 copies of *Iskra* (No. 1) were *seized* by the police, who got hold of the smuggler as well. Later one of them wrote to us, asking for more fare money. We replied that we could not give any more for this route— we would not dare to put it before our organisation—but if he would undertake specially to get one pood across (as he undertook to do when he talked with me), then let him come and pick it up.

There was not a word in reply. Do you know whether, perhaps, they have taken offence? What are they doing and planning? If you see any of them, please have a talk to find out how matters stand.

We are beginning to think about No. 2 of *Zarya*—it is time to do so. The Witte memorandum will soon be finished,** in about 2-3 weeks (for some reason Dietz is incredibly slow with it; so far only 9 sheets are ready). So far we have *no* material apart from Nevzorov's article on the historical preparation of Russian Social-Democracy which you already know about. We are hoping for a leading article by G. V. on recent events, his article *contra* Struve, your article (from editorial comments)—that's true, isn't it?; an article by Luxemburg is promised (a new introduction to her articles "Die sozialistische Krise in Frankreich",*** which articles we intend to translate), and Kautsky has promised an article on academicians and proletarians.

We have no foreign reviews. How do matters stand with the "Austrian" article? Isn't anything coming from America?—and from Switzerland? It is said that Danevich is ill. There is no one we can ask to write about Germany— apart from Parvus, who promised (?) a foreign review but that is not quite the thing.

---

* It would be good to come before our people with a joint draft of *Sotsial-Demokrat* and *Zarya*.

** "The Persecutors of the Zemstvo and the Hannibals of Liberalism" (see present edition, Vol. 5).—*Ed.*

*** "The Socialist Crisis in France."—*Ed.*

In the fourth issue of *Iskra* it is proposed to have an article on terrorism (by Alexei); there is: "The Autocracy and the Zemstvo" (continuation), "The Autocracy and Finance" (by Parvus), something for the social chronicle (there is a supplement on demonstrations) and the working-class movement. We are thinking of issuing No. 4 in a single sheet (No. 3 has expanded so much, to two sheets, 8 pages (seven pages are now ready), like No. 1—and part had to be left out!). We must exert every effort to expedite the publication of *Iskra*—to make it a monthly.

Good-bye! All the best. Regards to all your family. From my wife too.

Yours,
Petrov

P.S. Write to me at Rittmeyer's.

Before I forget: on the instructions of Elder Sister I inform you that 250 frs. has been received. The report on this is published in *Iskra* No. 3 ("From America through Axelrod"). I am sending you via Stuttgart 10 copies of *Zarya*—send them to Ingerman, Mokriyevich, etc. Elder Sister is writing an article for the Germans on the demonstrations.

Sent from Munich to Zurich

First published in 1925

Printed from
the original

14

TO N. E. BAUMAN[91]

May 24, 1901

We received your letter with the report for January, February, March and April. Thanks for the detailed and clear list of income and expenditure. But as regards your activity in general, we are still unclear what exactly this activity is and what its results are. You wrote that you have your hands full and there is no one to replace you, but you have still not kept your promise to describe this activity. Is your work confined to forwarding literature to the points named in the report? Or are you engaged in forming a group or groups? If so, where and what kind, what has been done already, and what are these groups for—for local work, for sending to us for literature, or for something else?

We ask about this because the question is very important. Things with us are going none too well. We are bad off financially, Russia gives almost nothing. Shipping is still unorganised and haphazard. Under these conditions, our "tactics" must aim *wholly* at 1) sending here the fullest possible amount of the money collected in Russia for *Iskra*, and reducing local expenditure to a minimum; 2) spending money almost exclusively on *shipment*, as we already have receiving agents functioning in Pskov and Poltava who are comparatively very cheap and no burden on our exchequer.

Please think this over carefully. Our daily bread, by which we barely manage to keep alive, consists as before solely of suitcases. For a couple of them we pay about a hundred rubles, and the chance nature of the persons sent entails a vast amount of delay, carelessness, loss, etc. Nothing is being done to organise the sending of "suitcasers" from Riga (which, according to both Raznotsvetov and

Ernst, is possible). There is no news from Leopold.[92] Nothing is being arranged in Finland, although this is also possible, as we are assured from various quarters. Is it reasonable, in such a state of affairs, to spend 400 rubles in four months on local reception and intermediaries for forwarding literature?

We think you should move into the immediate vicinity of the frontier for the sake of shipping at least 2-4 suitcases and 10-20 pounds per month by personal handling. What do you say to this?

Sent from Munich to Moscow

First published in 1928   Printed from
                                                 the original

15

TO P. B. AXELROD

May 25, 1901

Dear P. B.,

You have already heard, of course, from G. V. of the plan for our organisation and of the new "conciliatory" enterprise of Nevzorov, Danevich and Ryazanov (who have taken the title of the *Borba* group[93]). We answered their inquiry (whether we agreed to a preliminary conference between *Sotsial-Demokrat*, the Union, and *Zarya*, i.e., their representatives) *by consenting*. G. V. said here that, of course, it was necessary to agree and that he had already written to you about it. Today Ryazanov (who has already spent about two days here) told me that he had received a letter from Gurevich, who informed him that official agreement had been received only from us, that so far there was still nothing from the Emancipation of Labour group, that he had seen Krichevsky and Ivanshin and was almost sure of their agreement to the conference, that the place suggested is Brussels and the date about June 4, and that the Bund organisation abroad[94] also wished to attend the conference.

Please write to them *as soon as possible* about the *official* agreement to the conference on the part of the Emancipation of Labour group (as the representative of *Sotsial-Demokrat*), and about your attitude to the question of place and time.* On the first point we wrote that we are in favour of Zurich or some place closest to it (and that Switzerland, of course, is the most convenient place also for the Emancipation of Labour group) and that we should

---

* I am repeating Gurevich's address, just in case: Mr. E. Gourevitsch, 38 bis Rue Gassendi, 38 bis, Paris.

like the conference to be held quickly, if possible in May,
for in June we have not so much free time at our disposal.
(Our desire to hasten the conference is really to be explained
by the fact that it is more advantageous to us to get it over
quickly so as to begin our own organisation sooner and have
time for preparing for a decisive fight against the Union
in the event of a break. The fight, probably, will be shifted
to Russia, too, in the summer.)

Please support our desire to hasten the conference*
(putting forward any sort of grounds) and to hold it in
Switzerland. I think they can hardly object to Switzerland,
firstly, because two of the four (*Zarya* and *Sotsial-Demokrat*
against the Union and *Borba*) are in favour of Switzerland;
secondly, Switzerland is bound to be the natural place for
a congress of representatives of the Swiss, German and
French groups. Perhaps it would be possible to agree not
on Zurich but on Basle, for instance? Let me know, please,
when you send your official agreement.

I shall now tell you about Ryazanov. On the question
of *our* organisation (the *Iskra* organisation abroad) he at
first got into a huff when he learnt that we had no intention
of enlarging the editorial board and were proposing only
a deliberative role for them. He spoke with feeling about
Nevzorov being a man who had a great past and services
to his credit (exactly the way Nevzorov last summer spoke
about Ryazanov!)—he expressed indignation, resorted to
irony, and so on and so forth. But a little later, seeing that
all this hadn't the slightest effect on us, he became disposed
to make concessions. He declared that he, perhaps, would
agree to our plan ("Nevzorov would never agree"), but the
best thing would be a federation between *Sotsial-Demokrat*,
Zarya and *Borba*, that *Borba* was ready to give up the idea
of publishing its own organ (we never believed they could
set one up) and confine itself to a series of pamphlets.

On the whole, it looks as if it will be possible to work
with them; they may jib a little, but will nevertheless
join in.

As far as a rapprochement with the Union is concerned,
Ryazanov at first stated that he did not put any hopes at

---

* They are said to want it round about June 10. We don't mind.

all on the conference, that it was only Gurevich who entertained such an idea, and so forth. But when he learnt that we were not making the abolition of the Union a *conditio sine qua non*, and that we were ready to allow the existence of a scientific organ (*Zarya*) and a political newspaper (*Iskra*) side by side with a popular miscellany or workers' journal (*Rabocheye Dyelo*), he made a decisive change of front and declared that he had long ago spoken about this to Krichevsky, that he regarded it as the natural way of ending discord and that he himself was now ready to work for the realisation of such a plan. Let him do some work! Perhaps amalgamation *or federation* on such a basis will really occur—it would be a big step forward.

Another reason why we are in favour of Zurich, I would add, is that Alexei is anxious to have more time to talk over all kinds of matters with you.

If the questioning of all members of *Sotsial-Demokrat* (for an official answer to the *Borba* group) requires much time, please try, if possible, to shorten this time somehow. Delay in calling the conference is extremely undesirable.

Regarding participation of the Bund organisation abroad, we think it should be refused (without making a *casus belli* out of it in the last resort) on the grounds of paragraph 1 of the decisions of the Congress of the Russian Social-Democratic Labour Party in 1898. (On the strength of this paragraph the Bund is autonomous only in questions specifically concerning the Jewish proletariat and, consequently, cannot act as an independent party to negotiations.)

How about your article for *Iskra*? Do you intend to provide something for the second booklet of *Zarya*, about which G. V., of course, has told you?

With warmest greetings and best regards from all of us.

Yours,
Petrov

Sent from Munich to Zurich
First published in 1925

Printed from
the original

16

TO LYDIA KNIPOVICH[95]

How do you propose printing *Iskra* in Russia? At a secret printing-press or a legal one? If the latter, write immediately whether you have anything definite in view; we are ready to snatch at this plan with both hands (it is possible, we have been assured, in the Caucasus), and it would not require much money.* If the former, bear in mind that in our printed sheet (4 pages) there are about 100,000 characters [and that each month!]; would a secret printing-press be able to cope with that? Will it not waste a vast amount of money and people with excessively great risk? Would it not be better to use this money and energy on shipments, which Russia, in any case, cannot do without.

Written May 28, 1901
Sent from Munich to Astrakhan

First published in 1928

Printed from
the original

---

* If you have any more or less reliable contacts with legal printing-plants, talk the matter over with them without fail and write to us; we have our own, very practical (and tested) plan on this score.[96]

17

TO THE *ISKRA*[97] PROMOTION GROUP

Doctor* should take up residence at the frontier, in Polangen for example (we have connections with the non-Russian side in those places, and we have also our own depot), study the local conditions (he would have to know Lettish and German there, but perhaps one could manage without that), try to find a plausible occupation (we are assured that it is possible to live there by private practice), establish good relations with the local petty officials and accustom them to frequent crossings of the frontier. The frontier there is crossed not with a passport, but with a *Grenzkarte*** (valid for 28 days). With such frequent crossings it will be possible to carry across (on one's person or in a suitcase by our method, which requires a small case for medical instruments) a little at a time, some pounds of literature on each occasion. It is very important for us that the crossings should be regular and frequent, even if with very little at a time. If the person will undertake to arrange this and do the work *himself*, we will give him the fare money and a couple of months' living expenses, until he settles down.

Written June 5, 1901
Sent from Munich to Berlin

First published in 1928

Printed from
the original

---

* The identity of this person has not been established.—*Ed*.
** Frontier card, enabling people living in the frontier zone to cross the frontier.—*Ed*.

18

TO L. Y. GALPERIN[98]

ъ/з

A further shipment to Persia via Vienna was made only recently, so it is premature to talk of failure. It may be successful. Inform the addressee in Tabriz that he will be receiving books from Berlin and write us when they are received.

As regards arrangements for printing *Iskra* in the Caucasus, we have already sent X a *detailed* inquiry but have not yet had an answer.* We must know exactly what the plan is (whether a legal or an illegal printing-press), how feasible it is, what amount of printed matter it reckons on (can *Iskra* be printed monthly?), how much money is needed initially and per month. Our funds just now are very low, and we cannot make any promises until we have detailed information, which please send immediately.

Make every effort to obtain money. We have already written about this through X to one of your acquaintances and advise you to ask ZZ also to take up the matter; one of the members of the *Iskra* group already spoke to him about money at the beginning of last year (remind him of the conversation in a theatre in one of the capitals).[99]

As regards the Eastern shore of the Black Sea, you must look for routes without fail. Devote your efforts especially to the French steamships—we hope to find a means of contact with them from here.

Written between June 18 and 22, 1901
Sent from Munich to Baku
First published in 1928

Printed from the original

---

* See p. 70 of this volume.—*Ed.*

19

TO N. E. BAUMAN

To Rook

We have just received news from Nikolai (=Ernst) of the shipment to him of $4^{1}/_{2}$ poods, which he has in a safe place; that is the first thing. The second is that he *always* has an opportunity of getting our man together with the smuggler across the frontier and that such people are needed. So we make the following proposal to you: take a trip to the spot at once, travel with one of your passports to Nikolai in Memel, find out about everything from him, then cross the frontier by *Grenzkarte* or with a smuggler, pick up the literature lying on this side (i.e., in Russia) and deliver it everywhere. It is obvious that for success in this matter it is *essential* to have one more person from the Russian side to help Nikolai and exercise control over him, someone always ready to cross the frontier secretly, but chiefly occupied with receiving literature on the Russian side and forwarding it to Pskov, Smolensk, Vilna, Poltava. [We have lost faith altogether in Nikolai and his Co.; *we have decided not to give them another farthing* and we can hope to use this route only on condition that a wholly reliable man of ours takes a direct part in the shipments.] You would be a suitable man for this, for (1) you have already visited Nikolai once, and (2) you have two passports. It is a difficult and serious matter, requiring changes of residence, but it is also most important for us. Think it over carefully and reply immediately, without putting it off for a single day. If you are not prepared to undertake this job, we must find someone else for it immediately. Hence we once again earnestly request you to reply at once.

Written June 25 or 26, 1901
Sent from Munich to Moscow

First published in 1928

Printed from
the original

20

TO G. V. PLEKHANOV

July 7, 1901

Dear G. V.,

How is your work going? All this time I have been wanting to write you about the ending to Orthodox's article, i.e., the later addendum concerning Berdayev's article[100] in No. 6 of *Mir Bozhy*. Our *Struvefreundliche Partei*[101] *rejected* this ending by a majority of $2^3/_4$ votes against $1^1/_4$ (Alexei "divided himself" into $^3/_4$ and $^1/_4$)—I was left in the minority with my *"in favour"* They didn't like the note on romantic love either, nor the general character of the addendum. In my opinion, however, it gave a brief, sharp, clear and business-like rebuff to the gentleman in question; the concluding verses are especially good!

We are again told in letters from Russia that there is to be a congress of the Russian Social-Democratic Labour Party—in one town even an invitation has been received. It is extremely important to make haste with the programme. Write, please, whether you are thinking of undertaking and can undertake this work. Apart from you and P. B. there is really no one: the formulation requires intensive thinking out, but with the bustle existing here, for example, it is quite impossible to concentrate and give proper thought to it. Those old drafts of the programme and the article (that is, one draft and one article) which Alexei brought you—and which he quite wrongly took back—are hardly likely to be of much use, are they? What do you think? If, however, you need them, we shall immediately send them to you.

I have ordered Shakhovskoi and Tezyakov.[102] Why do you need them for the programme? You are not thinking of drawing up demands for the agricultural workers on the basis of them, are you? And what is your attitude to demands for the peasantry? Do you in general accept the possibility of such demands in the Russian Social-Democratic programme?

The proofs of your article have not yet come. *Zarya* No. 2 contains: Old Believer on *Russkoye Bogatstvo*, V. I. on Berdayev, I have written on the Witte memorandum and trounced the Preface[103] (I am thinking of sending it to you for your advice, but I don't know whether there will be enough time), Alexei has an essay on "The Tasks of the Socialist Intelligentsia"—you have seen it, what do you think of it? I shall write, too, against Chernov.* And will you do the review of the miscellany *At the Post of Honour*?

For *Iskra* (No. 6 is being set up and will appear in July, No. 7 should appear in August) we are expecting from you articles concerning the letter of a worker and on the "Rebirth of Revolutionism in Russia".

Parvus is still standing by his "organisation"!

Kautsky passed through here. He is going on holiday and does not promise to write anything just now.

Nevzorov has sent *Iskra* a "disgusting" (the comment of V. I. and Puttman) article against the article "Where To Begin"[104]—a hymn to the committees, a defence (evasive) of *Rabocheye Dyelo*, etc. We shall return it to the author (we shall make a copy and send it to you, if you like).

Yes, regarding the plan of federation or amalgamation with the Union, I hope you have seen our counter-plan? If not, ask Koltsov to get it from Dvinskaya. I doubt whether anything will come of this.

All the very best.

Yours....

Oh, yes, about the money from the Belgians for our movement. I think one-third should be given to *Rabocheye Dyelo*: for the sake of 50-100 francs it is not worth while to give cause even for talk.

Sent from Munich to Geneva

First published in 1926

Printed from
the original

---

* "The Agrarian Question and the 'Critics of Marx,'" (see present edition, Vol. 5).—*Ed.*

21

TO S. O. TSEDERBAUM[105]

We have just received a letter with the plan of Pakhomy's Brother, Yablochkov and Bruskov. We cannot conceal that not only are we unable to agree with any part of this plan (though the first part is perhaps debatable), but we were simply astonished by it, especially by the second part, namely: 1) that everyone move to St. Petersburg, 2) that a regional organ of the *Iskra* organisation in Russia be established. So astonished that we apologise beforehand for any too sharp word that may slip into our comments.

It is unbelievable! After a whole year of desperate efforts we have barely succeeded in starting to form a staff of leaders and organisers in Russia for this vast and most urgent task (this staff is still terribly small, for we have only 2-3 persons in addition to the three mentioned above, whereas an all-Russia organ requires more than one dozen such energetic collaborators, taking this word *not merely* in a literary sense), and suddenly the edifice is to be dismantled again and we are to return to the old primitive methods! I cannot imagine more suicidal tactics for *Iskra*! A regional organ like the existing *Yuzhny Rabochy*[106] means a mass of money and personnel expended all over again on editorial offices, technical facilities, delivery arrangements, etc., and for the sake of what? For the sake of five issues in eighteen months! Even this it will not be able to do now in eighteen months, for *Yuzhny Rabochy* had the advantage of being founded by a full-formed Committee, i.e., by a whole organisation at the apogee of its development. At present there are only three of you. If, instead of combating the narrowness which makes the St. Petersburger forget about Moscow, the Muscovite about St. Petersburg, the Kiev man about everything except Kiev, if instead of training people to handle all-Russia affairs (it takes years to train them for this, if we want to build a political party worthy of the name), if, instead of this, we shall again encourage primitive methods, local narrowness and the development of a Gothamite instead of an all-Russia Social-Democracy, it will be nothing but Gothamite foolishness, it cannot be anything else. It has been found out by experience how unequipped we are for creating a really political organ, how few contributors and reporters we have, how few people with political connections, how few practical workers to handle technical jobs and distribution.

Russia has *few* of them, as it is, without our splintering them still further and dropping an all-Russia undertaking that has already been launched and which needs all-round support, for the sake of founding a new local enterprise. At best, in the event of this new plan being a shining success, it will lower the standard of Russian Social-Democracy, lower its political significance, because there cannot be a "local" political newspaper, since in a local organ the general-political section is always bound to suffer. You write: a "mass" organ. We totally fail to understand what kind of animal this is. Do you mean to say that Pakhomy's Brother, too, has begun to think that we must descend to a lower level, from the advanced workers to the mass, that we must write more simply and closer to life? Do you mean to say our aim is to descend closer to the "mass" instead of raising this already stirring mass to the level of an organised political movement? Is it letters from factories and workshops that we lack, and not political exposures, political knowledge and political *generalisations*? And in order to extend and deepen our political *generalisations* we are invited to fragment our work as a whole into regional undertakings! And besides depreciating the cause politically they will inevitably depreciate it technically by the plan for a regional organ. By *combining* all forces on *Iskra*, we can set up a monthly newspaper (this has now been *proved* after a year's experience) with really political material, but in the case of a regional organ it is impossible just now to think even of four issues per annum. If we don't skip impatiently from one plan to another, and are not put out by temporary setbacks and the slow growth of an all-Russia undertaking, it would be quite possible after six months or a year to achieve a fortnightly organ (which is persistently in our thoughts). We assume, of course, that Pakhomy's Brother, Yablochkov and Bruskov stand by the previous line, approving both the political trend and the organisational plan of *Iskra*, but if they have altered their views on these matters, that is quite a different question, of course. We are quite at a loss to understand why these people have lost confidence in this plan, and so quickly too (because they cannot fail to see that the new plan destroys the old one). Is it because of shipments? So far we have attempted only *once* to arrange a route and this attempt has not yet led to a complete failure—and even after two or three *failures* we ought not to throw up the sponge. Have not these people begun to sympathise with publication in Russia, rather than abroad? Surely they know that *everything* was done for the former and about 1,000 rubles spent, but so far without result. We must say that in general we consider that any plan for publishing any sort of regional or local organ of the *Iskra* organisation in Russia is decidedly incorrect and harmful. The *Iskra* organisation exists to support and develop the paper, and to *unite* the Party through it, and not for a *dispersion* of our forces, of which there is more than enough without this organisation. As for everyone going to St. Petersburg, we can only say that we have very few Party workers like P., B. and Pakhomy's Brother and we need to preserve them. Living in one place, the danger of a general roundup is a hundred times greater. If they find that one person there is not enough (it's for them to decide), let them add to him the one who is being released in the autumn (Pakhomy's Brother), but not both. And then, for the sake of both security and united work, let them not forget that it is extremely desirable to change their place of residence from time to time. If, finally, success were achieved in winning over the Committee in St. Petersburg, it should, of course, be made to devote itself heart and soul to *Iskra* and its more frequent publication, and to oppose all new primitive undertakings. Primitivism is a much more dangerous enemy than Economism, for *vital* roots of Economism, we are profoundly convinced, are deeply buried in primitivism. And there will never be any political movement (political not in words only, but in fact, i.e., one directly influencing the government and preparing a general assault) until we overcome this primitivism and eradicate all belief in it. If St. Petersburg has bought 400 copies of *Yuzhny Rabochy*, the *Sotsialist*[107] group has set about distributing 1,000 copies of *Iskra*. Let them organise the distribution of this number of copies, let them arrange for it to contain a detailed St. Petersburg section (if necessary, it will be a special supplement), and then there will have been accomplished the very task that has overshadowed for you all other tasks of winning over St. Petersburg. Let us remind you that all "practical workers" are agreed that *Yuzhny Rabochy* has no advantages over *Iskra* as regards accessibility to workers, so that this argument, too, falls to the ground. It is absurd and criminal to disperse forces and funds—*Iskra* has no money, not a single Russian agent is obtaining a farthing for it, and yet everyone is thinking up some new undertaking requiring new funds. All this shows a lack of self-discipline. We must be more patient; by means of our plan we shall achieve our ends, albeit not so soon, whereas what can be reckoned on by implementing the proposed plan is clear from the lamentable experience of *Rabocheye Znamya*.[108] Our friends began to carry out their plan in such haste that Yablochkov travelled to St. Petersburg in defiance of the condition laid down, abandoning Odessa, in which the presence of our agent was essential. We demand that the new plan be discarded. If our arguments are thought unconvincing, let all new plans be put off until our congress, which we shall convene, if necessary, when the thing has been got going. As far as popular literature is concerned, the idea is to extend the publication of popular pamphlets. This letter expresses the opinion not only of our group but also of the Emancipation of Labour group.

Written in the second half
of July 1901
Sent from Munich to Vilna

First published in 1925

Printed from
the typewritten copy found
in police records

22

TO G. V. PLEKHANOV

July 25, 1901

Dear G. V.,

Yesterday I received the books on the agrarian question. Thank you for them. I am pretty deeply immersed in my "agrarian" article against Chernov (and partly Hertz and Bulgakov). I think this Chernov needs to be trounced *unmercifully.**

Velika was here just now and read extracts from your letter to her. As regards the proofs, we have already done "everything in our power", i.e., we have sent Dietz corrections to be inserted in the text if it is not too late; if it is, we shall specify them *without fail* at the end of the book so that there will be no great harm done really. My wife read the proofs and compared them with the manuscript (the phrase on which you have made the marginal note, "I didn't have that!" proved to be a slip of the pen on your part. As I have just seen from the manuscript, you actually did write "the May uprising". We have corrected this too). Since proof-reader mistakes are unavoidable, we shall from now on apply the "tactics" proposed by you: we shall send the author the *first* proofs (the second will be too late), for him to correct not individual letters and characters, since that will be done by the proof-reader and is indeed not important, but *only places where the sense is distorted* by the omission of words and phrases or by the replacement of one word by another.

---

* See "The Agrarian Question and the 'Critics of Marx'" (present edition, Vol. 5).—*Ed.*

I received my article* from P. B. with his letter. P. B. is also in favour of toning it down. Needless to say, I have already *introduced* all the mitigations concretely indicated by you and P. B. As regards changing the whole tone of the article, or replacing all attacks by tongue-in-cheek edification, although I like this plan of yours, I doubt whether I *could* do it. If I didn't feel any "irritation" against the author I would not have written like that. But since there is "irritation" (understandable not only to us but to every Social-Democratic reader of the preface), I am no longer able to conceal it, and cannot exercise cunning here. I shall try to tone it down still more and make still further reservations; perhaps something will come of it.

I shall pass on to Alexei your comments on his essay (he has long been looking forward to them). He probably forgot to tell you that *he himself* passed his subject about Mikhailovsky on to Ryazanov (the latter is now writing it). *I* understood that you were writing a review of *At the Post of Honour*, which we sent you.

All the very best.

Yours....

If you see Koltsov, give him many thanks from me for *Volnoye Slovo*.[109]

O yes, I almost forgot. I should like to ask your advice on the following question. This same swine Chernov quotes F. Engels's article "The German Peasant" in *Russkoye Bogatstvo*, 1900, No. 1, where *at the end* Engels says that it is necessary to "restore the Mark". I found this article. It turned out to be a translation of the *Anhang* to the *Entwicklung des Sozialismus von der Utopie zur Wissenschaft*— "Die Mark"; *moreover in "Russkoye Bogatstvo" at the end two paragraphs* (18 lines) *have been inserted which are absent in the original.* I compared all the rest of the translation paragraph by paragraph, but the devil knows where these two paragraphs have come from. This outrage ought to be exposed, only—isn't there a misunderstanding here

---

* "The Persecutors of the Zemstvo and the Hannibals of Liberalism" (see present edition, Vol. 5).—*Ed.*

perhaps? Isn't there *another text* of this article by Engels?
In a note to the Russian translation, the editors of *Rus-skoye Bogatstvo* say:
"This article of his (Engels) appeared in the eighties
[in 1882? the preface to *Entwicklung* is marked September
21, 1882] in a German magazine [? *Neue Zeit*? or *Zuricher Sozialdemokrat*?[110] Do you know?] without his signature
[?]. But in a copy of it, which Engels sent to one of his
friends [sic! Danielson? Did you hear anything about this
from Engels?] he signed it with his initials." In addition,
it is said, the historical part of the article is identical with
the preface to "Schlesische Milliarde" and with an article
in *Neue Rheinische Zeitung*[111] (*April-March 1849*).

Could you help me to get to the bottom of this? Wasn't
there *another text* of the article "Die Mark" in *Neue Rhei-nische Zeitung* or elsewhere? Could Engels *later* have thrown
out the end about "the restoration of the Mark"?

Sent from Munich to Geneva

First published in 1925   Printed from
                                               the original

23

TO P. B. AXELROD

July 26, 1901

Dear P. B.,

I have received and carefully read your letter (so has Alexeï). I was very glad that you set out your remarks in such detail.[112] Only you are wrong in thinking that I am too ("pretty") "stubborn". I have accepted *all* your suggestions about toning down definite passages (as well as all suggestions of G. V.), that is, I have toned it down everywhere. "A kopek on the ruble" will unite all the workers: I have added "in the opinion of the Economists" in brackets. Instead of "restriction of the autocracy" I have put "destruction", as you suggested. On pp. 82-83 I have *deleted* altogether what was incautious in the sense of our views on utilising the liberals (i.e., incautiously expressed ideas), as you advised. I have also inserted a note with a reference to your pamphlet *The Historical Situation*, pointing out that the question only slightly touched upon by me has been analysed in detail by you. I have inserted a couple of words to the effect that one can be glad of the greater understanding of the workers' movement shown by the liberals (in the person of R. N. S.). I have deleted altogether "regret" at the publication of the Witte memorandum with such a preface. I have also deleted some sharp remarks in the first and the second half of the article. In general, I am not at all so stubborn about toning down specific remarks, but as a matter of principle I cannot give up the idea that it is our right (and our duty) to trounce R. N. S. for his political juggling. He is precisely a political juggler—reading and re-reading the preface has definitely convinced me of this, and in my criticism I brought in everything that the last few months have shown us (i.e., *Verhand-*

*lungen** with "Calf", attempts at an agreement, etc.** I got a weight off my chest, so to speak, in settling accounts with this individual. I regarded elucidation of the constitutional nature of the Zemstvo as the crux of the whole article. Zemstvo liberalism is, in the sphere of its influence on society, the same thing as Economism in the sphere of the latter's influence on the workers. We must attack the narrowness of both the one and the other.

Tomorrow, probably, the question of the article will be *decided* here. If it goes to press now, I shall try to send you a copy of the first proof; you may have further suggestions, and we can still manage to touch it up (while the first and second proofs are being corrected).

I send you warm greetings and wishes for a good rest and recuperation. For this it would be best, perhaps, not to send you anything for the time being? So as not to spoil your holiday and treatment?

Yours,
Petrov

Write to Herrn Dr. Med. Carl Lehmann, Gabelsbergerstrasse 20 a/II, München (*für Meyer* inside).

Sent from Munich to Zurich
First published in 1925

Printed from
the original

---

* Negotiations.—*Ed.*
** See pp. 55-57 of this volume.—*Ed.*

24
TO G. V. PLEKHANOV

July 30, 1901

Dear G. V.,

I received your letter from the country and the new books (*Final Report, Blondel et Vandervelde et Destrée*), for which many thanks.

I did not get Tezyakov[113]; *probably it won't come at all,* as it was ordered from Kalmykova's store[114] and *she is being exiled* from St. Petersburg *for three years* and *is closing down the store* (the latest and quite accurate news!).

I am sending you Kuleman[115] today.

As regards the forgery in *Russkoye Bogatstvo* concerning Engels,* I shall take all possible steps.

As regards reviews, we have little definite information. All are busy with their own articles (Velika—against Berdayev, Puttman with magazine notes=against *Russkoye Bogatstvo*, I with my agrarian article,** etc.). Moreover, there is still time for reviews.

I have sent my article against R. N. S. to the press after toning down a number of sharp passages.*** I have also written a postscript to it, in which I draw a parallel between an article of Dragomanov's[116] ("Knock, and it shall be opened unto you") and that of R. N. S., to the advantage of the former. There, too, I am toning down a few expressions (on Velika's insistence). But the general tone of my strictures can no longer be subject to radical revision.

---

* See pp. 81-82 of this volume.—*Ed.*
** Lenin was engaged on his article "The Agrarian Question and the 'Critics of Marx,'" (see present edition, Vol. 5).—*Ed.*
*** "The Persecutors of the Zemstvo and the Hannibals of Liberalism" (see present edition, Vol. 5 and p. 81 of this volume.—*Ed.*

Letters from Russia say that our people are terribly taken with *Berdayev*. There you have someone who asks to be trounced, and *not only* in the specifically philosophical sphere! True, Velika is writing an article in connection with Berdayev's last article in *Mir Bozhy*.

I was very glad to learn that you and P. B. will be seeing each other and will start on the programme. It will be a tremendous step forward if we can come before our people with a draft like yours and P. B.'s. This is a matter that is most urgent.

All the very best.

Yours,
Petrov

Sent from Munich to the Canton
  of Vaux (Switzerland)

First published in 1925   Printed from
                                            the original

25
TO G. V. PLEKHANOV

October 21, 1901

Dear G. V.,

A few days ago I sent you *Neue Zeit* No. 1, with Engels's article on the programme.[117] I think you will find it of some interest for your work, i.e., for drawing up the draft programme. Then today we sent you proofs; when you have read them, please send them directly to Dietz marked *"Druckfertig"** as soon as possible.

I have selected a little material for a review of home affairs** and in a few days' time I shall tackle it in real earnest (at the moment I am indisposed—a touch of the flu after my trip[118]). Since after this work I shall have to get busy with *Iskra*, and then with the pamphlet, which I have been putting off for a long time,*** I have no time whatever left for the programme, and you are our only hope.

Could you recommend some Frenchman for letters from France? (Danevich will probably refuse.)

All the very best.

Yours,

Lenin

Sent from Munich to Geneva

First published in 1925

Printed from
the original

---

* "Ready for the press."—*Ed.*
** "Review of Home Affairs" (see present edition, Vol. 5).—*Ed.*
*** The reference is to *What Is To Be Done?* (see present edition, Vol. 5.—*Ed.*

26

TO G. V. PLEKHANOV

November 2

Dear G. V.,

We have received your letter. We are planning to print your article in *Iskra* No. 10. No. 9 will come out in a few days; the delay is due to its having swelled to eight pages.

Did you receive Nos. 1 and 3 of *Neue Zeit* (when you have finished with them, please *return* them)? I sent them to you because they contain articles by Engels and Kautsky on the programme,[119] which may, perhaps, be of use to you. When do you expect to finish the programme?

You do not write anything about the review of the collected writings of Marx.[120] We take it that you will send it all the same—it is absolutely necessary for *Zarya* No. 2-3. Volume 4 will be published on November 4, containing letters of Lassalle to Marx, but it is not worth while writing a review of it now, so as not to delay publication.

I am finishing my review of home affairs.* Alexei has written about Lübeck. We have reviews: yours on Frank, three by Alexei+yours on the collected writings of Marx+ perhaps Velika Dmitrievna's on *Svoboda*.[121] This will be enough.

Also,** *Zarya* No. 2-3 is ready and it is only a matter of the printing, which could be completed by the middle of November.

All the best.

Yours...

---

* See p. 87 of this volume.—*Ed.*
** And so.—*Ed.*

P.S. I ask about the programme so insistently because we have to know whether, immediately after *Zarya* No. 2-3 has come out, there will be material for No. 4 to be given to the compositors. Dietz is pressing me about this.

If Ryazanov's article has not yet been sent—send it *immediately*, otherwise he will positively tear Alexei to pieces. Ryazanov (and Parvus with him) has been mortally offended by the postponement of his article and wants, it seems, to take leave of us. "You don't know your job as editors!", Parvus said to us.

How do you like that?

Written November 2, 1901
Sent from Munich to Geneva

First published in 1926   Printed from
                                                      the original

27

TO THE *ISKRA* ORGANISATIONS IN RUSSIA

1) Yakov
2) The Moscow Committee
3) St. Petersburg+Nizhni
4) Bakunin?
5) "A Letter to the Russian Social-Democratic Press".[122]

We have just learnt that the Unionists are arranging a conference of the leading committees to decide the question of the conflict abroad.[123]

Every effort must be made to secure the adoption of the following measures by the largest possible number of committees and groups:

1) The conference must unfailingly be postponed at least until the spring (until Easter or thereabouts). Reasons: a) It is essential to have delegates *both* from *Iskra and* from the League abroad, and this requires time and money. A conference without delegates from *Iskra* and the League is invalid and senseless. b) It is essential to wait for the publication of the pamphlets of both sides giving the gist of the disagreements. Until these pamphlets come out the conference cannot have the knowledge needed for judgement and so its deliberations would be hanging in the air. *Iskra* No. 12 (appearing December 5, 1901) definitely promises that this pamphlet will be issued very shortly (in about a month and a half). All the disagreements will be analysed there in great detail. We shall show there how *pernicious* the *Rabocheye Dyelo* trend is, and reveal all their disgraceful vacillation and impotence in the face of Bernsteinism and Economism. This pamphlet is nearly ready and is rapidly approaching completion. Further, at the present time (mid-December, new style) reports on the

disagreements are being delivered abroad: one by a representative of *Rabocheye Dyelo*, another by a representative of the League. These reports too will very soon appear in print, and to call a conference before they appear is just a waste of money and a needless sacrifice.

2) We shall send a *special* representative to the conference, if it does take place. Hence it is *imperative* that we should be informed immediately (1) whether the conference has been fixed; (2) where; (3) when; and (4) the pass-word and rendezvous for the conference. The committees and groups must be *formally* requested to communicate this information on pain of the conference being declared invalid and of immediate publication of the fact that there is a desire to decide matters without having heard both sides.

3) If the committees or groups elect to the conference representatives with a bias in favour of *Rabocheye Dyelo*, it is essential to protest against this immediately and *formally*, and to demand representatives from *both Rabocheye Dyelo and Iskra* supporters (from the Majority and the Minority respectively).

4) In the event of the conference declaring against *Iskra*, it will be necessary to *withdraw* from committees and groups which do not agree to protest publicly against this—to withdraw and at once publish the fact in *Iskra* and give the reasons for it. Our people must begin right now to make arrangements for such a step.

5) We must be informed at once of the result, and kept informed immediately of *all* steps taken. *Every effort* should be made to ensure that *Iskra* supporters everywhere reach agreement and act in unison.

Written prior to December 18, 1901
in Munich

First published in 1928   Printed from
                                           the original

28

TO INNA SMIDOVICH[124]

We have received information that Akim is printing *Vperyod*.[125] We refuse to believe it and request you to ascertain whether this is not a misunderstanding. That people who have been collecting hundreds and thousands of rubles on behalf of *Iskra*, for the *Iskra* print-shop— people who represent the *Iskra* organisation in Russia— should go over secretly to another undertaking and that at a critical moment for us, when shipments have come to a stand, when the entire North and Centre (and the South too!) have flooded us with complaints at the absence of *Iskra*, and when the only hope was to have it reproduced in Russia, that people should have done this in such an underhand way, for Akim wrote us that he was printing No. 10 and we were so sure of it, while Handsome did not tell us a word about his magnificent plans—such behaviour, which violates not only all rules of the organisation, but also certain simpler rules, is simply unbelievable.

If this incredible news is true, we *demand* an immediate meeting to deal with this unprecedented depravity and, for our part, we earnestly request Yakov and Orsha to scrape together whatever money they can and immediately carry out their plan of coming here.

Written December 18, 1901
Sent from Munich to Kiev

First published in 1928

Printed from
the original

1902

29

TO L. I. GOLDMAN[126]

Do you consider it essential that the existence of an *Iskra* print-shop in Russia be kept secret? That is to say: are you against our widely showing the Russian copy abroad?[127]

As regards the general maladjustment of our affairs, of which, according to the person who has recently seen you,[128] you so bitterly complain, we can be of little assistance. The Russian members of the *Iskra* organisation should form a solid core and achieve a proper distribution of *Iskra* *throughout* Russia. That is wholly a matter for the Russian organisation. If we achieve it, success is assured. But without it, maladjustment is inevitable.* For the sake of proper distribution and *prestige* it would be extremely important to print *Iskra* in Russia, every third or fourth issue, choosing one of more permanent interest. Perhaps No. 13,[129] for example, should be chosen.

But once you do print, print a *much* larger number of copies; we should try at least once to *satiate* the whole of Russia. Do you remember how you yourself complained of the small circulation?

Once again, best regards and congratulations on your success!

Written January 3, 1902
Sent from Munich to Kishinev

First published in 1928

Printed from
the original

---

* Do you think Dementiev could act as distributor?

30

TO G. V. PLEKHANOV

February 7, 1902

Dear G. V.,

I am sending you the draft programme with Berg's amendments. Please write whether you will insert the amendments or present a complete counterdraft. I should like to know also which passages you have found unsatisfactory.

Regarding religion, in a letter of Karl Marx on the Gotha Programme I read a sharp criticism of the demand for *Gewissensfreiheit** and a statement that Social-Democrats ought to speak out plainly about their fight against *religiösem Spuk*.**[130] Do you consider such a thing possible and in what form? In the matter of religion we are less concerned about cautiousness than the Germans, as is the case, too, in regard to the "republic".

Will you please let Koltsov copy from your copy; it will not take much time.

How is your work going (if you are writing an article for *Zarya*, as we assume)? When do you think you will finish it?

You have still not sent me *Neue Zeit* (Nos. *1* and *3*) and the *letter on the agrarian programme*! Please send them or write why there has been this delay.

I have ordered *Conrad's Jahrbücher*[131] for 1902 for you. *Wirtschaftliche Chronik* for 1901 will come out in February— it will be sent to you then. Have you subscribed to *Torgovo-Promyshlennaya Gazeta*[132] and have you already begun to receive it?

---

* Freedom of conscience.—*Ed.*
** Religious spookery.—*Ed.*

Have you heard anything more about the *Rabocheye Dyelo* people? We haven't heard a thing.

My pamphlet is being set up.*

Vorwärts has refused to publish even a condensed reply and the matter has gone to the *Vorstand*.** It is said that Bebel is on our side. We shall see.

All the very best.

Yours,

Frey

Sent from Munich to Geneva
First published in 1928

Printed from
the original

---

* *What Is To Be Done?* (See present edition, Vol. 5).—*Ed.*
** Executive Committee (of the German Social-Democratic Party).—*Ed.*

31

TO G. V. PLEKHANOV

April 4, 1902

Dear G. V.,

I am sending you my article on the cut-off lands.* When you have read it, please send it to P. B. together with this letter, for *if* you keep to the plan which I originally supported (viz., that this article should be, so to speak, a general defence of our general draft), we must agree jointly on any necessary corrections. If, however, you reject this plan, then we shall have to make other arrangements.

In some places I have quoted the general part of the programme (the statement of principle) according to my draft; this will be altered, of course, if my draft is rejected. (I could then make some quotations from the Erfurt Programme,[133] if you had no objections.)

Velika Dmitrievna made some marginal comments without, however, suggesting definite changes in each particular case. Please write and give me your opinion on these points. On one of them, I should like to say a few words in my own defence. Velika Dmitrievna suggests deleting pages 79-82**; I, of course, would not go out of my way to defend them. But she has also discovered in them the programme's "encouragement of unfairness" in proposing not to give preference to small leaseholders (of nationalised land) but leasing to big and small alike *on condition* of fulfilment of the agrarian laws and (N.B.) proper cultivation of the land and livestock management.

---

* "The Agrarian Programme of Russian Social-Democracy" (see present edition, Vol. 6).—*Ed.*
** This refers to the MS. of "The Agrarian Programme of Russian Social-Democracy" (see present edition, Vol. 6, pp. 140-42).—*Ed.*

She argues: this will be a "crime", for "the rich will grab everything", while improved cultivation will deprive of work nine-tenths of the workers whom no agrarian laws will help.

I think this argument is incorrect, for (1) it presumes a very highly developed bourgeois society in which it is a rare peasant who can manage without wage-labour; (2) the "rich" can then obtain land only if large-scale farming is technically and economically "well organised", but this cannot be done all at once, hence the sudden transition that frightens Velika Dmitrievna cannot happen; (3) the ousting of workers by machines is, of course, the inevitable result of large-scale production, but we are pinning our hopes not on retarding the development of capitalist contradictions, but on their full development; moreover, improved cultivation of the soil presupposes a gigantic growth of industry and intensified efflux of population from the land; (4) the proposed measure will not only not help any "criminals" but, on the contrary, is the *sole conceivable* measure in bourgeois society for counteracting "crime", for it directly restricts *not only exploitation of the worker, but also plunder of the land* and deterioration of livestock. It is precisely the petty producer in bourgeois society who *especially squanders* the forces not only of people, but of the land and livestock.

If you, too, are in favour of deleting pp. 79-82, please give your advice on how to alter the note on p. 92.*

What is your opinion as to whether it is possible in general to publish the agrarian part of the programme (and the commentaries on it) separately from the programme as a whole, prior to the publication of the whole programme?

I received yesterday the proofs of V. I.'s article and sent them to Dietz. Yesterday I sent to your address the continuation of the proofs of her article. (To speed things up she could send the corrected proofs directly to Dietz.)

It is now three weeks since we last heard of poor Tsvetov. He has probably gone under. It will be a great loss to us!

All the very best.

Yours,

Frey

---

* See present edition, Vol. 6, p. 145.—*Ed.*

April 5. P.S. I have just received your letter. I have passed it on to our people. We shall answer in a few days. Please send Berg's draft (which you call commissional)[134] *immediately* to this address: *Frau Kiroff, Schraudolfstrasse, 29, III. 1.* bei *Taurer. This is very urgent,* for they *have no copy* and do not understand your comments. (Personally, I would have preferred publication of both drafts, in the form of the "third way" proposed by everyone, but the majority, apparently, is now of a different mind.) I shall send you the agrarian books. Velika Dmitrievna, it seems, is ready to soften her "detraction" of the legal Marxists.

Sent from Munich to Geneva

First published in 1928   Printed from
                                                           the original

32

TO P. B. AXELROD

May 3, 1902

Dear P. B.,

The other day I sent you a "letter for K.",* without adding a single line from me as I was extremely busy. I hope you will forgive me?

I should like to have a few words with you now about the article on the cut-off lands.** I corrected it, taking into account *all* the suggestions and demands of the high collegium. Now it is being sent to G. V. *to be forwarded on to you*: don't forget to ask him for it should he delay it (Dietz's printing-press is standing idle!). Berg is satisfied with my corrections, but he has informed me that the strongest objections to the article came from you. If it does not disturb your work too much—please write and tell me the cause of your dissatisfaction. I am very interested in this. (If you are writing an article, please don't drop it for my sake, as this conversation is not a "business" one, but largely *post festum*.)

I find it difficult, for instance, to understand your insertion "... the heavy oppression to which the peasantry is subjected..." (of the survivals of serfdom). Firstly, it is superfluous, as it adds nothing to the *thought*. Secondly, it is inaccurate (it is not only the peasantry that they heavily oppress; moreover their harmfulness does not lie only in the "oppression" of one or other social stratum).

The programme has already been sent for copying and will appear as the leading article in *Iskra* No. 21. The

---

* Unidentified.—*Ed.*
** "The Agrarian Programme of Russian Social-Democracy" (see present edition, Vol. 6).—*Ed.*

question whether or not I should write a criticism (permitted by the high collegium) I have not yet decided, for I want to read the programme in print over and over again "at leisure", and at present I have not yet fully recovered from the stunning effect of London.[135]

How are L. Gr. and Boris Nikolayevich? How is the former's work progressing? And how is the health of the latter? *We are counting on him very shortly (most probably)*, and may he, therefore, recover fully and quickly.

With warm greetings and best wishes for your health,

Yours...

P.S. Inform B. N. that in Voronezh about 40 people have been arrested (it is said), and a letter received today gives the names: "Karpov, Lyubimov, Korostenev, Kardashev, Butkovsky, Makhnovets and Gubareva, the last four were released without being interrogated. In Ufa there have been eight raids and two arrests: Boikov and Sazonov, students." The Voronezh people were arrested (April 1) apparently "on orders from St. Petersburg—Kiev" (sic!). That is the *entire* content of one *direct* letter to us.

In general, there have been arrests galore! It is *almost certain* that those arrested include our Nadezha, whom you saw and recognised both in Zurich and among us— yes, yes, the very same! It's a very bad business!

N.B. Get L. Gr. to send immediately the issue you received of *Pridneprovsky Krai*[136] containing blank spaces.

Sent from London to Zurich

First published in 1925   Printed from
                                                    the original

33
TO G. M. KRZHIZHANOVSKY[137]

May 6

We received the letter. Wood, apparently, has been taken. It is essential that Claire should save himself and therefore should go underground without delay. The meeting with Sasha[138] (Wood managed to write to us about it) led to the appointment of a committee for convening a congress in five months' time.

Our *main* task now is to prepare for it, i.e., to ensure that our own *reliable* people penetrate into the largest possible number· of committees and try to undermine the Southern Central Committee of the southern committees (=whirligig). This "whirligig", which is manipulated by a *Genosse* (someone has even accused him of being an *agent provocateur*, but that has not been verified yet), is the main obstacle (besides St. Petersburg). Hence the immediate task—that both Kurtz and Embryon join the committees at once. Next, that their example in one form or another is followed by Claire and Brodyagin. This is the main task, for otherwise we shall inevitably be ousted; subordinate everything else to this task, bear in mind the major significance of the Second Congress! Adapt...* to this end and think about an attack on the centre, Ivanovo and others, the Urals and the South. The formal aspect is now acquiring special significance.

Brodyagin suspects provocation. There cannot be any here, we are already in London. It is very likely that many threads have been picked up from some of our arrested

---

* A word crossed out in the manuscript has not been deciphered.— *Ed.*

people—that explains everything. Look after yourself as you would the apple of your eye—for the sake of the "main task".[139] If we (i.e., *you*) do not cope with it—it will be a great calamity.

Forward this letter to Brodyagin immediately and tell him to write to us without fail and more frequently; all his letters have arrived safely.

If it is confirmed that Wood has gone under, we must meet Claire or Brodyagin as soon as possible or correspond in great detail, if there are good addresses (?) for sending you *all* the details about Sasha (send an address for the bookbinding as quickly as possible).

Arrange the passport yourself, do not rely on us. Shouldn't Claire and Brodyagin change passports, since the former is already known to everyone?

Who will be the delegate from Moscow? Is he absolutely reliable? Has he a good successor? And so: again and again: join the committees. Is Nizhni reliable?

Written May 6, 1902
Sent from London to Samara

First published in 1928   Printed from
                                                    the original

34

TO G. V. PLEKHANOV

I have received the article with your comments.* You
have fine ideas of tact towards editorial colleagues! You
do not even shrink from choosing the most contemptuous
expressions, not to mention "voting" proposals which you
have not taken the trouble to formulate, and even "voting"
on style. I should like to know what you would say, if
I were to answer your article on the programme in a similar
manner? If you have set yourself the aim of making our
common work impossible, you can very quickly attain this
aim by the path you have chosen. As far as personal and
not business relations are concerned, you have already
definitely spoilt them or, rather, you have succeeded in
putting an end to them completely.

N. Lenin

Written May 14, 1902
Sent from London to Geneva

First published in 1925

Printed from
the original

---

* The reference is to "The Agrarian Programme of Russian Social-
Democracy" (see present edition, Vol. 6).—*Ed.*

35

TO G. V. PLEKHANOV

June 23, 1902

Dear G. V.,

A great weight fell from my shoulders when I received your letter, which put an end to thoughts of "internecine war". The more this last seemed inevitable the greater the gloom such thoughts aroused, since the consequences for the Party would be most unfortunate....

I shall be very glad, when we meet, to have a talk with you about the beginning of the "affair" in Munich,[140] not, of course, to rehash the past, but to discover for myself what it was that offended you at the time. That I had no intention of offending you, you are of course aware.

V. I. has shown me also your letter about the article, i.e., your proposal to be given an opportunity of expressing your opinion in your programmatic article. Personally, I am inclined to consider such a decision the best and I think that the possibility of registering a 25 per cent difference (if it has to be registered at all) has always existed for each of the co-editors (just as you have already mentioned a somewhat different formulation of the question of nationalisation in the same article—or of the liberals in the review in *Zarya* No. 2-3). I am ready now, of course, to discuss with you once again desirable alterations in my article* and I shall send you the proofs for this purpose. Select anything you like. We ought to finish *Zarya as quickly as possible*; as it is the negotiations are dragging out terribly. In any case, I shall at once inform both A. N. and Julius of your proposal.

---

* "The Agrarian Programme of Russian Social-Democracy" (see present edition, Vol. 6).—*Ed.*

I have not yet received the proofs of your article and so cannot answer your question about the passage on Marx.

The letter of a Socialist-Revolutionary,[141] in my opinion, is hardly worth publishing; they have their own press—let them polemise there (for that's what it is with them—sheer polemics). About Belgium, it would be good to publish Rosa Luxemburg's article, if this could be done quickly.

All the very best.

N. Lenin

P.S. In a day or two I am going to Germany to see my mother and take a holiday.[142] My nerves are worn to shreds and I am feeling quite ill. I hope we shall soon meet in London?

Sent from Londen to Geneva

First published in 1925

Printed from
the original

36
TO G. D. LEITEISEN[143]

July 24, 1902

Dear L.,

My sister's address is: Mme Elizaroff. *Loguivy* (par Ploubazlanec), Côtes du Nord. Anya and Mother really do not like it here very much and they may go to some other place—they don't know where yet (you can address your letter *Expédition*). I am going home tomorrow. I liked it here very much on the whole and have had a good rest, only unfortunately I was a bit premature in imagining myself well again, forgot about dieting and now am again having trouble with catarrh. Well, all that is of no consequence.

Are you going to stay long in that country of yours? It would be a good thing if you were to combine the pleasant with the useful (your job) and take a good long holiday. Drop me a line about yourself when you return.

How do you like the result of the negotiations with L. Gr. and Yuriev? Did you reach full agreement and do you now hope for better results?

There is good news from Russia of the committees making a turn towards *Iskra*, even that of *St. Petersburg* (sic!). Here is a curious little example. They sent a pamphlet to *Rabocheye Dyelo*. There is a note there (on p. 9—we have been told exactly!) reading: "See Lenin's excellent book."* The Unionists here raised the alarm, and wrote to St. Petersburg: be so good as to delete it, you are hitting both yourself and us by it. Reply: don't hinder us from putting matters on a new footing, but give the pamphlet to *Iskra*.

---

* *What Is To Be Done?* (See present edition, Vol. 5).—*Ed.*

This is *entre nous*, of course, for the time being. But it is characteristic!

I don't know whether St. Petersburg will maintain its new position.

All the very best.

Yours,
Lenin

Write to me in London.

P.S. I almost forgot. *Socialiste* notified me that my subscription expired in December 1901. Is that so? Haven't they made a mistake? I remember your going there once with Yurdanov's card. Didn't you keep some document, or do you remember without it?

Sent from Loguivy
(Northern coast of France)
to Paris

Printed from
the original

37

TO P. G. SMIDOVICH[144]

August 2, 1902

Dear Ch.,

I received your letter, and I reply, to start with, in a couple of words: I don't feel at all well, I am all done up.

On the point you have raised, I have *not* seen a *single* letter. I think you are under a misapprehension. Who could think of "unorganising" the workers' circles, groups and organisations instead of increasing and strengthening them? You write that I have not indicated how a strictly secret organisation can have contact with the mass of workers. That is hardly the case, for (although that is *vient sans dire*) you yourself quote the passage on p. 96 concerning the need *"in as large a number as possible* (Lenin's italics) and with the widest variety of functions" for "a large number (N.B.!) [*a large number*!] of other organisations" (i.e., besides the central organisation of professional revolutionaries).* But you are wrong in finding an *absolute* antithesis where I have merely established a gradation and marked the limits of the extreme links of this gradation. For a whole chain of links occurs, *beginning* from the handful making up the highly secret and close-knit core of professional revolutionaries (the centre) and *ending with the mass* "organisation without members". I point out merely the trend in the changing character of the links: *the greater the "mass" character of the organisation, the less definitely organised and the less secret should it be* —that is my thesis. And you want to understand this as meaning that there is no need for intermediaries between the mass and the revolutionaries! Why, the whole essence lies in these intermediaries! And since I point out the characteristics of the extreme links and stress (*and I do stress*) the need for intermediate links, it is obvious that the latter will have their place *between* the "organisation of revolutionaries" and the "mass organisation"—

---

* *What Is To Be Done?* (See present edition, Vol. 5, p. 466).—*Ed.*

between as regards the type of their structure, i.e., they will be less narrow and less secret than the centre, but more so than a "weavers' union", and so forth. In a "factory circle" (*needless to say*, we must aim at having a circle of intermediaries in each factory), for example, it is essential to find a "middle" course: on the one hand, the whole, or almost the whole, factory must inevitably *know* such and such a leading worker, trust him and obey him; on the other hand, the "circle" should arrange things so that *all* its members *cannot be* identified, so that the one in closest contact with the mass *cannot be* caught red-handed, cannot be exposed at all. Doesn't that follow logically from what is said in Lenin's book?

The ideal of a "factory circle" is quite clear: four or five (I am speaking by way of example) revolutionary workers—they must not *all* be known to the mass. One member, probably, must be known, and he needs to be protected from exposure; let it be said of him: he is one of us, a clever chap, *although he does not take part in the revolution* (not visibly). One member maintains contact with the centre. Each of them has an alternate member. They conduct *several* circles (trade-union, educational, distribution, spy-catching, arming, etc., etc.), the degree of secrecy, naturally, of a circle for catching spies, for example, or for procuring arms, being quite different from that of one devoted to the reading of *Iskra* or the reading of legal literature, and so on and so forth. The degree of secrecy will be inversely proportional to the number of members of the circle and directly proportional to the remoteness of the circle's aims from the *immediate struggle*.

I do not know whether it is worth while writing specially about this: if you think it is, return this letter to me together with yours, as material, and I shall think it over. I hope to meet the St. Petersburg comrade here and talk things over with him in detail.

All the very best.

Yours,
Lenin

Sent from London to Marseilles

First published in 1928

Printed from
the original

38
TO V. A. NOSKOV[145]

August 4, 1902

Dear B. N.,

I received both your letters and was very glad to see from them that the imaginary "misunderstandings" are really just *smoke*, as I already said in writing to Cook (I wrote that I was convinced of this).

You complain of our "agents". I want to talk this over with you—it is such a painful subject with me too. "Agents have been recruited too lightly." I know it, I know it only too well, I never forget it, but that is just the tragedy of our situation (believe me, tragedy is none too strong a word!)—that we *are obliged* to act in this way, that we are *powerless* to overcome the lack of management prevailing in our affairs. I am well aware that your words contained no reproach to us. But try to put yourself in our place and *adopt such an attitude* as to make you say not "your agents" but "*our* agents". You could, and in my opinion should, adopt such an attitude—and only then will *all* possibility of misunderstandings have been removed once for all. Substitute the first person for the second, keep an eye yourself on "our" agents, help to search for, change and replace them, and then you will speak not of our agents being "unpleasant" (such language is bound to be misunderstood: it is regarded as an expression of estrangement, it is regarded as such in general and by the members of our editorial collegium who have not had an opportunity of clearing up the question with you), but of the shortcomings of *our common* cause. The mass of these shortcomings weighs more and more heavily upon my mind as time goes on. The time is now fast approaching (I feel it) when the question will face us squarely: either Russia will appoint its people, put forward people who will come to our aid and set matters right, or.... And although I know and see that such people are being put forward and that their number is growing, this is taking place so slowly and with such interruptions, and the "creaking" of the machinery is so nerve-racking, that ... sometimes it becomes extremely painful.

"Agents have been recruited too lightly." Yes, but after all we don't make the "human material", we take and have to take *what we are given*. We couldn't live without it. A man is going to Russia—"I want to work for *Iskra*," he says. He is an honest man, devoted to the cause. Well, he goes, of course, and passes for an "agent", although *none* of us had ever handed out such a title. And what means have we for checking "agents", guiding them or appointing them to other places? More often than not we can't even get letters, and *in nine cases out of ten* (I speak from experience) all our plans in regard to the future activity of the "agent" end in smoke *as soon as the frontier is crossed*, and the agent muddles along just anyhow. Believe me, I am literally losing all faith in routes, plans, etc., made here, because I know beforehand that nothing will come of it all. We "have to" make frantic efforts *doing* (*for lack of suitable people*) other people's jobs. In order to appoint agents, to look after them, to *answer* for them, to unite and guide them *in practice*—it is necessary to be everywhere, to rush about, to see all of them on the job, at work. This requires a team of *practical organisers and leaders*, but we haven't got any; at least, very, very few to speak of.... That's the whole trouble. Looking at our practical mismanagement is often so infuriating that it robs one of the capacity for work; the only consolation is that it must be a vital cause if it is *growing*—and obviously it is—*despite* all this chaos. That means when the ferment is over we shall have good wine.

Now do you understand why the mere remark by an Iskrist: "those agents of 'yours' are rather lightweight" can almost drive us to distraction? Try taking the place of these "lightweights" yourselves instead, we feel like saying. We keep repeating and even writing in our booklets that the whole trouble is that "there are plenty of people and *there are no people*", yet we have this lack of people thrust under our nose. There is only one way out, only one solution that is *most imperatively* necessary, urgent in the most literal, unexaggerated sense of the word—for time will not wait and our enemies are growing too, including *Osvobozhdeniye*[146] and the Socialist-Revolutionaries and all the various new Social-Democratic groups, beginning with the lightheads of *Zhizn* and ending with the Borbist[147] intriguers. The solution is for the Iskrists in Russia to get together at last, *find the people* and *take the management of "Iskra" into their own hands*, for truly it is said: our land is great and abundant, but disorder reigns in it. People *must* be found, for *there are* people, but they must be guarded more carefully than the apple of one's eye, not merely in the direct sense of guarding from the police, but guarded for this urgent matter, without allowing them to be diverted by other, generally useful but *untimely tasks*. When, owing to a complete lack of people, we are *compelled* to seize on the most "lightweight", it is not surprising that we cannot stand by calmly watching others postponing our work "for later on".

If all the *present*, available supporters of *Iskra* were *at once*, without delaying, to take up the *management* of *Iskra*, its *independent* equipment with the means for sending across the frontier, its distribution, and supply of material, etc., we *would have already an actual Central Committee*, a C.C. disposing *de facto* of "agents" (for the C.C. and not the editorial board should dispose of the agents) and *managing* all practical matters.

It is being said: if there are no people, where is the C.C. to get them? But we do find the people, even if only lightweights. One heavyweight among ten lightweights does not take the lead, but the experience will not have been wasted. People learn in the course of the work: some drop out, others replace them, and *once things have been set going* it is ten times easier for the others to *take up* this work which has been running smoothly. If we were to set up a C.C. today (not formally), tomorrow it would be formal and would already be *drawing* capable people from every local organisation ten times more energetically than now. And it is only this "drawing from the local organisations" that can create a state of affairs under which these local organisations would be properly *served*.

That is why I am so *jealous*, so devilishly jealous about Semyon Semyonich[148] and why the glance (the mere glance) at an "outsider" worries me. I can't adopt any other attitude, for unless the Iskrists say: this is *my* business, unless they say it out loud, unless they come to grips with the job, tackle it tooth and nail, unless they begin to upbraid the others for lack of tenacity [you once said to me: upbraid the Iskrists! And I replied: it is not I but *you* should do so, for only one who takes part practically in the work *itself* and who knows it thoroughly has the right to do so]— unless the Iskrists do this, it means that they *want* to leave us "only with lightweights", and that would be the beginning of the end.

It is time to conclude. I am extremely desirous that you and Cook should have as concrete an idea as possible of our position, understand it and say not you, but *we*. In any case, it is essential that Cook should write to us frequently, and *directly*, and keep us in *closer* touch with Semyon Semyonich and the latter with us.

As to your visit here, if you still have to be in Zurich, that is a different matter. Why are you feeling bad? Is your health quite all right? Should you not take a little rest?

I am still unwell, so it is no use even thinking of a journey.

Write me your opinion of Zernova and Sanin. I have heard something about the latter from various persons and got the impression that he is no worker, that he is much too "wild".* Is it true that Zernova is a bad person, that is, not merely in the sense of being fond of "adventure" (that, in itself, is not so bad) but as being unreliable?

All the very best.

Yours,
Lenin.

Sent from London to Zurich
First published in 1925

Printed from
the original

---

* This word is in English in the original.—*Ed.*

39
TO E. Y. LEVIN[149]

Dear comrades,

We were extremely glad to receive your letter informing us of the views and plans of the remaining editors of *Yuzhny Rabochy*.[150] We whole-heartedly welcome your proposal for the closest contact and co-operation between *Yuzhny Rabochy* and *Iskra*. The most vigorous steps should immediately be taken to consolidate these close relations and pass to *united activities* resulting from the unity of our views. In the first place, we shall avail ourselves for this purpose of your proposal to negotiate with Chernyshev.[151] Let us have his address. Is he going to be abroad (as we have heard) and will he not visit us?* Secondly, let us know also who your official representative is. Give us at once a direct address for letters to you from abroad *and from Russia*, as well as a rendezvous address to you. We have already taken steps for members of the *Iskra* organisation in Russia to meet you and confer about everything in detail. Not to waste time, we ask you, too, to write to us about matters in greater detail. What are the immediate practical plans of the editorial board of *Yuzhny Rabochy*? Is it in contact with the southern committees and does it have formal relations with them? From your statement that you intend to conduct affairs as they were conducted *prior to the formation* of the League of Southern Committees and Organisations[152] we infer that both the composition and *trend* of the present editorial board of *Yuzhny Rabochy* differ from the composition and trend which existed in the spring, at the

---

* From abroad, write to Dietz in *two envelopes*, asking him to forward immediately to the editorial board of *Iskra*.

time of the conference. What exactly is the difference between these trends, and what is the position adopted here by the southern committees, i.e., which of them support the trend of the League of Southern Committees and Organisations and which of them are in favour of your trend? What is your opinion of the extent of this divergence, does it prevent Party unity, and what measures are desirable for speedy achievement of solidarity? In what relation do the six provincial groups you have written about stand to the southern committees (and to the two trends which you have mentioned)? We should very much like you to help us to clear up fully all these questions, for that would be of great assistance in bringing closer together your friends and the members of the *Iskra* organisation in Russia working in the south.

Written August 22, 1902
Sent from London to Kharkov

First published in 1924

Printed from
the original

40

TO V. P. KRASNUKHA AND YELENA STASOVA[153]

A *personal* letter to Vanya and Varvara Ivanovna. Please hand it immediately to them alone.

The news of Bouncer's "victory" has astounded us.[154] Was the departure of Kasyan and Hairpin really sufficient to deprive the Iskrists of the ability to act? Bouncer's protest could lead only to your proposing to him *to put it to the vote* and at once declaring by a majority, firstly, that on the substance of the question he is in an insignificant minority; and, secondly, that his complaint of violation of the Rules is ridiculous and petty-fogging (for, according to the Rules, the opinion should be asked of all who were present in St. Petersburg and the matter not deferred pend ing an inquiry of those who were absent).

If Bouncer raised (dared to raise) the question of dissociation, it was imperative at once to adopt a majority decision for his expulsion from the Union.

Obviously, Bouncer is brazenly heading "for war" and the Iskrists will be eternally disgraced if they do not reply to this by the most resolute and desperate war. Do not be afraid of any threats on the part of Bouncer, you have nothing to fear from publicity, treat the matter immediately as a war issue, as we have written above, and adopt the decisions proposed above as speedily as possible. Even if Bouncer carries still others along with him (even if only half or *less than* half of you are left) you should all the same go the whole hog and demand Bouncer's expulsion unconditionally, without being the least afraid of a "split" in the Union.

You should also put an ultimatum to the workers too: either a split in the Union and war, or a decisive condemnation of Bouncer by the workers and his expulsion.

We, for our part, are writing at once to 2a3b. We are *putting off* the publication of the St. Petersburg statement in *Iskra*.[155]

We repeat: the question has now become a *point of honour* with the *Iskra* people of St. Petersburg.... Of course, everything you do now must be done at a general meeting, to which Bouncer must be invited and minutes of the decisions taken. Send us the minutes at once.

Written September 24, 1902
    Sent from London
      to St. Petersburg

  First published in 1924   Printed from
                                                            the original

41

TO P. A. KRASIKOV[156]

Dear friend,

I cannot find my notes on our meeting here.[157] In any case they are not needed. The meeting was of a consultative nature and you two,[158] of course, remember what happened better than I do. I cannot reconstruct officially what took place, and I could not do so even if I had the jottings made exclusively for myself, sometimes not in words but by signs. If there is anything important that needs to be settled, write a definite proposal, send in an official inquiry to us (to the editorial board) and we shall answer at once. But if there is no occasion for it yet—well, we have reached full agreement on general tactics.

I was very, very glad to learn that you have rapidly gone forward in the matter of the O. C.[159] and set it up with six members. I am surprised only that you have co-opted others *before* the formal constitution, *before* the invitation of the Bund? Just the opposite was planned, wasn't it? Incidentally, this is not so important if you are sure that it will cause no inconvenience.

Be stricter with the Bund! Be stricter, too, in writing to the Bund and *Rabocheye Dyelo* abroad, reducing their function to such a minimum that in any case it cannot be of importance. You can entrust technical arrangements of the Congress to special delegates from you or to your special *agents*; don't hand over this matter to *anyone* and don't forget that the people abroad are weak in secrecy techniques.

Outline the congress *ordre du jour* only in general terms. Send us an enquiry asking to be informed of our (editorial) *ordre du jour*, who are our reporters and how many delegates there may be from us (from the editorial board). Speed things up with the Congress as much as you can.

Try to provide mandates for those who have fled from Russia; that will economise expenses.

Be sure to inform us exactly of each and every official step taken by the Organising Committee. And one thing more: *Rabocheye Dyelo* is dying and it would be very valuable if you (on behalf of the Organising Committee) were to send them an exhortation, in serious but not abusive terms, on the importance of uniting, on the value of conciliation, and so forth.

And so, make haste! In case of need, we shall raise a little money.

Written November 11, 1902
    Sent from London
      to St. Petersburg

First published in part in 1920
First published in full in 1928   Printed from
                                                   the original

42

TO E. Y. LEVIN

Lenin writing. We are very glad to note the successes
and energy of the O.C. It is most important to exert every
effort immediately to carry matters to a conclusion and
as quickly as possible. Try to replace speedily the member
from St. Petersburg (Ignat would be good) and write to us
in detail about the attitude adopted towards the Organising
Committee in various places (committees). Will Ignat see
Fyokla[160] soon? We need to know precisely and speedily.

We have drawn up the list of questions approximately
as follows (in the order for their discussion): 1) attitude
towards Boris[161]? (If only a federation, then we should
part at once and sit separately. We need to prepare
everyone for this.) 2) The programme. 3) The Party
Organ (the newspaper. A new one or one of those already
existing. Insist on the importance of this preliminary question). 4) Organisation of the Party (basic principle: two
central institutions, unsubordinated to each other. a) The
Central Organ—ideological leadership. Abroad? b) The Central Committee—in Russia. All practical direction. Regular
and frequent meetings between them and certain reciprocal
membership rights or sometimes reciprocal co-optation. It
is extremely important to prepare the ground in advance
for securing the adoption of this basic principle and for making it fully clear to everyone. Next, the greatest possible
centralisation. Autonomy of the local committees in local
affairs—with the Central Committee having the right of
veto in exceptional cases. District organisations only with
the consent and endorsement of the Central Committee).
5) Various questions of tactics: terror, trade unions, legali-
sation of the workers' movement, strikes, demonstrations,

uprising, agrarian policy and work among the peasantry and in the army, agitation in general; leaflets and pamphlets, and so on *and so forth*; here no special order has been adhered to. 6) Attitude to other parties (*Osvobozhdeniye*, Socialist-Revolutionaries, Poles, Letts, etc.). 7) Delegates' reports (*it is very important* that there should be reports from every committee, and as full as possible (they should be prepared *immediately* and for safety's sake copies should be given to the Organising Committee to be sent to us). Try always to characterise the local *Socialist-Revolutionaries* and give an estimate of their strength and connections in the reports). 8) Groups and organisations abroad (*Rabocheye Dyelo, Borba, Zhizn, Svoboda*.[162] A committee or the Central Committee to be charged with working out a plan for their unification). 9) May Day. 10) The 1903 Congress in Amsterdam.[163] 11) Internal organisational questions: finance, the type of organisation of the committees, the C.C. to take charge of shipment and distribution of literature, etc. Some of these, probably, will have to be discussed in committees.

I repeat, this is merely a preliminary draft and only the order of items 1-5 has been discussed here jointly. In this connection, among the members of the editorial board I was in favour of item 3 being put in one of the first places (i.e., in fact, third), but another member (Pakhomy) was for putting it after item 5. I consider it important to settle item 3 at the outset so as at once to give battle to all opponents on a fundamental and broad issue and to ascertain the entire picture of the Congress (alternatively: to separate on an important issue).

Find out whether you will have reporters and on what questions (*ad* 5—in detail).

What pamphlet does Ignat want published? Is it not the letter to Yeryoma*?

Be sure to obtain from *each* committee (and group) an official and *written* reply as to whether they recognise the Organising Committee. It is essential to have this at once.

I advise that the announcement about the Organising Committee should be issued in Russia as well (i.e., not

---

* The reference is to Lenin's "A Letter to a Comrade on Our Organisational Tasks" (see present edition, Vol. 6).—*Ed.*

only printed in *Iskra*); issue it even if only in hectographed form.

We shall send the general editorial draft of the questions and the list of our reporters when we have made contact about this with all the members of the editorial board who are living in various countries at present.

Appoint immediately members of the Organising Committee in the chief centres (Kiev, Moscow, St. Petersburg), and give secret addresses for rendezvous with them so that we can be sure that all those whom we send are under the full disposal of the Organising Committee. This is very, very important.

Finally, one thing more: Ignat's meeting with Fyokla must be arranged to take place *after* 1) he has seen all and everyone he possibly can; 2) you have received from everyone official recognition of the Organising Committee; 3) you have *officially informed "Rabocheye Dyelo" as well* that they will have a plenipotentiary member of the Organising Committee. Only under these conditions can the meeting of Ignat and Fyokla lead to further important practical steps. Ignat should therefore make haste with these preliminary measures and not forget that he should come to Fyokla's equipped with formally acknowledged and *the widest* (N.B.!) plenary powers.

Written not earlier than
December 11, 1902
Sent from London to Kharkov

First published in 1928   Printed from
                                                          the original

43

TO G. V. PLEKHANOV

December 14, 1902

Dear G. V.,

There has been no news from you for quite a time and a lot of business and questions have accumulated.

First of all, about articles for *Iskra*. For No. 30 (No. 29 will come out tomorrow or the day after) we have Julius's article "Autumnal Summing-up". One more article is *essential*. How about you? Please let us know whether you are writing anything and when you are thinking of sending it, and also about a *feuilleton*; it would be very good to have in No. 30 the *feuilleton* you proposed against Tarasov's "little page".[164] I shall await your reply.

Next, about a pamphlet against the Socialist-Revolutionaries. L. Gr. told me and wrote to you that it would be best if you undertook it, for you could give, in addition to "dogmatic" criticism, the *historical parallel* with the seventies. I fully agree with L. Gr. that such a parallel is very, very important; but there is no use, of course, in my even thinking about it. And in general I should be very glad if you would undertake this pamphlet. I have little heart for it myself; besides, in addition to current business, I am now faced with the task of preparing for lectures in Paris (Julius tells me that they want to invite me there for three or four lectures on the agrarian question). And so, absolutely everything points to the pamphlet being your job—it is most definitely needed against the Socialist-Revolutionaries, who must be picked to pieces in the most detailed and thoroughgoing manner. They are awfully harmful to us and our cause. Do write and tell us your decision.

L. Gr.'s answer to *Revolutsionnaya Rossiya*[165] was published in No. 29: you will receive it towards the end of
the week—and you have already seen the proofs.

I learnt today that you will be at the international conference in Brussels (probably at the end of December or
beginning of January[166]) and will read a lecture there. I
hope you will not fail to drop in on us. We are right next
door and the fare will be quite cheap during the holidays.
And here, firstly, your lecture is very badly needed, as
there are many *workers* here who are infected with anarchism
(I discovered this when I delivered my lecture on the Socialist-Revolutionaries, which did not interest our people
here[167]). You would certainly be able to influence them.
Furthermore, and this is the chief thing, we have a heap
of important subjects to discuss, especially as regards Russian affairs: the Organising Committee, after long preparation, has at last been formed there and it can play a *tremendous* role. It is of the highest importance that we should
jointly reply to a *whole series* of questions which it has *already addressed to us* (questions concerning measures for
uniting the Party, the agenda, *Tagesordnung*, at the general
congress, what reports there will be *from us*, etc.—extremely important questions in general, and now of particular
significance). Write, please, as to when exactly the conference in Brussels will be held, how long it will last and
whether you will be able to come here. Further, it may,
perhaps, not be out of place if at this conference you already make use in one way or another of the fact that the
Organising Committee has been set up. Write soon and we
shall get in touch with Russia: we may succeed even in
getting some sort of statement or letter from them addressed
to you, if needed.

Do you see the Zhiznites[168]? How is the "rapprochement"
with them progressing and what are the chances? And what
about the *Rabocheye Dyelo* people? You know, I believe
it would be a good thing if they too took part in your "Marxist circle" and if we began (informally) to come closer to
them. It is not worth while these days quarrelling with them,
and there is no reason to, as a matter of fact: by replacing
Rabocheye Dyelo by *Krasnoye Znamya*[169] they have in effect
adopted our plan for "division of literary functions", and

(apart from the *silly* "clairvoyant") there is nothing *harmful* in Martynov's pamphlet *Workers and Revolution.*

All the very best.

Yours,
Lenin

As for the Bulgarian,* I am to blame. I'm sorry. I did not write because there were no assignments to give, and it did not occur to me that you would worry.

Sent from London to Geneva
   First published in 1925

Printed from
the original

---

* Unidentified.—*Ed.*

44

TO V. I. LAVROV AND YELENA STASOVA[170]

December 27

We have received Vlas's letter. We shall give you what help we can. We have long been aware of your plight and have been thinking of assistance.

But you must immediately and without fail write us an accurate account of the split in St. Petersburg. Answer the following points: 1) Was the Organisation Committee (the summer one) elected by the League of Struggle[171] alone (=committee of intellectuals?) or by the Workers' Organisation[172] as well? 2) When exactly was it elected? 3) Is there a precise record of its powers (i.e., what it was charged with doing)? 4) Wherein lay the irregularity of its election, according to Bouncer and Co.? 5) Were there delegates from the Workers' Organisation (two?) in the Organisation Committee and by whom were they elected? 6) From what has Bouncer been chucked out—from the Organisation Committee or the Intellectuals' Committee or the Workers' Organisation? 7) What Workers' Organisation is it that now writes its declarations? A new one? A reorganised one? when? how? 8) Why have you not sent us the September leaflet of the Committee of the Workers' Organisation? 9) Why have you not issued even a handwritten leaflet against them?—or sent us a counter-declaration? Not one of their moves should be left unanswered. 10) What is this C.C. like now? Is there still an Organisation Committee? Are there workers on your side? Why haven't they formed a counter-organisation? Why don't your workers protest against Bouncer workers and their committee?

Send us immediately new, absolutely unused places of rendezvous for visitors. Do not give these (our) rendezvous to anyone else. Seek out beforehand a flat to shelter one person. Take special care to cover up traces of his contacts with the old members (Heron and others), who are probably being shadowed.

Written December 27, 1902

Sent from London
to St. Petersburg

First published in 1928

Printed from
the original

45

TO F. V. LENGNIK[173]

December 27

We have received the letter about the coup d'état* and are replying at once. We are astounded that Zarin could allow such a scandal! There you have the fruits of his mistake in not joining the Committee!—a step we were insisting on long ago. We shall not publish anything about the statement for the time being, for we have received neither the statement nor the letter against it. Commence hostilities by all means, make Zarin join, drew up a minute of the break (or the number of votes *pro* and *contra*), and issue a local leaflet on the causes of the split (or divergence). There is no sense in publishing the statement without such official documents about each of your steps. Be sure to put on record each step of the *Rabocheye Dyelo* supporters and of yours against them, and do not yield one iota. They must be shown up as being against the Organising Committee, whilst you are for it. It is on the basis of recognition (or non-recognition) of the Organising Committee that decisive battle should promptly be given *everywhere*; convey this most insistently to Zarin and his immediate *Genossen*.

And so, let Zarin display redoubled energy and fight for Kiev—that is his prime duty.

The literature is in Russia and should soon be in your hands. You *must* send not less than two poods to our people in St. Petersburg, *without fail*.

Written December 27, 1902
Sent from London to Kiev

First published in 1928

Printed from
the original

---

* This refers to the capture of the Kiev Committee by the Economists, supporters of *Rabocheye Dyelo*.—*Ed.*

1903

46

TO I. V. BABUSHKIN[174]

For Novitskaya from Lenin

Dear friend,

As regards the "examination",[175] I must say that it is impossible to propose an examination programme from here. Let all the propagandists write about the programme on which they are lecturing or wish to lecture, and I shall answer in detail. You ask for more questions to be put to you. Very well, only mind you answer them all: 1) What are the present Rules of the St. Petersburg Committee? 2) Is there "discussion"? 3) What is its position in relation to the Central Committee and the Workers' Organisation? 4) The attitude of the C.C. to the district organisation and to the workers' groups? 5) Why did the Iskrist workers tacitly permit Bouncer workers to call themselves a "Workers' Organisation Committee"? 6) Have measures been taken to keep track of every step of the St. Petersburg Zubatov organisation[176]? 7) Are regular lectures read (or talks arranged) in the workers' circles on the subject of organisation, on the significance of an "organisation of revolutionaries"? 8) Is propaganda widely conducted among the *workers* to the effect that it is they who should pass to an illegal position as frequently and extensively as possible? 9) Have measures been taken to ensure ten times as many letters from St. Petersburg, the flow of which has been held up for a disgracefully long time? 10) Is the idea being inculcated among all workers that *it is they* who ought to organise a printing-press for leaflets and the proper distribution of the latter?

There are ten questions for you. I send you warm greetings and await your reply. Mind you disappear at the first sign that you are being spied on.

Written January 6, 1903
    Sent from London
    to St. Petersburg

First published in 1928   Printed from
                                                 the original

47

TO YELENA STASOVA

We have received (from somewhere abroad) a new Bouncer document, dated October 1902, a programme and principles of organisation—muddled and pernicious. We are devilishly vexed and offended at your failure to send us immediately and directly (in two copies to different addresses) all the St. Petersburg productions. It is simply outrageous that up to now we have not had the first leaflet of the Bouncer people (the July "protest" against the recognition of *Iskra*) and only learnt about it from *Otkliki*[177]! Surely it is not difficult to send leaflets when all letters arrive quite all right! More outrageous still is the fact that you hold up your replies so long. Ignat has told us that his leaflet replying to the Bouncer drivel was written a long time ago, but that you held it up and substituted another one, longer, feebler and more watered-down, only in the end to publish none at all! If it couldn't be published, surely it could have been sent here in a letter!

For Christ's sake, explain what is the matter; is it due to sheer bungling oversight on the part of someone in the Committee (or of the whole Committee?) or to deliberate opposition and intrigue within the Committee?

We cannot rid ourselves of the impression inevitably created by all this: namely, that the Bouncers are steadily ousting you, deceiving you and before long will kick you out altogether.

We would strongly advise electing Bogdan in place of the missing member of the Organising Committee from

St. Petersburg[178]; he fully deserves it. And in general, apparently, things will never advance an inch without professional revolutionaries.

Written January 15, 1903
       Sent from London
       to St. Petersburg

First published in 1928   Printed from
                                                    the original

48
TO THE KHARKOV COMMITTEE OF THE R.S.D.L.P.

January 15

(From Lenin.) Dear comrades, many thanks for your detailed letter on the state of affairs; such letters are rarely written to us although we are in very great need of them and ten times as many are essential if we really want to establish a living connection between the editorial board abroad and the local Party workers, and make *Iskra* a full reflection of our working-class movement, both as a whole and as regards particular features of it. We therefore beg you to continue on the same lines, and at least sometimes to give us straight pictures of talks with workers (what do they talk about in the circles? What are their complaints? perplexities? requirements? the subjects of the talks? and so on and so forth).

The plan of your organisation, apparently, is suitable for a rational organisation of revolutionaries, insofar as it is possible to say "rational" when there is such a lack of people, and insofar as we can judge of the plan from a brief account of it.

Give us more details about the independents. Further questions: Are there no workers of the "Ivanovo-Voznesensk" school and tradition left in Kharkov? Are there any persons who once directly belonged to this Economist and "anti-intellectualist" company or only their successors? Why don't you write anything about the "leaflet of workers' mutual aid societies", and why don't you send it to us? We here have seen only a handwritten copy of No. 2 of this leaflet. What sort of group is issuing it? Are they out-and-out Economists or merely green youths? Is it a purely working-class organisation or is it under the influence of Economist intellectuals?

Are any traces left of the *Kharkovsky Proletary*[179] group?

Is *Iskra* read in the workers' circles? With explanations of the articles? Which articles are more eagerly read and what kind of explanations are required?

Is propaganda of secrecy methods and transition to an illegal position conducted among the workers on a large scale?

Try to make more use of the St. Petersburg Zubatov organisation and go on sending workers' letters.

Yours,
Lenin

Written January 15, 1903
    Sent from London

First published in 1924

Printed from
the original

49

TO YELENA STASOVA

January 16, 1903

We have just received No. 16 of *Rabochaya Mysl*[180] (from Geneva) and No. 2 and 3 of *Rabochaya Mysl Listki* from St. Petersburg. It is now as clear as daylight that the Bouncers are fooling you and leading you by the nose when they assure you of their agreement with *Zarya* and *Iskra*. Come out with a militant protest immediately (if you are not able to publish it, send it here at once, in any case a copy), wage war vigorously and carry it widely into the midst of the workers. Any delay and any conciliation with the Bouncers would now be not only arch-stupidity but absolutely disgraceful. And so long as you have Bogdan, you can't complain of being shorthanded (help has been sent). Reply at once what steps you are taking.

Sent from London to St. Petersburg

First published in 1928

Printed from the original

50

TO I. V. BABUSHKIN

January 16

We have received from Geneva *Rabochaya Mysl* No. 16 (evidently published and even written by *Svoboda*, i.e., by Nadezhdin) already labelled as the organ of the St. Petersburg Committee. It has a letter of the Bouncers making a correction, a trivial correction, strictly speaking not a correction at all but a *compliment* to *Svoboda*. If the Bouncers assure you of their solidarity with *Zarya* and *Iskra*, that is obvious deception, the sheer humbug of people who are playing for time in order to gain strength. We earnestly and insistently advise you therefore to issue immediately (and if you cannot issue it, send it here) a leaflet protesting in the name of the Committee and in general to refute all conciliatory manoeuvres and approaches, and to launch a vigorous war, a ruthless war, against the Bouncers, with an exposure of their defection from Social-Democracy to the "Revolutionary-Socialist" *Svoboda*. We approve the energetic behaviour of Novitskaya and once again ask you to continue in the same militant spirit, without allowing the slightest vacillations. War on the Bouncers and to hell with all conciliators, people of "elusive views" and shilly-shallyers! Better a small fish than a big beetle. Better two or three energetic and wholly devoted people than a dozen dawdlers. Write as often as possible and, *without delay*, give us access to your workers (and a characterisation of them) so that in case of arrests we shall not be stranded.

Written January 16, 1903
Sent from London
to St. Petersburg

First published in 1928

Printed from
the original

51
TO G. M. KRZHIZHANOVSKY

January 27

Old Man writing. I have read your angry letter of January 3 and am replying at once. Regarding correspondence, dogs,[181] etc., the secretary[182] will reply below: I can no longer make out who is to blame but we absolutely must be in constant touch, not less frequently than twice a month, but so far this has not been the case and we have heard nothing about you for long periods at a time. Don't forget that when we have no letters, we can't do anything, we do not know whether people are alive or not; we are compelled, simply compelled, to consider them almost non-existent. You did not answer my question about Brutus's transference; apparently, there is little hope of any good arrangement until this transference takes place. Now to business. In criticising us, you overestimate our strength and influence; we reached agreement here about the Organising Committee, we insisted on its meeting, on your being invited, and we wrote to you. We could do nothing more than that, absolutely nothing, and we do not answer for anything. The trouble is that Brutus was not in the Organising Committee, and all subsequent action was taken without him (as also without us). We have not accepted an unknown member (he is of the dawdler type, unintelligent; I knew him personally in Pskov, tied down by family and place, backward, no good at all, Pankrat had already been criticised because of him), we have not transferred the bureau, we have given absolutely no "power" to Pankrat. But when it turned out that Pankrat was the sole (N.B., N.B.) mobile person of the Organising Committee, the result could not but be power as well. You write: there are people, but we do not have them, do not know them, do not see them. We have worked ourselves up to

neurasthenia over the total lack of persons for the Organising
Committee, which requires mobile, flying, free and illegal
people. Pankrat alone went over to illegality, travelled,
began to fly, began to know everything—and assumed the
rank of corporal as a matter of course. We did not interfere,
naturally, because we neither could interfere nor wanted
to interfere; there was no other! Try to understand this.
Pankrat is indolent and careless, but he is clever, sensible,
knows the job, knows how to fight and is a man you can get
on with. Now he is stranded [in Paris] indefinitely, and we
are going for him baldheaded, driving him to Russia, as
otherwise the Organising Committee is nothing but a cipher.
"She" (Akim's brother) will go shortly, we shall try to get
"her" into the O.C.; "she", I believe, is energetic. Pen
does not want to go away. There are no passports, and
no copies. If Brutus moves to a nearby, lively place, we shall
help him to get the bureau back,[183] and everything will
be straightened out, perhaps. Otherwise everything will
proceed (if it does proceed) by the will of Allah, the will of
Pankrat, and "her" will, and we are powerless in the matter.

The literature has been sent off. Over 40 poods have been
shipped. We are publishing the statement of the Organising
Committee in No. 32, which will come out the day after
tomorrow.

Uncle, too, is still standing aside (like Brutus) and has
not even gone anywhere; if only he and Brutus would settle
in *Poltava* at least, they would take over the bureau.

I am very annoyed with Zarin; his letters convey nothing,
he is inert, knows nothing about Kiev, and has allowed a
split to take place under his very nose. To keep aloof from
local affairs to such an extent is simply outrageous! Is it
our fault that, of the two "equal members" of the Organising
Committee, Zarin "sits and says nothing", while Pankrat
at least is stirring a little? I think (I don't know for
certain) that Zarin is a person with little initiative and one
who is tied down by legality and place. And now such people, alas, remain aloof, and through no fault or will of ours.

Written January 27, 1903
Sent from London to Samara

First published in 1928   Printed from
                                                the original

52

TO THE UNION OF RUSSIAN SOCIAL-DEMOCRATS ABROAD[184]

To the Union of Russian Social-Democrats

In reply to the letter of the Union of Russian Social-Democrats to the League of Russian Revolutionary Social-Democracy, received by us on February 4, 1903, we hasten to inform the Union of Russian Social-Democrats that we entirely share its opinion as to the need to form a foreign section of the Organising Committee in Russia. It is true that we cannot at all agree with the opinion of the Union of the R.S.D. that the Organising Committee "wrongly or inaccurately ascribes its origin to private initiative", for the O.C. refers directly to the decision of the conference (the O.C. was in fact set up in fulfilment of such a decision). Moreover, the O.C. was formed by organisations which took part in the conference. The fact that the O.C. has not straight away and without inquiring the opinion of the remaining Party organisations declared itself an official Party body is, in our view, evidence of the Organising Committee's correct understanding of its tasks, and of its tact and caution, which are so important in a serious Party matter.

It should be said at once, though, that we do not attach any great importance to our above-mentioned disagreement with the Union of the R.S.D.; on the contrary, we have every hope that this disagreement will be easily dispelled with the development of the Organising Committee's activity.

Further, we would consider it inexpedient, even not quite lawful on our part, "to proceed *immediately* to constitute a foreign section of the O.C.", unless there was a direct invitation from the O.C. in Russia. We have been informed that the O.C. has already written to the Bund in Russia and to the Union of the R.S.D. Abroad. We do not have the text of either letter. In any case, it follows from the above that the O.C. in Russia is already taking steps in this direction. It would hardly be wise on our part to begin to act without waiting for the result of these steps of the Organising Committee.

We consider it our duty to bring the letter of the Union of the R.S.D. immediately to the notice of the O.C. in Russia and at the same time we shall communicate to the O.C. our opinion of the desirability of the O.C. in Russia immediately setting up its foreign section. We would suggest waiting for a reply from the O.C. in Russia. If, however, the comrades of the Bund Committee Abroad and of the Union of the R.S.D. consider that, before receiving this reply, it would be useful to arrange a *private meeting* of representatives of the Bund Committee Abroad, the Union of the R.S.D., and the League of Russian Revolutionary Social-Democracy, we would not, of course, refuse to take part.

The League of Russian Revolutionary Social-Democracy

Written February 4 or 5, 1903
Sent from London to Paris

First published in 1930   Printed from
                                                  the original

53

TO Y. O. MARTOV[185]

February 5, 1903

I am sending you a copy of the Union's letter and the draft of our reply.* The reply was sent to Plekhanov who was to await your letter from Paris. Arrange a meeting with P. Andr. and Boris immediately and answer Plekhanov *as quickly as possible* whether you are satisfied with the reply or whether changes are required. It would be desirable, of course, not to delay the reply to the Unionists, but if changes are voted it will entail a pretty long delay; perhaps unimportant changes can be disregarded. But, of course, if there is disagreement on the substance of the question, it will be necessary to hold up the reply (I am writing to Plekhanov about this) and have everyone vote.

In my opinion (with which V. I. and L. Gr. agree) the most important thing here is that 1) the foreign section of the O.C.[186] should be precisely a section of the Organising Committee in *Russia*. The Unionists' idea, I believe, is to have *two* sections with equal rights: one in Russia, the other abroad. By no means can we accept or allow such an interpretation. The O.C. in Russia must act cautiously (in this respect its announcement is admirably drawn up), but in *all* matters and in *all* approaches made to it, must *behave* with the utmost formality and rigour, that is to say, in such a way that it, the O.C. in Russia, controls everything and *no one* in the Party can do *anything* of a general Party character or in the way of general obligations, *unless authorised to do so by the Organising Committee in Russia.*

---

* See pp. 139-40 of this volume.—*Ed*.

Yet the Unionists, by their letter, recognise (or almost three-quarters recognise) the O.C. and the more they recognise it, the more formally and firmly must the Organising Committee behave. It is of the highest importance to adopt the right tone from the very beginning and to take such a stand that the Party position is made quite clear: *either* recognition of the *present* O.C. and *subordination* to it, *or* war. *Tertium non datur.** Even now there is every chance of obtaining *general* recognition, without offending or irritating anyone, but without giving way *in the slightest degree.*

2) The O.C. should reduce the functions of *its* foreign section to a minimum. The foreign section only "deals with" affairs *abroad* (in the sense of preparing for unity) and *assists* the Russian section. On every other question that goes the least beyond those limits, the foreign section of the O.C. *must request the opinion and decision of the Organising Committee in Russia.* I strongly urge, therefore, that the O.C. in Russia should *as soon as possible* write a letter to the Union, the League and the Bund proposing that they should form *a section of their own for exercising such-and-such functions.* It is essential that the O.C. in Russia should indicate the "limits of authority" to its foreign section, and I propose below an outline of these functions with *three* and only three strictly limited items. I earnestly request you to discuss this draft as quickly as possible with P. A. and Boris and confirm it (alternatively, put changes to the vote). (We shall send all these data to Yuri[187] as well, asking him to await the arrival of P. A. and Boris, who should do everything to hasten their arrival.)

(Of course, P. A. could write a letter to the League, the Union and the Bund Committee Abroad from here, but I think this is in the highest degree undesirable, for people will suspect a put-up job and a fiction. Better to wait a week or two, and have the letter sent without fail from Russia.)

I also believe we must think of electing a member of ours to the O.C. (the foreign section) and vote on it in advance, for owing to the members being in different

---

* There is no third way.—*Ed.*

places this can take much time and it will be unpleasant if things have to wait on this account. For my part, I vote for L. Gr.

I positively do not have time to write to Plekhanov as well. You will simply forward to him *at once both this letter and the reply to the Union*, and meanwhile I will drop him a line.

All the best.

Lenin

Sent from London to Paris
First published in 1925

Printed from
the original

54

TO THE NIZHNI-NOVGOROD COMMITTEE OF THE R.S.D.L.P.

To Nizhni

As regards the appeal, I (Lenin) find your decision reasonable[188]—I have not had time yet (nor a chance) to consult my associates.* The courage of the Nizhni-Novgorod workers, who asked that their personal well-being should not be taken into account, ought to be mentioned in *Iskra*; it would be desirable for you to write a letter about this to the editors.

We received via Berlin the "Letter to the *Iskra* Editorial Board from the Nizhni-Novgorod Committee", a long letter, about terrorism, with a defence (partial and conditional) of terrorism; the end is missing (apparently). Write *immediately*:

1) Did the Nizhni-Novgorod Committee send this letter officially?

2) Repeat the end of it (the letter has seven paragraphs and ends with the words: "They clear the atmosphere, which is often too heavy, they teach the government to handle the revolutionaries more carefully").

3) Let us know whether you allow stylistic corrections (in some places the style is very bad, due perhaps to incorrect, hasty and unclear copying).

We shall probably publish the letter together with our reply.

We earnestly and *insistently* beg you to inform us in your letters without delay of every official step taken by the Committee (dispatch of a document for travelling war-

---

* I may yet be able to return to this question.

rants..., list of leaflets, answer to another committee or to a group abroad, and so on and so forth). Otherwise there are bound to be misunderstandings,* mistakes and bureaucratic delays. Iskrists should pull together and inform *Iskra* speedily and comprehensively.

All the very best.

Written prior to February 23, 1903
Sent from London

First published in 1930

Printed from
the original

---

* For example, we have heard a lot of tittle-tattle and abuse about the Committee's leaflet *against* a demonstration on the day of the trial.[189] The leaflet itself we received not long ago *by chance*, from Berlin, and with delay. Good heavens! This is simply outrageous! Surely it wasn't difficult for the Committee to write to us about the *leaflet* and send us a copy of it *as soon as it came out*. For heaven's sake, take all the necessary steps to correct these shortcomings.

55
TO THE ORGANISING COMMITTEE WITH THE TEXT OF NADEZHDA KRUPSKAYA'S LETTER

I have received the letter of the O.C. I suggest answering like this:

"In our opinion, the question of the *'ordre du jour'* stands as follows. This question of the agenda will be definitely *settled* by the *Congress itself*, and only by the Congress. Consequently, it is quite useless to dispute about the right to vote on this point. Further, the *bulk* of the committees have already recognised the *'exclusive* initiative' of the O.C. in convening the Congress. Hence it follows that the *preliminary* preparation for the Congress, including *preliminary preparation* (or propaganda) of the *ordre du jour*, is *exclusively* a matter for the Organising Committee. It is, therefore, altogether superfluous to propose that anyone should *vote* as well on a *'preliminary' ordre du jour*; it *cannot* have any *decisive* significance. Furthermore, it will merely *cause* both delay and dissatisfaction, for there will be people who will be *offended* (committees that were not consulted), and people who will *inevitably* be dissatisfied and complaining. Consequently, from the standpoint of both formal loyalty and tact *no formal* decision should be taken about collecting the votes of the committees or of anyone at all. It would only undermine the authority of the Organising Committee if it renounces the *exclusive* initiative entrusted to it.

"If it is very inconvenient now to alter an adopted (and formally unexceptionable) decision, there may be, perhaps, the following way out: turn the voting (of the committees) into a *consultation* with them, that is to say, adopt a decision that as far as possible the O.C. will try to make use of meetings and talks for *consultation*.

"Finally, we advise making haste with the Congress. The sooner you convene it, the better. And set to work immediately and more actively *preparing the committees*, nominating delegates, winning over *Nikolayev* and Odessa. The important thing is to make perfectly sure of a safe majority of firm Iskrists."

Nevzorov disgraced himself yesterday, and Charles Rappoport and Krichevsky gave him a dressing down. There were no Iskrists.[190]

I shall be leaving probably on Sunday. The trains arrive not at 6 but at 3.45 and 10.45. With one of them, probably.

Yours....

Written March 5 or 6, 1903
Sent from Paris to Kharkov
First published in 1928

Printed from
the original

56

TO THE ORGANISING COMMITTEE

Letter to the O.C.

We have just received the rules of the Congress. It appears
that we did not understand you and replied about the *ordre
du jour* when you were asking about the *rules* of the Congress. We hasten to say that on the whole we are very satisfied with your draft, which is carefully and sensibly drawn up.
Clause 19, which has evoked dispute, seems reasonable to
us; to exclude certain organisations from the Congress (and,
in the final analysis, the rules are precisely regulations for
the exclusion of some and the granting of rights to others)
is in fact inconvenient and impossible without the agreement of the majority of the committees. Our only advice
would be to fix a formally binding period as short as possible
(for example, not more than a week) in the course of which
the committees and organisations are *obliged* to draw up
and send in their amendments to the draft rules. This is
essential in order to avoid delay, which is most of all to
be feared. (It is probably through fear of delay that Ignat,
too, protested. We understand his fears, but if you are able
to complete the interrogation quickly, the matter can be
put right.)

For our part, we shall write to the *Iskra* organisations
about our advice that your draft should be accepted immediately and completely. We earnestly request you to
make use of every facility to ensure that the dispatch and
communication of the draft (on the basis of § 19), the "session"
of the arbitration courts, and determination of the composition of the deputies will be completed within a month
at the latest.

In this connection we advise you informally to recommend all qualified organisations to appoint *as far as possible* one (or two) delegates from among comrades living abroad who are known for their past work—in order to avoid extra expenses and difficulties involved in sending delegates abroad.

We formally propose 1) to supplement your draft only by a note to § 19: "Organisations which have not presented their comments within a week from the date of receipt of the draft will be regarded as having accepted the draft rules of the Congress"; 2) to make provision for alternate delegates in the event of delegates being arrested before the Congress.

Written between March 6 and 9, 1903

Sent from Paris to Kharkov

First published in 1928

Printed from
the original

57

TO G. V. PLEKHANOV

March 15, 1903

Dear G. V.,

I have received your letter. You are writing "The Ides of March", that is excellent. The *dead-line* is March 25, 1903—the article must be here. *We expect it without fail.*

Maslov's book is being sent to me in a few days from Paris (I shall ask them to make haste) and I shall send it on to you *at once.*[191] It contains interesting data on the harm of the village commune, which I quoted in Paris.[192]

I had already ordered David's book and am now reading it. Terribly watery, poor and trite. I am trying to finish it quickly so as to send it on to you. Have you seen Kautsky's articles on this "neo-Proudhonist"[193]?

I have now set to work on a popular pamphlet for the peasants on our agrarian programme.* I should very much like to demonstrate our idea of the class struggle in the countryside on the basis of *concrete* data on the four sections of the village population (landowners, peasant bourgeoisie, middle peasantry, and semi-proletarians together with proletarians). What do you think of such a plan?

From Paris I came away with the conviction that only such a pamphlet could dispel the perplexities about the cut-off lands, etc.

About the Manifesto of February 26 I have written an article which will appear in No. 34.** I have categorically insisted that it should be the leading article in view of the *tremendous* importance of the Manifesto. It seems, how-

---

* *To the Rural Poor* (see present edition, Vol. 6).—*Ed.*

** "The Autocracy Is Wavering" (see present edition, Vol. 6).—*Ed.*

ever, that V. I. is *wavering* (!) and together with Y. O. is deciding the other way round: first about Marx.

In my opinion, this is even preposterous.

All the very best.

Yours,

Lenin

Sent from London to Geneva

First published in 1925   Printed from
the original

58

TO THE ORGANISING COMMITTEE

We advise that steps be taken immediately to have the O.C. together with the Polish Social-Democrats issue a formal declaration (as detailed and precise as possible) on their full solidarity with the Russian S.D.L.P. and their desire to join the Party. On the basis of such a formally published statement the O.C. could invite the Polish Social-Democrats to the Congress. Then, surely, no one will protest.[194]

Next (privately), we earnestly request you everywhere and among everyone to prepare the ground for a struggle against the Bund at the Congress. Without a stubborn struggle the Bund will not surrender its position. And we can never accept its position. Only firm determination on our part to go through to the end, to the expulsion of the Bund from the Party, will undoubtedly compel it to give way.

Make haste with the list; it is very important and must be done quickly, without waiting for a reply from the committees. By the way, were the committees given a short time within which to reply? Are you keeping a list of the delegates already appointed? (Send it to us as an additional precaution.)

Written March 31, 1903
Sent from London to Kharkov

First published in full in 1928

Printed from
the original

59

TO G. M. KRZHIZHANOVSKY

(The Old Man.)

There is little I can tell you this time. The main thing now, in my opinion, is to make every effort to expedite the Congress and ensure a majority of intelligent (and "our") delegates. Almost all our hope is on Brutus. As far as possible, he should himself keep an eye *on everything*, especially the delegates, and try to get the maximum number of our people appointed. The system of two votes from each committee is very favourable for this. Next, the question of the Bund is very important. We have stopped the polemic with it over the O.C., but not, of course, the polemic over principles. That is out of the question. We must make everyone understand, simply "ram it into every head", that it is necessary to prepare for war against the Bund if we want peace with it. War at the Congress, war even to the extent of a split—whatever the cost. Only then will the Bund be sure to surrender. We absolutely cannot accept, and never will accept, the stupid idea of federation. At the very most—autonomy according to the old Rules of 1898 with a delegate appointed by the C.C. taking part in the C.C. of the Bund. We must prepare our people, we must explain the stupidity and demonstrate the absurdity of the attack on Ekaterinoslav,[195] and so on. Please write speedily and let us know what the feeling is in this respect, how your propaganda is going and whether there is any hope of the majority taking the right stand. We should like to issue a pamphlet to the Jewish workers on the necessity of a close union and the stupidity of federation and "national" policy.

Written April 3, 1903

Sent from London to Samara

First published in 1928

Printed from
the original

60

TO THE ORGANISING COMMITTEE

April 6, 1903

In transmitting to the O.C. the inquiry of the foreign section of the O.C.,[196] we for our part earnestly advise you not to widen the functions of the foreign section in any way and not to allow it to extend its bounds by a single inch, as it is making every effort to do. In the interests of the work, the functions of the foreign section of the O.C. should in no way go beyond preparing the secret part of the Congress, collecting money and, at most, discussion of the conditions for uniting the Social-Democratic organisations abroad in the form of a *preliminary* preparation of this question. Regarding point 1 a), we are strongly against giving the address of the O.C.'s foreign section to the committees. The functions of the foreign section being what they are, this is quite pointless. It is not without its dangers in the sense of causing delay and confusion. As regards publicity, it should be frankly stated that everything will be published in *Iskra* (the formal basis for this is its recognition by the majority of the committees). Other organisations should be formally recommended to reprint all the statements of the O.C. from *Iskra*. As regards contact between the O.C. and its foreign section, we advise the following arrangement: the O.C. will communicate *with Deutsch* through the usual channels (*Deutsch* is the secretary of the O.C.'s foreign section, which also includes *Alexander and Lokhov*). And you will communicate with Deutsch through us, as before. This is quite natural; the foreign section of the O.C. elected a secretary and you have endorsed his election.

To the second question we advise that you reply by agreeing, and to the third by an explanation that the agenda will be presented and is already being prepared.

Sent from London to Kharkov
First published in 1928

Printed from
the original

61

TO YEKATERINA ALEXANDROVA[197]

Private, from Lenin

I have read your long letter, for which many thanks. Better late than never. You ask me not to be very cross. As a matter of fact, I was hardly cross at all, and was more inclined to smile at the recollection of my last conversation at the door of the "den"[198] with a certain Jacques, who considered at that time (at that time!) that we did too little bossing. That things take a long time adjusting themselves within the O.C., that there is still a huge amount of disorder and anarchy, I was quite aware and have not expected anything else. The only cure for that is persistent treatment (time and experience) and a single potent remedy (a general Party congress). I wrote long ago and I repeat it: hurry up, for heaven's sake, with this remedy as much as you can, otherwise there is a risk of your experience being *lost* altogether.

I am not going to write about the questions of 1) Yuri,[199] 2) the Bureau, and 3) Ignat's dispute with Bundist. In part, they have become obsolete; in part, they require to be settled on the spot, and as regards this last part my advice at best would be to no purpose (despite the opinion of my friend Jacques). This part you (all of you) have to decide for yourselves, "have to" not in the sense of *sollen** but of *müssen.***

I will say something about the Bund, the P.P.S.[200] and "heresy".

Formally, I think, our attitude to the Bund should be studiously correct (no hitting straight in the teeth), but

---

* Should.—*Ed.*
** Must.—*Ed.*

at the same time icily cold, buttoned up to the neck, and
on legitimate grounds we should press hard against the
Bund relentlessly and all the time, going right to the end
without being afraid. Let them get out, if they want to,
but we should not give them the slightest occasion, the
shadow of an excuse, for a break. We must, of course,
observe the formalities prior to the Congress, but there is no
point in showing our cards. You write: Bundist knows we
are working for *Iskra* but keeps silent, although we have no
right to do so in the name of the O.C. In my opinion, this
should not be done from the O.C. but from each member
personally, referring not to the O.C., but to *the committees
which have recognised Iskra*. The result is the same and
even much stronger (there are no "agents"), and the formal
aspect is irreproachable. Preparing the committees against
the Bund is one of the *most important* tasks of the present
moment, and it, too, is fully possible without any violation
of form.

Similarly, it was wrong to speak to the P.P.S. about the
"convictions of *members* of the Organising Committee".
It should have been said of the O.C.: we are preparing the
congress, and the *congress* will decide; and on the question
of "convictions" one should not remain silent but refer,
not to the O.C., but to *Iskra* and *still more* to the committees that have recognised *Iskra*. Furthermore, we should
obtain from the P.P.S. a formal if only short document
(a letter), and not say to them "we are anti-nationalists"
(why frighten people needlessly?), but gently persuade them
that our programme (recognition of the right of national
self-determination) is adequate for them too, drawing from
them definite counter-declarations and a *formal approach*
to the O.C. and the Congress. Our trump card against the
P.P.S. is that we recognise national self-determination in
principle, but within reasonable limits determined by the
unity of the proletarian class struggle.

Before I forget: I really do not know the representatives
of the Russian organisation of *Iskra* in the O.C. Nor do I
know why I should know this, and why there should be
"representatives". The Organising Committee has long ago
co-opted all sorts of good people, but they were not "representatives", were they? Or is this untrue?

It is important, I think, to make use of the distinction between the Russian organisation of *Iskra* and the O.C. precisely for the sake of formal irreproachability.

Now about "heresy". Either I misunderstand you, or this is a great mistake. In view of the extreme brevity of your letter on this (highly important) point, I can only take your words *à la lettre*. Four delegates "organise" both the C.C. and the Central Organ! Frankly, this is simply ridiculous, for you ought to know that the only people competent (i.e., *having the knowledge* and necessary experience) to "organise" the Central Organ are the members of the editorial board+*individuals* from outside for consultation, while the only people competent to organise the C.C. are experienced practical workers+individuals for consultation (if you know of such persons). Or do you, perhaps, know of a "foursome" who have *experience* and knowledge of all these things? If you do, then name them—seriously, I am not joking, for this letter of mine is a personal one and it is important for me to be clear about your idea.

You are out for a single centre of power and a "strong hand", if I am not mistaken. It would be a good thing and you are absolutely right that that is what we need. But no one can achieve it in such a forthright way as you are thinking of. For nine-tenths of current affairs, two central bodies are absolutely essential; they would immediately arise of themselves, even if we did not want this. For form's sake, however, we should try to achieve 1) a formal way of uniting these two central bodies (for example, a committee with delegates from both of them), 2) a reduction in the number of members of the two central bodies, or the selection of an executive committee within each central body, and— most important—3) a strict, *formal* distribution of functions among individual members of the central bodies, so that their whole membership should *know* precisely which member is charged with managing what, which member (in each centre) has the right to *decide* (and even to speak) in each sphere of problems, and in what way matters can be transferred to a plenary meeting of one or both of the central bodies.

I am confident that you will considerably moderate your demands and will agree that this is the maximum immediately desirable. Even that is very, very difficult and *I do not see* any people who are fully suitable, informed, and experienced enough for such a distribution of functions. There is a great deal, a vast amount of mismanagement *both* among you and *us* (you, members of the O.C., should not think only of yourselves, you "organise" the *whole* Party), and we must think out not *pia desideria*, but practical, *firm*, "first steps".

I have expressed my views to you *frankly* and I should be very glad of a further exchange of letters with you. Really and truly, you *ought* to write more often and in more detail on such questions. I have nothing against this letter being communicated to the whole O.C., I should even welcome it, but I leave the decision to you. You did well to mention *to whom* your letter was addressed.

All the best. Moderate your demands and hurry, hurry, hurry with the "potent remedy". Best regards.

Yours,
Lenin

Written later than May 22, 1903
    Sent from Geneva to Kiev

First published in 1928   Printed from
                                           the original

62

TO ALEXANDRA KALMYKOVA[201]

September 7, 1903

I have just received your letter and hasten to reply. Yes, I see that you are already well informed and that the sum of the information that makes you so is tinctured— as well it would be—a definite colour. I understand also that what has happened is bound to worry you.

But it is one thing to know and another to understand, as you justly write, and I am deeply convinced that it is impossible to understand what has happened from the stand-point of "the effect of a nervous breakdown". A nervous breakdown could only give rise to sharp animosity, fury and a reckless attitude to results, but the results them-selves are utterly inescapable and their advent has long been merely a question of time.

"Riffraff" and "praetorians"—you say. That is not the case. The political alignment was *im Grossen und Ganzen* as follows: five Bundists, three *Rabocheye Dyelo*-ists, four *Yuzhny Rabochy*-ists, six from the "Marsh" or indecisives, nine Iskrists of the soft line (or *Zickzackkurs*) and twenty-four Iskrists of the firm line; these are voting members, and, of course, approximate. There have been cases when everything was mixed up differently, but *à vol d'oiseau* this, on the whole, was how the groups worked out. The biggest shuffle (over equality of languages), when many Iskrists vacillated, left us with not less than 23 (out of a total of 33 Iskrists) and even among these 23 the "Martovites" were in a minority. And do you know the result of the vote at the meeting of the 16? Sixteen *members of the Iskra organisation*, and not "riffraff" nor "praetorians"? Do you know that here, too, Martov *was in the minority* both on the question of the person who had been the apple of discord *and on the question of lists*?

The minority of Iskrists of the soft or zigzag line defeated the majority (on the question of the Rules, and more than once) by a coalition of the Bund+the Marsh+the *Yuzhny Rabochy*-ists. And when the Bund and *Rabocheye Dyelo* withdrew, the majority of the Iskrists had their own back. *Voilà tout.* And not a single person has any doubt that, if the Bund had not withdrawn, Martov would have beaten us over the central bodies. And to make such a finale a reason for resentment, offence, a split in the Party! It is madness. The story goes that the "praetorians" ousted people because of a slanderous accusation of opportunism, that they cast slurs on and removed active people, etc. That is mere idle talk, the fruit of an imaginary grievance, *rien de plus.* No one, absolutely no one had "slurs" cast upon him or was removed, prevented from taking part in the work. Some one or other was merely removed from the *central body*—is that a matter for offence? Should the Party be torn apart for that? Should a theory of hypercentralism be constructed on that account? Should there be talk of rule by a rod of iron, etc., on that account? Never for a moment have I doubted or been capable of doubting that a trio of editors is the *sole* genuinely business-like trio, which does not break up anything, but adapts the old "family" collegium to the role of someone in an *official* capacity. It is precisely the family character of the Six that has been tormenting us all these three years, *as you know only too well*, and from the moment *Iskra* became the Party and the Party became *Iskra*, we *had to*, were *obliged to*, break with the Six and its family character. It was for this reason that already prior to the Congress I declared that I was going to demand freedom of election of the editorial board—or the trio—which is the sole basis also for sensible co-optation.

The break with the "family character" was absolutely essential and I am confident the Six would have peacefully accepted this trio but for the accompanying squabbles over § 1 and over the C.C. *It is only* these squabbles that in their eyes painted the trio in this "horrible", absolutely false hue. There is nothing "horrible" in it at all, and it was essential to impose a restraint on the *Zickzackkurs*, and the majority of the Iskrists (both at the Congress and within the *Iskra* organisation) understood this perfectly well.

No, I repeat, the finale is not an "unforeseen calamity", it is not a "division of the whole". That is untrue. It is untrue that one can curse the day of "promotion"—or all our old work would remain for ever a torment of Tantalus. And in the Party, on its formal basis, with subordination of *everything* to the Rules* (over which we quarrelled desperately not without reason, quarrelled over every trifle with Martov, who *beat* us on this point), in such a Party the old family editorial board (*not once* in three years—this is a fact—did it meet with the full number of six members) was *impossible*, the more so because the non-Iskrists entered the Party in a bunch by right, on formal grounds. And this called for a firm and consistent line, and not a zigzag policy. There is no returning to the old, and only a disordered imagination can picture Martov being led to the slaughter instead of to joint work with comrades, of whom each has his shade of the political line. *Actually*, I would add, this trio, *throughout these three years, in 99 cases out of a hundred,* had always been the decisive, politically decisive (and not literary) central body.

Now, after Martov *beat* the majority of the Iskrists by alliance with the Bund and *made every preparation* for beating them by this alliance on the question of the central bodies as well, I find "their" complaints about riffraff and praetorians, their laments about the "crystal" of *Iskra*'s editorial board ludicrous. He beat them by an alliance, I say, and not by a deal; I would not think of accusing them of a *deal* with the Marsh and the Bund, nothing of the sort. When "they" talk about "defamatory rumours" (of being allies of the Bundists) being spread against them, "they" are repeating their usual mistake of confusing the personal and the political. A deal would be personally ugly. The alliance did *not* depend *on their will*, their alliance was caused by their mistake; it was not they who went with the Bund+the Marsh, but the Bund+the Marsh+*Yuzhny Rabochy*, etc., who followed them, having grasped at once which of the Iskrists had to be supported from the anti-Iskrist standpoint. The Bund+the Marsh, etc., only

---

* That is why "arrangements among ourselves" are *impossible* now, absolutely impossible, both judicially and morally.

revealed politically Martov's organisational and tactical ✒
mistake.

For one who knows all the facts of the Congress and
especially the distribution of Iskrist votes (both at the Congress and in the underground organisation of *Iskra*) there
cannot be any doubt that there is no going back. The *Iskrists*
have parted company, but *Iskra* could not exist apart from
the Iskrists. And, I repeat, *among the Iskrists* Martov was
definitely in a minority, and a *split* in the Party (towards
which Martov is *fatally* heading, more and more each day)
will be a revolt of the minority, a minority that is in the
wrong both juridically and *still more in all essentials*.

We "cast slurs" neither on Martov nor on anyone else
for their mistake, but call *all* of them to the work.

As regards the "material means" of which you speak,
we are hard up just now, it goes without saying, and the
Californian[202] sources have gone up in smoke. But, if it
came to that, we could endure even extreme need, so long
as all the work of many years is not allowed to be wrecked
*through dissatisfaction with the composition of the central
bodies* (for objectively "their" dissatisfaction amounts *only*
to this).

"Must the bucket too be shared?"[203] you ask. I could
hardly answer this question, for I make no claim to impar-
tiality in "sharing", and you do not need an answer that
is not impartial. I am convinced that there are no "frac-
tional parts", but there is a senseless *attempt* to break to
pieces, smash and scatter the whole (to build a new hearth,
as you put it) owing to defeat on a *single* question where the
defeated Iskrists were utterly wrong.

All the best.

Sent from Geneva to Dresden
First published in 1927   Printed from a copy written out
         by N. K. Krupskaya

63

TO A. N. POTRESOV

To Alex. Nikolayevich

September 13, 1903

I tried to have a talk with Y. O. recently, when the atmosphere of the impending split was already in full evidence, and I want to try to have a talk with you too, in the hope that you, like Y. O., would not be averse to making an attempt at explanation. If this hope is unfounded, you will, of course, let me know, but meanwhile I shall do what I consider necessary.

The refusal of Martov to serve on the editorial board, his refusal and that of other Party writers to collaborate, the refusal of a number of persons to work for the Central Committee, and the propaganda of a boycott or passive resistance are bound to lead, even if against the wishes of Martov and his friends, to a split in the Party. Even if Martov adheres to a loyal stand (which he took up so resolutely at the Congress), others will not, and the outcome I have mentioned will be inevitable. (Not for nothing, by the way, does Auntie, too, write about "building a new hearth".)

And so I ask myself: over what, in point of fact, would we be parting company as enemies for life? I go over all the events and impressions of the Congress,[204] I realise that I often behaved and acted in a state of frightful irritation, "frenziedly"; I am quite willing to admit *this fault of mine to anyone*, if that can be called a fault which was a natural product of the atmosphere, the reactions, the interjections, the struggle, etc. But examining now, quite unfrenziedly, the results attained, the outcome achieved by frenzied struggle, I can detect nothing, absolutely nothing in these results that is injurious to the Party, and absolutely nothing that is an affront or insult to the Minority.

Of course, the very fact of finding oneself in the minority could not but be vexatious, but I categorically protest against the idea that we "cast slurs" on anybody, that we *wanted* to insult or humiliate anybody. Nothing of the kind. And one should not allow political differences to lead to an interpretation of events based on accusing the other side of unscrupulousness, chicanery, intrigue and other pleasantries we are hearing mentioned more and more often in this atmosphere of an impending split. This should not be allowed, for it is, to say the least, the *nec plus ultra* of irrationality.

Martov and I have had a political (and organisational) difference, as we had dozens of times before. Defeated over § 1 of the Rules, I could not but strive with all my might for *revanche* in what remained to me (and to the Congress). I could not but strive, on the one hand, for a strictly Iskrist Central Committee, and, on the other, for a trio on the editorial board that would remove the very cause of our old, hopeless quarrels, that would unite persons of whom each has his own political line, of whom each makes decisions and will always make decisions "without regard for persons" and in keeping with his own extreme conviction.

I said (during our conversation with you and Y. O. about the trio before the Congress) that I regarded the inclusion in the Six of an absentee member[205] as most harmful of all for the work; I also took exception at the time, very strong exception, to Zasulich's highly personal attitude (although Y. O. has forgotten it); I said quite definitely (when you named the *most probable* elected trio) that I too considered it the most probable and that even if it *remained alone*, without going in for any co-optation (although at the time we mentioned one of the possible co-optations), I saw nothing bad in that. Yuli Osipovich has forgotten this last statement of mine too, but I remember it very well. But it is, of course, useless to argue about this. That is not important; what is important is that with such a trio not one of those painful, long-drawn-out, hopeless quarrels with which we began the work of *Iskra* in 1900 and which were often repeated, making it impossible for

us to work for *months* on end—*not a single one of such* quarrels would be possible. That is why I consider this trio
the *only* business-like arrangement, the *only* one capable
of being an official institution, instead of a body based on
indulgence and slackness, the *only* one to be a real centre,
each member of which, I repeat, would always state and
defend his Party viewpoint, *not one grain more*, and ir-
respective of all personal motives, *all* considerations concerning grievances, resignations, and so on.

This trio, after what had occurred at the Congress, undoubtedly meant legitimising a political and organisational
line *in one respect* directed against Martov. Undoubtedly.
Cause a rupture on that account? Break up the Party because of it? Did not Martov and Plekhanov oppose me over
the question of demonstrations? And did not Martov and
I oppose Plekhanov over the question of the programme? Is
not one side of *every* trio *always* up against the other two?

If the majority of the Iskrists, both in the *Iskra* organisation and at the Congress, found this particular shade of
Martov's line organisationally and politically mistaken,
is it not really senseless to attempt to attribute this to
"intrigue", "incitement", and so forth? Would it not be
senseless to try to talk away this fact by *abusing* the Majority and calling them "riffraff"?

I repeat that, like the majority of the Iskrists at the
Congress, I am profoundly convinced that the line Martov
adopted was wrong, and that he had to be corrected. To
take offence at this correction, to regard it as an insult,
etc., is unreasonable. We have not cast, and are not casting,
any "slurs" on anyone, nor are we excluding anyone *from
work*. And to cause a split because someone has been exclud-
ed *from a central body* seems to me a piece of inconceivable
folly.

Lenin

Sent from Geneva to Montreux
(Switzerland)

First published in a shortened
version in 1904 in the pamphlet:
V. I. Lenin, *One Step Forward,
Two Steps Back*, and in full in 1927   Printed from
                                                        the original

64

TO G. M. KRZHIZHANOVSKY

Thanks to Smith for his long letter. Let him write to Yegor, making a last appeal to reason. Let Zarin go and see Yegor immediately, after obtaining authority (full authority) to decide matters in Yegor's countries. Arrange all this with strict precision. You must act formally and, as regards the Yegors,[206] you must prepare for a decisive war, and see to it at all costs that any attempt of theirs to get into the committees meets with a prompt and vigorous rebuff. You must be on your guard about this and prepare all the committees. All the Yegors are carrying out and *extending* the boycott; they are devilishly embittered, they have dreamed up a heap of imaginary grievances and insults, they imagine that they are rescuing the Party from tyrants, they are shouting about this left and right, they are stirring people up. Their dissension has already deprived us (I don't know for how long, *possibly* even *forever*) of two of our largest sources of money. Please make the most desperate efforts to obtain money—that is the chief thing.

And so, don't let Smith look on Yegor in the old way. Friendship is at an end here. Down with all softness! Prepare for the most vigorous resistance, send Zarin at once, nominate candidates (in the event of Smith's death*), and in the same event prepare Smith, too, for a trip "to Yegor",** appoint *members to the Council*,[207] put everything on a very formal footing and exert yourself to the utmost. We shall cope with the matter of literature. We are putting strong hopes on Vadim.

Written between September 10
and 14, 1903
Sent from Geneva to Kiev

First published in 1927

Printed from
the original

---

* Meaning here arrest.—*Ed.*
** Meaning to leave the country.—*Ed.*

65

TO ALEXANDRA KALMYKOVA

September 30

You write: "I have lived too long in the world not to know that in such cases truth is not on one side alone, but on both sides." I fully admit it. The trouble is that the other "side" does not realise the new situation, the new basis, and demands what used to be easily arrived at (if only after months of quarrelling), but is now unachievable. The basis has become *different*, that is a *fait accompli*; but they are still guided chiefly by the offensive turn this or that thing took at the Congress, by the frenzied way Lenin behaved, etc. I did act frenziedly, there is no denying it, and I frankly admitted as much in a letter to Old Believer.* But the thing is that the results achieved by "frenzied" struggle are *not frenzied at all*, yet the other side in its fight against frenzy goes on fighting against the results themselves, against the inevitable and necessary results. But you have long been aware of the direction in which things were going. You know how you expressed your firm conviction of an obstacle due to certain "old men", and you, of course, will not doubt that the ill-fated "trio" is not a dirty trick, not a Jacobin coup, but a straightforward, natural and the *best*, really and truly the best, way out from three years of "wrangling". The trio is a triangular construction and there is no room whatever for wrangling in it. You know what the sensitivity and "personal" (instead of political) attitude of Martov+Old Believer+Zasulich led to when, for example, they all but

---

* See pp. 164-66 of this volume.—*Ed.*

"condemned" a man *politically* for an incident of a purely personal character. At that time, without a moment's hesitation, you sided with the "flayers and monsters". Yet this is quite a typical case. Now, too, the root is the same, the same mixing of the personal and the political, the same suspicion that we want to *cast a slur on* people personally, although we only set them aside (or shift them) politically. And when you remind me: blame *must* also fall on you, I reply: I would not think of denying the personal aspect, but that is no reason for demanding a *political* correction. The hopelessness, the complete hopelessness, of the situation lies precisely in the fact that a political correction is being demanded on account of the sum total of personal grievances, of personal dissatisfactions with the composition of the central bodies. *Tout ce que vous voulez, mais pas de ça!** And if *political* divergence (as some desire) should be considered the cause, is it not ridiculous to *demand* for the sake of "peace" the co-optation of a larger number, or at least an equal number, of *political* opponents? It is ridiculous *nec plus ultra*!

The little example quoted by me above out of a large number of cases of wrangling is typical not only in substance but also in the form of the outcome. Do you know how we won the upper hand at that time? *We were in the minority*, but we won by sheer persistence, by threatening to bring everything into the open. They think they can do the same now. The trouble is that *now* is not *then*. Now the formal basis is *unremovable*. If it were not for this formal basis—why shouldn't there be six, once people have been roused to fury? We've stood three years of it, we can stand another three; we decided not by votes, but by persistence, so let us decide by persistence now too. But the thing is—it can't be done *now*. Yet people doggedly refuse to see or understand this change. And this is what makes the situation so hopeless. Now the dilemma is inexorable: *either* the divergence is over the question of persons, in which case it is ridiculous to make a political scandal and throw up work on account of it. *Or* the divergence is political—and then it is still more ridiculous to

---

* Anything but that!—*Ed.*

"correct" this by imposing definite persons of a different, shall we say, nuance.

They are taking (seem to be taking) the second course. In that case, join the trio, Martov, and *prove* before the Party the mistakes of the *two* in *your* collegium; unless you participate in the collegium you cannot obtain data for exposing these mistakes and putting the Party on its guard against them. Otherwise your accusations are empty *Parteiklatsch** over some future contingency.

If you take the first course, then don't stretch your resentment to the extent of throwing up the work, and the work will speedily cause "frenzy" to be forgotten. There is no more hopeless blind alley than that of throwing up one's work.

Written September 30, 1903
Sent from Geneva to Dresden

First published in 1927

Printed from a copy
written out by
N. K. Krupskaya

---

* Party tittle-tattle.—*Ed.*

66

TO THE ODESSA COMMITTEE OF THE R.S.D.L.P.

To the Odessa Committee

October 1, 1903

Dear comrades,

We too sincerely regret that a difference of opinion has arisen between the Odessa Committee and *Iskra* on the subject of factory stewards.[208] Our delay in replying to the letter of the Odessa Committee was due mainly to the fact that the editors were absent at the time. Generally speaking, the obstacle in this case (strange as it may seem) was the Second Congress of the Party.

As regards the essence of the matter, incidentally, a resolution was adopted at the Congress *recommending* participation in the election of factory stewards.

[Quote the text: resolution *No. 28.*]

This resolution was passed by a huge majority, and we think that matters can be put right, although it will take time. The Odessa Committee should *immediately* disseminate (without publishing) the text of this resolution among all *organised* workers and explain it to them. Later, when the resolution is published, it would be desirable for a leaflet to be issued over the signature of the Odessa Committee setting out the *Party* view on the question and calling on the workers to follow the tactics approved by the whole Party.

As regards the substance of the matter, we find that *constant* agitation in connection with the election of stewards would have a much greater educational and organising significance than agitation carried out *once only*—in connection with refusal to elect. And your own reports about patriarchal methods confirm this, pointing to the need for a *constant struggle* against espionage laws and methods of spying.

We fully concur with your desire for a more frequent exchange of opinions so as to avoid differences of opinion and contradictory statements in agitation. Write more often, not only for the press, and see to it that addresses (for letters to you) are effective regularly.

We shall try to write a leaflet on the connection between the economic and the political struggle, if only other work does not interfere.

We are publishing the manifesto of *Rabochaya Volya*[209] in full, as you desired.

Lenin

Sent from Geneva
First published in 1928

Printed from
the original

67

TO Y. O. MARTOV

To Comrade Martov from the Editors of the Central Organ of the R.S.D.L.P.

Comrade,

The editorial board of the Central Organ considers it its duty officially to express its regret at your refusal to participate in *Iskra* and *Zarya* (at present *Zarya* No. 5 is being prepared for the press). In spite of the numerous invitations to co-operate which we made immediately after the Second Party Congress, before *Iskra* No. 46, and which we repeated several times after that, we have not received a single literary item from you.

What is more, even the publication of the second edition of your pamphlet *The Red Flag* has been held up for many weeks owing to non-delivery of the end of the manuscript.

The editorial board of the Central Organ states that it considers that your refusal to co-operate has not been caused by any action on its part.

No element of personal irritation, of course, should be allowed to hinder work in the Central Organ of the Party.

If, however, your withdrawal is due to any divergence between your views and ours, we would consider a detailed exposition of such differences extremely useful in the interests of the Party. Moreover, we would consider it highly desirable that the nature and extent of these differences should be made clear to the whole Party as soon as possible through the pages of the publications edited by us.

Finally, for the sake of the cause, we once again bring to your notice that at the present time we are ready to co-opt you as a member of the editorial board of the Central

Organ so as to give you every opportunity to officially state and defend all your views in the highest Party institution.

Geneva, October 6, 1903[210]

Lenin. Plekhanov

Sent to Geneva
First published in full
in 1927

Printed from a copy
written out by
N. K. Krupskaya

68
TO G. D. LEITEISEN

October 10, 1903

Dear Leiteisen,

I received your letter and, in accordance with your request, I am replying at once. Whether there will be a congress and when, I do not know. I have heard that a majority of the three members of the League's board of management here pronounced against a congress and that it was decided to invite the opinion of the two absent members: you and Vecheslov; thus a settlement of the question has been postponed.

As far as I am concerned, I am personally against a congress. You think that the League ought to express itself and that a split in it is inevitable in any case; that two active militant sections would be better than a united inactive League. The point is, however, that a split in the League is not only inevitable, but is *already an almost accomplished fact*; two active militant sections *have already been formed* and until a split in the *Party* occurs these militant sections will *inevitably* remain in the united League. On the other hand, the Party Congress has completely upset the whole organisational basis of the League; its old Rules, which are well known to you, will, of course, in effect cease to exist after the Party Congress. The League must be renovated and it will, of course, be rebuilt on new lines by the Central Committee of the Party, which is charged with organising the Party committees and, in general, all Party institutions.

Consequently, one may say, it is left for the congress *to come together in order to part company*. To part company in two senses; in the sense of the mutual recrimination between us and the Martovites, and in the sense of the liquidation of the old League. Is it worth while coming together for this purpose? You will not cure the "split" (or, rather, the sulky withdrawal) in this way, but only still further embitter the two sides. What is the use of that? What is the use of a pageant of speeches when it is already almost certain that about thirty-five of the total forty members of the League have already *taken up their positions*?

Is the idea—to stage a *"dress rehearsal"*? i.e., to see approximately how we shall fight if it comes to a split in the Party? I cannot deny *this* significance of a congress, but *such* a game is not worth the candle.

The alignment of the remaining five (or about five) members of the League can be ascertained in a much easier way.

The League's work abroad will in any case proceed on new lines worked out by the Party's Central Committee. A League Congress *now* will generate more heat than light, i.e., it will contribute nothing to the work abroad.

I was very glad to learn that you are coming here and that we shall meet. Let me know in good time because I am still intending to go away on holiday for three or four days. I am swamped with work.

All the very best.

Yours,

Lenin

Sent from Geneva to Beaumont
(France)

First published in part in 1928
Published in full in 1929

Printed from
the original

69

TO G. M. KRZHIZHANOVSKY

To Claire

Dear friend,

I was very pleased to receive your latest news about the plan to take the skin off* Deer—it is high time! On the other hand, it is evident from letters that Deer and Vadim do not have a correct idea of the situation, and that there is no mutual understanding between us. This is very regrettable (even if Vadim's last letter giving advice in the form of an ultimatum is not to be taken seriously— Stake himself will reply to this, for, I repeat, I find it difficult to take *such* a thing seriously). Co-optation of Demon, Falcon, etc., is an erroneous step, in my opinion, for these people lack experience and self-dependence. The division of functions, too, is very dangerous, for it threatens to produce fragmentation. Meanwhile the committees continue to be neglected: in Kiev people are behaving foolishly and, strange to relate, neither Andreyevsky, nor Dyadin, nor Lebedev, have gone into the committees to fight. Kharkov, Ekaterinoslav, Don, and Gornozavodsky, too, are in the hands of the mutineers.** Positions must be occupied everywhere by our people at all costs. We must get at least one of our people, one who is wholly ours, on every committee without fail. The Caucasus is beginning to be stirred up[211]—there, too, they need our people's help. More important than a division of functions is for seats in each committee to be occupied by our agents, and then for all efforts to be devoted to transport and delivery.

---

* Meaning to place him in an illegal position.—*Ed.*
** Meaning the Mensheviks.—*Ed.*

When all is said and done, the most important thing, and our whole strength, lies in transport. We should not be content with one route alone, but have two or three, so as to put a stop to the continual interruptions.

It is extremely important to issue the announcement[212] as soon as possible, to issue it in Russia and distribute it everywhere. For heaven's sake, hurry up with this and write to us about it quickly and precisely. Brutus should be formally elected to the Council and his vote formally transferred to Stake. This is a matter that brooks no delay.

In my view, it is extremely important that Deer should be sent here if only for a couple of weeks, or even a week. This would be very, very useful, giving a view of everything *à vol d'oiseau*, enabling him to see the source of ferment and to achieve full mutual understanding. Surely, no one can grudge a mere 200 rubles and two or three weeks for the sake of this! Surely a legal foreign passport could be found for Deer! Think this over carefully. I strongly recommend this step, which is especially convenient in connection with Deer's plans. Truly, without having reached full agreement it is difficult to keep in step. And Deer's talk of "moral influence on the Old Man" shows (please don't take offence!) the utmost lack of mutual understanding. Why doesn't Deer write anything *about this*? The plan of co-opting Martov is simply ridiculous; it shows such a lack of understanding that there are certain to be instances when you will get into a mess, and with a scandal at that. No really, I can't even speak seriously about your co-opting Martov; if you have been thinking of it seriously, then we speak different tongues! We have all (including Stake) laughed until we cried over this "plan"!!

Lenin

Written October 20, 1903
Sent from Geneva to Kiev

First published in 1928   Printed from
                                                     the original

70

TO THE CAUCASIAN UNION
COMMITTEE OF THE R.S.D.L.P.

To the Caucasus

Dear comrades,

We have had news of your affairs both from Ruben in person and from Rashid-Bek by letter. We can only welcome your decision to remove Isari[213] temporarily, until the matter is examined *by the Central Committee*. The sum total of information concerning his behaviour at the Congress certainly points against him. The Congress showed his utter instability; after some waverings, Isari, nevertheless, at the decisive moment voted with the Majority and helped to secure adoption of the present composition of the editorial board of the Central Organ and of the Central Committee. But afterwards Isari suddenly went over to the other side, and is now fighting against the decisions of the Majority by methods that are hardly loyal! It's simply disgusting! Such a leader is not worthy of political trust. In any case, he should be treated with caution, to say the least, and should not be given any responsible posts—such is our deep conviction, both mine (Lenin's) and Plekhanov's.

Let the Caucasian comrades hold firmly to the course they have adopted. Let them turn a deaf ear to the slander against the Majority. The full minutes of the Congress will soon see the light of day and then things will be clear to all. Let them carry on their good teamwork with comradely faith in the Central Committee, and we are sure that the present "dissension" in the Party will be rapidly dispelled.

We are giving much thought now to the idea of organising here the publication of Georgian and Armenian literature. Competent comrades have taken this in hand, and we hope to raise the money. We need both literary and financial help.

We send greetings to the Caucasian comrades and ardent wishes for success in their work.

Lenin. Plekhanov

Written October 20, 1903
    Sent from Geneva

First published in 1928   Printed from
                                                          the original

71
TO THE DON COMMITTEE OF THE R.S.D.L.P.

Comrades,

We have received your letter with the resolution.[214] We earnestly request you to write to us on the following: 1) Have you heard reports from both the Minority and the Majority (one of your delegates, as you probably know, was on the side of the Majority), or only from the Minority? 2) What do you mean by the word "departure"? Departure —where to? Do you mean by this that someone has been removed from work, or has removed himself, for some reason or other, and for what reasons precisely? 3) What is it you call "abnormal conditions at elections"? 4) Who exactly, in your opinion, should be co-opted on to the Central Committee? and 5) who exactly on to the editorial board of the Central Organ?

Written in October 1903
Sent from Geneva

First published in 1904 in the book:
L. Martov, *The Struggle Against
the "State of Siege" Within the
Russian Social-Democratic Labour
Party*, Geneva

Printed from
the text of the book

72

TO THE MINING AND METALLURGICAL
WORKERS' UNION

Comrades,

We have received your resolution[215] and ask you to reply to the following questions. Please discuss them at a general meeting of all the members of the Committee (or send them to all the members, if they are not together) as an enquiry from the editorial board of the Party's Central Organ.

1) Has the Committee heard a report from the representative of the Majority at the Party Congress?

2) Does the Committee consider it normal to pass a resolution appraising the activities and decisions of the Congress before the minutes have been issued, and even before the Committee has enquired of the Central Committee or members of the Majority about matters which are not clear to it?

3) How could these disagreements on organisational questions *destroy* everything previously done by *Iskra* and the Organising Committee? How did the *destruction* manifest itself? *What exactly* was destroyed? We are not at all clear on this, and if you want to safeguard the Central Organ from any kind of error, it is your duty to explain to us what you regard as our error. Set the matter out in full detail and we shall carefully discuss your opinion.

4) What exactly are the "*sharp* disagreements on organisational questions"? We do not know. (We asked Martov and the former members of *Iskra*'s editorial board to expound these disagreements *in the pages of the publications edited by us*, but so far our request has not been complied with.*

---

* See pp. 173-74 of this volume.—*Ed.*

5) In what do you see the atmosphere of political intrigue and distrust? On the part of whom? Be more explicit. (If *we* distrusted Martov we would not have invited him to work in *Iskra*.)

6) If there really are "sharp disagreements on organisational questions" between us and the former editors, how can the two of us co-opt the four of them? That surely would mean making *their* tendency the dominant one? But the Congress pronounced in *our favour*, didn't it? What you want, therefore, is that the decision of the Congress should be revised on the basis of a private agreement.

7) Do you consider it normal that by threats of a split, boycott, etc., people should want to make Party officials (editors of the Central Organ, and the Central Committee) do something that these central bodies do not consider useful in the interests of the Party?

8) Do you consider it normal and permissible that Party members who have been left in a minority should abstain from work in the Central Organ, from supporting the Central Committee and obeying it, from helping the Party financially, and so forth?

Written in October 1903
Sent from Geneva

First published in 1904 in the book: L. Martov, *The Struggle Against the "State of Siege" Within the Russian Social-Democratic Labour Party*, Geneva

Printed from the text of the book

73

TO G. V. PLEKHANOV

November 1, 1903

Dear Georgi Valentinovich,

I am quite unable to calm down on account of the questions that are worrying us. This delay, this postponement of a decision, is simply dreadful, a torture....

No, really, I can quite understand your motives and considerations in favour of a concession to the Martovites. But I am deeply convinced that a concession at the present time is the most desperate step, leading to a storm and a shindy *far more certainly* than would war against the Martovites. This is no paradox. I not only did not persuade Kurtz to leave but, on the contrary, tried to persuade him to stay, but he (and Ru) flatly refuses now to work with the Martovite editorial board. What's going to happen? In Russia, dozens of delegates have been travelling all over; even from Nizhni-Novgorod they write that much has been done by the C.C., transport has been arranged, agents have been appointed, the announcement *is being published*, Sokolovsky in the west, Berg in the centre, and Zemlyachka and lots of others, have all settled down to work. And now comes the refusal of Kurtz. It means a long *break* (in the session and meeting of the *whole* C.C., now, it seems, already considerably enlarged). Afterwards, either a struggle of the C.C. against the Martovite editorial board or the resignation of the *whole* C.C. Then you+two Martovites in the Council must *co-opt a new C.C.*, and this without election by the Congress, with total disapproval on the part of the *great bulk* in Russia, and bewilderment, discontent and refusal on the part of these agents who have already gone out. Why, this will utterly discredit the Congress and sow complete discord and cause a scandal *in Russia* a hundred thousand times more terrible and dangerous than a scurrilous foreign pamphlet.

We are fed up with discord! That is what they write and *scream* about in letters from Russia. And to give way to the Martovites now would mean *legitimising* discord in Russia, for *in Russia* there has not yet been even a trace of disobedience and revolt. No statements of yours or mine will now restrain the delegates of the Majority at the Party Congress. These delegates will create a frightful rumpus.

For the sake of unity, for the sake of the stability of the Party—do not take this responsibility upon yourself, do not withdraw and do not give everything away to the Martovites.

Yours,

N. Lenin

Written in Geneva (local mail)
    First published in 1926

Printed from
the original

74

TO G. M. KRZHIZHANOVSKY

Dear friend,

You cannot imagine what is going on here—it's simply disgusting—and I beg you to do everything possible and impossible *to come here together with Boris, after obtaining the votes of the others.* You know that I am now fairly experienced in Party matters, and I categorically declare that any postponement, the slightest delay or vacillation, will spell ruin to the Party. You will probably be told about everything in detail. The gist of it is that Plekhanov has suddenly changed front, after the rows at the League Congress,[216] and has thereby cruelly and shamefully let down me, Kurtz and all of us. Now he has gone, without us, to haggle with the Martovites who, seeing that he was frightened of a split, double and quadruple their demands. They demand not only the Six, but also the entry of their people into the C.C. (they do not say as yet how many and whom) and of two of them into the Council, and a disavowal of the activities of the C.C. in the League (activities carried out with the full agreement of Plekhanov). Plekhanov was pitifully scared of a split and a struggle! The situation is desperate, our enemies are rejoicing and have grown insolent, all our people are furious. Plekhanov is threatening to throw the whole thing up immediately and is capable of doing so. I repeat, your *coming is essential* at all costs.

Written November 4, 1903
Sent from Geneva to Kiev

First published in 1928

Printed from
the original

75

TO THE CENTRAL COMMITTEE OF THE R.S.D.L.P.

Their conditions are: 1) co-optation of *four* on to the editorial board; 2) co-optation? on to the C.C.; 3) recognition of the lawfulness of the League; 4) *two* votes in the Council. I would propose that the C.C. put the following conditions to them: 1) co-optation of *three* on to the editorial board; 2) *status quo ante bellum* in the League; 3) *one* vote in the Council. Next I would propose endorsing at once (but for the time being without communicating it to the contending side) the following *ultimatum*: 1) co-optation of *four* on to the editorial board; 2) co-optation of two on to the C.C. at the discretion of the C.C.; 3) *status quo ante bellum* in the League; 4) *one vote* in the Council. If the ultimatum is not accepted—war to the bitter end. An additional condition: 5) cessation of all gossip, wrangling and talk concerning the strife at the Second Party Congress and after it.

For my part, I may add that I am resigning from the editorial board and can remain only in the Central Committee. I shall go *the whole hog* and publish a booklet about the struggle of the hysterical scandalmongers or discarded ministers.*

Written November 4, 1903
Sent from Geneva to Russia

First published in 1928

Printed from
the original

---

* Lenin's *One Step Forward, Two Steps Back* was published in May 1904 (see present edition, Vol. 7).—*Ed.*

76
TO V. A. NOSKOV AND G. M. KRZHIZHANOVSKY

November 5

1) Yesterday Lalayants set out to visit you.

2) I already wrote yesterday about the row here and that Plekhanov has taken fright and entered into negotiations with them.* They put forward the conditions: 1) restoration of the old editorial board, 2) co-optation of several persons on to the Central Committee, 3) two votes in the Council, 4) recognition of the League Congress as lawful. In other words, they agree to peace only on condition of complete surrender of the position, disavowal of Wolf and rendering the present Central Committee "harmless". My personal opinion is that any concessions on the part of the C.C. would be degrading and would completely discredit the present Central Committee. It is necessary that Deer and Nil come here as soon as possible, everything is at stake—and if the C.C. is not prepared for a determined struggle, a fight to the bitter end, it would be best to give up everything to them at once. To permit such demoralisation, to enter into such deals, means to ruin everything. I repeat, that is my personal opinion. In any case, come here at once so that we may jointly decide what to do.

Written November 5, 1903
Sent from Geneva to Kiev

First published in 1928

Printed from a copy
written out by
N. K. Krupskaya

---

* See p. 186 of this volume.—*Ed.*

77

TO G. V. PLEKHANOV

November 6, 1903

Georgi Valentinovich,

I have given much thought to your statement of yesterday that you will reserve for yourself "full freedom of action" if I do not agree to advise Konyagin to resign from the Party Council. I am quite unable to agree to this. Nor do I consider it possible to remain any longer in the unofficial position of *de facto* editor in spite of my resignation, since you say that full freedom of action as understood by you does not exclude your handing over the editorial board to the Martovites. I am compelled, therefore, to hand over to you all the official contacts of the editorial board of the Central Organ and all documents, which I am sending you under special cover. If any explanations are required in regard to the documents, I shall, of course, willingly give them. Some of the material has been given to contributors (Lebedev, Schwarz, Ruben), who will have to be told of everything being transferred to you.

N. Lenin

P.S. Please do not interpret the turnover of the editorial board in the sense of the notorious boycott. That would contradict what I said plainly in my statement to you of November 1 of this year.[217] I shall now, of course, bring my resignation from the editorial board to the knowledge of the comrades.

P.P.S. I am sending (tomorrow morning by messenger) three packets—aa, bb, cc—according to the importance of the material.

Issue No. 52 was to have been put out on November 16 with the announcement of the Central Committee.[218] For this the printing should begin on Monday; it will be all right even beginning it on Tuesday.

Written in Geneva (local mail)

  First published in 1926   Printed from
                                                      the original

78

TO G. M. KRZHIZHANOVSKY

November 8, 1903. To Smith

Dear friend,

Once more I earnestly beg you to come here, you in particular, and another one or two persons from the Central Committee. This is absolutely and immediately necessary. Plekhanov has betrayed us, there is terrible bitterness in our camp; all are indignant that, because of the rows in the League, Plekhanov has allowed the decisions of the Party Congress to be revised. I have definitely resigned from the editorial board. *Iskra* may come to a stop. The crisis is complete and terrible. Bear in mind that I am not fighting now for the editorial board of the Central Organ, I am quite reconciled to Plekhanov setting up a five-man board without me. But I am fighting for the C.C. which the Martovites, who have grown insolent after Plekhanov's cowardly betrayal, also want to seize; they are demanding the co-optation on to it of their own people without even saying how many! The fight for the editorial board of the Central Organ has been irretrievably lost owing to Plekhanov's treachery. The sole chance of peace lies in trying to give them the editorial board of the C.O. while holding on to the C.C. ourselves.

This is not at all easy (even this may be too late already), but we must try. We need Smith here, and best of all *two* more Russians from the C.C., the most imposing (no ladies) (e.g., Boris and Doctor). Plekhanov threatens to resign if the C.C. does not yield. For heaven's sake, don't believe in his threats; we must use more pressure on him, scare him. Russia must stand up firmly for the C.C. and content itself with handing over the editorial board of the C.O.

New people from the C.C. are needed here, otherwise there is absolutely no one to conduct negotiations with the Martovites. Smith is triply needed. I repeat the Martovites' "conditions": 1) negotiations on behalf of the editorial board of the C.O., and the C.C., 2) six on the editorial board of the C.O., 3) ? on the C.C. Cessation of co-optation on to the C.C., 4) two seats in the Council, 5) disavowal of the C.C. as regards the League, recognition of the latter's Congress as lawful. These are indeed peace terms put by victors to the vanquished!

Sent from Geneva to Kiev

First published in 1928

Printed from the original

79
TO M. N. LYADOV[219]

November 10, 1903*

Dear Lidin,

I should like to give you our "political news".

To begin with, here is a chronology of recent events. Wednesday (October 27 or 28?) was the third day of the League Congress. Martov yelled hysterically about "the blood of the old editorial board" (Plekhanov's expression) being upon us, and that on the part of Lenin there was something in the nature of intrigue at the Congress, etc. I calmly challenged him in writing (by a statement to the bureau of the Congress**) to make his accusations against me *openly* before the whole Party; I would undertake to publish *everything*. Otherwise, I said, it was mere *Skandalsucht*.*** Martov, of course, "nobly withdrew", demanding (as he still does) a court of arbitration; I continued to demand that he should have the courage to make his accusations openly, otherwise I would *ignore* it all as pitiful tittle-tattle.

Plekhanov refused to speak in view of Martov's discreditable behaviour. Some dozen of our people submitted a statement to the Congress bureau, branding Martov's "discreditable behaviour" in reducing the dispute to the level of squabbling, suspicions, etc. I would remark in parenthesis that my two hours' speech about "Comrade Martov's histor-

---

* The letter bears Lenin's note: "unmailed".—*Ed.*
** "Statement Concerning Martov's Report" (see present edition, Vol. 7).—*Ed.*
*** Mania for provoking a row.—*Ed.*

ical turn"* at the Party Congress towards *Versumpfung***
did *not* evoke even from the Martovites a *single* protest
about the issue being reduced to the level of squabbling.

Friday. We decided to introduce eleven new members
into the League. In the evening at a private meeting with
these "grenadiers" (as we jokingly called them), *Plekhanov
rehearsed* all the steps by which we should utterly rout
the Martovites. A stage scene. Thunderous applause.

Saturday. The C.C. read its statement about not endorsing the League's Rules and about the meeting being unlawful (a statement previously discussed with Plekhanov
in all details, word by word). All our people walked out
amid the Martovites' cries of "gendarmes" and so forth.

Saturday evening. Plekhanov "surrendered". He did not
want a split. He demanded the opening of peace negotiations.

Sunday (November 1). I tendered my resignation in
writing to Plekhanov (not wishing to be a party to such
depravity as the revision of the Party Congress under the
influence of a row abroad; to say nothing of the fact that
from the purely strategical aspect a more stupid moment
for concessions could not have been chosen).***

November 3. Old Believer gave Plekhanov, who began
the negotiations, a written statement of the conditions
of peace with the opposition: 1) Negotiations to be conducted by the editorial board of the C.O. and by the C.C.
2) Restoration of the old editorial board of *Iskra*. 3) Co-
optation on to the C.C., the number to be decided during
the negotiations. Cessation of co-optation on to the C.C. from
the moment negotiations begin. 4) *Two seats* (sic!) on the
Party Council and 5) recognition of the lawfulness of the
League Congress.

Plekhanov was not put out. He demanded that the C.C.
give way (!). The C.C. refused and wrote to Russia. Plekhanov declared that he would resign if the C.C. did not
give way. I turned over to Plekhanov (November 6) *all*
editorial matters, convinced that Plekhanov was capable

---

* "Report on the Second Congress of the R.S.D.L.P." (see present
edition, Vol. 7, pp. 73-83).—*Ed.*

** Sinking into the Marsh.—*Ed.*

*** See present edition, Vol. 7, p. 91.—*Ed.*

of surrendering to the Martovites not merely the newspaper
but the *entire C.C.* for nothing.*

The state of affairs: *Iskra* would hardly come out on
time. The Martovites were rejoicing over their "victory".
All our people (except the two Axelrod maids,[220] who
are faithful to Plekhanov even in his *Treulosigkeit***) dissociated themselves from Plekhanov and at a meeting (November 6 or 7) told him some home truths (on the subject
of the "second Isari").

A pretty picture, is it not? I shall not join the editorial
board, but I shall write. Our people want to defend the
C.C., insofar as that is possible, and to continue an intensified agitation against the Martovites—the right plan, in
my opinion.

Let Plekhanov leave us; the Party Council will then
turn over *Iskra* to a committee and convene an Extraordinary Party Congress. Do you mean to say the League Abroad
will be allowed by a majority of three or four votes to *revise*
the Party Congress? Do you mean to say it is proper, after
carrying the fight to the lengths of the greatest publicity
and almost a rupture, to sound the retreat and accept peace
terms dictated by the Martovites?

I should like to know your opinion.

I think that to act *à la* Plekhanov means subverting
the Party Congress and betraying its majority. I think
that we must agitate with all our strength here and in Russia for subordination to the Party Congress and not to the
League Congress.

A boycott of *Iskra* (even a Martovite *Iskra*) is, of course,
stupid. Moreover it would be a boycott not of a Martovite
but, possibly, of a Plekhanovite *Iskra*, for Zasulich and
Axelrod will soon give Plekhanov three votes in the Five.
And that's called an editorial board! As an illustration
to your witty remark about the saintly relics of Sarovsky,
I will quote the following statistical item: in the 45 issues
of *Iskra* under six editors, there were 39 articles and *feuil-
letons* written by Martov, 32 by me, 24 by Plekhanov, 8 by
Old Believer, 6 by Zasulich, and 4 by P. B. Axelrod. This

---

* See pp. 189-90 of this volume.—*Ed.*
** Treachery.—*Ed.*

in the course of three years! *Not a single* issue was made up (in the sense of technical editorial work) by anyone other than Martov or myself. And now—as a reward for the row, as a reward for Old Believer cutting off an important source of finance—they are to be taken on to the editorial board! They fought over "differences of principle", which, in Old Believer's letter of November 3 to Plekhanov were so expressively converted into figuring out how many seats they needed. And we have to legitimise this fight for seats, to make a deal with this party of discarded generals or ministers (*grève générale des généraux,** as Plekhanov said) or with the party of hysterical brawlers! What's the use of Party congresses if things are done by nepotism abroad, by hysteria and brawling?

Further about the notorious "trio", which the hysterical Martov sees as the pivot of my "intriguing". You probably remember from as far back as the time of the Congress my programme for the Congress and my commentary on this programme. I should very much like *all Party members to know this document*, and so once again I quote it for you precisely. "Item 23 (*Tagesordnung***). *Election of the Central Committee and the editorial board of the Central Organ of the Party.*

My commentary: "The Congress shall elect *three* persons to the editorial board of the Central Organ and *three* to the Central Committee. These six persons *in conjunction* shall, if necessary, co-opt by a two-thirds majority vote additional members to the editorial board of the C.O. and to the C.C., and report to this effect to the Congress. After the report has been endorsed by the Congress, subsequent co-optation shall be effected by the editorial board of the C.O. and by the C.C. separately."

Is it not clear that this means *renewal* of the editorial board, a thing which *cannot* be done without the consent of the C.C. (*four* out of six are necessary for co-optation), while the question of enlarging the original trio or leaving it as it was *is left open* (co-optation "*if necessary*")? I showed this draft to *everyone* (including Plekhanov, of course)

---

* A general strike of generals.—*Ed.*
** Agenda.—*Ed.*

prior to the Congress. Of course, renewal was necessary owing to dissatisfaction with the Six (and especially with Plekhanov, who in fact had the votes of P. B. Axelrod, who almost never took part, and of the pliable V. I. Zasulich), and, of course, in a private conversation with Martov, I *sharply* expressed this dissatisfaction, "scolded" all three—Plekhanov (especially) and Axelrod and Zasulich—for their caprices, and proposed even enlarging the Six to Seven, etc. Is it not hysteria to give a twist now to these private conversations and raise a howl that "the trio was aimed against Plekhanov" and that I had laid a "trap" for Martov, and so forth? Of course, when we agreed with Martov, the trio would be against Plekhanov, and when Plekhanov agreed with Martov (on the subject of demonstrations, for example) then the trio would be against me, and so on. The hysterical howling merely covers up a pitiful incapacity to understand that the editorial board must have real, and not fictitious, editors, that it must be a business-like and not a philistine collegium, and that *each* of its members should have his *own* opinion on *each* question (which was never the case with the unelected trio).

Martov *approved* my plan of two trios, but when it turned out to be against him in *one* question, he went into a fit of hysteria and began to howl about intrigue! It was not for nothing that in the corridors of the League Congress Plekhanov called him a "pitiful person"!

Yes ... the dirty squabble abroad—that is what overruled the decision of the majority of Russian Party workers. Plekhanov's betrayal, too, was partly due to fear of a row abroad, and partly to a feeling (*perhaps*) that in the Five he was sure to have three votes....

A fight for the C.C., for a new congress to be held soon (in the summer)—that is what is left to us.

———

Get hold of my notebook.* It was sent by Poletayev (Bauman) to Vecheslov *alone* and personally. Shergov could have taken it only by trickery, *only by a breach of trust.*

---

* The reference is to the "Report on the Second Congress of the R.S.D.L.P." (see present edition, Vol. 7).—*Ed.*

Read it to anyone you like, but don't let anyone have it, and return it to me.

You must oust Vecheslov from all positions. Take a letter for yourself from the C.C., tell the *Parteivorstand** that you are the agent of the C.C., and take *all* German contacts *wholly* into your hands.

I owe you an apology about your pamphlet. I have only managed to read it through once. It needs revising, but I have not had time to map out the revision.

Yours,
Lenin

Written in Geneva
First published in 1928

---

* The Executive Committee (of the German Social-Democratic Party).—*Ed.*

80
TO G. V. PLEKHANOV

November 18, 1903

Georgi Valentinovich,

I am sorry that I am a day late with my article*; I was not well yesterday and in general the work is going terribly hard these last few days.

The article turned out longer than I thought and had to be divided into two parts; in the second part I shall make a detailed analysis of Novobrantsev and draw conclusions.

I consider that my article should have a signature and so I am taking a pseudonym, otherwise, pending the announcement, it will probably be inconvenient for you.

Will you please also insert my statement** appended herewith in the issue of *Iskra* containing the announcement about the Congress. Of course, in the event of complete peace being established in the Party (which I am hoping for) and if you were to find it necessary, I could, among other peace terms, discuss also the non-publication of this statement.

Yours sincerely,

N. Lenin

Written in Geneva (local mail)
First published in full in 1928

Printed from
the original

---

* The reference is to "The Narodnik-like Bourgeois and Distraught Narodism" (see present edition, Vol. 7).—*Ed.*
** "To the Editorial Board of the Central Organ of the R.S.D.L.P." (see present edition, Vol. 7).—*Ed.*

81

TO THE CENTRAL COMMITTEE OF THE R.S.D.L.P.

Dear friends,

The new political situation was fully clarified after the publication of *Iskra* No. 53. It is clear that the Five in the Central Organ are out to hound both Lenin (even going so far as slander about his having expelled the *Yuzhny Rabochy* people from the Party and vile hints about Schweitzer[221]) and the C.C., and the Majority as a whole. Plekhanov says bluntly that the Five on the C.O. are not afraid of any Central Committee. The C.C. is being attacked both here and in Russia (letter from St. Petersburg about Martyn's journey). The issue squarely faces us. If time is lost and we fail to give the watchword for the struggle, *complete* defeat is inevitable owing, firstly, to the desperate struggle of the *Iskra* Five and, secondly, to the arrests of our people in Russia. *The only salvation is—a congress. Its watchword: the fight against disrupters.* Only by this watchword can we catch out the Martovites, win over the broad masses and save the situation. In my opinion, the only possible plan is this: *for the time being* not a word about the *congress*, complete secrecy. *All, absolutely all*, forces to be sent *into the committees and on tours.* A fight to be waged for peace, for putting a stop to disruption, for subordination to the Central Committee. Every effort to be made to strengthen the committees with our people. Every effort to be made to catch out the Martovites and *Yuzhny-Rabochy* people in disruption, pin them down by documents and resolutions against the disrupters; resolutions of the committees should pour into the Central Organ. Further, our people should be got into the wavering committees. Winning over the committees with the watchword: against disruption—this is the *most important* task. *The congress must be held not later than January*, therefore set to work energetically; we, too, shall put all forces into operation. *The object of the congress is to strengthen* the C.C. and the Council, and perhaps the C.O. as well, either by a trio (in the event of our being able to tear Plekhanov away, which is not very likely), or by a Six, *which I would join* in the event of a peace that is honourable for us. At the worst: *their C.O., our C.C. and Council.*

I repeat: either *complete* defeat (the C.O. will hound us) or *immediate preparation for a congress. It must be prepared secretly at first* during a maximum of one month, *after which during three weeks the demands of half the committees to be collected and the congress convened.* Again and yet again—this is the only salvation.

Written December 10, 1903
Sent from Geneva to Russia

First published in 1929

Printed from
the original

82

TO THE *ISKRA* EDITORIAL BOARD[222]

To the Editorial Board of the Central Organ

December 12, 1903

I, as representative of the C.C., received today from Comrade Martov an inquiry as to whether a report on the negotiations of the C.C. with the Geneva opposition could be published or not.[223] I believe it could, and I earnestly request the comrades on the editorial board of the C.O. to consider once again the question of peace and good will in the Party.

It is not too late yet to secure such a peace, it is not too late yet to keep from our people and our enemies the details of the split and the speeches about dishonourable conduct and falsified lists, speeches which will probably be utilised even by *Moskovskiye Vedomosti*.[224] I can guarantee that the Majority will readily agree to consign all this dirt to oblivion, provided peace and good will in the Party are secured.

Everything now depends on the editorial board of the C.O., which includes representatives of the former opposition that rejected the C.C.'s peace proposal of November 25, 1903.[225] I ask you, comrades, to take into consideration that since then the C.C. has already made two further voluntary concessions, by advising Comrade Ru to hand in his resignation and by trying to settle the League affair "amicably".

Meanwhile the boycott of the C.C., the agitation against it and the disruption of practical work in Russia continue. People write to us from Russia that the opposition are making a "hell" there. We have the most definite information that the agents of the Minority are systematically continuing their disruptive work, making a round of the committees. People in St. Petersburg write about Martyn's visit there with the same aim. Things have reached a point when the opposition are making their own transport arrangements and, through Dan, are offering the C.C. to share them on a fifty-fifty basis!

I consider it my duty to the Party to ask the editorial board of the C.O. for the last time that it persuade the opposition to subscribe to peace and good will on the basis of a sincere recognition of the two central bodies by both sides and cessation of the intestine war which renders any joint work impossible.

Written in Geneva (local mail)
    First published in 1929

                                                    Printed from
                                                    the original

83

TO G. M. KRZHIZHANOVSKY

Dear friend,

It is essential that we clear up in all details a question on which we apparently differ, and I beg you to forward this letter of mine for discussion by all members of the C.C. (or its Executive Committee[226]). The difference is this: 1) you think that peace with the Martovites is possible (Boris even congratulates us on peace! It is both comic and tragic!); 2) you think that an immediate congress is an acknowledgement of our impotence. I am convinced that on both points you are cruelly mistaken. 1) The Martovites are heading for war. At the meeting in Geneva, Martov bluntly shouted: "We are a force." They vilify us in their newspaper and basely sidetrack the issue, covering up their trickery by yelling about bureaucracy on your part. On every hand Martov continues to clamour about the C.C. being absolutely ineffective. In short, it is naïve and quite impermissible to doubt that the Martovites are out to seize the C.C. as well by the same methods of trickery, boycott and brawling. A fight with them on this level is beyond our strength, for the C.O. is a powerful weapon and our defeat is inevitable, especially in view of the arrests. By letting the time slip by you are heading for the certain and complete defeat of the entire Majority, you are silently swallowing the insults which the C.C. is suffering abroad (at the hands of the League) and asking for more. 2) A congress will demonstrate our strength, will prove that not merely in words but in fact we shall not permit a clique of brawlers abroad to boss the whole movement. It is now that a congress is needed, when the watchword is: the fight against disruption. Only this watchward jus-

tifies a congress, and justifies it completely in the eyes of
Russia as a whole. By losing this opportunity, you lose this
watchword and prove your impotent, passive subordination
to the Martovites. To dream of strengthening our positions
by positive work in face of the attacks on the part of the
C.O. and the Martovites' boycott and agitation is simply
ludicrous. It means slowly perishing in an inglorious struggle against the intriguers, who will say afterwards (and
are already saying): see how ineffective this Central Committee is! I repeat, don't harbour any illusions. Either
you dictate peace to the Martovites at a congress, or they
will kick you out ingloriously or replace you at the first
setback caused by arrests. The congress now has an aim,
namely: to put an end to the intolerable disruption, to
sweep away the League, which flaunts every and any C.C.,
to take the Council firmly into its hands and put the Central
Organ in order. How to put it in order? At *worst* by leaving
even the Five (or by restoring the Six); but this worst event
is improbable if we get a big majority. Then we shall either
rout the Martovites completely (Plekhanov *is beginning
to talk* of a new *Vademecum*, seeing that there is no peace,
and is threatening to attack both contending sides. That's
just what we want!), or we shall say frankly that we have
no guiding C.O. and we shall convert it into an organ for
discussion, with freedom for signed articles of the Majority
and the Minority (or even better: relegate the polemic with
the Martovites to pamphlets, and in *Iskra* fight only against
the government and the enemies of Social-Democracy).

And so, abandon the naïve hope of working peacefully
in such an impossible atmosphere. Send all the *main* forces
out on tours, let Deer travel, *secure* immediately the absolute support of your own committees, then launch an
attack on those of the others, and—a congress, a congress
not later than January!

P.S. If Martov asks Deer concerning publication[227]—
let Deer without fail transfer his vote to Stake; without
fail, otherwise there will be an arch-scandal! When Martov
and Dan speak to Stake at rendezvous they treat him with
intolerable insolence!

P.P.S. Today, 18th, another dirty trick of the Martovites: their refusal to publish in No. 54 my letter on why

I resigned from the editorial board,* on the pretext that Hans was against publication of documents (they have become inveterate liars! Hans was against it provided there was *peace!*). The refusal is accompanied by a heap of disgusting statements, such as that the C.C. has been trying to lay hands on the C.O., that negotiations have gone on for restoring confidence in the C.C., and so on. The tactic is clear: hypocritically to disguise the opposition of the Dans, Martyns, etc., to the C.C. and on the sly to fling mud at the C.C. in the newspaper. On no account shall I leave the vile No. 53 unanswered. Wire immediately: 1) do you agree to the publication of my letter *outside Iskra*? 203 shares; 2) do you agree to devote all efforts immediately to the congress? 204 shares. If the answer to both questions is "yes", then wire: 407 shares. If it is "no" to both, then 45 shares.

The day after tomorrow I shall send you my letter of resignation from the editorial board. If you do not agree to an immediate congress and intend to suffer Martov's insults without saying anything, then I shall probably have to resign from the Central Committee as well.

Written December 18, 1903
Sent from Geneva to Kiev

First published in 1929   Printed from
                                                          the original

---

* See present edition, Vol. 7.—*Ed.*

84

TO N. Y. VILONOV[228]

Dear comrade,

I was very glad to have your letter because here abroad we have too little opportunity of hearing the frank and independent voices of those engaged in local activities. For a Social-Democratic writer living abroad it is extremely important to have a frequent exchange of opinions with advanced workers who are active in Russia, and your account of the impact our dissensions have upon the committees interested me very much. I shall, perhaps, even publish your letter if the occasion offers:[229]

It is impossible to answer your questions in a single letter, since a detailed account of the Majority and the Minority would take up a whole book. I have now published in leaflet form my "Letter to the Editors of *Iskra* (Why I Resigned From the *Iskra* Editorial Board),"* where I give a brief account of the reasons why we parted company and try to show how the matter is misrepresented in *Iskra* No. 53 (beginning with No. 53, the editorial board consists of four representatives of the Minority in addition to Plekhanov). I hope that this letter (a small printed sheet of eight pages) will soon be in your hands, because it has already been taken to Russia and it will probably not be difficult to distribute it.

I repeat: in this letter the matter is set out very briefly. It cannot at present be set out in greater detail until the minutes of the Party Congress and of the League Congress have been issued (it is announced in *Iskra* No. 53 that the minutes of both these congresses will be published in full

---

* See present edition, Vol. 7.—*Ed.*

very soon. I have information that the minutes of the Party Congress will be issued as a book of over three hundred pages; nearly 300 pages are now ready and the book will probably come out in a week or two at the latest). Most probably a pamphlet* will have to be written when these two sets of minutes are published.

My personal view of the matter is that the split is primarily and mainly due to dissatisfaction with the composition of the central bodies (the Central Organ and the Central Committee). The Minority wanted to keep the old six-man board of the C.O., but the Congress selected three of the six, apparently finding them better suited for political leadership. The Minority was similarly defeated over the composition of the Central Committee, that is to say, the Congress did not elect those whom the Minority wanted.

In consequence of this the dissatisfied Minority began exaggerating minor differences of opinion, boycotting the central bodies, mustering its supporters and even preparing to split the Party (very persistent and, probably, trustworthy rumours are current here that they have already decided to found, and have begun to set up, their own newspaper to be called *Kramola*.** No wonder the *feuilleton* in *Iskra* No. 53 has been set up in a type which does not exist at all in the Party print-shop!).

Plekhanov decided to co-opt them on to the editorial board to avoid a split, and wrote the article "What Should Not Be Done" in *Iskra* No. 52. After No. 51, I resigned from the editorial board, for I considered this modification of the congress under the influence of the rows taking place abroad to be incorrect. But personally, of course, I did not want to prevent peace if peace were possible, and therefore (since *now* I do not consider it possible for me to work in the Six) I withdrew from the editorial board, without, however, refusing to contribute.

The Minority (or opposition) wants to force its people into the Central Committee too. For the sake of peace, the C.C. agreed to take two of them, but the Minority is still not satisfied and continues to spread vile rumours about

---

* Lenin has in view his pamphlet *One Step Forward, Two Steps Back* which appeared in May 1904 (see present edition, Vol. 7).—*Ed.*
** Meaning "Sedition".—*Ed.*

the C.C. being ineffectual. In my opinion, that is the most outrageous violation of discipline and Party duty. Moreover, it is sheer slander, for the C.C. was elected by the Congress from persons for whom the *majority* of the *Iskra* organisation had expressed support. And the *Iskra* organisation, of course, knew better than anyone else who was fitted for this important role. A Central Committee of three persons[230] was elected at the Congress—all three long-standing members of the *Iskra* organisation; two of them were members of the Organising Committee; the third had been invited to serve on the O.C. but did not do so because he was personally unwilling, yet for a long time he worked for the O.C. on general Party matters. It follows that the most reliable and experienced persons were elected to the C.C. and I consider it a shabby trick to shout about their "ineffectiveness", when it is the Minority itself that *hinders* the C.C. from working. All the charges against the C.C. (about formalism, bureaucracy, and so forth) are nothing but malicious inventions devoid of any foundation.

It goes without saying that I fully share your opinion as to the unseemliness of an outcry against centralism and against the congress on the part of people who previously spoke in a different tone and who are dissatisfied because on one particular issue the congress did not do what they wanted. Instead of admitting their mistake, these people are now disrupting the Party! I believe, the comrades in Russia should vigorously oppose all disruption and insist that the congress decisions be implemented and prevent the squabble about who should be on the C.O. and the C.C. from hindering the work. The squabbles abroad among the writers and all the other generals (whom you too harshly and bluntly call intriguers) will cease to be dangerous to the Party only when the leaders of committees in Russia become more independent and capable of firmly demanding the fulfilment of what their delegates decide at the Party congress.

Concerning the relations between the Central Organ and the Central Committee, you are quite right that neither the one nor the other should be given the upper hand once for all. The congress itself, I think, should make a separate

decision on each occasion. At present, too, according to
the Rules, the Party Council stands above both the C.O.
and the C.C. And the Council has two members from the
C.O. and two from the C.C., the fifth member having been
elected by the congress. Hence the congress itself has decided who should be given the upper hand on this occasion.
Stories about us wanting the C.O. abroad to overrule the
C.C. in Russia are sheer gossip in which there is not a word
of truth. When Plekhanov and I were on the editorial
board we had even in the Council *three* Social-Democrats
from Russia and *only two* from abroad. Now, under the
Martovites, the reverse is the case! Now judge for yourself
what their talk is worth!

I send you warm greetings and earnestly request you to
let me know whether you received this letter, whether
you have read my letter to the editorial board and Nos. 52,
53 of *Iskra*, and how in general things are now in the Committee.

With comradely greetings,

Lenin

Written between December 17
and December 22, 1903
Sent from Geneva to Ekaterinoslav

First published in 1929   Printed from
                                                the original

85

TO THE CENTRAL COMMITTEE OF THE R.S.D.L.P.

December 22, 1903

To the Central Committee from Lenin, member of the C.C.

I have read the C.C.'s announcement circulated to the committees,[231] and can only shrug my shoulders. A more ridiculous misunderstanding I cannot imagine. Hans has been cruelly punished by this for his credulity and impressionability. Let him explain to me, in the name of all that's holy, where he gets the temerity to speak in such an unctuous tone about peace when the opposition (Martov included) *has formally rejected peace* in the reply to the Central Committee's ultimatum? Is it not childishness, after this formal rejection of peace, to believe the chatter of Martov who, firstly, does not remember today what he said yesterday and, secondly, cannot answer for the whole opposition? Is it not naïve to speak and write about peace when the opposition is on the war-path again, is clamouring at meetings in Geneva that it is a force, and is beginning a mean persecution in *Iskra* No. 53? And to tell a downright lie to the committees!—for example, that the conflict with the League is "completely at an end"? To keep silent about the first Council (with Ru)?

Finally, this silly advice that I should go away from here! I could understand if it has been given by members of the family or relatives, but for such piffle to be written by the Central Committee! Yes, it is now that the literary war begins. No. 53 and my letter, published in leaflet form,* will demonstrate that for you.

---

* The reference is to the letter "Why I Resigned From the *Iskra* Editorial Board" (see present edition, Vol. 7).—*Ed.*

I am so angry at your announcement to the committees that for the moment I cannot think how you are to be extricated from a ludicrous situation, unless it is by declaring that the contents of *Iskra* No. 53, and especially the article "Our Congress", have destroyed all your faith in the possibility of peace. Personally, I see no other way out.

Reply to the committees (and to Martov himself) that the disgracefully false article "Our Congress" has provoked a polemic in the press, but that you (the C.C.) will try to carry out positive work. Plekhanov was against the article "Our Congress" and against Martov delivering a public lecture.

Sent from Geneva to Russia

First published in 1929   Printed from
                                                          the original

86

TO THE EDITORS OF *ISKRA*[232]

To the Editorial Board of the Central Organ

Comrades,

In connection with the resolution adopted on December 22 by the editorial board of the Central Organ, the representative of the C.C. abroad considers it necessary to point out to the editors the extreme unseemliness of this resolution, which can only be put down to excessive irritation.[233]

If Lenin, acting not as a C.C. member but as a former editor, expounded something which you thought incorrect, you can thresh this out in the press.

Comrade Hans did not conclude on behalf of the C.C. any agreement about non-publication of the negotiations and he could not do so without our knowledge. The editorial board cannot fail to be aware of this. Probably Comrade Hans made a suggestion about non-publication of the negotiations *in the event of a formal peace being concluded.*

Not evasively, but quite categorically, the C.C. representative abroad twice informed the editorial board of the C.O. that he permitted Lenin's letter to be published.*

If the editorial board had not been moved by a spirit of excessive irritation, it would easily have seen how extremely out of place were its remarks about the number of C.C. members living abroad. To this and other unseemly attacks of the editorial board (like the ludicrous charge of some kind of alleged "secret" printing), the C.C. represen-

---

* The reference is to the letter "Why I Resigned From the *Iskra* Editorial Board" (see present edition, Vol. 7).—*Ed.*

tative abroad replies merely by a call to remember Party duty and put a stop to *acts* capable of making literary polemics the occasion for a split.

The Central Committee Representative Abroad

Written December 24-27, 1903,
   in Geneva (local mail)
·First published in 1929   Printed from
                                                     the original

———

87

TO THE CENTRAL COMMITTEE OF THE R.S.D.L.P.

December 30, 1903

We have received your letter of December 10 (old style). We are surprised and angered by your silence on burning issues and your unpunctuality in correspondence. It is really impossible for matters to be conducted in this fashion! Get another secretary if Bear and Doe are unable to write every week. Just think, so far nothing substantial has been received from Deer! So far (after 20 days) there has been no reply to our letter of December 10 (new style).* At all costs this scandalous state of affairs must be put an end to!

Further, we categorically insist on the need to know where we stand in the struggle against the Martovites, on the need to reach agreement among ourselves and to adopt an absolutely definite line.

Why haven't you sent Boris over here, as Hans here wanted? If Boris were here, he would not be writing us ridiculous speeches about peace. Why hasn't Hans fulfilled his promise to write to the Old Man an exact account of Boris's mood? If you can't send Boris, send Mitrofan or Beast in order to clear up the matter.

I repeat over and over again: Hans's main mistake lies in having trusted to his latest impression. No. 53 ought to have sobered him. The Martovites have taken possession of the C.O. for the purpose of war, and now war is being waged all along the line: attacks in *Iskra*, brawling at public lectures (recently in Paris Martov read a lecture about the split to an audience of 100 and engaged in a

---

* See pp. 200-01 of this volume.—*Ed.*

fight against Lebedev), the most shameless agitation against the Central Committee. It would be unpardonable short-sightedness to think that this could not spread to Russia. Things here have reached a stage when the C.O. has broken off relations with the C.C. (the C.O. resolution of December 22, sent to you), and when the C.O. has published *a false statement* (*Iskra* No. 55) alleging an *agreement* about non-publication of the negotiations).

It is high time you gave serious thought to the political situation as a whole, took a broader view, got away from the petty, everyday concern with pence and passports, and, without burying your head in the sand, got clear on where you are going and *for the sake of what* you are dilly-dallying.

There are two tendencies among us in the C.C., if I am not mistaken (or, perhaps, three? What are they?). In my opinion they are: 1) to procrastinate, without convening a congress and turning a deaf ear, as far as possible, to attacks and grossest insults, and to strengthen the position in Russia; 2) to raise a storm of resolutions against the C.O., to devote *all* efforts to winning over the shaky committees and to prepare a congress in two, or at most three, months' time. And so, I ask: what does your strengthening of the positions consist in? Only in your losing time, while the adversary is mustering his forces here (and the groups abroad matter a lot!), and in your putting off a decision until you suffer defeat. Defeat is inevitable and will be fairly rapid—it would be sheer childishness to ignore that.

What will you leave us after the defeat? Among the Martovites—fresh and increased forces. Among us—broken ranks. For them—a strengthened Central Organ. For us—a bunch of persons badly handling the transportation of a Central Organ that abuses them. That is a sure path to defeat, a shameful and stupid postponement of *inevitable* defeat. You are merely closing your eyes to this, taking advantage of the fact that the war abroad is slow in reaching you. Your tactics literally amount to saying: after us (after the present composition of the C.C.), the deluge (a deluge for the Majority).

I think that even if defeat is inevitable, we must make our exit straightforwardly, honestly and openly, and that is possible only at a congress. But defeat is by no means inevitable, for the Five are *not* solid, Plekhanov is not with them, but *in favour of peace*, and a congress could *show up* both Plekhanov and them, with their supposed differences of opinion. The only serious objection to a congress is that it will necessarily legitimise a split. To this I reply: 1) even that is better than the present position, for then we can make our exit honestly instead of prolonging the disgraceful position of being spat upon; 2) the Martovites have missed the moment for a split, and their withdrawal from the Third Congress is improbable, for the present struggle and full publicity remove the possibility of a split; 3) a deal with them, if that were possible, is best of all done at the congress.

Discuss this matter seriously and send your reply at long last, giving the opinion of each (absolutely each) member of the Central Committee.

Don't bother me about leaflets; I am not a machine and in the present scandalous situation I can't work.

Sent from Geneva to Russia
First published in 1929

Printed from
the original

1904

88

TO THE CENTRAL COMMITTEE OF THE R.S.D.L.P.

P.S.[234] January 2, 1904. I have just received the proofs of Axelrod's article in *Iskra* No. 55[235] (No. 55 will be out in a couple of days). It is much more disgusting even than Martov's article ("Our Congress") in No. 53. We have here "ambitious fantasies" "inspired by the legends about Schweitzer's dictatorship"; we have here again accusations about "the all-controlling centre" "disposing at its personal (sic!) discretion" of "Party members who are converted (!) into cogs and wheels". "The establishment of a vast multitude of government departments, divisions, offices and workshops of all kinds." The conversion of revolutionaries (really and truly, sic!) "into head clerks, scribes, sergeants, non-commissioned officers, privates, warders, foremen" (sic!). The C.C., it says (according to the Majority's idea), "must be merely the collective agent of this authority (the authority of the *Iskra* editorial board), and be under its strict tutelage and vigilant control". Such, it says, is "the organisational utopia of a theocratic nature" (sic!). "The triumph of bureaucratic centralism in the Party organisation—that is the result"... (really and truly, sic!). In connection with this article I again and again ask all C.C. members: is it really possible to leave this without a protest or fight? Don't you feel that by tolerating this silently you are turning yourselves into nothing more nor less than gossip-mongers (gossip about Schweitzer and his pawns) and spreaders of slander (about bureaucrats, i.e., yourselves and the Majority as a whole)? And do you consider it possible to conduct "positive work" under such "ideological leadership"? Or do you know of any other means of honest struggle apart from a congress?

((The Martovites, apparently, have Kiev, Kharkov, Gornozavodsky, Rostov and the Crimea. This makes ten votes+the League+the editorial board of the C.O.+two in the Council=16 votes out of 49. If all efforts are at once directed towards Nikolayev, Siberia and the Caucasus, it is *fully* possible to leave them with one-third.))

Sent from Geneva to Russia
    First published in 1929   Printed from
                                                                 the original

89

TO G. M. KRZHIZHANOVSKY

January 4, 1904

Old Man writing. I have just received Deer's letter with a reply to mine of December 10* and I am answering immediately. You don't have to ask me for a criticism of Deer's views! I will say straight out that I am furious with Deer's timidity and naïveté.

1) To write to the C.O. from the C.C. in Russia is the height of tactlessness. Everything must go *through* the C.C.'s representative abroad, and no other way. I assure you, this is essential if you want to avoid a terrific row. The C.O. must be told once and for all that there is the C.C.'s plenipotentiary representative abroad and that's flat.

2) It is not true that there was some sort of agreement about the League minutes. You said plainly that you were leaving the question of publishing or shortening them to us. (As a matter of fact there was no "agreement" for *you* to make on this. Not even for the *entire* C.C.). You are hopelessly muddled up on this, and if you were to write a single incautious word, it will all appear in the press with an immense hullabaloo.

3) If in your letter to the C.O. about No. 53 you did not use a single word of protest against the obscenities about Schweitzer, bureaucratic formalism, etc., then I am bound to say that we have ceased to understand each other. In that case I shall say no more and come out as a private writer against these obscenities. In print, I shall call these gentlemen hysterical tricksters.

---

* See pp. 200-01 of this volume.—*Ed.*

4) While the C.C. is muttering about positive work, Yeryoma and Martyn are stealing Nikolayev from it. This is a downright disgrace and another warning to you, the hundredth, if not thousandth. *Either* we win over the committees and convene a congress, *or* ignominiously retire from the scene under the hail of obscene attacks by the C.O., which denies me access to *Iskra*.

5) To speak of a conference of the committees and of an "ultimatum" (after they have *ridiculed* our ultimatum!) is simply ridiculous. Why, the Martovites will simply burst out laughing in reply to this "threat"! What do they care about ultimatums when they brazenly hold back money, attack the C.C. and *openly* say: "We await the first break-down."

Can Deer have forgotten already that Martov is a pawn in the hands of cunning persons? And after this to still talk about the attitude of Martov and George towards Deer and Nil! It is offensive to read this naïveté. In the first place, both Martov and George don't care a hang about all your Deer and Nils. Secondly, George is pushed right into the background by the Martovites and he says plainly that they don't listen to him (which is clearly evident from *Iskra*). Thirdly, I repeat for the hundredth time that Martov is a cipher. Why didn't that good soul Hans make friends here with Trotsky, Dan and Natalya Ivanovna? What a pity the dear fellow missed such a chance (the last chance) to make a "sincere", "happy peace".... Would it not be wiser to write letters directly to these "masters" than to weep on the neck of that rag doll, Martov? Just try and write, it will sober you up! And until you have written to them and personally received a spit in the face from them, don't bother us (or them) about "peace". We here can clearly see who is doing the *chattering* and who the *bossing* among the Martovites.

6) I gave my arguments in favour of a congress already last time. For heaven's sake, don't pussyfoot to yourself; postponing the congress would only be a proof of our impotence. And if you continue harping on peace, it will not only be Nikolayev that the enemies will take from you.

It's either war or peace. If peace—then it means that you are giving way to the Martovites, who are waging a vigorous and clever war. In that case you will suffer in silence while mud is being flung at you in the C.O.' (=the ideological leadership of the Party!). In that case we have nothing to talk about. I have already said in the press *everything* there was to be said, and will go on saying everything in the full sense of the word.

It is clear to me that the hounding we feared if I were to take *Iskra* on my own, has started all the same, only now my mouth is stopped. And it is childishness to rely on Andreyevsky's talk about the influence of Lenin's name.

If it's war, I would ask you in that case to explain to me by what means, other than a congress, a *real* and honest war can be carried on.

I repeat that a congress now is not pointless, for Plekhanov is no longer with the Martovites. Publication (which I shall secure at all costs)[236] will finally separate him from them. And he is already at loggerheads with them.

The Martovites will not even mention the Six at the Third Congress. A split would be better than what we have at present, when they have dirtied *Iskra* with tittle-tattle. But they will hardly seek a split at the Third Congress, and we shall be able to hand over *Iskra* to a neutral committee, taking it away from both sides.

7) Against the League, I shall do my utmost to achieve a decisive war.

8) If Nil is still for peace, let him come and talk a couple of times with Dan. That will be enough, I'm sure!

9) We need money. There is enough for two months, and after that not a farthing. Don't forget we are now "keeping" a bunch of scoundrels, who spit on us in the C.O. That is called "positive work". *Ich gratuliere*!*

Sent from Geneva to Kiev

First published in 1929   Printed from
                                                    the original

---

* My congratulations!—*Ed.*

90

TO THE *ISKRA* EDITORIAL BOARD[237]

As the representative of the C.C., I consider it necessary to point out to the editors that there are absolutely no grounds for raising the question of lawfulness, etc., on the basis of heated speeches at lectures or on the basis of literary polemics. The Central Committee as such has never had, and does not have, the slightest doubt of the lawfulness of the editorial board co-opted, as *Iskra* No. 53 quite justly stated, in complete accord with Clause 12 of the Party Rules. The Central Committee would be ready to state that publicly as well, if necessary. If the editorial board sees these polemics as attacks upon itself, it has every opportunity of replying. It is hardly reasonable to resent what the editorial board regards as sharply worded statements in the polemic, when no mention is made anywhere of boycott or any other disloyal (from the viewpoint of the C.C.) form of activity. We would remind the editorial board that the C.C. has *repeatedly* expressed its full readiness to publish, and made a *direct proposal to publish*, immediately both Dan's letter and Martov's "Once Again in the Minority", without being at all put out by the very sharp attacks to be found in these documents. In the view of the C.C., it is essential to give all Party members the widest possible freedom to criticise the central bodies and to attack them; the C.C. sees nothing terrible in such attacks, provided they are not accompanied by a boycott, by standing aloof from positive work or by cutting off financial resources. The Central Committee states even now that it would publish criticism against itself, seeing in a free exchange...*

Written January 8, 1904
in Geneva (local mail)
First published in 1929

Printed from
the original

---

* The sentence was completed by F. V. Lengnik as follows: "of opinions a guarantee against possible mistakes on the part of the central bodies".—*Ed.*

91
TO G. V. PLEKHANOV, CHAIRMAN
OF THE PARTY COUNCIL[238]

Comrade,

We would propose getting together for a meeting of the Council on Monday, January 25, at 4 p.m., in the Landolt restaurant. If you appoint a different place and time, please let us know not later than Sunday, for one of us lives far away from Geneva.

As regards secretarial duties, we think it should be possible to restrict ourselves to the services of Comrade Martov, who was already appointed secretary of the Council at its first meeting.

We would emphatically protest against Comrade Blumenfeld as secretary for, in the first place, he does not observe the rules of secrecy (he informed Druyan of Lenin's membership of the Central Committee); secondly, he is too expansive, so that there is no guarantee of calm and business-like qualities, and there is even the danger of a row and of having the door locked. Thirdly, we may have to discuss him personally on the Council, as purchaser of Party literature.

If you consider a special person necessary as secretary, we propose for this Comrade Bychkov, who is one of the old members of the *Iskra* organisation and a prominent Party activist (a member of the Organising Committee); moreover he is the most impartial and capable of recording everything calmly.

Council members....

P.S. I shall have to come to Geneva specially for the Council meeting, and the mail takes rather a long time reaching Mornex. I would ask you therefore to send me a letter not later than Sunday (*during the day*), if the meeting is fixed for Monday, otherwise the notice will not reach me in time.

Alternatively, I would ask you to postpone the meeting until Wednesday.

My address is: Mornex....

Written January 23, 1904
in Geneva (local mail)

First published in 1929

Printed from
the original

92

TO G. V. PLEKHANOV, CHAIRMAN
OF THE PARTY COUNCIL

Comrade,

We are unfortunately compelled to enter our emphatic protest against the editorial board's proposal of Comrade Gurvich as secretary.

Firstly, there were a number of conflicts with him in the C.C.

Secondly, he has expressed in writing (we can send you a copy) such an attitude to the Council, the highest Party institution, that his participation in the Council meeting is quite impossible.

Thirdly—and chiefly—we shall probably have to raise in the Council the question of *Comrade Gurvich personally*, as a representative of the League's board of management, who, in our opinion, has shown a wrong attitude to the Central Committee. It is inconvenient to have as secretary a person whose activities are being questioned.

We draw attention also to the fact that, appreciating the importance of the Council as an instrument for unity and agreement (and not for disunity and discord) we *immediately* proposed as secretary someone who has taken *no* part in the dissensions and against whom there has been no protest by the other side.

We are sure that the other side, too, the editorial board of the Central Organ, could easily propose a candidate who has not taken part in the dissensions and who could not be the *subject* of discussion on the Council.

Yours sincerely, *L.*

Vritten January 27, 1904
in Geneva (local mail)

First published in 1929

Printed from
the original

93

TO THE CENTRAL COMMITTEE OF THE R.S.D.L.P.

For the C.C. (to be handed to N.N.*)

The meetings (three sittings) of the Party Council ended yesterday. These meetings brought into sharp focus the whole political situation within the Party. Plekhanov sided with the Martovites, outvoting us on every question of any importance. Our resolution condemning boycott, etc. (boycott *by either side*), was not put to the vote; a line was merely drawn in principle between impermissible and permissible forms of struggle. On the other hand, a resolution of Plekhanov's was adopted saying it was desirable that the C.C. co-opt an *appropriate* (sic!) number from the Minority. After this we withdrew our resolution and submitted a protest against this policy of place-hunting on the part of the Council. Three Council members (Martov, Axelrod and Plekhanov) replied that it was "beneath their dignity" to examine this protest. We stated that the only *honest* way out was a congress. The Council rejected it. The three members passed resolutions legitimising (!) the editorial board's sending out its representatives separately from the C.C., and instructing the C.C. to give the editorial board literature in the amount required for distribution (!). That means giving it them for their own transportation and delivery, for they now send out one "agent" after another, who *refuse* to execute commissions for the Central Committee. In addition, they also have transport ready (they proposed sharing the cost of carriage fifty-fifty).

Iskra (No. 57) has an article by Plekhanov calling our C.C. *eccentric* (there being no Minority on it) and inviting it to co-opt the Minority. How many is unknown; according

---

* N.N. — unidentified.—*Ed.*

to private information, not less than *three* out of a very
short list (of 5-6, apparently), perhaps with a demand also
for the resignation of someone from the Central Committee.

One must be blind not to see now what is afoot. The
Council will bring pressure to bear on the C.C. *in every
possible way*, demanding complete surrender to the Martovites.
Either—an immediate congress, the immediate collection of resolutions on a congress from 11-12 committees,
and the immediate concentration of all efforts on agitating
for a congress. Or—the resignation of the whole C.C., for
no C.C. member will consent to the ignominious and ludicrous role of accepting people who *foist themselves* on the
C.C., people who will not rest content until they have
taken everything into their hands, and who will drag every
trifle before the Council so as to get their own way.

Kurtz and I insistently demand that the C.C. *be convened
immediately at all costs* to decide the matter, taking
into account, of course, our votes as well. We repeat emphatically and for the hundredth time: either a congress
at once, or resignation. We invite our dissentients to come
here, so as to judge the situation on the spot. Let them try
in practice to get along with the Martovites and not write
us hollow phrases about the value of peace!

We have no money. The C.O. is overloading us with
expenses, obviously pushing us towards bankruptcy, and
obviously counting on a financial crash in order to take
extraordinary measures which would reduce the C.C. to
a cipher.

We need two or three thousand rubles immediately at
all costs. Without fail and immediately, otherwise we shall
face *complete* ruin within a month!

We repeat: think it over carefully, *send delegates here*
and take a straightforward view of the matter. Our last
word is: either a congress or the resignation of the whole
Central Committee. Reply at once as to whether you give
us your votes. If not, let us know *what is to be done if
Kurtz and I resign*, let us know without fail.

Written January 31, 1904
Sent from Geneva to Russia

First published in 1929   Printed from
                                                 the original

94
TO G. M. KRZHIZHANOVSKY

To Hans from Old Man

Dear friend,

I have seen *Beast* and only learnt about your affairs from him. In my opinion, you must make Deer go away at once and change his skin. It is stupid and ridiculous of him to await the blow. The only way out is to go underground and travel about. It only seems to him that such a step is difficult and hard to take. Deer should try it and he will quickly find that his new position will become a normal one for him. (I utterly fail to understand or share Konyaga's arguments against it.)

Next, about the whole political situation. Things are in a terrible tangle. Plekhanov has gone over to the Martovites and is overpowering us in the Council. The Council has expressed a desire that the C.C. should have additional members (this is published in *Iskra* No. 58). The Council has given the editorial board the right to send out agents and receive literature for distribution.

The Martovites evidently have their own war fund and are only waiting for a suitable moment for a coup d'état (such a moment as a financial crash—we are without money—or a break-down in Russia, etc.). I have no doubt about this and Kurtz and I are demanding that C.C. members who do doubt it should come here to convince themselves, for it is ridiculous and undignified to have people pulling different ways.

I believe we should now 1) kick up a row in the committees against the C.O. by means of the most militant resolutions; 2) carry on a polemic against the C.O. in leaflets of the committees; 3) adopt resolutions on a congress in

the committees and publish them locally; 4) set Schwarz, Vakar and others to work on leaflets for the Central Committee.

Hans should be warned that he will definitely be used to give false evidence against me, that is certain. If Hans does not want this to happen, let him immediately send a written categorical statement: 1) that there was no agreement about non-publication of the negotiations; 2) that in the Council on November 29, 1903, Hans did not promise to co-opt on to the C.C.; 3) that Hans understood that the Martovites would take over the C.O. for the purpose of peace and that they balked his expectations by launching war, beginning with No. 53. We shall publish this statement *only if* they provoke us.

Written between February 2 and 7,
            1904
     Sent from Geneva to Kiev
       First published in 1929   Printed from
                                                   the original

95
TO THE CENTRAL COMMITTEE OF THE P.P.S.

Comrades,

Please send us more detailed information as to what kind of conference you are planning, which organisations will be represented, and when and where it will be held. Further, be so good as to inform us what would be your attitude to the participation of Polish Social-Democrats in the conference.

On receipt of all supplementary information from you, we shall submit your proposal, in accordance with our Party Rules, to the Party Council.

With comradely greetings,
On behalf of the C.C....

Written February 7, 1904
Sent from Geneva

First published in 1925

Printed from
the original

96

TO THE CENTRAL COMMITTEE OF THE R.S.D.L.P.

Old Man writing. I have read the letters of Zemlyachka and Konyagin. Where he got the idea that I have now realised the uselessness of a congress, God only knows. On the contrary, I insist as before that this is the only honest way out, that only short-sighted people and cowards can dodge this conclusion. I insist as before that Boris, Mitrofan and Horse should be sent here without fail, for people need to see the situation (especially that which arose after the Council meetings) for themselves, and not waste their time preaching to the winds from afar, hiding their heads under their wings and taking advantage of the fact that the C.C. is a long way off and it would take a year and a day to reach it.

There is nothing more absurd than the opinion that working for a congress, agitating in the committees, and getting them to pass well-thought-out and forceful (and not sloppy) resolutions *precludes* "positive" work or contradicts it. Such an opinion merely betrays an inability to understand the political situation which has now arisen in the Party.

The Party is virtually torn apart, the Rules have been turned into scraps of paper and the organisation is spat upon—only complaisant Gothamites can still fail to see this. To anyone who has grasped this, it should be clear that the Martovites' attack must be met with an equal attack (and not with fatuous vapourings about peace, etc.). And for an attack, all forces must be set in motion. All technical facilities, transport and receiving arrangements should be handled *exclusively* by auxiliary personnel, assistants and agents. It is supremely unwise to use C.C.

members for this. The C.C. members must *occupy* all the committees, mobilise the Majority, tour Russia, unite their people, launch an onslaught (in reply to the Martovites' attacks), an onslaught on the C.O., an onslaught by means of resolutions 1) demanding a congress; 2) *challenging* the editors of the C.O. to say whether they will submit to the congress on the question of the composition of the editorial board; 3) branding the new *Iskra* without "philistine delicacy", as was done recently by Astrakhan, Tver and the Urals. These resolutions should be published in Russia, as we have said a hundred times already.

I believe that we really do have in the C.C. bureaucrats and formalists, instead of revolutionaries. The Martovites spit in their faces and they wipe it off and lecture me: "it is useless to fight!"... Only bureaucrats can fail to see now that the C.C. is not a C.C. and its efforts to be one are ludicrous. Either the C.C. becomes an organisation of *war against the C.O.*, war in deeds and not in words, of war waged in the committees, or the C.C. is a useless rag, which deserves to be thrown away.

For heaven's sake, can't you see that centralism has been irretrievably shattered by the Martovites! Forget all idiotic formalities, take possession of the committees, teach *them* to fight for the Party against the circle spirit abroad, write leaflets for them (this will not hinder agitation for a congress, but assist it!), use auxiliary forces for technical jobs. Take the lead in the war against the C.O. or renounce altogether ludicrous pretensions to "leadership"... by wiping off the spittle.

Claire's behaviour is shameful, but Konyaga's encouragement of him is still worse. Nothing makes me so angry now as our "so-called" C.C. *Addio*.

Old Man

Written in February 1904
Sent from Geneva to Russia

First published in 1929

Printed from
the original

97

TO THE EDITORIAL BOARD OF *ISKRA*

The C.C. informs the editorial board of the C.O. that it regards the instruction that letters *intended for the C.C.* are to be handed to the C.O. as an illegitimate and unscrupulous confiscation and a violation of trust.

The C.C. states also that it has already fully taken the measure of Comrade Blumenfeld, who has now been entrusted with the sorting out of letters, on account of his unreliability in matters of secrecy and his proneness to make rows.

The C.C. will therefore bring to the knowledge of all Party members such confiscation and its inevitably harmful consequences for our work.

The C.C.

Written February 26, 1904
in Geneva (local mail)

First published in 1930

Printed from
the original

98

TO THE CENTRAL COMMITTEE OF THE R.S.D.L.P.

Comrades,

Having received notification of your collective decision of the C.C. majority against a congress and the desirability of putting an end to "squabbling", and having discussed this notification among the three of us (Kurtz, Beast and Lenin), we unanimously adopted the following decision:

1) Kurtz and Lenin will *temporarily* resign membership of the Council (while remaining members of the C.C.) until the true nature of our differences with the majority of the Central Committee has been cleared up. (We stated in the Council that we see no other honest way out of the squabbling except a congress, and we voted for a congress.) We stress that we are withdrawing temporarily and conditionally, by no means resigning altogether, and greatly desiring a comradely clarification of our differences and misunderstandings.

2) In view of (a) the need for C.C. members on the Council to live abroad; (b) the need for personal consultation with the C.C. members in Russia; (c) the need for a C.C. member abroad after the departure of Kurtz, Beast and Lenin (Kurtz and Beast are leaving for Russia, Lenin is taking his official and full holiday for not less than two months); (d) the need to arrange that the conduct of affairs here that give rise to "squabbling" should be in the hands of *those* C.C. members who *disagree* with us, for we are *powerless to combat* the squabbling otherwise than as we are doing,

— in view of all this, we most earnestly request the C.C. to send here *immediately* and without fail at least *one* of its members from Russia.

We ask you to inform us at once of the receipt of this letter and of your reply.

P.S. To avoid gossip and false rumours, we have informed the Council of our resignation in the following form (copy in full):

"*To the Chairman of the Party Council*

"Comrade, in view of the departure of one of us, and the holiday being taken by the other, we are regretfully compelled to relinquish temporarily the post of C.C. members on the Council. We have informed the Central Committee of this.

"With Social-Democratic greetings,

Kurtz,
Lenin"

Written March 13, 1904
Sent from Geneva to Russia

First published in 1929   Printed from
                                                the original

99

TO F. V. LENGNIK

I add my personal request to Stake that he should on no account resign.[239] If Valentin is unwilling to consult on everything and to hand all, absolutely all, information to Stake, then let Valentin resign. Let Stake bear in mind that the whole course of events is now in our favour; a little more patience and persistence, and we shall win. Make sure to acquaint everyone with the pamphlet,* especially Brutus. After the pamphlet we must make a further attack on Brutus. Brutus will be ours; for the time being I shall not accept his withdrawal; you should not accept it either; put his resignation in your pocket for the time being. There is no question of Zemlyachka's resignation, remember that; Nil does not even claim that she has resigned. Inform Zemlyachka about this and stand firm. I repeat: our side will gain the upper hand within the Central Committee.

Written May 26, 1904
Sent from Geneva to Moscow

First published in 1930

Printed from
the original

---

* The reference is to *One Step Forward, Two Steps Back* (see present edition, Vol. 7).—*Ed.*

100

TO G. M. KRZHIZHANOVSKY

Dear friend,

You will, of course, grasp the gist of the matter from our agreement with Nil.[240] For heaven's sake, don't be in a hurry to make decisions and don't despair. Be sure first to read my pamphlet* and the Council minutes. Do not let your temporary withdrawal from affairs worry you; better abstain from some of the voting, but do not withdraw altogether. Believe me, you will still be very, very much needed and all your friends are counting on your early "resurrection". Many people in the Party are still in a state of bewilderment and confusion, at a loss to grasp the new situation and faint-heartedly losing confidence in themselves and in the right cause. On the other hand, it is becoming more and more evident to us here that we are gaining from delays, that the squabbling is dying out of itself and the essential issue, that of principles, is irrevocably coming into the forefront. And in this respect the new *Iskra* is pitiably feeble. Don't believe the stupid tales that we are out for a split, arm yourself with a certain amount of patience and you will soon see that our campaign is a splendid one and that we shall win by the force of conviction. Be sure you reply to me. It would be best if you could wangle things so as to come out here for a week or so—not on business, but just for a holiday, and to meet me somewhere in the mountains. I assure you that you will still be very much needed, and although Konyaga

---

* *One Step Forward, Two Steps Back* (see present edition, Vol. 7).—*Ed.*

mistakenly dissuaded you from one plan of yours—a thing put off is not a thing lost! Gird up your loins, we are still full of fight.

Yours,

Lenin

Written not earlier than
May 26, 1904
Sent from Geneva to Russia

First published in 1930

Printed from
the original

101

TO L. B. KRASIN[241]

From Old Man to Horse, private

In connection with the documents sent you (the agreement with Nil and my official letter to the C.C.*), I should like to have a talk with you, but I do not know whether we shall succeed in meeting. Your "friend"[242] was here recently and he spoke of your possible arrival, but Nil contradicted this news. It will be a great pity if you do not come; your coming would be absolutely essential in all respects, as there are misunderstandings galore and they will increase more and more, hindering all work, unless we succeed in meeting and having a detailed talk. Write to me without fail whether you are coming and what you think of my pamphlet. In general, you are unpardonably inactive where letters are concerned.

In my opinion, Boris (and *Konyaga*, too, apparently) have got stuck in an obviously obsolete point of view. They are still "living in November", when squabbling overrode everything else in our Party struggle, when it was permissible to hope that everything would "come right of itself" given a certain personal tractibility, etc. This point of view is now antiquated and to persist in it means either being a parrot senselessly repeating one and the same thing, or a political weathercock, or renouncing any leading role whatsoever and becoming a deaf-and-dumb cabman or factotum. Events have irrevocably shattered this old point of view. Even the Martovites refuse to have anything to do with "co-optation"; the theoretical

---

* *"Letter to the Members of the Central Committee"* (see present edition, Vol. 7).—*Ed.*

drivel that fills the new *Iskra* has already *de facto* pushed all squabbling far into the background (so that now only the parrots can call for a cessation of squabbling); by the force of events the issue has *boiled down*—for heaven's sake grasp this—it has boiled down to whether the Party is satisfied with the new *Iskra*. If we don't want to be pawns, we absolutely must understand the present situation and work out a plan for a sustained and inexorable struggle on behalf of the Party principle against the circle spirit, on behalf of revolutionary principles of organisation against opportunism. It is time to get rid of old bugbears which make out that every such struggle is a split, it is time to stop hiding our heads under our wings, evading one's Party duties by references to the "positive work"... of cabmen and factotums; it is time to abandon the opinion, at which even children will soon be laughing, that agitation for a congress is Lenin's intrigue.

I repeat: the C.C. members are in very serious danger of becoming extremely backward eccentrics. Anyone who possesses a particle of political honour and political honesty must stop shifting and shuffling (*even* Plekhanov has not succeeded in that, leave alone our good Boris!), and must adopt a definite position and stand by his convictions.

All the very best. Awaiting your reply,

Yours,
Lenin

Written not earlier than May 26,
1904
Sent from Geneva to Baku

First published in 1930

Printed from
the original

102

TO YELENA STASOVA AND F. V. LENGNIK

We have just received Absolute's letter about the meeting and do not understand it at all. On whose initiative is the meeting being arranged? Who will attend it? Will Nikitich, Deer and Valentin be there? It is essential to know everything in the greatest possible detail. For what may happen is this: Deer, Nikitich and Mitrofan may transfer their votes to Nil or Valentin, which will give them a majority, and they may carry out a coup d'état; it is easier to do this abroad, where the Council is at hand to sanction their decisions. In general a meeting here of the soft members[243] may turn out to be very dangerous at the present time. Judging by the way Nil behaves, one could expect anything from him. He says, for example, in connection with Plekhanov's letter: "We must reply that we do not agree with Lenin's policy, but we don't want to give him up." What he understands by Lenin's policy, God alone knows. He refused to discuss matters with Falcon: "You will learn my opinion from Valentin." He talks to the Minority in a very friendly way, quite different from the way he talks to the Majority. Falcon wanted to go away today, but just now we are in some perplexity. The "soft" ones alone may decide, if it is to their advantage, that transfer of votes is not allowed, in which case Falcon ought not go away—it will be an extra vote and, besides, support for Lenin is needed. If, however, there are no grounds for thinking that the meeting will end in a coup, then there is no need for Falcon to hang about. In the first event, wire: *"Geld folgt"** (meaning: Falcon to travel immedi-

---

* "Money follows".—*Ed.*

ately); in the second event, wire: *"Brief folgt"** (meaning: Falcon to remain abroad). The address for the telegram is...**

Reply also by letter without delay and in as much detail as possible. Settle the time more exactly. What do you mean by: prepare lodgings? Do you too think that all the "stone-hards" can go away without everything falling into the hands of the hard-soft "Matryona-ites"? If, for example, Valentin remains while the others go away, he can break a lot of china. In that case, perhaps, Falcon's presence will be needed in Russia. Think all this over very carefully. At present we do not share your optimism concerning the C.C., but we are optimists as regards our victory.

If the meeting is a general one, let Stake once more make desperate efforts to drag Deer out here and explain to him that the transfer of his (Deer's) vote to Konyaga or Boris could mean a coup d'état and Lenin's withdrawal for a desperate struggle.

Written June 19, 1904
Sent from Geneva to Moscow

First published in 1930

Printed from a copy written out
by N. K. Krupskaya with corrections
and an addition by V. I. Lenin

---

* "Letter follows".—*Ed.*
** Space was left in the manuscript for the address.—*Ed.*

103

TO Y. O. MARTOV, SECRETARY
OF THE PARTY COUNCIL

Reply to Comrade Martov

Comrade,

I received your undated letter while travelling, and without having the Council minutes at hand. At all events I consider it in principle absolutely impermissible and unlawful that outside a Council meeting members of the Council should give their votes or make arrangements on any matters that come within the competence of the Council. I cannot therefore comply with your request about voting for candidates. If I am not mistaken, the Council decided that all Council members should represent our Party at the congress.[244] Consequently, the question has been settled. If any Council member is unable to go, then, in my opinion, he can appoint someone else in his place; I do not know, of course, whether it is customary for international congresses to permit such substitution, but I do not know of any obstacle to it in our Party Rules or in the Party's usual regulations. Personally I am also unable to go and would like as a substitute for myself Comrade Lyadov, who has plenipotentiary powers from the C.C., and Comrade Sergei Petrovich, member of the Moscow Committee.

With Social-Democratic greetings,
N. Lenin, Council member

P.S. *Re* the communication to the C.C., I shall write to the Geneva agents, who are in charge of all matters during my absence.

Written August 10, 1904
in the Swiss mountains
    Sent to Geneva

First published in 1930

Printed from
the original

104

TO M. K. VLADIMIROV[245]

For Fred

Dear Comrade,

I have received your last letter. I am writing to the old address, although I am afraid that letters are not reaching you; the previous letter was answered in considerable detail. The comradely trust which is evident in all your letters induces me to write to you personally. This letter is not written from the collegium and is not intended for the Committee.

The state of things in your Committee, which is suffering from a lack of people, lack of literature and complete lack of information, is similar to the state of things in Russia as a whole. Everywhere there is a terrible lack of people, even more so in the Minority committees than in those of the Majority, complete isolation, a general mood of depression and bitterness, stagnation as regards positive work. Ever since the Second Congress, the Party is being torn to pieces, and today things have gone very, very far in this respect; the tactics of the Minority have terribly weakened the Party. The Minority has done all it could to discredit the C.C. as well, beginning its persecution already at the congress, and carrying it on intensively both in the press and orally. In even greater measure it has discredited the C.O., which it has turned from a Party organ into an organ for settling personal accounts with the Majority. If you have been reading *Iskra* there is no need to say anything to you about this. In their attempts to dig up fresh disagreements they have now trotted forth as their slogan "liquidation of the fourth, *Iskra*, period", and are burning everything that they worshipped

yesterday, totally distorting the perspective and interpreting Iskrism in a way its worst enemies used to interpret it. The Party functionaries, who remember what they stood for yesterday, do not follow the lead of the C.O. The vast majority of the committees adhere to the standpoint of the Congress majority and are breaking their spiritual ties with the Party organ more and more.

The present state of affairs, however, is having such an effect on positive work, and hindering it to such an extent, that among a whole number of Party functionaries a mood has developed that makes them immerse themselves in positive work and stand completely aloof from the embittered internecine struggle which is taking place in the Party. They want to close their eyes, stop up their ears and hide their heads under the wing of positive work; they are running away to escape from things which no one, being in the Party, can now escape from. Some of the C.C. members have adopted such a "conciliatory" attitude in an attempt to blanket the growing disagreements, to blanket the fact that the Party is disintegrating. The Majority (the non-conciliatory Majority) says: we must quickly find some way out, we must come to some arrangement, we must try to find the framework within which the ideological struggle can proceed more or less normally; a new congress is needed. The Minority is against a congress; they say: the vast majority of the Party is against us and a congress is not to our advantage; the "conciliatory" Majority is also against a congress, it is afraid of everyone's growing animosity against the C.O. and the C.C. To think that a congress could lead only to a split would mean to admit that we haven't got a Party at all, that Party feeling is so poorly developed among all of us that it cannot overcome the old circle spirit. In this respect we have a better opinion of our opponents than they have of themselves. Of course, it is impossible to guarantee anything, but an attempt to settle the conflict in a Party manner, and to find a way out, must be made. The Majority, at any rate, does not want a split, but to go on working under the conditions which have now been created is becoming more and more impossible. Already more than ten committees have expressed themselves in favour of a congress (St.

Petersburg, Tver, Moscow, Tula, Siberia, Caucasus, Ekaterinoslav, Nikolayev, Odessa, Riga, Astrakhan), but even
if the great majority of the committees pronounce for a
congress it will not take place so very soon, for both the
C.O. and the C.C., and probably the Council as well, will
oppose the wishes of the majority of the comrades in Russia.

With regard to literature, the C.C. comrade with whom
we talked about this replied that it was being punctually
supplied to your Committee. Obviously, there has been
some confusion. Persons were sent to you twice, but in
Russia they were directed to other places. We shall try to
send you new things as opportunity arises.

With comradely greetings,

Lenin

Written August 15, 1904
in the Swiss mountains,
    sent to Gomel

First published in 1934

Printed from a copy
written out by
N. K. Krupskaya

105

TO THE *ISKRA* EDITORIAL BOARD

To the C.O. of the R.S.D.L.P.

August 24, 1904

Comrades,

Being rather far from Geneva, I learnt only today that the editors of the Central Organ intend to publish a "declaration" said to have been adopted by the Central Committee.[246]

I consider it my duty to warn the editors of the C.O. that already on August 18, 1904, I made a statement contesting the lawfulness of this declaration,* i.e., the lawfulness of the decision on this question allegedly adopted by a majority of the C.C.

There are at present six members of the C.C. (owing to Comrade Mitrofan's resignation and, if the rumour is to be believed, the recent arrest of Zverev and Vasiliev).

According to my information, it is even probable that only three members out of the six had the audacity to speak for the whole C.C. and to do so not even through the two representatives abroad, who are formally bound by the agreement of May 26, 1904 (this agreement was signed by Glebov, Zverev and myself).

I enclose herewith a copy of my statement of August 18, 1904, and I must state that the editorial board of the C.O. will be responsible for giving press publicity to the *whole incident and conflict* in the event of the "declaration" being

---

* "To Five Members of the Central Committee" (see present edition, Vol. 7).—*Ed.*

published before the matter of my protest against the validity of the decision has been settled within the C.C.

N. Lenin,

C.C. member and representative abroad

P.S. In any case I consider it absolutely obligatory that publication of the "declaration" should be withheld until I have thrashed out the matter with Comrade Glebov who, according to my information, is today leaving Berlin for Geneva. Not even I, a member of the C.C., have any knowledge of the latter's decision concerning the publication of this declaration.

If, nevertheless, the editorial board decides to publish the declaration, then I consider it is morally bound to publish also my protest against its lawfulness.

Written in the Swiss mountains,
    sent to Geneva

First published in 1930

Printed from a copy
written out by
N. K. Krupskaya

106

TO MEMBERS OF THE MAJORITY COMMITTEES AND ALL ACTIVE SUPPORTERS OF THE MAJORITY IN RUSSIA WITH THE TEXT OF A LETTER TO LYDIA FOTIYEVA

Dear Lydia Alexandrovna,

Please send the following letter to all *our friends* in Russia as soon as possible (desirably today):

"Please begin immediately collecting and dispatching all correspondence to our addresses with the inscription: 'For Lenin'. Money, too, is badly needed. Events are taking a sharper turn. The Minority is obviously preparing a coup through a deal with part of the Central Committee. The worst is to be expected. Details in a few days."

Send this letter immediately

(1) to *St. Petersburg*, to the address of Mouse, (2) to *Tver*, (3) to *Odessa* (to both addresses), (4) to *Ekaterinoslav*, (5) to Siberia, (6) to the Urals, (7) to *Riga* (to both addresses), (8) to Rosa, (9) to Nizhni-Novgorod (the address for letters: Library of the Vsesoslovny Club, in a brochure), (10) to Saratov (to Golubev's address), and generally to all the addresses of friends on whom we can fully depend.

Best regards.

Leon* should not leave so soon, her document will be sent out, but not before a day or two.**

Written about August 28, 1904,
in Switzerland

First published in 1930

Printed from
the original

---

* Unidentified.—*Ed.*
** The lines printed in small type are Krupskaya's text.—*Ed.*

107

TO V. A. NOSKOV

To Comrade Glebov, Member of the C.C.

August 30, 1904

Comrade,

I cannot take part in the voting on co-optation[247] proposed by you until I receive your written reply to my protest of August 18, 1904, and detailed information on the decisions allegedly adopted by the Central Committee. I cannot come to Geneva at the present time.

Lenin, C.C. member

Written in the Swiss mountains,
sent to Geneva

First published in 1930

Printed from the original

108

TO V. A. NOSKOV

To Com. Glebov. In reply to your note of August 30, 1904, we inform you that the lawfulness and validity of the C.C. decisions to which you refer have been contested by C.C. member, Comrade Lenin. In the capacity of C.C. agents who have been kept informed of the whole course of the conflict within the C.C. we, in turn, also contest the lawfulness of this decision and state that the decision of the C.C. cannot be recognised as lawful, for it begins by stating as a fact what is known to be untrue: here abroad we ourselves have seen *two* C.C. members who were not informed of the meeting of the Central Committee. Since you have once told us a direct untruth (about an alleged ban imposed by the Central Committee on Comrade Lenin's book*) we are the more inclined to doubt statements emanating from you. We therefore request you to furnish us immediately with exact data for checking the lawfulness of the C.C. decision (composition of the meeting** and written statements of each participant). While having no intention whatever to oppose lawful decisions of an actual majority of the C.C. we shall pay no attention to any statement of yours until this lawfulness has been proved to us.

Written August 30 or 31, 1904
 in the Swiss mountains,
  sent to Geneva
First published in 1930   Printed from
                                                          the original

---

* *One Step Forward, Two Steps Back* (see present edition, Vol. 7) — *Ed.*

** To avoid misinterpretation, we state that after publication of the untrue statement (in the declaration) concerning the composition of the meeting, we have absolutely no possibility of arriving at the truth except by getting to know the composition of the meeting.

109
TO V. A. NOSKOV

To Comrade Glebov

September 2, 1904

Comrade,

Please let me know whether you intend to reply to my protest in connection with the decision allegedly adopted by a majority of the Central Committee.

At what "preceding regular meeting of the C.C." did Comrade Osipov announce his resignation?

When exactly and by whom were the C.C. members who were absent when Osipov made this statement informed about this?

Did Comrade Valentin report to the Central Committee about his (Valentin's) dispute with Comrade Vasiliev in connection with the supposed resignation of Comrade Osipov?

When and to whom did Comrade Travinsky formally announce his resignation? Please let me have a copy of this announcement and all the details. Perhaps someone has already written to me about this, but the letter has gone astray?

Until the lawfulness (of the composition of the C.C. and its decision of... July) has been "verified" by *all* members of the C.C., I do not regard either Comrade Glebov or myself entitled to represent the C.C. in the Party Council.

N Lenin,
C.C. member

Written in the Swiss mountains,
sent to Geneva
First published in 1930

Printed from
the original

110

TO Y. O. MARTOV, SECRETARY OF THE PARTY COUNCIL

To Comrade Martov

September 2, 1904

Comrade,

In reply to your invitation of August 31, 1904, to a sitting of the Council, I must state that until the lawfulness of the composition of the C.C. and of its last, allegedly regular, meeting has been verified by all C.C. members, I do not consider either Comrade Glebov or myself entitled to represent the C.C. in the Party Council. Until such a check is made I regard all official steps undertaken by Comrade Glebov (and participation in the Council is also an official step) as *unlawful*.

I shall confine myself to pointing out one *obvious untruth* and one *inaccuracy* in the "verification" of the C.C.'s composition carried out by three C.C. members at their "meeting" of . . . July. 1) Regarding the resignation of Mitrofanov, I have the written statement of Comrade Osipov. About the resignation of Travinsky, I have had no definite written statement from anyone. Three C.C. members at least prematurely accepted the resignation, without consulting the other members. 2) Regarding the notorious resignation of Comrade Osipov I have a written communication of C.C. member Vasiliev about his dispute with Comrade Valentin and the decision to examine the dispute at a general meeting of the Central Committee. About Osipov's resignation, too, I have not had a single communication. The statement of the three C.C. members that Osipov formally announced his withdrawal at the preceding regular meeting of the C.C. is an *obvious lie,*

documentarily refuted by the agreement of May 26, 1904, signed by Zverev and *Glebov*. This agreement, which was concluded *months after* the "preceding regular meeting of the C.C." and after Osipov is alleged to have joined the St. Petersburg Committee, records the C.C. as consisting of nine members, i.e., *including Osipov*.

N. Lenin,
C.C. member

Written in the Swiss mountains,
    sent to Geneva

First published in 1930

Printed from
a copy written out by
N. K. Krupskaya

111

TO Y. O. MARTOV,
SECRETARY OF THE PARTY COUNCIL

To Comrade Martov

Duplicate

September 7, 1904

Comrade,

In connection with the copies you have sent me, I have to state that the Council need not have troubled to repeat its invitation, seeing that I have already replied to it by a refusal. Never have I expressed a desire that investigation of the "conflict" in the C.C. should be submitted to the Council. On the contrary, I have plainly stated in letters to Comrade Glebov and to Comrade Martov that only the C.C. members as a whole are competent to verify the lawfulness of its composition. The Council is not authorised even by the Rules to examine conflicts within the Central Committee.*

Since the Bureau of the International Congress has accepted the transference by me of *my* mandate,[248] I am no longer accountable in any way to any Council. I shall willingly give explanations (in writing or in print) concerning *definite* issues to anyone who wants them.

N. Lenin,
C.C. member

Written in the neighbourhood
of Geneva, sent to Geneva

First published in 1930

Printed from
the original

---

* See pp. 253-55 of this volume.—*Ed.*

112
TO PARTICIPANTS IN THE CONFERENCE OF THE SOUTHERN COMMITTEES[249] AND TO THE SOUTHERN BUREAU OF THE C.C., R.S.D.L.P.

Comrades,

In reply to your resolution on the desirability of an Organising Committee of the Majority being set up, we hasten to inform you that we entirely agree with your idea. We should prefer only to call the group not an Organising Committee, but a Bureau of the Majority Committees. We do not consider it possible for us to appoint the B.M.C. ourselves, and are restricting ourselves to recommending comrades Martyn, Demon and K., Baron, Sergei Petrovich, Felix and Lebedev, who (as you know) have actually begun the work of uniting the Majority committees. We think that, given the direct support of several committees, these comrades could act as a special group uniting the activities of supporters of the Majority.

(Participants of the Meeting of the 22[250])

Written later than October 5, 1904
Sent from Geneva to Odessa

First published in 1930

Printed from
the original

113

TO THE MAJORITY COMMITTEES

1) To be written to *all* our committees:
"Immediately and without fail write *officially* to the C.C. in Russia (sending us a copy of your letter) requesting that the Committee be supplied with all publications of the new publishing house of Bonch-Bruyevich and Lenin,[251] and that they be supplied regularly. Get a reply from the C.C. and send it to us. Make use of a personal meeting with C.C. members and ask them about their reply in the presence of witnesses. Have you received the supplement to Nos. 73-74—the decisions of the Council[252]? You must protest against this scandalous affair, it is a downright falsification of the congress, a downright incitement of the periphery against the committees and a shifting of the squabble to the Council. If you have not received these decisions, enquire about them also from the C.C. and keep us informed. We shall issue shortly a detailed examination of these Council decisions."

2) The *full* reply of the 22 concerning the Organising Committee to be sent to *Odessa*, *stipulating* that the place they received it from is to be kept secret. The letter to be inscribed "for Baron, Osip and Leonsha *exclusively*". Let Odessa send us, Felix and Mouse immediately their reply, their amendments, or their agreement, etc. Let Odessa send immediately Nikolayev's decision concerning the congress.

Written later than October 5, 1904
Sent from Geneva to Russia
First published in 1930

Printed from the original

114
TO THE SIBERIAN COMMITTEE

Geneva, October 30, 1904

To the Siberian Committee from N. Lenin

Comrades,

I should like through you to answer Comrade Simonov, who was here as a representative of the Siberian Union and who, before departing, left me a letter (I was not in Geneva at the time) setting out his conciliatory point of view. It is this letter, the contents of which are probably known to you from Comrade Simonov, that I should like to talk to you about. Comrade Simonov's point of view amounts to this: they (the Minority) are, of course, anarchists and disrupters, but there is nothing to be done with them; a "truce" is necessary (Simonov stresses that, in contrast to other conciliators, he does not speak of peace but of a truce) in order to find some way out of an intolerable situation, and to gather strength for a further struggle against the Minority.

I found Simonov's letter extremely instructive as coming from such a rarity as a *sincere* supporter of conciliation. There is so much hypocrisy among the conciliators that one finds it refreshing to meet the views (even if incorrect) of a man who says what he thinks. And his views are certainly incorrect. He himself realises that it is impossible to be *reconciled* with falsehood, confusion and squabbling, but what is the sense of talking about a *truce*? For the Minority will use such a truce merely for strengthening their positions. Factional polemics (cessation of which was hypocritically promised by the hypocritical C.C. in its recent letter to the committees, a letter that you too have prob-

ably already received) have not ceased but have assumed
the especially vile forms that were condemned even by
Kautsky, who sides with the Minority. Even K. Kautsky
said in his letter to *Iskra* that a "hidden" polemic is worse
than any other, for the issue becomes confused, hints remain obscure, straightforward answers are impossible. And
take *Iskra*; the leading article in No. 75, the subject of
which is very remote from our differences, will be found
interspersed, without rhyme or reason, with senilely embittered abuse against the Ivanovs on the Council, the sheer
ignoramuses, etc., etc. From the standpoint of our deserters
from the C.C., this, probably, is not factional polemics!
I say nothing, in substance, of the arguments used by the
author of the leading article (apparently Plekhanov): that
Marx was *mild* towards the Proudhonists. Can you imagine
a falser use of historical facts and great names of history?
What would Marx have said if the slogan of mildness was
used to cover up *muddling* the distinction between Marxism
and Proudhonism? (And is not the new *Iskra* wholly occupied in muddling the distinction between *Rabocheye Dyelo*-
ism and Iskrism?) What would Marx have said if mildness
had been made a cover for asserting in print the correctness
of Proudhonism against Marxism? (And is not Plekhanov
now playing the fox in print by pretending to recognise
that the Minority is correct in principle?) By this com-
parison alone Plekhanov gives himself away, betrays the
fact that the relation of the Majority to the Minority is
equivalent to the relation of Marxism to Proudhonism, to
that very relation of the revolutionary to the opportunist
wing which figures also in that memorable article "What
Should Not Be Done". Take the decisions of the Party
Council (No. 73 and the supplement to Nos. 73-74) and you
will see that the cessation of the Minority's secret organisation, proclaimed in the above-mentioned letter of the C.C.
to the committees, signifies nothing but the passing of three
C.C. members into the secret organisation of the Minority.
In *this* sense the secret organisation has really disappeared,
for all three of our so-called central institutions—not
only the C.O. and the Council, but also the Central Committee—have now become a secret organisation (for struggle
against the Party). In the name of a struggle ("on prin-

ciple") against formalism and bureaucracy, they are now declaring war on the "headings", declaring that the publishing house of the Majority is not a Party one. They falsify the congress, counting the votes falsely ($16 \times 4 = 61$, for five members of the Council figure in the total 61, but in half the organisations the Council figures as an organisation with two votes!), concealing the resolutions of the committees from the Party (it is concealed that Nizhni-Novgorod, Saratov, Nikolayev and the Caucasus were in favour of a congress: see the last resolutions in our pamphlet *To the Party* and *The Fight for a Congress*[253]). They bring squabbling into the Council, interminably distorting the question of representation at the Amsterdam Congress[254] and having the audacity to publish charges of "deceit" against the Northern Committee, when this incident had not only not been investigated (although the C.C. had decided to investigate it as far back as *July*), but the comrade accused by some slanderer has so far *not even been questioned* (during three months, August, September and October, this comrade was abroad and saw Central Committee member Glebov, who had taken the decision for an investigation but did not take the trouble to present the charges to the accused person himself!). They encourage disruption in the name of the Council, inciting the "periphery" to attack the Majority committees, and uttering a deliberate lie about St. Petersburg and Odessa. They condemn as an "abuse" the voting of one and the same comrades in different committees, when at the same time three Council members—Plekhanov, Martov and Axelrod—vote *three* times *against* a congress: once on the editorial board, once in the Council and once in the League! They assume the powers of a congress by declaring credentials invalid. Isn't that falsifying the congress? And can it be that Comrade Simonov would advise a truce in relation to *these* tactics as well?

Take the report to the Amsterdam Congress[255] which has recently been issued in Russian. Deliberately flouting the will of the Party, the Minority speak in the name of the Party, repeating in a covert form the same lie about the old *Iskra* which was always being propagated by Martynov and Co., and which is now being served up by Balalaikin-

Trotsky. Or maybe Comrade Simonov wants a truce with this Balalaikin too (whose pamphlet is published *under the editorship of Iskra* as plainly stated in *Iskra*)? Maybe here, too, he believes in the cessation of factional polemics promised by the C.C.?

No, the belief that a truce with hypocrisy and disruption is permissible is one that is unworthy of a Social-Democrat and profoundly erroneous at bottom. It is faint-heartedness to think that "there is nothing to be done" with writers, even notable ones, and that the only tactic left in relation to them is that formulated by Galyorka ("Down with Bonapartism") in the words "You curse but bow down". To the conversion of all the Party's central institutions into a secret organisation for struggle against the Party, to the Council's falsification of the congress, the Majority replies by a further and inevitable strengthening of its unity. Disdaining hypocrisy, it openly puts forward a programme of struggle (see the resolution of the 22 endorsed by the Caucasian Union,[256] and the Committees of St. Petersburg, Riga, Moscow, Odessa, Ekaterinoslav and Nikolayev. The C.O., of course, concealed this resolution from the Party although it received it two months ago). The southern committees have already taken a decision to unite the committees of the Majority and to set up an Organising Committee to combat the flouting of the Party. There is not the slightest doubt that such an organisation of the Majority will be set up in the near future and will act openly. Despite the lying stories of deserters from the C.C., the adherents of the Majority are growing in number in Russia, and the young literary forces, repelled by the muddled and hypocritical *Iskra*, are beginning to rally from all sides to the newly-started publishing house of the Majority (the publishing house abroad of Bonch-Bruyevich and Lenin) with the aim of giving it every possible support by transforming, enlarging and developing it.

Comrade Simonov had no reason to be down-hearted. He was wrong to jump to the conclusion that, however nasty it was, there was nothing to be done about it. There is something to be done! The more grossly they flout the idea of a congress (Balalaikin-Trotsky, writing under the editorship of *Iskra*, has already declared a congress to be

a *reactionary attempt* to reinforce the plans of the Iskrists.
Ryazanov was more sincere and honest when he called
the congress a packed affair) and the more grossly they
flout the Party and its functionaries in Russia, the more
merciless becomes the rebuff they encounter and the more
closely does the Majority rally its ranks, uniting all persons of principle and recoiling from the unnatural and
intrinsically rotten political alliance of Plekhanov, Martynov and Trotsky. It is precisely such an alliance that we
see now in the new *Iskra* and in *Zarya* No. 5 (a reprint of
Martynov's article has appeared). Anyone who sees a little
further than his nose, whose policy is not determined by
interests of the minute and coalitions of the hour, will
understand that this alliance, which breeds only confusion
and squabbles, is doomed, and that the adherents of the
trend of the old *Iskra*, people who are able to distinguish
this trend from a circle even of notable "foreigners", must
and will be the grave-diggers of this alliance.

I should be very glad, comrades, if you would inform
me of the receipt of this letter and whether you have succeeded in forwarding it to Comrade Simonov.

With comradely greetings,

N. Lenin

First published in 1930

Printed from
the original

115

TO A. M. STOPANI[257]

To Tu—ra from Lenin, private

Dear Comrade,

I was extremely glad to have your letter. Please write punctually every week, even if only a few lines, and make sure that all addresses are usable and that you have reserve addresses for letters and rendezvous. It's a downright scandal that the adherents of the Majority are so scattered! No common work is possible without regular contact and we have had nothing from you for over six months.

I absolutely and fully agree with everything you write concerning the need to unite the Majority, to rally its committees and prepare for a united congress capable of enforcing the will of the Party workers in Russia. Very close contact is essential for all this, otherwise we shall drift apart and you will know absolutely nothing of our common affairs.

The C.C. has now wholly fused with the Minority and has *virtually* become part of its secret organisation, the aim of which is to fight against a congress at all costs. The new decisions of the Council plainly falsify both the counting of votes and the will of the committees (supplement to *Iskra* Nos. 73-74. Have you seen it?). Now we must be prepared for the fact that they will not convene a congress on any account, will not shrink from any violation of the Rules, nor from any further flouting of the Party. They openly jeer at us, saying "where is your strength?" We should indeed be behaving like children if we confined ourselves to *faith* in a congress, without preparing straightaway to counter force by force. For this purpose we must: 1) immediately unite all the Majority committees and set up a Bureau of the Majority Committees (the initiative has already been taken by Odessa+Nikolayev+Ekaterinoslav) to combat the Bonapartism of the central bodies 2) exert every effort to support and extend in every way the Majority's publishing house (started here by Bonch-Bruyevich and myself; Bonch-Bruyevich is only the publisher). A group of writers in Russia has already set to work on this and you should immediately begin collecting and sending all kinds of material, correspondence, leaflets, comments, and so on and so forth, especially from workers and about the workers' movement. Do this without fail and immediately. (If from now on you do not begin to send us an item every week, we shall break off relations with you.)

In the matter of the Bureau, what has been done already is this. The Odessa+Nikolayev+Ekaterinoslav committees took the following decision (quote in full) ...==The 22 answered them as follows ...==[258]

You must try to go to Tiflis as soon as possible and hand over both the one and the other. Let them speedily join. It will, of course, be possible to add members from the Caucasus to the Bureau. And so, let all the committees of the Caucasus immediately give their opinion about the idea of a Bureau, that is to say, write to us and to St. Petersburg (or Riga?) (address..., key...), whether they agree to a Bureau and whether they want changes or additional candidates. For heaven's sake see to it that this matter of prime importance is dealt with properly, sensibly and quickly.

Some comrades are demanding a conference of the Majority committees in Russia. We here think this is not only expensive but bureaucratic and ineffectual. But we must press on with might and main. It is not worth while coming together to elect a Bureau; it is much better to reach agreement on this by letter or by a tour made by one or two comrades. When the Bureau speaks out and is joined by Ekaterinoslav+Odessa+Nikolayev+St. Petersburg+Moscow+Riga+the Caucasus, then this Bureau will at once be speaking as the representative of the organised Majority.

And so, for heaven's sake, make haste and answer speedily.

All the very best.

Yours,

N. Lenin

Written November 10, 1904
Sent from Geneva to Baku

First published in 1930

Printed from
the original

116
TO A. A. BOGDANOV

Dear friend,

Please tell Rakhmetov immediately that he is acting like a real pig towards us. He cannot imagine how eagerly everyone here is expecting from him definite and precise, encouraging reports, and not the telegrams he sends us. This eternal suspense and uncertainty is real torture. It is absolutely impossible that Rakhmetov should have nothing to write about: he has seen and is seeing many people, he has spoken with Zemlyachka, he has been in touch with Beard, the Moscow lawyers and writers, etc., etc. He must keep us *au courant*, pass on contacts, inform us of new addresses, forward local correspondence, tell us about business meetings and interesting encounters. Rakhmetov has not sent us a single new contact! It's monstrous. *Not a single* item of correspondence, not a single report about the group of writers in Moscow. If Rakhmetov were to be arrested tomorrow, we'd find ourselves empty-handed, as if he had never lived! It's a crying shame; he could have written everything and about everything without the slightest danger, and all he has done is to hint at some young forces and so on. (What is known about Bazarov, Frich, Suvorov and the others?) Not less than once a week (that's not much, surely), two or three hours should be spent on a letter of 10-15 pages, otherwise, I give you my word, all contact is virtually broken. Rakhmetov and his boundless plans become a boundless fiction, and our people here are simply running away, drawing the horrified conclusion that there is no sort of majority and that nothing will come of the majority. In their new form, the tactics of the Minority have become quite clear, namely, to ignore and keep silent about the Majority's writings and the Majority's existence, to keep polemics out of the C.O. and talk importantly about positive work (recently the editors of the C.O. issued in print, "for Party members only", a letter to Party organisations concerning a plan for the participation of Social-Democrats in the Zemstvo campaign—staggering pomposity about staggering banalities. An analysis and scathing criticism of this letter has been issued here by Lenin*). It is essential that the Majority should come forward with an organ of its own[259]; the necessary money and workers' letters for this are lacking. We must work hard to get both the one and the other; unless we have the most detailed and exhaustive letters nothing will come of it. Contacts are not being transmitted, there is no possibility of attacking one and the same personage from different angles, there is no co-ordination in the work of the bulk of the Bolsheviks who travel about Russia arranging things each on his own. This dispersal of efforts is felt everywhere; the committees are again lagging behind the situation, some of them unaware of the Council's new decisions (the supplement to *Iskra* Nos. 73-74, a special ten-page leaflet), others not giving serious thought to them and not realising that these decisions are tantamount to the most complete and brazen falsification of the congress. Only children could fail to see now that the Council and C.C. will stop at nothing to *sabotage* a congress. We must counterpose this by a *force*=a press organ+the organisation of the Majority in Russia, otherwise we are bound to die. Lenin has not yet seen Lightmind; it is strange that the latter has moved to the side lines and maintains a waiting attitude!

And so, give Rakhmetov a triple dressing-down and make him write a diary as a punishment. Why hasn't Mme Rakhmetova gone where she promised? We repeat: all and sundry will run away (even Galyorka is groaning and moaning), for there is no sign of any contact with Russia, no sign that Rakhmetov is alive, working for the common cause, that he is worried and concerned about it. Without letters there is nothing but complete isolation!

Written November 21, 1904
Sent from Geneva to Russia

First published in 1930

Printed from
the original

* The reference is to the pamphlet *The Zemstvo Campaign and Iskra's Plan* (see present edition, Vol. 7).—*Ed.*

117

TO NADEZHDA KRUPSKAYA

December 3, 1904

Today I sent a business letter to Bonch. I forgot to add an important thing—that *3,000* copies (of Leiteisen's dictionary) be printed; this is essential for price calculation. Tell Bonch about this at once.

I am sending you the statement of the Union Committee and of the Caucasian representative of the C.C.,[260] received today by Raisa.* *In my opinion*, it is *absolutely necessary* to re-issue this immediately *in leaflet form* in our publishing house. Do this at once without fail; the Nikolayev and other resolutions can be added to the leaflet, but it should be kept quite small, 2-4 (maximum) pages (without any headings, merely with a mention below of the publishers).

I have just received your letter. I don't understand what the matter is with the "plan" of Lyadov and Rakhmetov, but there is something wrong here. *I shall try to come as quickly as possible* and hasten Destroyer's arrival.

I warmed the attached sheets but without success. Perhaps you'll try some other reagents.

A free evening has occurred unexpectedly. I am sending you on the other side a letter which I advise you to forward *immediately* to all three from me personally,** without a powwow. It will give them a good shake up; afterwards we could find out whether the news was exaggerated or not. The fact remains that disunity is beginning, and a warning

---

* Unidentified.—*Ed.*
** See pp. 271-73 of this volume.—*Ed.*

must be issued and the culprits denounced most forcefully at the very start. I strongly advise you to send this letter off *at once* to all three from me personally. Tomorrow I shall talk to Destroyer and, I'm sure, he'll be for me, so will Vasily Vasilyevich and Schwarz, but it will be best if the text is mine personally. I wanted to write to Martyn Nikolayevich and give him a piece of my mind, but I don't think it's any good; I shall come and talk it over, as he is harmless here for the time being. As to the damage that has started in Russia, my letter will go some way in paralysing it. A pity you did not make Martyn Nikolayevich write to me at once in Paris about everything—a great pity, it was so important.

I have re-read the letter to Rakhmetov; a hard word here and there could, perhaps, have been omitted, but I *earnestly advise* you to send the letter off at once from me personally in this sharply worded form.

I called on Leiteisen. He read me Plekhanov's letter to him. Plekhanov, of course, swears at Lenin for all he is worth. He writes that "Trotsky's pamphlet is trashy, like himself". He asks Leiteisen "not to side with the Minority, but with him" (Plekhanov). He complains of "the tragedy of his life, when, after twenty years, there isn't a comrade who believes him". He says that he asks for "comradely confidence but not subordination to authority", and that he is "seriously thinking of resigning" ... for the time being this is *entre nous*.

Deutsch wrote to Leiteisen the other day, *asking for financial assistance*—he says they have no money. Zasulich wrote the same thing (earlier) to Yefron, swearing at Galyorka and considering Sergei Petrovich to be Galyorka(!).

I hope to leave on Monday, the day after tomorrow, to read on Tuesday and Wednesday in Zurich, to be in Berne on Thursday, and home on Friday. It may take a few days longer though.[261]

Write to me in Zurich through Argunin (in two envelopes, but see that the inner one is fairly strong, and be cautious). Have they written from Lausanne, have they asked me to go there? Have they given an address?

Yours,

N. Lenin

Be sure to write immediately to *all* our committees to send us a *formal order* to reprint *openly* for everyone the editorial board's letter on the Zemstvo. Do this, just to be on the safe side. *No excuses*, please. Get hold of the letter itself (or republish it) and circulate it in envelopes to the Majority committees.

Sent from Paris to Geneva

First published in 1930

Printed from
the original

118

TO A. A. BOGDANOV, ROZALIA ZEMLYACHKA AND M. M. LITVINOV[262]

From Lenin to Rakhmetov, Zemlyachka and Papasha, private

December 3, 1904

Dear friend,

I received news of Martyn Nikolayevich's arrival (I have not seen him myself) from which I infer that things are in a bad way with us. The Bolsheviks in Russia and those abroad are at sixes and sevens again. From three years' experience I know that such disunity can do enormous damage to our cause. I see evidence of this disunity in the fact: 1) that Rakhmetov's arrival is being held up; 2) that the weight of emphasis is being shifted from the press organ here to something else, to a congress, a Russian O.C., etc.; 3) that deals of some kind between the C.C. and the writers' group of the Majority, and almost idiotic enterprises of the Russian organ, are being connived at or even supported. If my information about this disunity is correct, I must say that the bitterest enemy of the Majority could not have invented anything worse. Holding up Rakhmetov's departure is sheer unpardonable stupidity, verging on treachery, for gossip is increasing terribly and we risk losing impact here because of the childishly foolish plans for devising something immediately in Russia. To delay the Majority's organ abroad (for which only the money is lacking) is still more unpardonable. The whole crux now lies in this organ, without it we shall be heading for certain, inglorious death. We must get some money at all costs, come what may, if only a couple of thousand, and start immediately, otherwise we are cutting our own throats. Only hopeless fools can put *all* hopes on a congress, for it is clear that the Council will torpedo any congress, wreck it even before it is convened. Understand me properly, for heaven's sake; I am not suggesting that we abandon all agitation for a congress and renounce this slogan, but only children could now confine themselves to this, and fail to see that the essence lies in *strength*. Let there be a spate of resolutions about the congress as before (for some reason Martyn Nikolayevich's tour did not yield a single repeat resolution, which is a pity, a great pity), but *this is not the crux of the matter*—how can anyone fail to see this? An Organising Committee or a Bureau of the Majority is necessary, but without a press organ this will be a pitiful cipher, a sheer farce, a soap bubble which will burst at the first setback caused by police raids. At all costs an organ and money, money to us here, get it by any means short of murder. An Organising Committee or a Bureau of the Majority should authorise us to start an organ (as quickly as possible) and make a round of the committees, but should the O.C. take it into its head to *first* get "positive work" going, and *put off* the organ *for the time being*, then such an idiotic Organising Committee would ruin the whole thing for us. Finally, to publish anything in Russia, to make any sort of deal with the dirty scum of the C.C. means committing an outright betrayal. That the C.C. wants to divide and split up the Bolsheviks in Russia and those abroad is obvious; this has long been its plan and none but foolish greenhorns could be taken in by it. To start an organ in Russia with the help of the C.C. is madness, sheer madness or treachery; this is what follows and will inevitably follow from the objective logic of events, because the organisers of an organ or a popular newspaper are bound to be fooled by every mangy tyke of a Central Committee. I plainly prophesy this and I give such people up in advance as a hopeless case.

I repeat: first and foremost comes an organ, and again an organ, and money for an organ; to spend money on anything else now is the height of folly. Rakhmetov must be dragged out here at once, without delay. Making a round of the committees should have the primary aim of securing local correspondence (it is inexcusable and disgraceful that we have no correspondent items all this time! It's a down-right shame and a spoke in our wheel!); all agitation for a congress should be merely an *incidental* matter. All the Majority committees should immediately and *in actual practice* break with the C.C. and transfer all relations to the O.C. or the Bureau of the Majority; this O.C. *must immediately* issue a printed announcement of its formation, and make it public at once without fail.

Unless we nip this disunity among the Majority in the bud, unless we come to an agreement on this both by letter *and* (*most important*) by a meeting with Rakhmetov, we here will all *give the whole thing up as a hopeless job*. If you want to work together, you must all pull together and act in concert, by agreement (and not in defiance of and without agreement). Damn it all, it's a downright disgrace and scandal that people go out to get money for an organ and engage instead in all kinds of piddling lousy affairs.

In a few days I shall come out in print against the C.C. still more vigorously. If we don't break with the C.C. and the Council we shall deserve only to be spat on by everyone.

I await a reply and Rakhmetov's arrival.[263]

N. Lenin

Sent from Paris to Russia
First published in 1930

Printed from
the original

119

TO M. M. LITVINOV

To Papasha from Lenin

Dear friend,

I hasten to reply to your letter, which pleased me very, very much. You are a thousand times right that we must act vigorously, in a revolutionary way, and strike the iron while it's hot. I agree, too, that it is the Majority committees that must be united. The need for a centre in Russia and an organ here is now clear to all of us. As far as the latter is concerned, we have already done all we could. Private is working with might and main, he has enlisted participants, has thrown himself whole-heartedly into the job and is trying his hardest to find a millionaire, with considerable chance of success. Finally, you are a thousand times right in that we must act openly. The question at issue between us touches only on a minor point and should be discussed calmly, viz.: whether to have a conference of committees or direct formation of a Bureau of the Majority Committees (we prefer this title to Organising Committee, although of course it is not a matter of the title) which would be recognised at first by some, and afterwards by all, of the Majority committees. You are for the former, we are for the latter. If a conference abroad were possible, I would be wholly in favour of it. In Russia, however, it would be devilishly dangerous, bureaucratic and ineffectual. Meanwhile Odessa+Nikolayev+Ekaterinoslav have already come to terms and authorised the "22" to "appoint an Organising Committee". We replied by recommending the title "Bureau of the Majority Committees" and seven candidates (Mermaid, Felix, Zemlyachka, Pavlovich, Gusev, Alexeyev, Baron). We are writing to Odessa and St. Petersburg about this. Alexeyev is already on his way to you. Will it not be best to carry out the election of candidates through Riga, St. Petersburg+Moscow, and immediately afterwards make a *public* statement about this (we are sending you a draft of the announcement*), and then rush off to the Northern Committee, the Caucasus, Saratov, Nizhni-Novgorod, etc., asking them to subscribe and supplementing the Bureau as liberally as possible by a couple or so of *their* candidates (although it is not very likely that the subscribing committees will demand large additions to the members of the Bureau). I definitely cannot imagine our meeting with difficulties over the composition of the Bureau.

The advantages of this method are: speed, cheapness, safety. These advantages are very important, for speed counts above all now. The Bureau will be the official body for uniting the committees and will in fact completely replace the C.C. in the event of a split. The membership of the literary group for our future central organ is already fully designated (a five- or six-man board: Private, Galyorka, myself, Schwarz+*Lunacharsky*+perhaps *Bazarov*). Tackle the transportation job yourself and do so energetically. We have got hold here of a former Bundist who has done a lot of work on two frontiers; he promises to arrange things for 200-300 rubles monthly. We are only waiting for the money before putting him in touch with you.

The disadvantage of your method is the red tape. I consider it quite useless to present ultimatums to the C.C. and Council. The C.C. is playing the hypocrite and I don't doubt now for a moment that they have sold themselves completely to the Minority and are out to falsify the congress. We should not harbour any illusions. Now, when they control all the central bodies, they have a thousand means for falsifying the congress and *have already begun to do so*. We shall prove this in print by analysing the Council's decisions (*Iskra* Nos. 73-74, supplement). We, of course, stand and will continue to stand for a congress, but we must cry from the house-tops that they are already falsifying the congress and that we shall expose their falsification. As a matter of fact, I now put the congress in the ninth

---

* See present edition, Vol. 7, pp. 503-05.—*Ed.*

place, allotting the first to the organ and the Russian centre. It's absurd to speak of disloyalty when they have pushed us into it themselves by making a deal with the Minority. It is a lie to say that the secret organisation of the Minority has been dissolved; it has not; three members of the C.C. have entered this secret organisation, that is all. All three central bodies now constitute a secret organisation against the Party. Only simpletons can fail to see that. We must reply by an open organisation and expose their conspiracy.

Please strengthen everyone's faith in our organisation and in the future organ. We need only to be patient a little longer, while Private finishes his job. Collect and send us local correspondence (*always* inscribed: for Lenin) and material, *especially* from workers. You and I differ on a minor point, as I would be only too glad to have a conference. But really, the game is not worth the candle; it will be much better to come out at once with an announcement from the Bureau, for we shall easily reach agreement on its membership and conflicts on this score are improbable. And once the Bureau proclaims itself it will quickly gain recognition and will begin to speak on behalf of all the committees. Think this over carefully once more and reply speedily.

Written December 8, 1904
Sent from Geneva to Russia

First published in 1926   Printed from
                                                                the original

120

TO ROZALIA ZEMLYACHKA

To Zemlyachka from Old Man

December 10, 1904

I have just returned from my lecture tour and received your letter No. 1. I spoke with Mermaid. Did you get my abusive letter (sent also to Papasha and Sysoika)?* As regards the composition of the O.C., I, of course, accept the general decision. I don't think Private should be drawn into this—he should be sent out here immediately. Further, it is essential to organise a special group (or to supplement the O.C.) for making regular rounds of the committees and maintaining all contacts between them. Our contacts with the committees and with Russia in general are extremely inadequate and we must exert every effort to get more local correspondents' reports and ordinary letters from comrades. Why don't you put us in touch with the Northern Committee? With the Moscow printing workers (this is very important!)? With Ryakhovsky? With Tula? With Nizhni-Novgorod? Do this immediately. Further, why don't the committees sent *us* their repeat resolutions concerning the congress? This is essential. I am very much afraid that you are too optimistic about the congress and about the C.C.; you will see from the pamphlet *The Council Versus the Party* (it is already out) that they go to any lengths, perform the devil knows what tricks, in their desire to sabotage the congress. In my opinion, it is a definite mistake on the part of the O.C. not to issue a printed announcement. In the first place, an announcement is necessary in order to offset our open way of acting to the Minority's

---

* See pp. 271-73 of this volume.—*Ed.*

secret organisation. Otherwise the C.C. is bound to catch
you out, to take advantage of Sysoika's ultimatums and
talk of your "secret" organisation; this will be a disgrace
for the Majority, a disgrace for which you will be wholly
to blame. Secondly, a printed announcement is necessary
in order to inform the mass of Party workers about the new
centre. You will never be able to do this even approximately
by any letters. Thirdly, a statement about the unity of the
Majority committees will be of tremendous moral significance as a means of reassuring and encouraging despondent
members of the Majority (especially here abroad). To ne-
glect this would be a great political mistake. I therefore
insist, again and again, that immediately after the Northern
Conference the Bureau of the Majority (or the O.C. of the
Majority committees) should issue a printed statement
mentioning the consent and *direct authorisation* of the
Odessa, Ekaterinoslav, Nikolayev, four Caucasian, Riga,
St. Petersburg, Moscow, Tver, and Northern committees,
etc. (perhaps the Tula and Nizhni-Novgorod committees),
i.e., 12-14 committees. This will not only not harm the
struggle for a congress but will be of tremendous assistance
to it. Answer at once whether you agree or not. Regarding
the Zemstvo campaign, I strongly recommend that both
my pamphlet* and the letter of the *Iskra* editorial board
should be published in Russia immediately and openly
(without the stupid heading "for Party members"). I may
write another pamphlet, but the polemic with *Iskra* must
be republished without fail. Finally, and this is particularly important and urgent: may I sign the local manifesto
about a new organ** on behalf of the Organising Committee of the Majority committees (or better the Bureau of the
Majority Committees)? May I speak here in the name of the
Bureau? May I call the *Bureau* the publisher of the new
organ and organiser of the editorial group? This is extremely
necessary and urgent. Reply immediately, after seeing
Private; tell him, and repeat it, that he must come here

---

* *The Zemstvo Campaign and Iskra's Plan* (see present edition,
Vol. 7).—*Ed.*
** "A Letter to the Comrades (With Reference to the Forthcoming
Publication of the Organ of the Party Majority)" (see present edi-
tion, Vol. 7).—*Ed.*

immediately, without delay, if he doesn't want to run the risk of being arrested and doing great harm to our cause. People everywhere abroad chatter an awful lot; I have heard them myself when on a lecture tour in Paris, Zurich, etc. A last warning: either he clears out and comes here at once or ruins himself and throws all our work back a year. I do not undertake to present any ultimatums about a congress to anyone here, as that would only evoke ridicule and jeers; there is no point in play-acting. Our position will be ten times cleaner and better if we come forward openly with the Bureau of the Majority and openly declare for a congress, instead of carrying on silly backdoor negotiations, which at best will serve only to delay matters and allow new intrigues on the part of people like Glebov, Konyagin, Nikitich and other rotters. The entire Majority here is fretting and worrying, longing for an organ, demanding it everywhere. We cannot publish it without direct authorisation from the Bureau, but publish it we must. We are doing everything we can to raise money and hope to succeed; you too must try to raise some. For heaven's sake, hurry up with the authorisation to publish in the name of the Bureau, and print a leaflet about it in Russia.

Sent from Geneva to Russia

First published in 1930

Printed from
the original

121

TO THE CAUCASIAN UNION COMMITTEE OF THE R.S.D.L.P.

To the Caucasian Union from Lenin

Dear Comrades,

We have just received the resolutions of your conference.[264] Send us without fail a more carefully made copy—there is a lot that is undecipherable. Without fail, too, carry out as soon as possible your splendid plan—to send your special delegate here. Otherwise it will really be extremely difficult, almost impossible, to reach agreement and remove mutual misunderstandings. This is an urgent necessity at the present time.

You still have little knowledge of all the documents and all the dirty tricks of the Council and the Central Committee. There is not the slightest doubt that they have already side-tracked the Third Congress and will now split all the committees. It is essential immediately 1) to set up a Bureau of the Majority Committees, 2) to entrust it with all matters concerning the congress and all leadership of the committees, 3) to support our organ *Vperyod*,[265] 4) to publish your resolutions (do you authorise us to do this?) and an announcement about the Bureau.

Please reply quickly.

Yours,

Lenin

We do not understand what relationship your (Caucasian) Bureau bears to the All-Russia Bureau of the Majority Committees. Write speedily, and best of all send a delegate.

Written later than December 12, 1904
Sent from Geneva

First published in 1926

Printed from the original

122

TO THE CAUCASIAN UNION COMMITTEE
OF THE R.S.D.L.P.

Dear Comrades,

I have received your letter concerning *Borba Proletaria-ta*.[266] I shall do my best to write and shall tell my editorial comrades about it too. I am heavily occupied at present with work for the new organ. A detailed letter on this matter has already been sent to you.* Let us have your reply as soon as possible and please send more, more and still more, workers' letters. The success of the organ depends now on you in particular, for the beginning is especially difficult.

Yours,
N. Lenin

Written December 20, 1904
Sent from Geneva

First published in 1930

Printed from
the original

---

* "A Letter to the Comrades (With Reference to the Forthcoming Publication of the Organ of the Party Majority)" (see present edition, Vol. 7).—*Ed.*

123

TO MARIA ESSEN[267]

From Lenin to Nina Lvovna, private

December 24, 1904

Dear Beastie,

I have long been intending to write to you, but have been hard pressed for time. We are now all in high spirits and terribly busy; yesterday the announcement concerning publication of our newspaper *Vperyod* came out. The entire Majority rejoices and is heartened as never before. At last we have stopped this sordid squabbling and shall get down to real team-work with those who want to work and not to make rows! A good group of writers has formed, we have fresh forces. Money is scarce, but we should be getting some soon. The Central Committee, by betraying us, has lost all credit; it has co-opted (in an underhand way) the Mensheviks and is raising a hue and cry against the congress. The Majority committees are uniting, they have already elected a Bureau and now the organ will cement this unity. Hurrah! Cheer up, we're all coming to life again. Sooner or later, one way or another we certainly hope to see you too. Drop me a line how you are getting on, and, above all, keep cheerful; remember, you and I are not so old yet— we have everything before us.

Affectionately yours,
Lenin

Sent from Geneva to Russia
First published in 1926

Printed from
the original

124

TO ROZALIA ZEMLYACHKA

To Zemlyachka from Lenin, private

December 26, 1904

Dear friend,

I have received your authorisation. In a day or two I shall be writing for the press on your business.* I recently received also the minutes of the Northern Conference.[268] Hurrah! You have done a splendid job and you (together with Papasha, Mouse and others) are to be congratulated on a huge success. A conference like that is a very difficult thing under Russian conditions; apparently, it has been a great success. Its significance is tremendous; it fits in most appropriately with our announcement of our newspaper (*Vperyod*). The announcement has already been issued. The first number will come out at the beginning of January, new style. The task now is: 1) To issue in Russia as quickly as possible a printed leaflet about the Bureau of the Majority Committees. For heaven's sake, don't put this off even for a week. It is devilishly important.

2) Once again to make a round of the committees of the south (*and Volga*), stressing the importance of giving *every* support to *Vperyod*.

Transportation will be taken care of, so long as we have Papasha. Let him take energetic steps for passing on his heritage in case of arrest.

Get Rakhmetov away quickly from dangerous areas and send him to destination. Be quick!

When we have money, we shall send a lot of people.

---

* "Statement and Documents on the Break of the Central Institutions with the Party" (see present edition, Vol. 7).—*Ed.*

We are publishing an article in *Vperyod* No. 1, about
the St. Petersburg disgrace (the Minority's disruption of
the demonstration).*

Hurry up with the public announcement about the Bureau, and be sure to list all the thirteen committees.[269]
Hurry, hurry and again hurry! We shall then have the
money.

Yours,

Lenin

My best regards to all friends.

Sent from Geneva to Russia

First published in 1926

Printed from
the original

------

*The article referred to is: "Time to Call a Halt!", published
in *Vperyod* No. 1 (see present edition, Vol. 8).— *Ed.*

125

TO A. I. YERAMASOV[270]

To Monk from Lenin, private

Dear Comrade,

I was very glad to learn that it is now possible to establish more regular contact with you. It would be good if you were to take advantage of this to write me a few lines about how you feel and what the immediate prospects are. Up till now all news of you has come through intermediaries, which always makes mutual understanding rather difficult.

Throughout the year our Party affairs have been in a scandalous state, as you have probably heard. The Minority has wrecked the Second Congress, created the new *Iskra* (Have you soon it? What do you think of it?) and now, when the vast majority of the committees that have expressed themselves at all have vigorously rebelled against this new *Iskra*, the Minority has wrecked the Third Congress as well. It has become all too obvious to the Minority that the Party will not tolerate their organ of tittle-tattle and squabbling in the struggle, of reversion to *Rabocheye-Dyelo*-ism in matters of principle, to the famous organisation-as-process theory.

The situation now has been made clear. The Majority committees have united (four Caucasian and the Odessa, Ekaterinoslav, Nikolayev, St. Petersburg, Moscow, Riga, Tver, Northern and Nizhni-Novgorod committees). I have begun here (with new literary forces) to publish the newspaper *Vperyod* (an announcement has been issued, No. 1 will appear at the beginning of January, new style). Let us know what you think of it and whether we can count on your support, which would be extremely important for us.

Written between December 23, 1904
and January 4, 1905
Sent from Geneva to Russia

First published in 1930

Printed from
the original

126

TO THE ST. PETERSBURG ORGANISATION
OF THE R.S.D.L.P.

The Moscow Zubatovist Workers' Society has a branch in St. Petersburg with the same Rules (workers of machine industry) and partly even with the same membership, that is, with those who previously worked in the St. Petersburg Zubatovist Society (Ushakov, Starozhilov and Gorshkov, Pikunov and Mokhnatkin, Nikiforov, and others). This Society is sponsored by Litvinov-Fallinsky, Chizhov and Langovoi. It is strongly recommended that *extreme* caution be exercised in contacts with this Society owing to the *huge* risk of *agent provocateurs*. The Society has now gone a bit left, but is completely at the service of the bourgeoisie and the police.

(This information comes from a well-informed person.)

Written in October-December 1904
Sent from Geneva

First published in 1925

Printed from
the original

1905

127
TO A COMRADE IN RUSSIA

January 6, 1905

Dear friend,

Thank you for your detailed letter. It will be very welcome if you tackle local affairs more energetically.

As for my view of the arguments of the editorial board in its second "secret" leaflet[271] quoted by you, I can only say the following so far. First of all one is struck by the glaring absurdity of "secret" when 1) there is nothing secret about it, and 2) the same ideas were repeated in No. 79 (the Ekaterinodar demonstration, the article of a correspondent, and the editors' comment). No. 79 is analysed in *Vperyod* No. 1.* You will receive it before Monday and will see how we present the issue. Secrecy technique by means of a leaflet nowadays is simply absurd, and I would attack it particularly sharply.

In essence, the "ideas" of the editors in this new production of theirs offer, as it were, two points of vantage: 1) Old Believer's position, to which the editors refer and which is clarified in *Iskra*, and 2) playing *at* parliamentarism, "parades and manoeuvres", lack of faith in the proletariat, a bashful attempt to *retract* on the question of panic (as much as to say, those words about panic were perhaps "superfluous" (!)).

> *This should be strongly emphasised*

Ad 1. Old Believer's position, which clearly emerged also in No. 77 (*the leading article*)—N.B., N.B., in my

---

* See Lenin's article "Good Demonstrations of Proletarians and Poor Arguments of Certain Intellectuals" (present edition, Vol. 8).— *Ed.*

opinion, is sheer muddle. I shall analyse it in the press.[272]
To justify his muddled resolution he is obliged to "invent"
a *good* bourgeoisie. A "bourgeois democracy" is invented
distinct from the Zemstvo people and liberals (as if the
Zemstvo people were not bourgeois democrats!), which,
practically speaking, includes the *intelligentsia* (by attentively reading No. 77 and No. 79 you will clearly see that
bourgeois democracy is identified with the "radical intelligentsia", "democratic intelligentsia" and "intellectualist
democracy"—e.g., No. 78, p. 3, column 3, 9th line up,
and passim).

To class the intelligentsia, in contrast to the Zemstvo
people, etc., as bourgeois democrats is sheer nonsense.
To call on them to become an "independent force" (No. 77,
Iskra's italics) is claptrap. The real basis of broad
democracy (the peasants, handicraftsmen, etc.) is ignored
here, as are also the *Socialist-Revolutionaries*, who are
the natural and inevitable *left* elements of the radical
intelligentsia. I can only outline these propositions here,
as it is necessary to deal with them in greater detail in
the press.

Old Believer is chockful of pretentious drivel about the
"democratic intelligentsia" being the "motor nerve" (!) of
liberalism, and so on. His attempt to represent as a "new
word" the term "third element", used to describe the uplift
intelligentsia, the intellectuals among the Zemstvo employees, etc., is amusing. See my review of home affairs
in *Zarya* No. 2-3, where there is a *whole chapter* entitled
"The Third Element".* Only the new *Iskra* could find a
"new word" here.

It is not true that the Social-Democrats, as a vanguard,
can influence only the democratic intelligentsia. They can
influence and *are influencing* the Zemstvo people too. Our
influence on them and on Mr. Struve is a fact overlooked
only by people enamoured of the "evident, tangible
results" of gala performances.

It is untrue that, apart from the Zemstvo people and
democratic intelligentsia, there is no one to influence (peasants, handicraftsmen, etc.).

---

* See present edition, Vol. 5, pp. 281-89.—*Ed.*

It is untrue that it is the intelligentsia, in contrast to the liberals, that constitutes "bourgeois democracy".

It is untrue that the French Radicals and Italian Republicans have not obscured the class-consciousness of the proletariat.

It is untrue that the "agreement" (of which the editors wrote in the first leaflet) *could* have referred to Old Believer's "conditions". That is absurd. The editors are hedging, clearly aware that *in fact* the conditions have gone by the board.

Ad 2. In my opinion, the second point stands out particularly clearly in a sentence of the second leaflet:

"We should, in our view, follow our class enemy and temporary political ally in that very sphere in which they are fulfilling the role of political leader entrusted them by history, that of emancipating the nation; *in this sphere the proletariat should measure its strength against the bourgeoisie*".*

This is playing *at* parliamentarism with a vengeance! "Measure its strength"—to what depths our despicable intellectualist gasbags degrade this great concept by reducing it to the demonstration of a handful of workers at a Zemstvo meeting! What a hysterical fuss, trying to snatch an advantage from a momentary situation (just now the Zemstvo people are "in the limelight"—fire away about the sphere in which they fulfil the role entrusted them by history! For pity's sake, gentlemen! Don't talk so pretty!). "*Full* contact of the proletariat with the bourgeoisie that is politically in the limelight." What can be "fuller" than that! "Argufying" with the Mayor of Ekaterinodar himself!

The defence of the idea about the "highest type of mobilisation" is not quite clear, for here you are paraphrasing and not quoting. But this idea contains the *key* to their confusion. The distinction between an "ordinary" and a "political demonstration" (does the second leaflet really say that in so many words? Is it a printed leaflet? Can you get a copy? a specimen?) is a real *gem*. This, I think, is where the opponent should be brought to bay, for it is

---

* The italics are Lenin's — *Ed*

here that he comes to grief. It is not demonstrations in the Zemstvos that are bad, but high-faulting judgements about the highest type that are *fatuous*.

I shall leave it at that for the time being. I am preparing for my lecture today.[273] It is said that the Mensheviks have decided not to come.

No. 1 of *Vperyod* comes out today.[274]

Write in some detail about your impression of *Vperyod*, obtain letters for it, especially for the workers' section.

[I advise you to compare the second leaflet of the editorial board with No. 77 and No. 78. Old Believer, and No. 79.]

Yours,

N. Lenin

Written in Geneva
First published in 1934

Printed from
the original

128

TO ROZALIA ZEMLYACHKA

To Zemlyachka from Lenin, private

I have received your huffy letter and hasten to reply.
You have taken offence for nothing. If I did say hard things,
I meant them lovingly, really, and with the reservation:
provided Lyadov's information was correct. The tremendous work you have done to win over fifteen committees
and organise three conferences[275] is highly appreciated by
us, as you could have seen from the preceding letter concerning the Northern Conference.* We have not taken and
are not taking a single step without you. The young lady
who went to St. Petersburg promised to use her personal
connections to obtain money, and we wrote to N. I.[276] for
you, and not at all through any desire to ignore you (the
inscription "private" was intended solely as a safeguard
against our enemies). The misunderstanding about our letters to N. I. we shall explain to her immediately. To the
devil with N. I., of course.

Many thanks to the committees for sending addresses.
Please send some more. Gusev has gone, Lyadov will be
going when we have money.

Lyadov set out the matter of the organ in Russia somewhat incorrectly, and I beg your pardon if I lost my temper
a bit and offended you.

As regards the open action of the Bureau I shall not argue
this point any more. A fortnight, of course, is a trifle. Believe me, I fully and positively intend to reckon with the
opinion in Russia on all points, and I only ask you seriously:
for heaven's sake, inform me more frequently about this

---

* See p. 283 of this volume.—*Ed.*

opinion. If I am guilty of succumbing to the mood of the Bolsheviks abroad, I can hardly be blamed, since Russia writes rarely and exasperatingly little. I fully accept the choice of the Northern Conference,[277] and, believe me, I do so right willingly. Try to raise money and write telling me that you are not angry.

Wholly yours,

Lenin

Written at the beginning
of January 1905
Sent from Geneva
to St. Petersburg

First published in 1925

Printed from
the original

129

TO THE SECRETARY
OF THE MAJORITY COMMITTEES' BUREAU

January 29, 1905

Dear friend,

I have a great favour to ask you: please give Rakhmetov a scolding, yes, a good sound scolding. Really, he acts towards us like the *Osvobozhdeniye* people[278] or priest Gapon[279] towards the Social-Democrats. I have just been looking at the table of our correspondence with Russia.[280] Gusev sent us six letters in ten days, but Rakhmetov two in thirty days. What do you think of that? Not a sign of him. Not a line for *Vperyod*. Not a word about the work, plans and connections. It's simply impossible, incredible, a disgrace. No. 4 of *Vperyod* will come out in a day or two, and immediately after it (a few days later) No. 5, but without any support from Rakhmetov. Today letters arrived from St. Petersburg dated January 10, very brief ones. And no one arranged for good and full letters about the Ninth of January![281]

I have had no reply whatever to my letter to Rakhmetov about literary contributions!*

Neither is there anything about the Bureau and the congress.[282] Yet it is so important to hurry up with the announcement concerning the Bureau and with the convening of the congress. For heaven's sake, don't trust the Mensheviks and the C.C., and go ahead everywhere and in the most vigorous manner with the split, a split and again a split. We here, carried away by enthusiasm for the revolution, were on the point of joining with the Mensheviks

---

* See present edition, Vol. 8, pp. 43-46. —*Ed.*

at a public meeting, but they cheated us again, and shamefully at that. We earnestly warn anyone who does not want to be made a fool of: a split, and an absolute split.

Sent from Geneva
to St. Petersburg

First published in 1925

Printed from
the original

130

TO AUGUST BEBEL

Geneva, February 8, 1905

Comrade,

On the very day you wrote to me[283] we were preparing a letter to Comrade Hermann Greulich,* in which we explained how and why the split in the Russian Social-Democratic Labour Party has now become an accomplished fact. We shall send a copy of this letter to the Executive Committee of the German Social-Democratic Party.

The Third Congress of our Party will be convened by the Russian Bureau of the Majority Committees. The *Vperyod* editorial board and the Bureau are only provisional central bodies. At the present time, neither I nor any of the editors, contributors or supporters of *Vperyod* known to me can assume the responsibility of taking any new, important steps binding on the whole Party without a Party Congress decision.[284] Thus, your proposal can be submitted only to this Party Congress.

Please excuse my poor German.

With Social-Democratic greetings,

N. Lenin

Sent to Berlin

First published in German
and Russian in 1905

Printed from
the original
Translated from the German

---

* "A Brief Outline of the Split in the R.S.D.L.P." (see present edition, Vol. 8).—*Ed.*

131

TO S. I. GUSEV[285]

To Khariton

February 15, 1905

Dear friend,

Many thanks for the letters. Be sure to keep this up, but bear in mind this: 1) never restrict yourself to making a precis of letters or reports handed over to you but be sure to send them on (apart from your own letters) *in full*; 2) be sure to put us in *direct* touch with new forces, with the youth, with newly-formed circles. Don't forget that the strength of a revolutionary organisation lies in the number of its connections. We should measure the efficiency and results of our friends' work by the number of *new* Russian connections passed on to us. So far *not one* of the St. Petersburgers (shame on them) has given us a *single* new Russian connection (neither Serafima, nor Sysoika, nor Zemlyachka, nor Nik. Iv.). It's a scandal, our undoing, our ruin! Take a lesson from the Mensheviks, for Christ's sake. Issue No. 85 of *Iskra* is chockful of correspondence. You have been reading *Vperyod* to the youth, haven't you? Then why don't you put us in touch with one of them? Remember, in the event of your being arrested we shall be in low water unless you have obtained for us a *dozen* or so new, young, loyal friends of *Vperyod*, who are able to work, able to keep in contact, and able to carry on correspondence even without you. Remember that! A professional revolutionary must build up dozens of new connections in each locality, put all the work into their hands while he is with them, teach them and bring them up to the mark not by lecturing them but by work. Then he should go to another place and after a month or two return to check up on the young people who have replaced him. I assure you that there is a sort of idiotic, philistine, Oblomov-like fear of the youth among us. I implore you: fight this fear with all your might.

Yours,
Lenin

Sent from Geneva
to St. Petersburg

First published in 1925

Printed from
the original

132

TO S. I. GUSEV

February 25, 1905

We have just this moment learnt from Lyadov's letter that the C.C. has agreed to a congress.[286] I adjure the Bureau by all that is holy not to believe the C.C. and not on any account to relinquish a single jot of their complete independence in convening the congress. The Bureau has no right to yield an inch to the C.C. If it does we here will raise a revolt and all the rock-firm committees will be with us. The C.C. has been invited to the congress, and let it come with the Mensheviks, but we and we alone are convening the congress. *Vperyod* No. 8, with the Bureau's announcement and our energetic addendum,* will come out on Tuesday (February 28, 1905). For heaven's sake, do everything to ensure that this letter is forwarded quickly to Lyadov, Sysoika and Zemlyachka.

Yours,
Lenin

Sent from Geneva
to St. Petersburg

First published in 1925

Printed from
the original

---

* See present edition, Vol. 8.—*Ed.*

TO S. I. GUSEV

To Nation

Dear friend,

Thanks tremendously for the letters. You are simply rescuing us from the effects of our foreign environment. Be sure to keep it up. For heaven's sake, obtain correspondence from the workers themselves. Why don't they write? It's a downright disgrace! Your detailed account of the Committee's agitation at the elections to the Shidlovsky Commission[287] is magnificent. We shall print it.

One more question: did you accept on the Committee the six workers mentioned? Reply without fail. We advise you by all means to accept workers on the Committee, to the extent of one-half at least. Unless you do this you will not be fortified against the Mensheviks, who will send strong reinforcements from here.

No one from the Bureau writes about the congress. This worries us, for Mermaid's optimism (and partly yours) that the C.C.'s consent to the congress is a gain, inspires grave misgivings. To us it is as clear as daylight that the C.C. wanted to fool you. You should be a pessimist as far as the C.C. is concerned. Don't believe it, for Christ's sake! Make the most of the moment to induce the Minority committees, especially those of the "Marsh", to turn up. It's tremendously important to give special attention to Kiev, Rostov and Kharkov; *we know* that there are *Vperyod* supporters, *workers* and intellectuals, in all these three centres. *At all costs* delegates from these committees should be brought to the congress with a *consultative* voice.* The

* Write all this to Mermaid and Demon.

same applies to the Moscow print-workers. Altogether it is most deplorable that the Bureau did not publish our decision to have the workers' organisations invited to the congress: *this is a tremendous mistake.* Rectify it quickly and without fail.

I strongly advise carrying out agitation among all the *300* organised workers in St. Petersburg for sending one or two delegates to the congress with a *consultative* voice *at their own expense.* The idea will no doubt appeal to the workers, and they will set to work with a will. Don't forget that the Mensheviks will try their damnedest to discredit the congress in the eyes of the workers by saying: there were no workers present. This has to be taken into consideration and special attention must be paid to workers' representation. The workers of St. Petersburg will certainly collect three hundred rubles for two workers' delegates (or some Maecenas will make a special donation for it)— agitation among the workers for sending the cap round will have a tremendous effect, everyone will know of it. This would be of enormous importance. Be sure to read this in the Committee and at meetings of organisers and agitators. Do all our organisers and agitators speak to the workers about direct connections with *Vperyod*?

All the very best.

Yours,
Lenin

P.S. Both Bureau leaflets (No. 1 on an uprising and No. 2 on the attitude towards the liberals) are excellent and we are reprinting them in full in *Vperyod.*[288] If only they were to keep this up! By the way: why has the writers' group declared that it belongs to the organisation of the St. Petersburg Committee? The reason this is not advisable is this. A writers' group attached to the Committee would have no mandate to the congress. If it was a *special* group, not belonging to any committee, but an *all-Russia* "writers'" group belonging to the Russian S.D.L.P.", it would have the right (*with the Bureau's permission*) to send a delegate with a *consultative* voice. Arrange this, please! We shall not publish the fact that it is a group attached to the St. Petersburg Committee. Let

1) the S.P.C. part with it; 2) let it become a separate and special group at least for a time; 3) let it "submit a request" (there's bureaucracy for you!) for its delegate to be admitted to the congress with a consultative voice; 4) let the Bureau give permission. I can't believe that a dozen writers will be unable to raise 200 rubles for a delegate! I'm sure it would be useful to have their delegate at the congress (for example, Rumyantsev or someone else). Inform the Bureau of this or, better still, *do all this yourself without any reports at all.*

Written at the beginning
of March 1905
Sent from Geneva
to St. Petersburg

First published in 1925

Printed from
the original

134

TO S. I. GUSEV

To Nation from Lenin

March 11, 1905

Dear friend,

I have just received Nos. 10 and 11.* Many thanks, particularly for the scolding in No. 10. I love to hear people scold—it means they know what they are doing and have a line to follow. You've given the "old wolf" a proper trimming; the mere perusal of it made him scratch himself. No. 11, though, showed that you are far too optimistic if you hope so easily to come to terms with the St. Petersburg Mensheviks. Oh, I fear the Danaans[289] and advise you to do the same! Have you noticed that everything that is not to their advantage remains a matter of words, undocumented—for example, the C.C.'s agreeing to a congress. Issue No. 89 of *Iskra* appeared today with the Council's decision of March 8, 1905, against a congress—a lying, raging decision ("by acting the way they do, the participants in a congress place themselves outside the Party"), which gives the number of "qualified Party organisations, apart from the central bodies", as of January 1, 1905, as thirty-three (a shameless lie, non-existent committees, like that of the Kuban and the unendorsed Kazan Committee, have been invented, while in the case of two others, those of Polesye and the North-West, the date has been mixed up, January 1, 1905, being stated instead of April 1, 1905). Clearly there can be no question of the Council's participation in the congress, nor, consequently, of the League and the Central Organ. I'm very glad of this, *and I don't believe* that the

---

* Gusev's letters to Lenin.—*Ed.*

Mensheviks in Russia will go; I don't believe it. So far not one of you has sent us a single written statement of a single Menshevik committee agreeing to a congress. Be under no illusion! If the St. Petersburg Mensheviks agree to make concessions, demand from them, as a *conditio sine qua non*, *recognition of the congress* to be convened by the Bureau, and recognition of the St. Petersburg Committee as the only *legal committee connected with the working-class movement* —to be given in writing, and copies to be sent to *Vperyod* without fail (over their own signatures) and on behalf of all the members, specified by name, of the St. Petersburg Minority group. Even then do not allow them *any contacts at all*—otherwise you will win yourselves internal enemies, mark my words!

Inform Rakhmetov immediately by express telegram that around March 20, 1905, there will be a most important conference here with the Socialist-Revolutionary Party and a *host* of other parties about an agreement for an uprising[290] —Rakhmetov's presence is *essential*, let him come posthaste and lose no time.

In conclusion I tell you once again: you do not know the Minority forces throughout Russia and are under an illusion. This is a mistake. The Mensheviks at present are stronger than we are; it's going to be a long and hard fight. The icons abroad[291] raise a heap of money. I consider it simply *indecent* for us to raise the question of an agreement with the Bund, etc., *after* their (and the Lettish) conference with the C.C.[292] (minutes in *Posledniye Izvestia*[293] and in *Iskra* No. 89). It would be idiocy; it would look as if we were thrusting ourselves upon them. We shall be told: we don't know you, we have already reached agreement with the C.C. It will end in disgrace, believe me!

All the very best. *Lenin*

Sent from Geneva
to St. Petersburg

First published in 1925

Printed from
the original

135

TO S. I. GUSEV

To Gusev from Lenin

March 16, 1905

Dear friend,

I have just learnt that, at the request of the Bund, the conference here of *eighteen* Social-Democratic and other *revolutionary* parties (including the Socialist-Revolutionary Party and the P.P.S.) has been postponed to the beginning of April. It is extremely important for us to settle jointly with Rakhmetov a number of fundamental questions concerning our participation in this conference (its aim is to reach agreement on an uprising). *Iskra* is carrying on a most vile intrigue. If Rakhmetov has not left yet, make every effort to see that he goes immediately, and let me know at once without fail exactly what you know about the time of his departure.

We are pretty worried here about the congress. It's all very well for you, Igor and Lyadov to write about the Old Man being nervy. Who wouldn't be nervy when we are surrounded here by enemies who take advantage of every item of news and who get their news more quickly than we do. Really, this is unpardonable on the part of the Bureau. As regards the East, for example, all we know is that Zemlyachka is touring the Urals and that Lyadov visited Saratov. The reply from the latter place is vague, nothing definite. We do not know what arrangements have been made for publishing leaflets over the signature of the "Committees of the Eastern District". It is a disgrace and a scandal! Recently the Socialist-Revolutionaries showed us one such leaflet, a stupid one, against Gapon! Obviously, this is a C.C. intrigue, but surely two members of the Bureau who

visited the East could have learnt something and written
us about it in good time, so as not to put us in an idiotic
position in face of the enemy! Don't they feel ashamed
at putting *Vperyod* in such an extremely awkward position?
And more than awkward, because *Iskra* brazenly takes
advantage of everything. In *Iskra* No. 89 the Council excom-
municates everyone who goes to the congress. The votes
are again falsified there. They count 75 votes as of January
1, 1905 (33×2=66+9 from the C.C., Central Organ and
Council). They have invented the Kazan and Kuban committees, which were never endorsed, and lie about the Polesye and North-Western committees having been endorsed
as of January 1, 1905. Actually, they were not endorsed
until April 1, 1905. We exposed this lie in *Vperyod* No.
10.*

Here is something that should be borne in mind: for
the congress to be lawful from *Iskra*'s point of view, there
must be *nineteen* committees attending it. By our reckoning,
this is wrong. But if there were 28 (apart from the League)
fully qualified organisations in *Russia* as of January 1, 1905,
then the participation of *14-15* at the congress is extremely
desirable, *almost essential*. Meanwhile, we have 13—1
(Ekaterinoslav)+2 (Voronezh and Tula)=14, and that only
by counting Tiflis, a doubtful. Of course, the congress is
necessary all the same, if only of a dozen committees,
and the sooner the better. Any kind of congress, so long as
it is a congress. But why is there no news of the Bureau
having visited a *single* neutral or Menshevik committee?
Was it not decided that the Bureau would invite and visit
all of them? Why hasn't Lyadov visited the Kuban Committee? Why, in travelling through, did he not invite to
the congress the Don, Kharkov, Gornozavodsky and Kiev
committees? And the various groups in these towns? An
excellent means of stirring the workers is to invite them
to the congress *themselves*. Why isn't this being done? It
would really have enormous significance! Why isn't there
a scrap of news about Kursk, the Polesye Committee and
others? We shall do everything we can from here, but not

* See "Whom Are They Trying to Fool?" (present edition, Vol.
8). —*Ed*

much can be done from here. There are slight chances of
making contact with Kazan, Siberia, Kursk, Polesye, and
Saratov, but all this is problematical. And yet, if all these
five, plus the Urals, were at the congress, then its full lawfulness, even according to *Iskra*'s reckoning, would be
beyond doubt. Do write.

Yours,

Lenin

Sent from Geneva
to St. Petersburg

First published in 1925   Printed from
                                                  the original

136

TO THE ODESSA COMMITTEE OF THE R.S.D.L.P.

To the Odessa Committee from Lenin

Dear friends,

I should like to say a few words to you about congress delegates. If you are sending them from Russia, then my letter does not apply. But I heard that you are thinking of giving a mandate to one of the people here. If this rumour is true, then I would advise giving mandates to *both* of your candidates here, i.e., to Josephine and Danila—one with a vote and the other with a consultative voice (i.e., write a letter to the congress that the Odessa Committee *requests the congress* to let Josephine attend with a *consultative* voice, as a member of the Southern Bureau and a very useful worker in a consultative capacity, or, for example, Danila, as having an excellent knowledge of the local areas and having worked with remarkable energy among the Odessa proletariat). You may rest assured that the congress will grant such a request from the Committee. Please read this letter to *all* the Committee members and send me a reply.[294]

P.S. Are you taking workers into the Committee? This is essential, absolutely essential! Why don't you put us in direct contact with workers? Not a single worker writes to *Vperyod*. *This is a scandal.* We need at all costs *dozens* of worker correspondents. I would ask you to read this part of the letter, too, not only to all Committee members, but also to all Majority organisers and agitators.

Regards to everyone!

Yours,

Lenin

Written March 25, 1905, in Geneva

First published in 1925

Printed from the original

137

TO S. I. GUSEV

To be handed to Gusev from Lenin, private

April 4, 1905

Dear friend,

You wrote yourself that you were now being shadowed. What's more, I have gathered information fully confirming this fact from St. Petersburgers who have recently arrived from the scene of activities. There can be no doubt at all about it. I know from my own experience and from that of lots of comrades that one of the most difficult things for a revolutionary is to leave a danger spot *in good time.* Whenever the time comes to drop work in a given locality, that work becomes particularly interesting and *particularly needed*; so it seems always to the person concerned. I consider it my duty, therefore, to *demand* of you most insistently that you abandon St. Petersburg for a time. This is absolutely essential. *No* excuses *of any kind*, no considerations for the work, should put off this step. The harm caused by an inevitable arrest will be enormous. The harm caused by going away will be insignificant, and merely apparent. Advance young assistants *for a time*, for a month or two, to fill the top posts, and rest assured that, with an extremely brief and temporary setback, the cause, on the whole, will gain by it tremendously. The young people will acquire more experience in key posts, and any mistakes they may make will be speedily corrected by us. An arrest, however, would ruin all our major opportunities for organising central work. Once more, I insistently advise going out *immediately* to the provinces for a month. There's heaps of work to be done everywhere, and everywhere general guidance is needed. If there is a *will* to go (and a will there must be) the thing can always be arranged.

I'm not writing anything about the agreement of March 12, 1905.[295] Cursing will do no good. I suppose they could not act otherwise. The thing now is to prepare energetically for the congress and to increase the number of delegates. Don't be too free with money, take care of it; it will be needed more than ever after the congress.

Sent from Geneva
to St. Petersburg

First published in 1925

Printed from
the original

138

TO OLGA VINOGRADOVA[296]

To Beggar from Lenin

Dear Comrade,

I have read with interest your letter[297] (No. 6) about the primary nucleus of the organisation among handicraft workers. At the factories this nucleus should be represented by the factory committee, but what about the handicraft industries? You stand for trade union circles, but what about your opponents—? I didn't quite grasp what they stand for. Neither do I know, unfortunately, what these old trade union "councils" were. When did they exist? How were they formed? How did they combine Social-Democratic and trade union work?

Not being familiar with the practical aspect of this practical question, I hesitate to express an opinion *as yet*. Further letters may tell me more—then we shall see. One must study experience and be careful in changing things, that is true. But it's not quite clear to me what Economism has to do with it. Don't the factory committees, too, mainly discuss factory interests (which are also trade union interests)? Yet no one has objected to the factory committee being the primary nucleus of the *Social-Democratic* organisation. The important thing is living conditions, conditions of assembly, conditions under which people meet, conditions of joint work, because the primary nucleus should meet frequently and regularly and function in a particularly lively fashion. Finally, is a single type of organisation obligatory here? Would not a variety of types be better for adaptation to various conditions and for acquiring richer experience?

Thanks for the letters. Keep on writing, for it is not often we have news about the *day-to-day* (the most interesting) aspect of the work.

Lenin

Written April 8, 1905
Sent from Geneva to Odessa

First published in 1925

Printed from
the original

139

TO THE INTERNATIONAL SOCIALIST BUREAU

To the Secretariat of the International Socialist Bureau

Geneva, July 8, 1905

Dear Comrades,

Your letter of July 6 somewhat surprised us. You should already have known that Citizen Plekhanov is no longer the representative of the Russian Social-Democratic Party in the International Socialist Bureau.

In *Iskra* No. 101, Citizen Plekhanov published the following letter, which we translate literally, and which, one would think, he should have brought to the notice of the Bureau:

"Comrades, the decisions of the conference [of the breakaway section of the Party],[298] which have dealt a mortal blow to the central institutions of our Party, compel me to divest myself of the title of editor of the Central Organ and fifth member of the Council (elected by the Second, *lawful* Congress).

"*G. Plekhanov.*

"P.S. I take this opportunity publicly to ask that section of the Party which recognises the decisions of the 'Third' Congress[299] as binding, whether it wishes me to continue to represent this, now—alas!—dissevered Party in the International Socialist Bureau. I can remain the representative of the R.S.D.L.P. *only* if this is the wish of *both* sections.

"Montreux, May 29, 1905."

The editorial board of *Proletary*,[300] the Central Organ of the Party, replied to this statement of Citizen Plekhanov's with the following paragraph, published in No. 5, for June 13, 1905:

"In regard to Comrade Plekhanov's postscript we can state that the question of the Party's representation in the

International Bureau by Comrade Plekhanov has now been submitted to the C.C. of the Party for its decision."

The question has not yet been settled and, consequently, at the present time Citizen Plekhanov cannot, in the capacity of representative of the Party,[301] sign any document emanating from the International Bureau.

In view of this we draw your attention, dear comrades, to the fact that it is very inconvenient for us to communicate with the Bureau through a comrade who himself declares *publicly* that he cannot represent the Party so long as it does not definitely authorise him to do so. We again repeat our request to the International Secretariat that, pending settlement of the question of representation in the International Socialist Bureau, everything that concerns us (letters, manifestoes, documents, funds, etc.) should be sent to the address of the Party's Central Committee (V. Oulianoff, Rue de la Colline, 3, Genève).

Accept, dear comrades, the assurance of our fraternal sentiments.

Sent to Brussels
First published in 1931   Printed from
                                                the handwritten copy
                                             Translated from the French

140

TO THE CENTRAL COMMITTEE OF THE R.S.D.L.P.

From Lenin to the members of the C.C., private

July 11, 1905

Dear friends,

A number of letters from all over Russia, Alexandrov's news, a talk with Tick and several other new arrivals— all this strengthens my conviction that there is some internal defect in the work of the C.C., a defect of organisation, in the way the work is arranged. The general opinion is that there is no Central Committee, that it does not make itself felt, that no one notices it. And the facts confirm this. There is no evidence of the C.C.'s political guidance of the Party. Yet all the C.C. members are working themselves to death! What's the matter?

In my opinion, one of the principal causes of it is that there are no regular C.C. leaflets. Leadership by means of talks and personal contacts at a time of revolution is sheer utopianism. Leadership must be public. *All other* forms of work must be wholly and unconditionally subordinated to this form. A responsible C.C. litterateur should concern himself first of all with writing (or obtaining from contributors—though the editor himself should always be prepared to write) a leaflet twice a week on Party and political topics (the liberals, the Socialist-Revolutionaries, the Minority, the split, the Zemstvo delegation, the trade unions, etc., etc.) and republishing it in every way, immediately mimeographing in 50 copies (if there is no printing-press) and circulating it to the committees for republication. Articles in *Proletary* could, perhaps, sometimes be used for such leaflets—after a certain amount of revision. I cannot understand why this is not being done! Can Schmidt and Werner have forgotten our talks on this? Surely it is possible to write and circulate at least one leaflet a week? The Report on the Third Congress* has not been re-printed[302] in full anywhere in Russia all this time. It is so outrageous, such a fiasco for all the C.C.'s famous "tech-niques" that I simply cannot understand what Winter was thinking about, what Sommer and the others are thinking about! After all, are there not committee print-shops in existence?

Apparently, the C.C. members completely fail to under-stand the tasks of "keeping in the public eye". Yet without that there is no centre, there is no Party! They are working themselves to the bone, but they are working like moles, at secret rendezvous, at meetings, with agents, etc., etc. It is a sheer waste of strength! If you are short-handed, then put third-rate forces on the job, even tenth-rate ones, but attend to the political leadership yourselves, issue leaflets first and foremost. And then—personal appearances and speeches at district meetings (in Polesye no one attend-ed the meeting. A scandal. They all but broke away!), at conferences, etc. Something like a C.C. diary should be published, a C.C. bulletin, and every important question should be dealt with in a leaflet issued twice a week. It is not difficult to publish one: 50 copies can be run off on a hectograph and circulated, one of the committees can print it and have copies sent to us. The thing is to *act*, to act *all the time* openly, to stop being dumb. Otherwise we here, too, are completely cut off.

Perhaps the C.C. should be enlarged? Half a dozen more agents taken on? People could be found for this, I'm sure. In fact, I want to suggest a practical step right now: in view of the almost total absence of correspondence between the C.C. members (we have had only two letters from Werner and Winter, and from Alexandrov only news from the road, "travel impressions", nothing more), it is absolutely essential to *carry out* our joint decision of May 10, 1905, concerning the holding of a meeting by September 1, 1905.[303] For heaven's sake, don't put this off, don't be stingy about spending 200-300 rubles. Without this, there is a great

---

* See present edition, Vol. 8, pp. 433-39.—*Ed.*

danger that we shall not be able to set things going properly.
At the moment they are not moving at all. This is evident
from all reports.

There are still six weeks to go to September 1. It is possible to wind up affairs and make arrangements for a trip
in good time, after corresponding among others with Alexandrov as to who should go. I await a reply.

Sent from Geneva to Russia

First published in 1926   Printed from
                                               the original

TO THE CENTRAL COMMITTEE OF THE R.S.D.L.P.

From Lenin to the C.C.

Dear friends,

In regard to your recent letters I should say that I agree with all the decisions except two. 1) I emphatically protest against the appointment of Matryona as an agent and earnestly request you to revise it. He is a muddle-headed fellow, who can cause us great harm, desert us a dozen times, put us to shame by his stupidity, etc. Let him work in the Committee—as an agent he is no good at all, unless you put him on a "technique" job. As regards Stanislav, please let me know who he is, tell me more about him. For my part I would strongly recommend Lalayants as an agent. In Odessa and the Southern Bureau he displayed outstanding ability as an organiser; according to the general opinion he has got real live work going there. He was the guiding spirit of all the local work—so a number of Odessites reported, some of whom were anything but favourably disposed towards the "rockfirm". Last but not least he is a man of exceptionally high principle. 2) Regarding Plekhanov, I am extremely surprised at your silence on a question that had been raised here in Winter's time. Have we the right to appoint as the representative of the Party someone who does not want to come into the Party and refuses to recognise the Third Congress? He has now declared in print that he does not consider the Third Congress lawful and will act as representative *only* of both sections. A number of comrades here had pointed out, when Winter was still here, that, in appointing Plekhanov, we would only pamper him and spoil him altogether. I was in favour of Plekhanov at first, but I now see that he can only be appointed on certain conditions. Just imagine concretely what it will mean to have as our representative on the Bureau someone to whom no one speaks, and who *cannot* be made to "represent" the *C.C.* and not himself! We have now at last secured direct contact between the Bureau (the I.S.B.) and us, and we see that there are quite a number of small business matters, financial and others (requests on behalf of Russia and concerning Russia, about which I wrote to them recently; the method of representation, about which they asked me a few days ago, etc.). The Bureau wrote about another "proposal of Bebel's"[304] (which has not yet reached us); evidently, the old fellow is out to "make peace" again (Kautsky has published a mean article in connection with the German edition of the "Report"[305]). Think what our position will be if Plekhanov is the representative and Plekhanov has to deal with Bebel on the question of "peace"! I understand very well what strong reasons there are to make us all, and especially you, desire "peace", desire the appointment of Plekhanov, but I have become convinced that such a step, without a *real* guarantee of peace, will be only a false step, will confuse the issue still more, will cause new splits, violations of agreements, altercations and *fresh* resentment, and will only make unity *more remote.* In my opinion, all the talk about unity will be so much empty phrase-making so long as a *realisable* plan for it has not been worked out from experience; things are going in this direction, we must wait a few months, let everyone assess the absurdity of the decisions of the conference, let *experience* destroy their idiotic "organisational statute", let *experience* cut down their claims (for, in general, things are going better with us, and we are obviously going forward to victory)— and then direct negotiations will be started between the central bodies without intermediaries, then we shall work out (whether at once or after two or three attempts, I do not undertake to say, of course) a *modus vivendi*. But now it is necessary to fight.

My proposal is to make a "proposal" to Plekhanov on your lines, *but on condition* that he is willing to recognise the Third Congress, come into the Party and submit to its decisions. By such a step we shall observe the conventions and eliminate any possible confusion.

Pending your reply I shall not propose anything to Plekhanov. I earnestly beg you to postpone a decision until we meet in September.

I am extremely surprised that you write nothing about the "Open Letter"[306] written by Reinert that was sent to me. I don't understand the why and wherefor. Why is there not a word about this in the *decisions*? Write quickly whether it is to be published in the Central Organ. If it is, then I should like very much to ask for a slight alteration concerning tactical differences so that it may not come into contradiction with my pamphlet, which Lyubich will tell you about.[307] I hope we shall see eye to eye on this and, if possible, I would ask to be allowed to make this alteration myself.

I am extremely surprised that the "Report" is not being issued in Russia in full. It's scandalous! Make all the technical staff hurry up with this, for heaven's sake!

We are extremely grateful for the detailed decisions, letters from committees and leaflets you have sent us. At long last something like regular contacts between us are being established! Please, don't drop this custom and find a good St. Petersburg secretary. We are badly in need of information from St. Petersburg about Party affairs, the liberals, questions of Party life that are being discussed in the circles, etc., etc. Do not forget that the Bund and the Mensheviks are better informed than we are here!

All the very best.

N. Lenin

Written July 12, 1905
Sent from Geneva to Russia

First published in 1926

Printed from
the original

142

TO THE CENTRAL COMMITTEE OF THE R.S.D.L.P.

No. 1

July 28, 1905

Dear friends,

The two following important questions must be decided as quickly as possible: 1) The question of Plekhanov. We have instructed a special agent (Lyadov) to tell you how the matter stands. I shall repeat it briefly. Plekhanov acted with incredible impudence by writing to the International Socialist Bureau that both sections of the Party had recognised (!) him, and in every way denouncing and denigrating our Third Congress. I have a copy of his letter sent to me from the Bureau. It will be sent on to you. With great difficulty I established direct contact with the International Socialist Bureau and refuted Plekhanov. Plekhanov then refused to be the representative. You know that I was by no means unconditionally opposed to Plekhanov's appointment, but now it would be quite unthinkable. It would be such a disavowal of me that my position would become impossible. It would discredit us altogether in the eyes of the International Socialist Bureau. Do not forget that almost all the Social-Democrats abroad are on the side of the "icons" and think nothing of us, look down on us. An incautious step on your part will spoil everything. Therefore I earnestly request Werner and Schmidt to confirm, as quickly as possible, if only provisionally, the steps I have taken. That is one thing. Secondly, Plekhanov should be offered a scientific organ in the name of the C.C. of the R.S.D.L.P., but on condition that he recognise the Third Congress and all its decisions as binding on him. If he turns this down, the blame will fall on him, while we shall have demonstrated our conciliatory spirit. If he accepts, we shall take a further step to meet him. And so: I earnestly advise you to rescind the decision about representation, and, as regards the scientific organ, to draft the proposal with the above condition.[308] 2) About the proposal for mediation on the part of the International Socialist Bureau. The full text will be sent to you, although Lyadov has already taken it for you. For the purpose of reconciliation, the International Socialist Bureau proposes a conference between us and the Minority, under the chairmanship of members of the I. S. Bureau. The foreign Social-Democrats (Bebel and others) are strongly urging the I.S.B. to bring pressure to bear on us. Letters of this kind have come even from the British (the Social-Democratic Federation; I have a copy of the letter, in the usual conciliatory vein, about it being a crime to quarrel at such a time, etc.[309]). I wrote to the I. S. Bureau that it was not within my competence to settle this question, and that the decision had to come from the whole C.C., to which, I said, I was writing immediately. Then I enquired whether they had in mind mediation only, or a court of arbitration that was binding on both sides; it was important for me, I said, to write on this point to the C.C. So far there is no reply from them.

My opinion is as follows. The conference should certainly be agreed to. It should be fixed for round about September 1. We should send to it without fail one or two C.C. members from Russia (do not forget that our meeting is fixed for September 1, and that it is extremely necessary in all respects). Mediation should be accepted with thanks. A binding decision by arbitration should be refused on the strength of the Third Congress resolution,[310] which has bound us unconditionally and which states that the conditions for complete amalgamation with the Minority should be submitted to the Fourth Congress for confirmation. The Third Congress instructed us to prepare and work out these conditions, but not to endorse them finally. In fulfilment of the instruction of the Third Congress, we accept mediation and will try to work out a fully detailed modus for agreement now and for gradual amalgamation. If we can manage it, we shall implement the agreement at once, and submit the plan for amalgamation to the Fourth Congress, which will then have to be convened at the same time and in the same place with the obligatory attendance of all Minority organisations. It is extremely important to bear in mind that the Mensheviks have no central body whose decisions are binding on them. *Iskra* is not subordinated to the Organisation Committee. We should not play the role of fools entering into an agreement with people who have neither the right nor the power to speak for the whole Minority. It is essential therefore to make it clear at once that the delegates from the Minority at the meeting with the I. S. Bureau should be both from the Organisation Committee and from *Iskra*, and in addition should promise to invite the opinions of all Minority organisations as soon as possible, giving a list of them to us. Incidentally, if from the point of view of Russia it is of more importance to you that the Mensheviks of Russia should preponderate, then you will discuss whether special *Iskra* delegates are necessary. You will know best. But do not forget that without the consent of *Iskra* all agreements will be a fiction. One more question: should we inform the I. S. Bureau of the secret resolution of the Third Congress? Have we the right to do so? I am in doubt about this. Of course, informing the European socialist comrades is not "publishing", and they can be made to undertake not to publish. But is this advisable? Decide for yourselves. It is easy to give a satisfactory explanation even without informing them about the Third Congress resolution which binds us.

I shall publish the open letter to the Organisation Committee in *Proletary* No. 11 (No. 10 is already coming out). I did not publish it earlier because I was waiting for an explanation from you, which only arrived yesterday. We earnestly request you to make a note on each document whether it is to be published and published immediately.

And so, reply as soon as possible on behalf of Werner and Schmidt at any rate: 1) Will you write the reply to the I. S. Bureau yourselves or do you instruct me to do so? 2) Do you approve my reply or not? 3) If not, I would ask you to hurry up with a reply, so that we can reach full agreement; any misunderstanding in such a matter, lack of clarity or lack of information, is fraught with the greatest danger.

P.S. Please send my letters on to Dubois, I haven't got his address.

Sent from Geneva to Russia

First published in 1926

Printed from
the original

143

TO A. V. LUNACHARSKY[311]

August 2, 1905

Dear An. Vas.,

Yesterday I sent you a "business" letter and asked for *Iskra* No. 105* and Plekhanov's L. Feuerbach** to be sent to you. Today I'd like to talk to you on things other than current petty business.

Our people in Geneva are down in the dumps. It's surprising how little is needed for people who are not quite self-dependent and not used to independent political work, to lose heart and start moping. And our Geneva Bolsheviks are terrible mopers. A serious struggle is on, which the Third Congress, of course, did not put an end to and merely opened a new phase of it; the Iskrists are lively busybodies, brazen as hucksters, well skilled by long experience in demagogy—whereas among our people a kind of "conscientious stupidity" or "stupid conscientiousness" prevails. They can't put up a fight, they're awkward, inactive, clumsy, timid.... They're good fellows, but no damn'd good whatever as politicians. They lack tenacity, fighting spirit, nimbleness and speed. Vas. Vas. is extremely typical in this respect: a charming fellow, an utterly devoted worker and honest man, but he'll never make a *politician*, I'm afraid. He's much too kind—one can hardly believe that the "Galyorka" pamphlets were written by him. He brings

---

* The leading article is said to be utter piffle! Will you write something against it as quickly as possible? If you agree, *send a telegram.*
** Meaning Plekhanov's preface to the second Russian edition of Engels's pamphlet *Ludwig Feuerbach and the End of Classical German Philosophy.—Ed.*

no fighting spirit either to the newspaper (he is always regretting that I do not allow him to write kind articles about the Bund!) or to the colony. A spirit of despondency reigns and I am for ever being reproached (I have only been three weeks in the country, and travel to town for four to five hours *three* and sometimes *four* times a week!) because things are not going well with them, because the Mensheviks are smarter, etc., etc.!

And our C.C., for one thing, is not much of a "politician" either, it's much too kind, it, too, suffers from a lack of tenacity, resourcefulness and sensitivity, from inability to take political advantage of every trifle in the Party struggle. Secondly, it has a lofty contempt for us "foreigners" and keeps all the best people away from us or takes them from here. And we here abroad, find ourselves behindhand. There is not enough ferment, stimulus or impulse. People are incapable of acting and fighting by themselves. We are short of speakers at our meetings. There is no one to pour cheer into people, to raise key issues, no one capable of lifting them above the Geneva marsh into the sphere of more serious interests and problems. And the whole work suffers. In political struggle a halt is fatal. There are thousands of demands and they are continually increasing. The new-Iskrists are not dozing (they have now "intercepted" the sailors[312] who arrived in Geneva, have enticed them, probably by their usual political showmanship and overloud *marktschreien**, "utilising" post facto the Odessa events for the benefit of their coterie). We are *impossibly* short of people. I don't know when Vas. Vas. intends to write, but as a speaker and political centre he is beneath criticism. He is more likely to spread despondency among people than to rouse them and call them to order. Schwarz is absent; he writes from over there zealously and well, even better than he did here, I should say, but that's all he does. As for personally exercising an influence on people and being able to direct them and meetings, he is rarely capable of doing that even when in Geneva. It is a large, important centre here. There are lots of Russians. Crowds of travellers. Summer is an especially busy time, for among

---

* Mountebank crying of wares.—*Ed.*

the multitude of Russian tourists coming to Geneva there is a certain percentage of people who should and could be made use of, aroused, drawn in and guided.

Think it over and write to me in greater detail (preferably to my private address: 3. Rue David Dufour). Do you remember writing me that your absence from Geneva would be no loss, because you wrote a lot even from afar. You do write a lot, and we keep the newspaper going *somehow* (just somehow and no more, though we desperately need a lot more). But not only is there a loss, but a tremendous loss, which is felt more and more sharply every day. Personal influence and speaking at meetings make all the difference in politics. Without them there is no political activity and even writing itself becomes less political. Faced by an enemy who has powerful forces abroad, we are losing more ground each week than we can probably make up in a month. The fight for the Party is not over, and it will not be brought to real victory without straining every nerve....

All the best.

Yours,

N. Lenin

Sent from Geneva to Italy
First published in 1934

Printed from
the original

144

TO THE CENTRAL COMMITTEE OF THE R.S.D.L.P.

From Lenin to the Members of the C.C.

August 14, 1905

Dear friends,

I have just read in *Iskra* No. 107 the minutes of the meeting of July 12, 1905, between the C.C. and the Organisation Committee.[313] It is most regrettable that so far the promised minutes have *not* been received from you. There have been no letters either. Really, it is impossible to work in this way. I knew nothing about the plan to issue the "Open Letter" or the plan of negotiations, or the plan for some sort of concessions. Is such an attitude to a member of the collegium permissible? Think of the position you put me in! The position is absolutely impossible, for it is precisely here, abroad, that I have to answer everybody frankly—you will admit this yourself on calm reflection.

Your reply to the Organisation Committee gives rise to a number of perplexities. I can't make out whether you are trying to be cunning or what? Can you have forgotten that there is the straightforward resolution of the Third Congress that the terms of unification must be endorsed by a new congress? How could one talk seriously of co-opting to the C.C. when there are two rival organs? How could one leave unanswered the toleration of two central organs, i.e., a complete violation both of the Rules and of the decisions of the Third Congress? How was it possible not to present the Mensheviks with a principled ultimatum on the organisational question: (1) congresses instead of plebiscites as the supreme organ of the Party; (2) unconditional subordination of Party literature to the Party; (3) direct elections to the C.C.; (4) subordination of the minority to the majority, etc.?

Haven't you taken warning from the unfortunate example of the transportation "agreement", which was immediately wrecked by Frockcoat, causing so much fresh bitterness?[314] Nothing can do such harm to the cause of future unity as a fictitious agreement which satisfies no one and leaves grounds for a struggle; such an "agreement" will *inevitably* lead to a new rupture and redoubled bitterness!

Or are you being cunning? Are you hoping to "take in" the Organisation Committee, or to set the Mensheviks in Russia at loggerheads with those abroad? Has there not been sufficient experience on this score, proving the futility of such attempts?

I repeat in all seriousness: you are putting me in an *impossible* position. I am not exaggerating. I earnestly request you to answer these questions: 1) shall we have the meeting on September 1, as we decided, or have you rescinded this decision? 2) if you have rescinded it, then how, when and where will your meeting (of C.C. members) be held and what measures do you intend to take to enable me to cast my vote and (what is *much more* important) discover your *real* intentions. A meeting is devilishly necessary on a thousand matters. We have no money. The Germans, for some reason, are not giving any. If you do not send 3,000 rubles, we shall go under. Practically all the minutes have been set up,[315] 1,500 rubles are needed for the publication. The treasury is empty as *never* before.

What is this resolution of the Orel-Bryansk Committee? (*Iskra* No. 106.)[316] There is some muddle here. For heaven's sake, tell us what you know. Couldn't someone be sent there—Lyubich from Voronezh, for example?

Sent from Geneva to Russia

First published in 1926

Printed from
the original

145

TO A. V. LUNACHARSKY

Dear An. Vas.,

I have received your letter. You had better write to my private address: 3. Rue David Dufour.

I don't know what to do about Kostrov's pamphlet. I have not yet read it in the press, but from the old manuscript I know what kind of stuff it is. You are quite right about its being plain "Black-Hundred literature".[317] You ask—how to reply?

Vas. Vas. has written a paragraph for *Proletary*—an uninteresting one, I don't feel like publishing it. Olin has delivered a lecture, he is writing, too, but I don't think he'll manage it. Two things are required here, in my opinion: firstly, "a brief outline of the history of the split". A popular one. Starting from the beginning, from Economism. Properly documented. Divided into periods: 1901-03; 1903 (Second Congress); August 26, 1903-November 26, 1903; November 26, 1903-January 1904; January-August 1904; August 1904-May 1905; May 1905 (Third Congress).

I think it could be written so clearly, exactly, and concisely that even those to whom Kostrov addresses himself would read it.

Secondly, we need a lively, sharp, *subtle* and detailed characterisation (literary-critical) of these Black Hundreds. As a matter of fact, this falsity is at the bottom of things both with L. M. (did you read the disgraceful stuff in No. 107? Schwarz is replying with an article. I don't know whether it is worth while?) and with Old Believer. A number of such articles and pamphlets should be collected, the gross lie should be shown up, *nailed down*, so that it would be impossible to wriggle out of it, and branded as definitely "Black-Hundred literature". The new-Iskrists have now provided plenty of material and if it is carefully gone over and these dirty methods of *tittle-tattle*, talebearing, etc., are exposed in all their beauty, a powerful effect could be produced. L. M.'s obscure "personal hints" alone—what undiluted filth it is!

I may perhaps tackle the first subject myself, but not just now, not soon; I have no time for it* (afterwards, I daresay, it will be too late!).

I would not tackle the second subject and I think that *only* you could do it. A nasty job, a stinking one, there's no denying it, but, after all, we are not fine gentlemen, but newspapermen, and it is impermissible for Social-Democratic publicists to allow "foulness and poison" to go unbranded.

Think this over and drop me a line.

A pamphlet on the mass political strike has to be produced—that should not be difficult for you.

You should certainly continue writing popular pamphlets as well, selecting something topical. What precisely, I do not know. Perhaps about the Bulygin Duma? It will be necessary to await the publication.[320]

It would be good to write about workers' organisation. Compare our Rules (Third Congress) and the Conference Statute, analyse the two, explain the idea, importance and methods of *revolutionary* organisation of the proletariat (particularly for an uprising), the difference between Party organisations and those aligned with the Party, etc. In part, this would be an answer to Kostrov, a popular one, for the masses, on a burning topic of the day. Have a try!

All the very best,

Yours,

N. Lenin

Written between August 15 and 19, 1905
Sent from Geneva to Italy
First published in 1934

Printed from the original

---

* I am now going to answer Plekhanov (*Sotsial-Demokrat* No. 2).[318] He has to be pulled to pieces thoroughly, for he, too, has a heap of abominations and miserable arguments. I hope that I shall succeed.

Further, I am turning over in my mind a plan for a popular pamphlet: *The Working Class and Revolution*[319]—a description of democratic and socialist tasks, and then conclusions about an uprising and a provisional revolutionary government, etc. I think such a pamphlet is essential.

146

TO P. N. LEPESHINSKY[321]

To Comrade Olin, who signed as secretary of the Geneva group of the R.S.D.L.P. organisation abroad

Decision of the C.C. representative abroad, which must *be read out in full* at the next meeting of the group (i.e., today, August 29, if this decision arrives during the meeting).[322]

Today, August 29, 1905, at 8 p.m., copies of the letter from the Geneva group to the forwarding office and of the reply of the latter to the former reached the C.C. representative abroad.

In connection with these documents, the representative abroad of the C.C. of the R.S.D.L.P. points out to the Geneva group that it has displayed lack of understanding of Party discipline and has violated the Party Rules. The forwarders are agents of the Central Committee. Any dissatisfaction with C.C. agents is a matter for examination primarily by the Central Committee itself. According to the Rules, the C.C. deals with all conflicts arising within the Party, and particularly so in the case of conflicts between members of the Party's various organisations and C.C. agents. Therefore, by inviting C.C. agents to a meeting of the group, the latter took a step that was, formally speaking, incorrect in general and tactless in particular.

If, however, this invitation was not supposed to be a formal act, then it should not have been made in writing and officially.

The "personal behaviour" of "officers" is either merely personal (unconnected with and independent of the office they hold), in which case its investigation by the group amounts to *squabbling*; or else, the personal behaviour has to do with the office, in which case every Party member, who is dissatisfied with this behaviour, and who insists on a *formal*, *official* investigation, is *obliged* first and foremost to address himself formally to the C.C. The Geneva group of the R.S.D.L.P., by allowing questions concerning dissatisfaction with C.C. agents to "come up" before the group as a matter of *formal* examination prior to this being *formally* reported to the C.C., has thereby again showed failure to understand the discipline and Rules of the Party.

The difference I have just mentioned between *squabbling* and *criticism of an officer* (criticism which is *obligatory* for every Party member, and which should be made in an open way and addressed directly to the central institutions or the Congress, and not underhand, private, parochial criticism), this difference is evidently not clearly grasped by the group.

The C.C. representative abroad therefore considers it his duty to warn all young comrades of the group. In the "colonial" conditions of life abroad people can always be found who are liable to contract the disease of squabbling, gossip and tittle-tattle, people who very badly fulfil the functions which the C.C. or the Congress entrusts to them, but who are eager to gossip about the unsatisfactory fulfilment of other functions by other Party members. Some comrades, through inexperience, curiosity or spinelessness, may often listen seriously to these people. Such people, however, should not be listened to, but should be sharply called to order and *not allowed* to raise formal questions concerning the "personal behaviour of officers" *until* these questions have been formally submitted for consideration to the appropriate Party institutions and examined and *decided by them.*

Party members abroad easily succumb to the disease I have indicated, but all young comrades with healthy nerves should keep a strict eye on themselves and others, for the *only* way of combating this disease is to see to it that any inclination towards squabbling and tittle-tattle is *immediately and relentlessly nipped in the bud.*

That is why the C.C. representative abroad has decided:

I. To *request* the Geneva group to *withdraw* its letter of August 28 to the forwarding office.

This would be the best and speediest way of ending a bad business which, by the very force of events, threatens to lead to the most unpleasant quarrels and rifts.

The group is not obliged, of course, to meet the *request* which I am making *in the name of the C.C.* I venture to make this *request* because I am dealing with *comrades*, with whom so far I have never had any formal conflict.

II. Should the group reject my request then point I of the decision falls away. In that case, I propose that the group:

1) Inform me whether it intends to comply with the Party Rules as explained above, i.e., to comply with the *decision made by me in the name of the C.C.* (an appeal against this decision can be made (a) at a full meeting of the C.C. or (b) at a Congress, but it is binding until annulled by a higher body).

2) Send me, in accordance with Clause 11 of the Party Rules, all information concerning the make-up of the group and "all its activities" (votings, etc.) in connection with the present unfortunate business.

N. Lenin,
the Representative Abroad
of the C.C. of the R.S.D.L.P.

Written August 29, 1905,
in Geneva (local mail)

First published in 1931   Printed from
                                                     the original

147
TO P. N. LEPESHINSKY

At the request of Comrade Vas. Vas. I am explaining the passage he indicated in my decision (that people can be found who do their work badly, but who are eager to gossip about the shortcomings of others). The suggestion that I meant to accuse someone, etc., is without grounds. *Every* Party worker has his shortcomings and drawbacks in the work, but we must be *careful* that criticism of shortcomings or their examination at the central Party bodies does not overstep the boundary where tittle-tattle begins. The whole point and substance of my decision are meant to serve as a *warning* and a *request* that an immediate stop be put to a matter that has been wrongly and badly begun.

N. Lenin

Written August 29, 1905
in Geneva (local mail)

First published in 1931

Printed from
the original

148

TO A. V. LUNACHARSKY

Dear An. Vas.,

Your plan for a pamphlet on *Three Revolutions* pleased me immensely. I'd drop the reply to Plekhanov for the time being if I were you—let that enraged doctrinaire bark away to his heart's content. To delve specially into philosophy at such a time! You must work as hard as you can for Social-Democracy—don't forget that you are committed *for your entire working time.*

As for the Three Revolutions, tackle this straight away. This subject has to be dealt with in a *thorough* manner. I am sure you could make a success of it. Describe, in a popular way, the tasks of socialism, its essence and the conditions for its realisation. Then—victory in the present revolution, the significance of the peasant movement (a separate chapter), what could *now* be regarded as complete victory; a provisional government, revolutionary army, uprising—the *significance and conditions* of new forms of struggle. Revolution *à la* 1789 and *à la* 1848. Finally (better to make this the second part and the preceding one—the third), about the bourgeois character of the revolution, more fully about the *economic* aspect, then thoroughly expose the *Osvobozhdeniye* people in all their *interests*, tactics and political intrigue.

This is a rich theme indeed, and a militant one, against the *Iskra* vulgarisers. Please tackle it at once and take your time over it. It is extremely important to produce a popular thing on this subject, something forceful and pointed.

Now about the split. You misunderstood me. It's no use your waiting for me, for these are different subjects: one is the history (we shall try to manage that); the other—an outline of their polemical methods. A literary-critical outline on the subject, let us say, of "cheap and shoddy literature". Here an analysis is to be given in a whole pamphlet of several chapters, with quotations, showing up all this disgusting claptrap of Old Believer, Martov and the rest in their polemic with *Proletary*, as well as the rehash of this theme in "Majority or Minority", etc. Pillory them for their *paltry method* of warfare. Make them into a *type*. Draw a full-length portrait of them by quotations from their own writings! I am sure you'd pull it off, if only you collect a few quotations.

All the very best.

Yours,

Lenin

P.S. I have received the article about Kuzmin-Karavayev. Also the 1848 feuilleton.

Written at the end of August 1905
Sent from Geneva to Italy

First published in 1934

Printed from
the original

149

TO THE CENTRAL COMMITTEE OF THE R.S.D.L.P.

From Lenin to members of the C.C.

September 7, 1905

Dear friends,

Today I received news of your agreement to a conference on the Duma with the Bund, the Letts, etc.[323] Only today, although the thing happened a month ago! It is left for me to write you another "protest" (an occupation which, it seems, is becoming my profession)....

Definitely, I shall accuse you formally before the Fourth Congress of the crime called "restoration of duocentrism in defiance of the Rules and will of the Party". Really, I shall. Just think—is it not duocentrism that you have introduced! I am *obliged ex officio* to run the organ of the Central Committee. Is that not so? But how can I do that when I *do not get a scrap* of writing on any question of tactics, and a for-r-r-rmal enquiry about the "pre-arranged" meeting on September 1 (new style) is left without reply! Just think what the outcome will be if there is disharmony between us! Is it so difficult to get someone to write in good time, if only on matters of "state importance"?

I have written about the Duma in Nos. 12, 14 and 15 of *Proletary*. I am also writing in No. 16, which will come out on September 12 (new style)*. In *Posledniye Izvestia* (September 1, new style, No. 247) the Bund talked itself pop-eyed. We'll give them a whipping they won't forget till

---

* See "The Boycott of the Bulygin Duma, and Insurrection", "'Oneness of the Tsar and the People, and of the People and the Tsar'", "In the Wake of the Monarchist Bourgeoisie, or in the Van of the Revolutionary Proletariat and Peasantry?" and "The Theory of Spontaneous Generation" (present edition, Vol. 9).—*Ed.*

they're able to sit up again. These Bundists are such dolts and trumpeters, such nitwits and idiots, they are the limit! *Iskra* has got tangled up in lies, especially Martov in the Wiener *Arbeiter-Zeitung* (August 24, new style—translation in *Proletary* No. 15). For heaven's sake, don't rush in with an official resolution and do not give way an inch to this Bundist-new-Iskrist conference. Is it true that there will be no minutes? How can one possibly confer with these prostitutes without minutes?

I strongly warn you against the Armenian Social-Democratic Federation.[324] If you have agreed to its participation in the conference, you have made a *fatal* mistake, which must be rectified *at all costs*. It is represented in Geneva by a couple of disrupters who publish sheer trivia here and have no *serious* connections with the Caucasus. It is a *Bund creatura*, nothing more, specially invented to cultivate Caucasian Bundism. If you allow these people to attend a *Russian* conference, that is, a conference of organisations working in Russia, you will get yourself into a terrible mess. All the Caucasian comrades are against this gang of disruptive writers (I know this from many people); and we shall soon trounce them in *Proletary*. You will only evoke protests from the Caucasus and a *fresh* squabble instead of "peace" and "unity". For pity's sake! How can one ignore the Caucasian Union, which is working so hard in Russia, and hobnob with the dregs of the Geneva marsh! I beg you most earnestly, don't do it.

I have received the decision about dividing the money equally with the Organisation Committee. It will be carried out to the letter.

All the best.

N. Lenin

Sent from Geneva to Russia

First published in 1926

Printed from
the original

150

TO P. A. KRASIKOV

September 14, 1905

Dear friend,

I hasten to reply to your pessimistic letter. I cannot verify the facts, but it seems to me that you are exaggerating; that's the first point. The C.C.'s leaflets are good, and *Rabochy* No. 1 is very good.[325] This is a big thing. At the moment financial affairs are bad, but connections exist and the prospects are very good. One big enterprise, very solid and profitable, has been set up, so the "financier"[326] is *certainly* not asleep. The second point: you take a wrong view of things. To wait until there is complete solidarity within the C.C. or among its agents is utopian. "Not a circle, but a party", dear friend! Focus attention on the local committees; they are *autonomous*, they give full scope, they free one's hands for financial and other connections, for statements in the press, and so on and so forth. Mind you don't make the same mistake you are blaming others for; don't moan and groan, and if you don't like working as an agent, push on with committee work and urge those who think like you to do the same. Assuming that you do have differences of opinion with the "agents". It is far more advisable for you to get your views accepted in the committee, especially if it is a united, principled committee, and to conduct an open, straightforward, vigorous policy in it than to argue with the "agents". If you are right about the anaemia of the committees and a plethora of "agents", the remedy for this malady is in your own hands: flock into the committees. The committee is autonomous. The committees *decide* everything at congresses. The committees can pass resolutions. The committees have the right to go into print. Don't sit idle, looking up at the "heads", but get down to business on your own. You now have a broad, free field and independent, rewarding work in a most important committee. Throw yourself into it, pick a willing team, approach the workers boldly and widely, run off leaflets, *order them from us*, Schwarz, me, *Galyorka*, loudly voice your Party opinion in the name of the committee. In this way, I assure you, you will do a thousand times more to influence the whole Party and the C.C. in the direction you desire than by bringing personal influence to bear on the agents and members of the C.C. It strikes me that you are looking at things in the old parochial way, and not from the Party standpoint. The C.C. is elective, the congress is not far off, you have your rights, make use of them and bring all energetic, resolute supporters on to the same road: into the committees! Pressure must be brought to bear formally, through the committees, and not personally through talks with the agents. No one is obliged to be an agent if he wants to work in the committees!

You write that the agent Myamlin stated that *Iskra*'s Khlestakovian report is fair.[327] Very well. That is his right. But in *Letuchy Listok* No. 1, the C.C. stated that two-thirds of the Party is on our side. That means that Myamlin has hit out at himself! Your job is to curb the Myamlins and expose and discredit them through *your own* committee, and not through talks with them. The committees will elect people who appoint the Myamlins, but it is not the Myamlins who decide the fate of the Party. Let energetic people capture the committees: there you have a slogan for all, which I advise you to spread, to drum into people's heads and to implement.

The agent Myamlin stands for two central organs. Again: who will decide? The committees and their delegates to the fourth congress. Prepare one, two or more committees— there you have a rewarding and *practical* task. Suppose the Myamlins are victorious. The *committees* have the right to start their own organ of the press, even a single committee! That is why you err and drift into the old, pre-party point of view when you write: "They are printing Trotsky's leaflets" (there is nothing wrong in that if the leaflets are fairly good and vetted. I advise the St. Petersburg Committee, too, to print his leaflets vetted, say, by you), or when you write: "A fall from grace *à la* Boris is imminent." I don't understand it. Suppose there are Borises. This junk is always plentiful. Suppose the Borises and Myamlins prove to have the majority (of the *committees*, don't forget that, of the *committees*). Then "all the preceding work is undone", you conclude. Why? How can *Proletary* become undone, what can cause its undoing? Even the absurdity of "two central organs" will not cause the undoing of *Proletary*, it will only introduce absurdity into the Rules. Life will only preserve *Proletary* and sweep away the absurdity. Even the Myamlins will not dare to close down *Proletary*. And finally, let us assume the worst of possible endings, in the vein of your pessimism: suppose the closing down does take place. I shall then ask: what is the St. Petersburg Committee for? Is it likely that *Proletary* will be weaker as the organ of the St. Petersburg Committee than as one of "two" central organs? Take immediate energetic measures to have the St. Petersburg Committee establish not formal, but business-like, close, permanent ties with *Proletary*, and you will strengthen your position and the impact of your ideas so much that you will defy a hundred Myamlins. The St. Petersburg Committee is a force three times as great as all the "agents" put together. Make *Proletary* the organ of the St. Petersburg Committee and the St. Petersburg Committee the thorough-going executor of the *ideas* and tactics of *Proletary*; there you have a *real* struggle against Myamlinism, and not a struggle by complaints and groaning. Hundreds of addresses can be found in St. Petersburg, and a host of opportunities for organising workers' correspondence, revitalising contacts, placing orders for leaflets, republishing articles from *Proletary* in leaflet form, retelling them in leaflets, re-writing them in the form of leaflets, etc., etc. Leaflets can and should deal also with general Party problems (the other day the Kostroma Committee sent us a resolution against Plekhanov being appointed to the International Bureau: a downright smack in the eye, and no mistake!). Myamlinism must be combated by *exemplary* organisation of committee agitation, by *militant leaflets to the Party* and not by wry complaints to the C.C.!

What article of mine in No. 5 (?) of *Zarya* (on Proko-povich) are you referring to?[328] I am puzzled. Why are you dissatisfied with Ruben? Put me in direct touch with him and Lalayants without fail.

All the very best. Write oftener and cheer up! The Myam-lins be damned!

Yours,
N. Lenin

Sent from Geneva
to St. Petersburg

First published in 1926

Printed from
the original

151

TO S. I. GUSEV

To Nation from Lenin

September 20, 1905

Dear friend,

Thanks for letter No. 3. We may publish part of it.[329] You have made a start with the talks with the editorial board not merely on formal questions (on the Rules, contacts, addresses, and so on), not only on subjects for reportage (such and such events occurred), but on the subject of the *gist* of your views, your *understanding* of our tactics, and *how precisely you* put these tactics into effect in lectures, at meetings, etc. Such talks between practical workers in Russia and ourselves are *extremely valuable* to us, and I request you most earnestly to advocate, remind and insist everywhere that anyone who wants to consider the Central Organ *his own* C.O. (and every Party member should want that), should not restrict himself to formal answers or reports, but should *talk* with the editorial board about the views he is advocating, *talk not for publication*, but to create an ideological connection. To regard such talks as a mere pastime is to lapse into narrow-minded practicalism and leave to chance the entire principled, ideological aspect of all our practical work, all agitation, for without a clear, well-thought-out ideological content agitation degenerates into phrase-mongering. And to work out a clear ideological content it is not enough to be merely a contributor to the C.O., it requires also joint discussions about how the practical workers *understand* one or other proposition, how *they are putting into actual practice* particular views. Without this, the editorial board of the C.O. is left in the air, it will not know whether its advocacy is accepted, whether there is any response to it, how practical life modifies it, what amendments and additions are needed. Without it, Social-Democrats will sink to a level where the writer scribbles and the reader reads from time to time. Consciousness of connection with the Party is still weak among us, it has to be strengthened by word and deed.

I shall try to make use of your example by publishing part of your letter. On the whole we are in agreement and see eye to eye with you (your ideas coincide with mine in *Two Tactics*). In particular, it seems to me that you are wrong in attacking the Mensheviks for the words "preparation of the *masses* for an uprising". If there is a mistake here, it is not a cardinal one.

All the very best.

Yours,
Lenin

Sent from Geneva to Odessa
First published in 1926   Printed from
                                                 the original

152

TO THE CENTRAL COMMITTEE OF THE R.S.D.L.P.

I received your *Letuchy Listok* No. 2 for June 24, 1905, only today, October 3, 1905, new style. (It takes the "United Centre" *three* months to inform its members....)

The article: "Fundamentals of Party Organisation" is very good. I can imagine what it's like to have to chew over the ABC to the Mensheviks! But you have to. The writer of the article has made an excellent job of it. I am thinking of publishing it in *Proletary*.[330] It is late, of course, but better late than never.

This article has set me thinking that you can and should see to it that the C.C. is not mute but always articulate. The time is past for ideological leadership through "whisperings" in secret meeting places and rendezvous with agents! Leadership should be through political literature. *Rabochy* is not suitable for that, it has a different role to perform. You *must decidedly* issue a C.C. bulletin in a format not exceeding *two printed pages*, but you should issue it *twice a week*. It would contain a short article on a political, tactical or organisational subject, then brief, minor items of three lines each. Only (1) it must be printed, for the hectograph is now very bad (is there not some small equipment that operates *rapidly*?) and (2) it must be done punctually and frequently.

Your plan of converting *Rabochy* into a smaller weekly newspaper is not clear to me. In my opinion, a popular organ is one thing (I am not in favour of it, but the Congress decided on it, so that's that), and a *bulletin* of really guiding political articles of a general kind is another. You have three or four good contributors, so it would be as easy as anything to get two small articles every week, and the significance would be tremendous!

Written October 3, 1905
Sent from Geneva to Russia

First published in 1926

Printed from
the original

153

TO THE CENTRAL COMMITTEE OF THE R.S.D.L.P.

October 3, 1905

Dear friends,

I have received a pile of documents and listened to Delta's detailed story. I hasten to reply on all the points.

1) I shall not be able to come at the scheduled time, as there can be no question of my leaving the newspaper now.[331] Voinov is stuck in Italy. Orlovsky had to be sent away on business. There is no one to replace me. Therefore the thing is being postponed until Russian October, as arranged by you.

2) I repeat my most urgent request that you send a formal reply to the International Bureau. As to whether you are sending someone to the conference abroad. Exactly whom and when. As to whether you are appointing someone—also precisely. Otherwise you will discredit yourselves incredibly in the eyes of the International Bureau.

3) About Plekhanov, also formally and conclusively— yes or no. Who should be appointed? Postponement of this question is extremely dangerous.[332]

4) About legal publishing, make a formal decision quickly. My draft agreement with Malykh,[333] has done you no harm whatever, as it is only a draft. I merely repeat that Malykh provided a livelihood for lots of people here, whom the Party is unable to maintain. Do not forget that. I would advise both concluding an agreement with Malykh and continuing to do business with the others after the manner of Schmidt.

5) As regards opposition to the C.C. on the part of almost all the agents, I have the following to say. Firstly, co-opting Insarov and Lyubich, which I fully welcome, will probably

improve matters very much. Secondly, some of the agents are evidently exaggerating somewhat. Thirdly, would it not be advisable to put some of the agents on the committees with instructions to concern themselves with the whole area of two or three neighbouring committees? Unity of tactics should not be overestimated: a certain variety in the actions and plans of the committees will do no harm.

6) I consider it extremely important to start preparing for the fourth congress.[334] It is high time. It will probably be six months late at least, if not more. All the same, it is high time. I think we are a little to blame for the laxity among some of the committees and for allowing them to waive the decisions of the Third Congress concerning the conditions of admission for the Mensheviks. If these committees, which at one and the same time recognise and do not recognise the Third Congress, do not define their attitude to the fourth congress, there will be chaos. Some of them will not attend the fourth congress. Another scandal. Some of them will attend it and desert to the other side at the congress. We should not confuse the policy of uniting the *two* parts with the *mixing-up* of both parts. We agree to uniting the two parts, but we shall never agree to mixing them up. We must demand of the committees a distinct division, then two congresses and amalgamation. Two congresses at the same time, in one place, and they will discuss and accept the drafts for amalgamation prepared beforehand.

But just now we must vigorously *oppose* any *mixing-up* of the two sections of the Party. I would advise giving the agents a watchword of this kind in the most definite form and instructing them to put it into effect.

If this is not done there will be an unholy mess. The Mensheviks have everything to gain by confusion and they will go out of their way to breed it. They won't be "any the worse for it" (since nothing can be worse than their disorganisation), whereas we value our organisation, embryonic though it is, and will defend it tooth and nail. It pays the Mensheviks to mix things up and make another scandal out of the fourth congress, for they are not even contemplating a congress *of their own*. We must direct all our efforts and all our thoughts towards cementing and better organising *our* section of the Party. These tactics may seem "egoistic", but they are the only reasonable ones. If we are well united and organised, if we get rid of all the whiners and turncoats, then our hard core, even if not very large, will carry with it the whole mass of "organisational nebulosity". But if we have no such core, the Mensheviks, having disorganised themselves, will disorganise us as well. If we have a hard core, we shall soon force them into amalgamation with us. If we have no core, then it will not be the other core (it is non-existent) that will win the day, but the *muddleheads*, and then, I assure you, there will be fresh squabbles, a fresh, inevitable split and resentment a hundred times worse than before.

So let us prepare for real unification by increasing *our own* strength and working out *clear* drafts for standards of rules and tactics. And the people who chatter idly about unification, who *mix up* the relations between the sections of the Party, should, in my opinion, be ruthlessly removed from our midst.

All the best.

Yours,

N. Lenin

Sent from Geneva to Russia

First published in 1926

Printed from the original

154

TO THE CENTRAL COMMITTEE OF THE R.S.D.L.P.

October 5, 1905

Dear friends,

I have just received Reinert's new letter. I have gone carefully into his proposal, talked it over with Delta and revised my negative reply in the letter of October 3, 1905.

I can return Orlovsky in a week's time. They could then, perhaps, manage without me somehow for a week or two. I would write a few articles in advance and do some writing during the journey. But your plan, nevertheless, seems to me highly irrational. According to the news now filling the foreign press, feeling in Finland is running very high. It is openly reported that a number of outbreaks are imminent and that an uprising is being prepared. Troops are being sent there in force. The coastal and naval police have been reinforced fourfold. After the *John Grafton* incident,[335] special attention is being paid to ships approaching the coasts. Arms have been discovered in many places and the search for them has been stepped up. It is considered within the bounds of possibility that clashes will be deliberately provoked to provide a pretext for using armed force.

To arrange a general meeting there under such circumstances means taking a quite unnecessary risk. It would be an absolutely desperate undertaking. A trifling accident (the likelihood of which in Finland now is particularly great) would be enough to wreck everything, both the C.C. and the C.O., for then everything here would go to pieces. We must face the facts: it would mean handing over the Party wholly to the Menshevik leaders to be torn to pieces. I am sure that when you have thought the matter over you will agree that we are not entitled to do that.

Please discuss whether the plan could not be altered in the following way. All of us to meet in Stockholm. Compared to the present plan this would mean for you some slight inconveniences and tremendous advantages. The inconveniences lie in the half-a-day's delay (counting from Abo, near which it is proposed to meet) or a maximum of one day each way. Two days in all, possibly even 4 days. That is a mere trifle. The advantages are greater safety. A total break-down would then be ruled out completely. That means we shall not in the slightest jeopardise the C.O. and the whole C.C.; we shall not be doing anything stupid or desperate. Some of you can travel quite legally; they cannot be arrested. The rest will obtain passports of other people or will travel without passports (Delta says it is easy for the Finns to arrange for crossing the frontier). In the event of an arrest being made, it would be, firstly, an isolated case and not wholesale break-down and, secondly, there would be absolutely no evidence, so that in the event of legal proceedings it would be impossible for the police to dig up anything serious. We are then guaranteed meeting for two to three days in complete safety, with all the documents available (I shall bring them with me and you will send yours by post, etc.), and with the possibility of drawing up any minutes, manifestos, etc., that we like. Finally, we would then try out whether I could travel to Stockholm more frequently, in order to work for you and for the leaflets, etc., from there (the Mensheviks, I believe, did something of the kind in the South).

Please discuss this plan carefully. If you approve, send me a telegram addressed: Kroupsky, 3, rue Dawid Dufour, Genève, signed Boleslav with just a number indicating the date when I ought to be in Stockholm (30 = I should be there by September 30; 2 or 3 = I should be there by October 2 or 3, and so on).

All the best.

N. Lenin

Sent from Geneva to Russia
First published in 1926

Printed from
the original

155

TO THE CENTRAL COMMITTEE OF THE R.S.D.L.P.

October 8, 1905

Dear friends,

I hasten to inform you of an important change that has taken place in regard to representation on the International Bureau. The South-Russian Conference of Mensheviks[336] adopted a resolution on this question in which (1) there is a gross lie about me personally. I am replying in No. 20 of *Proletary*,* which will come out the day after tomorrow; (2) they ask Plekhanov to represent *their section of the Party*.

This is exactly what we need! Plekhanov, of course, will accede to their request. His quasi-neutrality, which is so disastrous to us, will be shown up, and that is just what we wanted to prove. Let there be two representatives on the International Bureau: one from the Majority and one from the Minority. That will be the best thing. Moreover, if Plekhanov represents the Minority *that will be better still*. It is an excellent precedent for future unity. I earnestly request you: abandon now all thought of Plekhanov and appoint your own delegate from the Majority. Only then will our interests be fully taken care of. It would be good to appoint Orlovsky. He knows languages, he is a good speaker, and an impressive personality. Most contacts are by writing, almost all of them, and we, of course, would begin consultations. As a matter of fact, there would be nothing to consult about: I assure you from experience that this representation is *a mere formality*. At one time

---

* See "Representation of the R.S.D.L.P. in the International Socialist Bureau" (present edition, Vol. 9).—*Ed.*

Plekhanov often entrusted this representation to Koltsov, and no harm ever came of it, although Koltsov was no good at all as a "parliamentarian" and an impossible, clumsy lout in general.

All the best.

N. Lenin

Sent from Geneva to Russia

First published in 1926

Printed from
the original

156

TO A. V. LUNACHARSKY

October 11

Dear An. Vas.,

Your article deals with a subject that is extremely interesting and very timely.[337] Recently, in a leading article, *Leipziger Volkszeitung*[338] ridiculed the Zemstvo members for their September Congress, for "playing at a Constitution", for *already* posing as parliamentarians, etc., etc. The mistake of Parvus and Martov needs analysing from *this* aspect. But your article gives no analysis. I believe the article should be revised along one of two lines: either the weight of emphasis should be shifted to our new-Iskrists, who are "playing at parliamentarism", and you should demonstrate in detail the relative, temporary importance of parliamentarism, the futility of "parliamentary illusions" in an era of revolutionary struggle, etc., by explaining the whole thing from the beginning (for Russians this is very useful!) and introducing a bit of Hilferding,[339] just by way of illustration; or else you should take Hilferding as a basis—the article will then need less revision—give it a different heading, but describe more clearly Hilferding's method of presenting the question. Of course, you may find another plan of revision, but please set to work on it at once, without fail. You have time for it, since the article could not go into this issue (the Moscow events[340]+ the old material have taken up all the space). So, the deadline is Tuesday, October 17. Please make it a comprehensive article and send it by October 17. It would be better to revise it along the first lines, it may then turn out to be an editorial!

If we already had a parliament, we would certainly support the Cadets,[341] Milyukov and Co. contra *Moskov-*

skiye Vedomosti. For example, when balloting, etc. Such action there would not in the slightest degree violate the independence of the class party of Social-Democracy. But in an era not of parliament, but of revolution (you make the distinction in the very heading), support for people *who are incapable of fighting in a revolutionary way* is 1) violation of the independence of our Party. The deal cannot be clear and above-board. It is precisely the "sale" of our right to revolution, as you say, and not the *use* of our right for the purpose of support. In a parliament we give support without in any way disappearing. Now we are disappearing by *obliging* the Milyukovs to speak *for us* on definite terms. Further, what is most important 2) such support is betrayal of the revolution. There is no parliament as yet, it is only an *illusion* of the Milyukovs. We must fight in a revolutionary way *for* a parliament, but not in a parliamentary way for a revolution; we must fight in a revolutionary way for a *strong* parliament, and not in an *impotent* "parliament" for a revolution. In Russia now, *without* the victory of the revolution, *all victories* in "parliament" (the Duma or the like) are *nothing*, worse than nothing, for they blind the eyes by a *fiction*. Parvus has not understood this.

The Cadets have already become *regierungsfähig** (the Trubetskois and Manuilovs in the role of rectors, etc.), they have already climbed to the second storey of freedom of assembly (at the price of debasing assemblies), the storey of quasi-parliamentarism. All they need is that the proletariat, while remaining *actually in the basement*, should imagine itself on the second storey, should fancy itself a parliamentary force and agree to "conditions" about "support" and so on. That is a rich theme! We now are strong owing to the revolutionary struggle of the people and weak in a quasi-parliamentary respect. *With the Cadets it is just the reverse*. They calculate on dragging us into quasi-parliamentarism. *Iskra* has allowed itself to be fooled. It is on this point that a *detailed* analysis of the relation of "'parliamentarism' to revolution" would be appropriate (cf. Marx on the class struggles in France in 1848).[342]

---

* Fit to govern.—*Ed.*

These ideas outlined by you (I am stating them, of course, in a very general and inexact way) must be amplified, mulled over, and served up. People in Russia are now badly in need of having the relation between parliamentarism and revolution explained to them from the very beginning. But Martov and Co. go into hysterics and scream: if only we would become legal! If only we would act openly! It doesn't matter how, so long as it's legal! It is now of all times that we need steadfastness, the continuation of the revolution, struggle against a wretched semi-legality. *Iskra* has failed to understand this. Like all opportunists, they do not believe in the energy and stubbornness of the workers' revolutionary struggle. Moscow is a lesson to them. And here we have that vulgarian Parvus applying to Russia the tactics of petty deals!

Did you receive my letter? All the very best to you and to An. Al.

Yours,
Lenin

Written October 11, 1905
Sent from Geneva to Florence

First published in 1931

Printed from
the original

157

TO S. I. GUSEV

To Nation from Lenin

October 13, 1905

Dear friend,

The resolution of the Odessa Committee on the trade union struggle ("decisions" No. 6 or 5—it is not clear; in letter No. 24. It is dated September 1905) seems to me highly erroneous. The excitement of the struggle against the Mensheviks naturally explains this, but one must not fall into the other extreme. And that is just what this resolution does. I venture, therefore, to make a critical analysis of the Odessa Committee's resolution, and would ask the comrades to discuss my remarks, which are in no way due to a desire to find fault.

The resolution is in three (unnumbered) parts in the preamble, and five (numbered) parts in the resolution proper. The first part (the opening paragraph of the preamble) is quite good: to undertake "leadership of *all* manifestations of the class struggle of the proletariat" and "never to forget the task" of leading the trade union struggle. Splendid. Further, the second point, that the task of preparing for an armed uprising comes "into the forefront", and (the third or final point of the preamble) "in consequence of this the task of leading the trade union struggle of the proletariat inevitably recedes into the background". This, in my opinion, is wrong theoretically and incorrect from the point of view of tactics.

It is wrong theoretically to equate the *two tasks* as if they were on the same level: "the task of preparing for an armed uprising" and "the task of leading the trade union struggle". The one task is said to be in the forefront, the other in the background. To speak like that means comparing and contrasting things of a different order. The armed uprising is a method of political struggle at a given moment. The trade union struggle is one of the constant forms of the whole workers' movement, one always needed under capitalism and essential at all times. In a passage quoted by me in *What Is To Be Done?* [343] Engels distinguishes three basic forms of the proletarian struggle: economic, political, and theoretical—that is to say, trade union, political, and theoretical (scientific, ideological, and philosophical). How can one of these basic forms of struggle (the trade union form) be put on a level with a *method* of another basic form of struggle at a given moment? How can the whole trade union struggle, as a "task", be put on a level with the present *and by far not the only* method of political struggle? These are incommensurable things, something like adding tenths to hundredths without reducing them to a common denominator. In my opinion, both these points (the second and third) of the preamble should be deleted. Alongside "the task of leading the trade union struggle" can be put only the task of leading the general political struggle as a whole, the task of waging the general ideological struggle as a whole, and not some particular, given, modern tasks of the political or ideological struggle. In place of these two points mention should be made of the necessity of never for a moment forgetting the political struggle, the education of the working class in all the fullness of Social-Democratic ideas, and the need to achieve a close, indissoluble connection between all manifestations of the workers' movement for creating an integral, truly Social-Democratic movement. This indication could be the second point of the preamble. The third could mention the necessity of warning against the narrow conception and narrow formulation of the trade union struggle, which are zealously disseminated by the bourgeoisie. I am not, of course, putting forward a draft for the resolution, I am not touching on the question whether it is worth while making special mention of this; for the time being I am merely examining what expression of your thought would be theoretically correct.

Tactically, the resolution in its present form puts the case for an armed uprising rather lamely. An armed uprising is the highest method of *political* struggle. Its success from the point of view of the proletariat, i.e., the success of a proletarian uprising under Social-Democratic leadership, and not of any other kind of uprising, requires extensive development of all aspects of the workers' movement. Hence the idea of contraposing the task of an uprising to the task of leading the trade union struggle is supremely incorrect. In this way the task of the uprising is played down, belittled. Instead of summing up and crowning the *entire* workers' movement as a whole, the result is that the task of the uprising is dealt with as a thing apart. Two things are, as it were, mixed up: a resolution on the trade union struggle in general (this is the *subject* of the Odessa Committee's resolution), and a resolution on the disposition of forces in the present work of the Odessa Committee (your resolution goes off on this tack, but that's quite another pair of shoes).

I pass on to the numbered points of the part comprising the resolution proper.

Ad I. "To expose the illusions" "which are bound up with the trade unions"... this is more or less passable, although it were best deleted. Firstly, it belongs to the preamble, where the inseparable connection of all aspects of the movement should be pointed out. Secondly, the nature of the illusions is not stated. If this is to be inserted at all, there should be added: bourgeois illusions as to the possibility of meeting the economic and other needs of the working class in capitalist society.

..."strongly emphasising their [the unions'?] narrowness compared with the ultimate aims of the workers' movement". It follows that all trade unions are "narrow". What about *Social-Democratic* trade unions which are linked with the political organisation of the proletariat? The crux of the matter is not that trade unions are "narrow", but that this one aspect (and narrow just because it is one aspect) should be bound up with others. Consequently, these words should either be thrown out or further mention should be made of the need to establish and strengthen the *connection* between one aspect and all the others, the need to imbue the trade unions with *Social-Democratic* content, *Social-Democratic* propaganda, and to draw them into *all* Social-Democratic work, etc.

Ad II. All right.

Ad III. For the reasons stated, it is incorrect to compare the task of the trade unions with the "most urgent and primary task" of an armed uprising. There is no need to speak of the armed uprising in a resolution on the trade union struggle, for the former is a means for the "overthrow of the tsarist autocracy" which is mentioned in point II. The trade unions could broaden the basis from which we shall draw strength for an uprising, so that, I say once again, it is erroneous to contrapose one to the other.

Ad IV. "To wage a vigorous ideological struggle against the so-called Minority", which is reverting to "Economism" "in problems of the trade unions". Isn't this too general for a resolution of the Odessa Committee? Doesn't it seem an exaggeration? After all, there has been no criticism in the press of any resolution of the Mensheviks on the "trade unions". It has merely been pointed out that the liberals praise them for a tendency to fall over backwards in their zeal on this question. The only [inference] to be drawn from this is that we too must show zeal, without however "falling over backwards" in the attempt. I think this point should either be deleted altogether, leaving only a warning against narrowness and mentioning the struggle against the tendencies of the bourgeoisie and liberals to distort the tasks of the trade unions, or it should be formulated specially in connection with some particular resolution of the Mensheviks (I do not know of such resolutions at the present time, unless some kind of Akim resolutions appeared among you in the South).

Ad V. Now this is the real thing. The words "and, if possible, leadership" I would replace by "and leadership". We do everything "if possible". The insertion of these words here of all places may be misinterpreted in the sense that we strive less for leadership, etc.

Generally speaking I think we should be careful not to exaggerate the struggle against the Mensheviks on this issue. This is probably just the time when trade unions will soon begin to spring up. We must not stand aloof, and above all not give any occasion for thinking that we ought to stand aloof, but endeavour to take part, to influence, etc. For there is a special section of workers, elderly family men, who will make very little contribution to the political struggle at present, but very much to the trade union struggle. We must make use of this section, merely guiding their steps in this field. It is important that at the very outset Russian Social-Democrats should strike the right note in regard to the trade unions, and at once create a tradition of Social-Democratic initiative in this matter, of Social-Democratic participation, of Social-Democratic leadership. In practice, of course, there may not be enough forces, but that is quite another question; even so, given an ability to make use of all the available forces, some will always be found for the trade unions as well. Forces have been found for writing a resolution on the trade unions, i.e., for ideological guidance, and that's the crux of the matter!

I wish you all the best and ask you to drop me a line about receipt of this letter and about your thoughts in connection with it.

Yours,

N. Lenin

Sent from Geneva to Odessa

First published in 1926   Printed from
                                           the original

158

TO MARIA ESSEN

October 26, 1905

Dear Beastie,

I received your long letter a few days ago. Many thanks. We get very little news from St. Petersburg, and few leaflets of any kind. Please do not abandon your intention to send us absolutely all news of every kind as well as correspondence.

As regards Party affairs, it seems to me that your pessimism is a bit exaggerated. I judge by things over here. I continually hear from the "periphery" that *Proletary* is obviously on the decline, that things are going from bad to worse, that the newspaper is running to seed and so on and so forth. But things are not as bad as they seem. With the gigantic movement that there is now, no single C.C. in the world, under conditions where the Party is illegal, could satisfy a thousandth part of the demands made on it. That our slogans, the slogans of *Proletary*, are not just a voice crying in the wilderness, can be clearly seen even from the legal newspapers, which report meetings of 10,000-15,000 in the University, etc. My word, our revolution in Russia is a fine one! We hope to return there soon—things are heading that way with remarkable speed.

We shall certainly arrange a meeting with the C.C. This question is already settled and everything has been arranged.

As regards differences of opinion, you seem to be exaggerating too. I see no disagreements here between *Proletary* and the C.C. Timing the uprising? Who would undertake to fix it? Personally, I would willingly postpone it until the spring, and until the Manchurian army comes home; I am inclined to think that in general it will be to our advantage to postpone it. But, then, nobody asks us anyway. Take the present tremendous strike.

That the C.C. is focussing its attention on leadership through the press is, in my opinion, the right tactics. I only wish that in addition to *Rabochy*, which is very useful at the present time, we had *agitational* bulletins, small ones of two, or a maximum of four, pages, lively, frequent, issued at least once a week, and sometimes twice. With the present gigantic, incredible growth of the movement, the Party can be led only through the press. And we must produce lively, mobile, speedy, brief leaflet-bulletins, giving the main slogans and the results of the main events.

Concerning stoppage of the Central Organ, there is a misunderstanding here. They were afraid of the whole business going bankrupt, but had no intention of suppressing the C.O. Generally speaking the importance of the foreign-based section of the Party is now diminishing *hour by hour*, and this is unavoidable. We shall not abandon *Proletary*, of course, under any circumstances, until we can get it published in Nevsky Prospekt in St. Petersburg. But we must now pay a great deal of attention to a legal newspaper as well. We here abroad already have to put the shutters up (propagandist literature), and we shall soon close down altogether and open up in St. Petersburg.

In preparing for the uprising, I would advise at once carrying out extensive propaganda everywhere for the organisation of a *large number*, hundreds and thousands, of *autonomous* combat squads, very small ones (from *three* persons upwards), which would arm themselves as best they can and prepare themselves in every way. The time of the uprising, I repeat, I would *willingly postpone* until the spring, but it is difficult, of course, for me to judge from a distance.

All the very best.

Yours,

N. Lenin

Sent from Geneva
to St. Petersburg

First published in 1926

Printed from
the original

159

TO THE CENTRAL COMMITTEE OF THE R.S.D.L.P.

To the C.C.

Please write to me immediately whether you authorise me to invite Plekhanov on to our broad Editorial Committee (the 7-man one) and the editorial board of *Novaya Zhizn*.[344] Wire (signature—Boleslav. Address—Krupskaya): yes or no. I shall make another attempt at a rapproachement with him, although there is not much hope.

Written October 27, 1905
Sent from Geneva
to St. Petersburg

First published in 1926

Printed from
the original

160

TO G. V. PLEKHANOV

Dear Georgi Valentinovich,

I am writing this letter to you because I am convinced that the need for Social-Democratic unity is a question that can no longer be put off, and the possibility for it is now greater than ever. Two reasons prevent me from further postponing a direct approach to you: 1) the founding of a legal Social-Democratic newspaper, *Novaya Zhizn*, in St. Petersburg, and 2) the events of the last few days.[045] Even if these events do not lead to our returning to Russia very soon, at any rate this return is now very, very near, and the Social-Democratic newspaper provides an immediate basis for the most serious joint work.

That we Bolsheviks earnestly desire to work together with you is something I need hardly repeat to you. I have written to St. Petersburg asking all the editors of the new newspaper (at present there are seven of them: Bogdanov, Rumyantsev, Bazarov, Lunacharsky, Orlovsky, Olminsky and myself) to send you a joint and official request to join the editorial board. But events will not wait, postal communication is interrupted, and I do not think I am justified in postponing an essential step for what is really a mere formality. In fact, I am absolutely sure of general agreement and joy on account of this proposal. I am very well aware that all Bolsheviks have always regarded disagreement with you as something temporary, due to exceptional circumstances. It goes without saying, the struggle often involved us in steps, statements and actions which were bound to make future unity more difficult, but there has always been a *readiness* on our part to unite, a consciousness of the *extreme abnormality* of the best force among Russian

Social-Democrats standing aloof from the work, a consciousness of the entire movement's *extreme need* of your guiding,
close and immediate participation. And we all firmly
believe that if not today, then tomorrow, and if not tomorrow, then the day after, our union with you will come about
despite all difficulties and obstacles.

But it would be better if it were today rather than tomorrow. Things have now taken such a turn that *we may be
too late*, and we intend to exert every effort not to be late.

Would you care to work together with us? I should be
extremely glad if you would agree to meet me and talk
this over. I am confident that a personal meeting would
remove many misunderstandings, and many seeming difficulties in the way of unity would vanish at once. But
should you not agree in general, or not agree just now,
I venture to take the liberty of touching on some of these
difficulties in advance.

These difficulties are: 1) Your disagreements with many
members of the new editorial board. 2) Your disinclination
to join either of the two halves of the Social-Democratic
Party.—The first difficulty, I think, is wholly removable.
We are in agreement with you on approximately nine-
tenths of the questions of theory and tactics, and to quarrel
over one-tenth is not worth while. You wanted, and still
want, to correct some assertions, which you regard as erroneous, in my writings. But nowhere at any time have
I gone out of my way specially to impose my views on any
Social-Democrat, and none, positively none, of the new
editors has entered into an engagement to be "Leninist".
Barsov's speech at the Third Congress was an expression
of the general view in this respect. You consider that the
philosophical views of three of the seven persons mentioned
are erroneous.[346] But these three, too, have not attempted,
and are not attempting, to link these views of theirs with
any official Party matter. And these three—I am not speaking at random but on the basis of precise knowledge of
the facts—would be extremely glad to work jointly with
you. For you and us to part company politically now, at
a time when your general sympathy with the views of the
Majority is known, among other things, from your lecture,
is evident from your latest writings, and is evident indi-

rectly from the position adopted by Parvus, who is perhaps most in agreement with you—to part company politically now would be extremely undesirable, extremely inopportune, and extremely harmful for the Social-Democratic movement.

And a new legal newspaper, which will have an audience of tens, if not hundreds, of thousands of workers—indeed, all the coming work in Russia at a time when your immense knowledge and vast political experience are terribly needed by the Russian proletariat—all this will provide *new ground*, on which it will be so much easier to forget the past and work together on a real live job. To pass from work in Geneva to work in St. Petersburg is a transition that is exceptionally favourable, psychologically and from the Party standpoint, for going over from disunity to unity, and I very much hope that we shall not miss such an opportunity, which has not occurred since the Second Congress and which, probably, will not occur again so soon.

Here, however, is the second difficulty. Perhaps you do not want unity with one half of the Party. You will demand unity of the whole Party as a *conditio sine qua non* for your participation in the work. You are quite right in holding that such unity is desirable and necessary. But is it possible *at present*? You yourself are inclined to answer this in the negative, for not long ago you were proposing a federation. *Today* the broadest tribune for our influence on the proletariat is a *daily* newspaper in St. Petersburg (we shall be in a position to issue it in an edition of 100,000 copies and bring the price down to one kopek). Is a joint editorial board with the Mensheviks conceivable *at present*? We think it is not. And so do the Mensheviks. And so do you, judging from your proposal for a federation. Are three newspapers really necessary? Cannot we get together for a *political* organ of revolutionary Social-Democracy when there are really no organisational disagreements between us, and the Party's coming out into the open tomorrow will dispel all lingering fears about conspiracy. And the revolution itself will sweep away our tactical differences with astonishing speed; besides, you have not expressed any disagreement with the *resolutions* of the Third Congress;

and these *resolutions*, after all, are the sole Party directive that unites all of us Bolsheviks.

It seems to me that under such circumstances your coming over to us is fully possible, and it will not make future unity more difficult, but will rather facilitate and accelerate it. Instead of the present struggle, which is being protracted owing to your standing aloof, the revolutionary Social-Democratic movement as a whole will be in a stronger position. The struggle, too, will gain by it by becoming steadier, more disciplined. The general body of Social-Democrats will at once feel confident, hopeful—a different atmosphere will immediately be created, and the new newspaper, hour by hour, will win for itself a leading position in the Social-Democratic movement, without looking backwards, without going into details of the past, but only firmly and steadfastly leading the working class in the present arena of struggle.

I conclude by once again asking you to agree to meet me and by expressing the general confidence of us Bolsheviks in the usefulness, importance and necessity of working jointly with you.

Sincerely yours,
V. Ulyanov

Written at the end of October 1905,
    in Geneva (local mail)

First published in 1926

Printed from
the original

161
TO MOTYA AND KOSTYA,* MEMBERS
OF THE ODESSA ORGANISATION OF THE R.S.D.L.P.
(MAJORITY)

To Motya and Kostya, Members
of the Majority of the Odessa organisation

Dear Comrades,

I have received your "Letter to the Comrades". I shall
not publish it—indeed you do not ask me to do so. But
I consider it my duty to reply to you. I have more than
once stated in print what I am repeating to you now. It
is useless to complain and mourn over the split. We must
work hard to do away with it, we must think *how* to unite,
and not indulge in platitudes and lamentation. Complaining about the struggle of *two* parties and creating a *third*,
and a *secret* one at that, as you have done, hiding yourselves
from both organisations—means *intensifying* the split. If
you have been expelled for violating the rules of the organisation, it serves you right, and it's no use trying to
muddle things by making out that you were expelled for
your opinions, for your conciliatory attitude, and not
because of your disruptive activities.

An "inaugural congress" is an empty *phrase*. Just think
a *bit*, the tiniest *little bit*, what groups precisely should
send their delegates, and how many from each? Just think
a tiny bit how you would react to the idea of an inaugural
meeting *without* a basis of voting rights. Would you not
call it charlatanry?

---

* The bearers of these pseudonyms have not been identified.—*Ed.*

Why do you say nothing about the idea of *two* congresses, that of the Majority and the Minority, held at the same time and in the same place? This idea was put forward by the C.C. and by *Proletary*.[347] Would it not be easier to hold two congresses from the *existing* two parties than to start by creating a *third* (on which you will waste *months*, if not years) and then to convene *three* congresses? What idiot is going to submit to an "inaugural congress" without knowing beforehand whether the Social-Democrats will really be represented there, which of them exactly, and in what proportions?

The slogan of "two congresses" has in its favour 1) the assent of one party of the two; 2) full readiness for a congress on the part of the Majority and the fact that *its* standards for convocation and the *rights* of its congress were made known; 3) the possibility of achieving the same thing very rapidly in the groups and organisations of the *other* party: by publicly listing all groups, getting their opinions, and publishing draft rules of the congress.

But all that your slogan of an "inaugural congress" has in its favour is the whining of certain whimperers, for *not a single section* of the Party knows the *basis* of this congress in any respect whatever. You are simply people of little faith and weak nerves. The sight of an unclean disease and ugly pimples has made you turn away. This is understandable, humanly speaking, but irrational. We think that one must not turn away, that a third party will not get us anywhere, whereas the two existing ones will unite after all, albeit not at once and not without painful treatment.

Vritten end of October-beginning
of November 1905
Sent from Geneva to Odessa

First published in 1931   Printed from
                                                 the original

1907

162
TO MAXIM GORKY

Wednesday, August 14, 1907

Dear Alexei Maximovich,

We arrived here today with Meshkovsky and tomorrow we are going to Stuttgart.[348] It is very, very important that you, too, should be there.[349] For one thing, you were appointed officially by the C.C. (with a consultative voice). Secondly, it would be very good to see you, as it may be a long time before we meet. Thirdly, it is only a matter of a day's journey from where you are and it will last *not more than* a week (it is not London!). It will not be at all late if you leave on Sunday or even Monday.

In short, everything is in favour of your coming. I wish you would, health permitting. Don't miss this opportunity of seeing the international socialists *at work*—it is something quite, quite different from a general acquaintance and mere chatting. The next congress will not be held for another three years. Besides, we shall never be able to discuss all our business by mail unless we meet. In short, come without fail. *Au revoir*!

My best regards to Maria Fyodorovna.[350]

Yours,
N. Lenin

Sent to the Isle of Capri (Italy)
First published in 1930

Printed from
the original

163

TO A. V. LUNACHARSKY

Dear An. Vas.,

I have received your pamphlet at last—the first part arrived quite a long time ago.[351] I kept waiting for the end so as to read it as a whole, but I waited in vain. So far the third supplement is still missing ("How Marx Regarded", etc.). This is most unfortunate for, not having the complete manuscript, one is afraid of giving it to the press to be set up. If this third supplement has not been sent yet, please try to send it as quickly as possible. The money (200 rubles) has been sent to you; did you receive it?

As regards the content of your pamphlet, I liked it very much, as did all our people here. A most interesting pamphlet and excellently written. The only thing is, there are many unguarded statements, so to speak—I mean the kind of things which various S.R.s, Mensheviks, syndicalists, etc., will *pick on*. We discussed collectively whether we should touch it up or give an explanation in the preface. We decided on the latter course, as it would be a pity to touch it up; it would impair the integral character of the exposition.

The conscientious and attentive reader will be able to understand you correctly, of course; nevertheless, you should *specially guard yourself* against false interpreters, whose name is legion. For example, we must of course criticise Bebel, and I do not approve of Trotsky, who recently sent us a hymn of praise to Essen and German Social-Democracy in general. You are right in pointing out that in Essen Bebel was wrong both on the question of militarism and on the question of colonial policy (or rather on the character of the radicals' fight at Stuttgart on this subject).[352] But it should be mentioned in this connection that these are the mistakes of a person with whom we are going the same way, and which can only be rectified in this, Marxist, Social-Democratic way. For there are many people among us (you probably do not see their press) who maliciously chuckle over Bebel *for the sake of glorifying* Socialist-Revolutionarism, syndicalism (*à la* Yezersky, Kozlovsky, Krichevsky—see *Obrazovaniye*, etc.) and anarchism.

In my opinion, *all* your ideas can and should always be set forth in such a way that criticism will be aimed not at orthodoxy, not at the Germans in general, but at *opportunism*. Then it will be *impossible* to misinterpret you. Then the conclusion will be clear, namely, that Bolshevism, taking a lesson from the Germans and profiting by their experience (this demand of yours is a thousand times correct!), will take *all that is vital* from syndicalism *in order to kill Russian syndicalism and opportunism*. To do this is easier and more natural for us Bolsheviks than for anyone else, for in the revolution we have always fought against parliamentary cretinism and Plekhanovite opportunism. And it is we alone who, from the revolutionary and not from the pedantic Cadet standpoint of Plekhanov and Co., can refute syndicalism, which produces no end of confusion (particularly dangerous confusion in the case of Russia).

Proletary No. 17 has come out and has been sent to you, and so has *Zarnitsy*.[353] Have you received them? Do you read *Tovarishch*? How do you like it now? What about your remembering old times and poking fun at them in verse? Write please.

All the very best.

Yours,
Lenin

Written between November 2 and 11, 1907
Sent from Kuokkala (Finland) to Italy

First published in 1934   Printed from
                                                 the original

1908

164
TO MAXIM GORKY

January 9, 1908, Geneva

Dear Al. M.,

My wife and I arrived here a few days ago. We both caught cold on the way. We are settling down here just anyhow, for the time being temporarily, so everything is bad. I was very glad to have your letter: it would really be fine to make a trip to Capri! I shall definitely find time one of these days to visit you. At present, unfortunately, it is impossible. We have come here with the commission to establish a newspaper: to transfer *Proletary* here from Finland. We haven't decided yet finally whether we shall choose Geneva or some other city. In any case we must hurry and we have our hands full with the new arrangements. It would be nice to pay you a visit in the spring or summer, when things here are well under way! What is the best time for Capri?

How is your health? How do you feel? Does your work go well? I heard while passing through Berlin that you and Lunacharsky have been touring Italy and, in particular, have been in Rome.[354] Do you like Italy? Do you meet many Russians?

It would be best for me to visit you when you are not engaged on anything big, so that we can wander about at leisure and chat together.

Have you received my book (the first volume of collected articles for twelve years)[355]? I asked for it to be sent to you from St. Petersburg.

My very best regards to Maria Fyodorovna. *Au revoir!*

Yours,
N. Lenin

My address is: Mr. Wl. Oulianoff,
17, Rue des deux Ponts, 17, (chez Küpfer), Genève.

Sent to the Isle of Capri (Italy)
First published in 1924

Printed from
the original

165

TO MAXIM GORKY AND MARIA ANDREYEVA

January 15, 1908

Dear A. M. and M. F.,

I received your express letter today. The idea of dropping in on you on Capri is delightfully tempting, dash it! You have painted such an attractive picture that I have definitely made up my mind to come out, and I shall try to bring my wife with me. Only I am still uncertain about the date; at present I must give all my attention to *Proletary*, it must be *established* and work got going smoothly at all costs. That will take a month or two at least. But it must be done. By the spring we shall find ourselves drinking the white wine of Capri, looking at Naples and chatting with you. Incidentally, I have begun to study Italian and, as a learner, I pounced at once on the address written by Maria Fyodorovna: *expresso* instead of *espresso*! Let's have that dictionary!

As for the shipment of *Proletary*, you have brought it on your own head by writing. You won't be able to wriggle away from us now so easily! A heap of commissions have to be given straight away to M. F.:

1) To find the secretary of the union of steamship employees (there must be such a union!) serving on steamers that maintain communications with Russia.

2) To find out from him where the ships *come from* and *go to*, and *how often*. He must arrange *weekly shipments* for us without fail. How much will that cost? He must find someone for us who is *punctual* (are there punctual men among the Italians?). Will they want an address in Russia (in Odessa, say, for delivering the newspapers or could small quantities be kept *temporarily* with some

Italian innkeeper in Odessa? This is *extremely important* for us.

3) If M. F. cannot take care of this herself—making all the arrangements, finding the necessary people, instructing them, checking, etc., let her be sure to put us in touch with this secretary—we shall then write to him directly.

This thing is urgent. In two or three weeks' time we hope to publish *Proletary* here and it will have to be dispatched at once.[356]

Well—until we meet on Capri! Now, A. M., take care of yourself.

Yours,

V. Ulyanov

Sent from Geneva
to the Isle of Capri (Italy)

First published in 1924

Printed from
the original

166

TO THEODORE ROTHSTEIN[357]

January 29, 1908

Dear Comrade,

About two-and-a-half to three months ago in Finland I received your letter with the reminder about the debt, which I handed over to the C.C.[358] Now the "Finnish smash-up" has compelled me to move to Geneva, involving considerable time and trouble. Today one of the comrades here has told me that you are insistently reminding about the debt and that the Englishman is even threatening publication in the press (!), etc.

I shall immediatcly write again to Russia to say that the debt must be repaid. But, you know, it is *extremely* difficult to do this now! The Finnish smash-up, the arrests of many comrades, the seizure of papers, the need to remove printing-presses and to send many comrades abroad—all this has entailed *heavy* and unforeseen expenditure. The Party's financial plight is all the more unfortunate because during two years everyone has grown out of the habit of working illegally and has been "spoilt" by legal or semi-legal activities. Secret organisations have had to be organised almost afresh. This is costing a mint of money. And all the intellectualist, philistine elements are abandoning the Party; the exodus of the intelligentsia is enormous. Those remaining are pure proletarians who have no opportunity of making open collections.

It should be explained to the Englishman and brought home to him that the conditions at the time of the Second Duma when the loan was made were quite different, that the Party will, of course, pay its debts, but it is impossible, inconceivable to demand this just *now*, that it would be usury, and so on.

We must convince the Englishman. It is hardly likely he will be able to get the money. And making a row will lead him nowhere.

If I am not mistaken, the members of the *factions* signed separately and the responsibility is by *factions* too.

All the best.

Yours,

N. Lenin

P.S. Not knowing your address, I have written to Quelch, asking him to obtain some literature. *I am extremely grateful to him*; I'm afraid he can't always make out my terrible English!

My address is: Vl. Oulianoff, 17, Rue des deux Ponts, Genève.

Sent from Geneva to London

First published in 1930

Printed from
the original

167
TO MAXIM GORKY

February 2, 1908

Dear A. M.,

I am writing to you about two matters.

Firstly, about the Semashko affair. If you do *not* know him personally, it is not worth while your intervening in the matter described below. If you do know him, it *is* worth while.

L. Martov made a "statement" in the Berne Social-Democratic newspaper to the effect that Semashko was not a delegate at the Stuttgart Congress, but merely a *journalist*. Not a word about his being a member of the Social-Democratic Party. This is a vile attack by a Menshevik on a Bolshevik who is in prison. I have already sent my official statement as the representative of the R.S.D.L.P. in the International Bureau.[359] If you know Semashko personally, or knew him in Nizhni-Novgorod, you should write *without fail* to the same newspaper saying that you are shocked at Martov's statement, that you are personally acquainted with Semashko as a Social-Democrat, and that you are sure that he is not implicated in the affairs inflated by the international police. I am quoting below the newspaper's address and the full text of Martov's statement, which M. F. will translate for you. Write to the editors yourself in Russian, and ask M. F. to append a German translation.

The second matter. All three of us have come together here now, having been sent from Russia to establish *Proletary* (Bogdanov, I and one "Praktik"). Everything is in running order, in a day or two we shall publish an announcement.[360] You are on our list of contributors. Drop us a line as to whether you could give us something for the first issues (something after the manner of your *"notes on philistinism"* in *Novaya Zhizn*, or fragments from a story you are writing[361], etc.

All the very best. Best regards to M. F.!

Yours,
V. Ulyanov

The following was published in *Berner Tagwacht*[362] (address of the editorial office: Kapellenstrasse 6, Bern. Social-Democratic organ) No. 24, January 30, 1908.

"Erklärung. In einigen Zeitungen stand zu lesen, dass der unlängst in Genf verhaftete D-r Simaschko ein Delegierter der Genfer Gruppe der russischen Sozialdemokratie in Stuttgart gewesen sei. Dem gegenüber erkläre ich, dass D-r Simaschko nicht Mitglied der russischen Section auf dem genannten Kongresse war und kein Delegiertenmandat besessen hat. Er war dort nur als Journalist tätig.

"L. Martoff, Delegierter der russischen Sozialdemokratie auf dem Stuttgarter Kongress."*

That's all. The disgusting thing about it is that Social-Democracy indirectly, as it were, shakes the dust off its feet, and repudiates Semashko!

Sent from Geneva to the Isle
of Capri (Italy)

First published in 1924   Printed from
the original

---

* *"Statement.* Some newspapers reported that Dr. Semashko, recently arrested in Geneva, was a delegate in Stuttgart of the Russian Social-Democratic group in Geneva. In contradiction to this, I declare that Dr. Semashko was not a member of the Russian section at the said Congress and had no delegate's mandate. He was there only in the capacity of journalist.

"*L. Martoff*, delegate of Russian Social-Democracy at the Stuttgart Congress."—*Ed.*

168
TO MAXIM GORKY

February 7, 1908

Dear A. M.,

I shall consult A. A. about your statement; since you did not know him personally I think it is not worth while publishing it.[363]

To what Bolshevik symposium have you sent the article on cynicism? I am puzzled, because people write to me a good deal about Bolshevik symposia, but I have never heard of this one. I hope it is to the St. Petersburg one.[364] Send me a copy of your letter to Sienkiewicz, if you have one (indicating *when* it was sent)—but Sienkiewicz will no doubt publish it since it is an opinion poll.[365]

Your plans are very interesting and I should like to come. But, you will agree, I cannot very well throw up the Party job, which needs organising immediately.[366] It is difficult to get a new job going. I can't throw it up. We shall have it going in about a couple of months or so, and then I shall be free to tear myself away for a week or two.

I agree with you a thousand times about the need for *systematically* combating political decadence, renegadism, whining, and so forth. I do not think that there would be any disagreement between us about "society" and the "youth". The significance of the intellectuals in our Party is declining; news comes from all sides that the intelligentsia is *fleeing* the Party. And a good riddance to these scoundrels. The Party is purging itself from petty-bourgeois dross. The workers are having a bigger say in things. The role of the worker-professionals is increasing. All this is wonderful, and I am sure that your "kicks" must be understood in the same sense.

Now—how are we to exert influence, what exactly should our literature be? Symposia *or Proletary*? Of course, the easier thing is to reply: not *or*, but *and*—the reply will be irreproachable but of little practical value. We must have legal symposia, of course; our comrades in St. Petersburg are working on them by the sweat of the brow, and I, too, have been working on them after London, while sitting in Kwakalla.[367] If possible, *all* efforts should be made to support them and continue these symposia.[368]

But my experience from London up to November 1907 (half a year!) has convinced me that no *systematic* legal literature can now be produced. I am convinced that what the *Party* now needs is a regular political organ, consistently and vigorously pursuing a policy of struggle against disintegration and despondency—a *Party* organ, a political newspaper. Many people in Russia do not believe in a foreign-based organ. But this is an error, and our collegium knew what it was doing when it decided to transfer *Proletary* here. That it is difficult to organise, set it up and run it—goes without saying. But it *has* to be done and it will be done.

Why shouldn't literary criticism be included in it? Too little space? I don't know, of course, your system of working. Unfortunately, when we have met, we spent more time chattering than talking business. If you don't like writing small, short, periodical (weekly or fortnightly) articles, if you prefer to work on *big* things—then, of course, I would not advise you to interrupt it. It will be of greater benefit!

If, however, you are inclined towards joint work in a political newspaper—why not continue and make a regular feature of the genre which you began with "Notes on Philistinism" in *Novaya Zhizn*, and began very well, in my opinion? I wrote to you about this "with an ulterior motive" in one of the first letters, thinking: if it appeals to him, he will seize on the idea. And it seems to me that in your last letter you are seizing on it after a fashion. Or am I mistaken? How great would be the gain, both for Party work through the newspaper, which would not be so one-sided as it previously was, and for literary work, which would be more closely linked with Party work, with systematic, continuous influence on the Party! There should be not "forays", but a solid onslaught all along the line, without stops or gaps; Bolshevik Social-Democrats should not only attack all kinds of duffers piecemeal, but should conquer all and everything as the Japanese conquered Manchuria from the Russians.

Of the three subjects that you mention for the symposia (philosophy, literary criticism, and current tactics) one-and-a-half would go into the political newspaper, into *Proletary*, viz.: current tactics and a good half of the literary criticism. Ah, there is nothing good about all those special, long articles of literary criticism scattered through various semi-Party and non-Party periodicals! We should try to take a step away from this old, intellectualist, stuffed-shirt manner, that is, we should link literary criticism, too, *more closely* with Party work, with Party leadership. That is what the adult Social-Democratic Parties in Europe are doing. That is what we should do, too, without being afraid of the difficulties of the first steps of collective news-paper activity in this field.

Large works of literary criticism—in books, partially in periodicals.

Systematic, periodic articles, in the concert of a political newspaper, linked with Party work, in the spirit of what was begun by *Novaya Zhizn*—tell me, have you any incli-nation towards this, or not?

The third subject is philosophy. I am fully aware of my un-preparedness in this sphere, which prevents me from speaking about it in public. But, as a rank-and-file Marxist, I read attentively our Party philosophers, I read attentively the empirio-monist Bogdanov and the empirio-critics Bazarov, Lunacharsky, etc.—and *they* drive me to give *all* my sym-pathy *to Plekhanov*! It takes physical strength to keep oneself from being carried away by the mood, as Plekhanov does! His tactics are the height of ineptitude and baseness. In philosophy, however, he upholds the right cause. I am for materialism against "empirio-" etc.

Can, and should, philosophy be linked with the trend of Party work? With Bolshevism? I think this should not be done at the present time. Let our Party philosophers put in some more work on theory for a while, let them dispute and ... *seek a meeting of minds*. For the time being, I would stand for *such* philosophical disputes as those between materialists and "empirios" being separated from integral Party work.

I look forward to your reply, meanwhile I must conclude.

Yours,
Lenin

Sent from Geneva to the Isle
     of Capri (Italy)

First published in 1934   Printed from
                                                          the original

169

TO A. V. LUNACHARSKY

To Anat. Vas.

February 13, 1908

Dear An. Vas.,

Yesterday I sent you a short note about Bringmann. I hasten to reply to your letter of February 11.

I don't quite understand why you should feel hurt by my letter. Not on account of philosophy, surely!

Your plan for a section of *belles-lettres* in *Proletary* and for having A. M. run it is an excellent one, and pleases me exceedingly. I have in fact been dreaming of making the *literature and criticism* section a permanent feature in *Proletary* and having A. M. to run it. But I was *afraid*, terribly afraid of making the proposal outright, as I *do not know* the nature of A. M.'s work (and his work-bent). If a man is busy with an important work, and if this work would suffer from him being torn away for minor things, such as a newspaper, and journalism, then it would be foolish and criminal to disturb and interrupt him! That is something I very well understand and feel.

Being on the spot, you will know best, dear An. Vas. *If you consider* that A. M.'s work *will not suffer* by his being harnessed to regular Party work (and the Party work will gain a great deal from this!), then try to arrange it.

Proletary No. 21 will come out on February 13(26). So there is still time. It is desirable to have the manuscripts by *Friday*, which will give us plenty of time to put them in the issue which comes out on Wednesday. If it's something urgent we could manage it even if the copy arrives on Sunday (to avoid delay, write and send it directly to my address), or even (in an extreme case!) on Monday.

You, too, must write without fail. Won't you send us for No. 21 either a political article on Russian affairs (10,000-16,000 characters) or an article on Ferri's resignation[369] (8,000-10,000 characters)? Better still, not "either...or", but "both...and".

I send you my best regards and ask you to reply whether A. M.'s contribution to *Proletary* is being arranged. If it is, let him begin at once, *without waiting* for the "meeting" and an agreement.[370]

Sent from Geneva to the Isle
    of Capri (Italy)

First published in 1924   Printed from
                                                            the original

170

TO MAXIM GORKY

February 13, 1908

Dear Al. M.,

I think that some of the questions you raise about our differences of opinion are a sheer misunderstanding. Never, of course, have I thought of "chasing away the intelligentsia", as the silly syndicalists do, or of denying its necessity for the workers' movement. There can be no divergence between us on any of *these* questions; of that I am quite sure, and since we cannot get together at the moment, we must start work together at once. At work we shall best of all find a common language.

I am very, very pleased with your plan of writing short paragraphs for *Proletary* (the announcement has been sent to you). Naturally, if you are working on something big, *do not break it off.*

Regarding Trotsky, I wanted to reply last time, but I forgot. We (i.e., the editorial board of *Proletary*, Al. Al., myself and "Inok"—a very good colleague from the home Bolsheviks) decided straight away to invite him on to *Proletary*. We wrote him a letter, proposing and outlining a theme. *By general agreement* we signed it the "Editorial Board of *Proletary*", so as to put the matter on a more collegial footing (I personally, for example, had had a big fight with Trotsky, a regular fierce battle in 1903-05 when he was a Menshevik). Whether there was something in the form of our letter that offended Trotsky, I do not know, but he sent us a letter, not written by him: "On Comrade Trotsky's instructions" the editorial board of *Proletary* was informed that he refused to write, he was too busy.

13—1158

In my opinion, this is mere posturing. At the London Congress,[371] too, he acted the *poseur*. I don't know really whether he will go with the Bolsheviks....

The Mensheviks here have issued an announcement about the monthly *Golos Sotsial-Demokrata*[372] over the signatures of Plekhanov, Axelrod, Dan, Martov and Martynov. I shall get it and send it to you. The struggle may become sharper. But Trotsky wants to stand "above the contending factions"....

It is in regard to materialism as a world outlook that I think I disagree with you in substance. Not the "materialist conception of history" (our "empirios"[373] do not deny that), but philosophical materialism. That the Anglo-Saxons and Germans owed their philistinism to "materialism", and the Romance peoples their anarchism, is something I emphatically dispute. Materialism, as a philosophy, was *everywhere pushed into the background* by them. *Neue Zeit*, that most sober and well-informed organ, is indifferent to philosophy, was never a zealous supporter of philosophical materialism, and of late has been publishing the empirio-critics without a single reservation. It is wrong, absolutely wrong to think that dead philistinism could be deduced from the materialism which Marx and Engels taught! All the philistine trends in Social-Democracy are most of all at war with philosophical materialism, they lean towards Kant, neo-Kantianism, the critical philosophy. No, the philosophy which Engels substantiated in *Anti-Dühring* keeps philistinism at arm's length. Plekhanov does harm to this philosophy by linking the struggle *here* with the factional struggle, but after all no Russian Social-Democrat ought to confuse the present Plekhanov with the old Plekhanov.

Al. Al. has just now left me. I shall communicate with him again about the "meeting". If you insist—it could be arranged for a couple of days and very soon at that.

All the best.

Lenin

Sent from Geneva to the Isle
of Capri (Italy)

First published in 1924

Printed from
the original

171

TO MAXIM GORKY

March 16, 1908

Dear A. M.,

It's a pity I can't manage to go and see you. A reply has come from Brussels[374] and here there is no delay. But there is no money and no time, and I cannot abandon the newspaper.

Judging from the fact that you own a nanny-goat, I see that you are in a good humour, the right frame of mind, and life is normal with you. With us things are going none too well. We are pretty much at loggerheads with Al. Al. over this philosophy. I am neglecting the newspaper because of my hard bout of philosophy: one day I read one of the empirio-critics and swear like a fishwife, next day I read another and swear still worse. And Innokenty scolds me— and quite right too—for neglecting *Proletary*. Things are not running smoothly.

Ah, well, it's only natural. Things will come right.

It would be fine if you could manage to write for *Proletary* without your major works suffering.

With warm greetings and best regards to A. Vas. and Maria Fyodorovna.

Yours,
Lenin

Sent from Geneva to the Isle
    of Capri (Italy)

First published in 1924

Printed from
the original

172

TO MAXIM GORKY

To A. M., private

March 24, 1908

Dear A. M.,

I have received your letter concerning my fight with the Machists. I quite understand and respect your feelings and I ought to say that I get something similar from my St. Petersburg friends, but I am very deeply convinced that you are mistaken.

You must understand—and you will, of course—that once a Party man has become convinced that a certain doctrine is grossly fallacious and *harmful*, he is obliged to come out against it. I would not be kicking up a row if I were not absolutely convinced (and I am becoming more and more convinced of this every day as I study the original sources of wisdom of Bazarov, Bogdanov and Co.) that their book is ridiculous, harmful, philistine, fideist—the whole of it, from beginning to end, from branch to root, to Mach and Avenarius. Plekhanov, at bottom, is *entirely* right in being against them, only he is unable or unwilling or too lazy to say so *concretely*, in detail, simply, without unnecessarily frightening his readers with philosophical nuances. And at all costs I shall say it *in my own way*.

What kind of "reconciliation" can there be here, dear A. M.? Why, it is ludicrous even to mention it. A fight is *absolutely* inevitable. And Party people should devote their efforts not to slurring it over, putting it off or dodging it, but to ensuring that essential Party work *does not suffer* in practice. That is what *you* should be concerned about, and nine-tenths of the Bolsheviks in Russia will help you in this and heartily thank you for it.

How is this to be done? By "neutrality"? No. There cannot and *will not be* any neutrality on such an issue. If it is possible to speak of neutrality, it can only be in a *relative* sense: we must *separate* all this fight from the faction. So far, you have been writing "from the outside", keeping away from the factional publications; go on writing in this way. Only so will the faction not be committed, not be *involved*, not be compelled tomorrow or the day after to *decide*, to *vote*, i.e., to turn the *fight* into a chronic, protracted, hopeless affair.

That is why I am *against* allowing any kind of philosophy in the journal.[375] I know I am being abused for this: he wants to stop other people's mouths, while he has not yet opened his own! But just think it over coolly.

A journal with philosophy. No. 1—three articles of Bazarov, Bogdanov and Lunacharsky against Plekhanov. One article of mine saying that *Studies in the Philosophy of Marxism*=Berdayevism and reactionary clericalism.

No. 2—three times three keyed up articles of Bogdanov, Bazarov and Lunacharsky against Plekhanov and Lenin. One article of mine, proving from another angle that *Studies in the Philosophy of Marxism*=reactionary clericalism.

No. 3—howling and cursing.

I could write six or a dozen articles against *Studies in the Philosophy of Marxism*, one article against each author and each aspect of his views. Can this drag on in this way? How long? Will *this* not make a split *inevitable* through endless exacerbation and embitterment? Will *this* not bind the faction to make a decision: decide, analyse, and end the "discussion" by a vote....

Think this over carefully, if you fear a split. Will the practical workers undertake to distribute books with such a "fight"? Isn't another way better: go on writing as before, *outside* the factional publications. Do your scrapping on the side, *for the time being* the faction can wait. If there is a chance of *weakening* the inevitable animosity, it can only be in this way, I think.

You write: the Mensheviks will gain from a fight. You are mistaken, deeply mistaken, A. M.! They will gain if the Bolshevik faction does not dissociate itself from the philosophy of the three Bolsheviks. *In that case*, they will

definitely win. But if the philosophical fight goes on out-side the faction, the Mensheviks will be definitely reduced to a political line and that will be the death of them.

I say: *separate* the fight from the faction. Of course, such a separation, on living persons, is rather difficult and painful. It needs time. It needs solicitous comrades. Here the practical workers will help, here you should help, here it is a question of "psychology", and you know best. I think you could help a lot here—provided that, on reading my book against the *Studies*,* you don't become as furious against me as I became against them.

As regards the journal, think it over carefully and answer me soon. I am a little doubtful whether it is worth while for us to make the journey to you together *at present.* Why jangle nerves unnecessarily? Why draw out the torture ... there is no avoiding a fight. Would it not be better to settle this business of the journal simply, without long negotia-tions and ceremonial and futile meetings. I am merely putting questions to you in order to consult you.

Best regards to M. F. I shall most certainly come to Capri and try to bring my wife along, only I should like to do this independently of the philosophical fight.

All the very best.

Yours,
Lenin

P.S. I enclose *important* information about a spy among you.

Sent from Geneva to the Isle
      of Capri (Italy)

First published in 1924   Printed from
                                                    the original

---

* The reference is to *Materialism and Empirio-criticism* which Lenin was engaged on at the time (see present edition, Vol. 14). — *Ed.*

173

TO MAXIM GORKY

How is it there is no news from you, dear A. M.? You wrote that you had long finished your big work and were going to help us in *Proletary*. But when? What about your doing a small article on Tolstoy or something of that sort? Send us a line whether you intend to do so.[376]

Al. Al. is on his way to you. I can neither abandon the paper nor get away from my work. But this is only a delay, I shall come all the same.

What do you think of *Proletary*? It is an uncared-for waif. Never before have I so neglected my paper: I spend whole days reading the accursed Machists, and dash off articles for the newspaper in incredible haste.

Well, all the best.

Yours,

Lenin

To M. F. thousand greetings! I shall bicycle down to see her!

Get Anat. Vas. to write for *Proletary* too! Let me do some philosophic barking by helping *Proletary* in the meantime!

Written in the first half
of April 1908
Sent from Geneva to the Isle
of Capri (Italy)

First published in 1924

Printed from
the original

174

TO A. V. LUNACHARSKY

To Anat. Vas.

April 16, 1908

Dear A. V.,

I have received your letter. I am *very* glad that you are undertaking work for *Proletary*. This is absolutely *necessary*, *particularly* in regard to the subjects you mention +Italian letters. Mind you don't forget that you are a contributor to a Party newspaper and don't let those round you forget it.

All the very best.

Yours,

Lenin

P. S. *Privately*, about philosophy: I cannot return your compliments and I think you will soon take yours back. As for me, I have parted company (and probably for a long time) with the preachers of "the union of scientific socialism and religion" and with all Machists as well.

Sent from Geneva to the Isle
of Capri (Italy)

First published in 1934

Printed from
the original

175

TO MAXIM GORKY

April 16, 1908

Dear Al. M.,

Today I received your letter and hasten to reply. It is useless and harmful for me to come: I *cannot* and will not talk to people who are preaching the union of scientific socialism and religion. The time for notebooks[377] is past. It's no use arguing, and it's stupid to jangle one's nerves for nothing. Philosophy must be *separated* from Party (factional) affairs: the decision of the Bolshevik Centre[378] makes this obligatory.

I have already *sent to be printed* the most formal declaration of war.[379] There is no longer any room for diplomacy here—of course, I am speaking of diplomacy not in the bad sense, but in the good sense of the word.

"Good" diplomacy on your part, dear A. M. (if you, too, have not come to believe in God), should consist in separating our joint (i.e., including myself) *affairs* from philosophy.

A talk on other matter than philosophy won't come off now: it would be unnatural. Incidentally, if these *other* matters, *not* philosophical, but *Proletary* matters, for example, really demand talks just *now*, and at your place, I could come (I don't know whether I shall find the money: there are difficulties at present), but I repeat: only on condition that I do not speak about philosophy or religion.

And I definitely intend coming to have a talk with you when I am free and through with my work.

All the very best.

Yours,

Lenin

Best regards to M. F.: she is not for God, by any chance, is she?

Sent from Geneva to the Isle
of Capri (Italy)

First published in 1924

Printed from
the original

176

TO MAXIM GORKY

April 19, 1908

Dear A. M.,

I have received the telegram from you and M. F. and am sending my refusal today or tomorrow morning. I repeat, *on no account* is it permissible to mix the disputes of writers about philosophy with a *Party* (i.e., *factional*) matter. I have already written about this to An. Vas.[380] and to avoid any misinterpretations or incorrect conclusions from my refusal to come *I repeat it for all the comrades.* We should continue to conduct our factional work harmoniously: none of us has regretted the policy which we pursued and implemented at the time of the revolution. Hence, it is our duty to *defend* it before the Party. We can only do this all together, and we should do it in *Proletary* and in all Party work.

If, in the course of it, A should inveigh against B, or B inveigh against A, on account of philosophy, we *must* do this as a thing apart, that is, without interfering with the work.

I shouldn't like you and the comrades to put a bad construction on my refusal to come. I am very sorry, but the whole situation and the state of the editorial board prevent my coming.

All the very best.

Yours, *Lenin*

We are expecting to receive the promised article about the Rome strike from An. Vas. as soon as possible. We are expecting help for *Proletary* from all writers: we are all answerable to our comrades in Russia, who are dissatisfied with it. Let Al. Al. *concern himself* seriously about money! They are crying out in Russia for lack of money.

Sent from Geneva to the Isle
   of Capri (Italy)

First published in 1924   Printed from
                                           the original

177
TO V. V. VOROVSKY[381]

Dear friend,

Thanks for your letter. Both your "suspicions" are wrong. I was not suffering from nerves, but our position is difficult. A split with Bogdanov is imminent. The true cause is offence at the sharp criticism of his philosophical views at lectures (not at all in the newspaper). Now Bogdanov is hunting out every kind of difference of opinion. Together with Alexinsky, who is kicking up a terrible row and with whom I have been compelled to break off all relations, he has dragged the boycott out into the light of day.

They are trying to bring about a split on empirio-monistic and boycott grounds. The storm will burst very soon. A fight at the coming conference is inevitable. A split is highly probable. I shall leave the faction as soon as the policy of the "Left" and of true "boycottism" gets the upper hand. I invited you, thinking that your speedy arrival would help to pacify. In August (new style) we are nevertheless counting on you without fail as a participant in the conference. Be sure to arrange things so as to be able to travel abroad. We shall send money for the journey to all the Bolsheviks. Issue the slogan locally: mandates to be given only to local, and only to active Party workers. We earnestly request you to write for our newspaper. We can now pay for articles and will pay regularly.

All the best.

Do you know of any publisher who would handle the work on philosophy I am writing?[382]

Written July 1, 1908
Sent from Geneva to Odessa

First published in 1924

Printed from
the typewritten copy found
in police record

178

TO P. YUSHKEVICH[383]

Sir,

I do not agree to diluting Marxism nor to a free tribune in publications I know nothing of.

N. Lenin

Written November 10, 1908
Sent from Geneva to St. Petersburg

First published in 1933

Printed from
the original

1909

179

TO ROSA LUXEMBURG[384]

May 18, 1909

Werte Genossin,

I sent you yesterday by registered book-post a copy of my book on philosophy—in memory of our conversation about Mach when we last met.[385]

If possible, I should like to ask you to write a note about this book for *Neue Zeit*[386] for the *"Verzeichnis der in der Redaktion eingelaufenen Druck-Schriften"**. If this necessitates any formality, such as sending the book direct to the editors (who do not understand Russian), please drop me a line about it and I shall try to send a special copy to the editors of *Neue Zeit.*

You, of course, have heard from Comrade Tyszka about our internal struggle among the Bolsheviks. Your article against the otzovists and ultimatumists[387] has pleased everyone very much[388]; it is a pity that you write *so rarely* in Russian; you prefer the rich Social-Democratic Party of the Germans to the poor Social-Democratic Party of the Russians.

All the best! Regards to Tyszka. With greetings.

N. Lenin

P.S. The note of *Die Neue Zeit* editors to Rothstein's (excellent) article in No. 33 leads me to think that Kautsky himself is none too pleased now with his defence of the I.L.P. in Brussels[389].... Am I right?

Sent from Paris to Berlin

First published in 1925

Printed from
the original

---

* "List of printed matter received by the editorial board."—*Ed.*

180

TO A. I. LYUBIMOV[390]

Dear Mark,

I am sending you for Lyova my reply to the Capriotes.[391] If he considers it necessary, let him make a copy for Inok, and then send the letter to Capri—I don't know the address. I think it could be sent in two envelopes: the outer one inscribed "Signor Massimo *Gorki*, Villa Blaesus, *Capri*, Italie", and the inner one: "For the Executive Committee of the School".

I don't know any other address.

As regards Trotsky, I must say that I shall be most vigorously opposed to *helping* him if he rejects (and he has already rejected it!) *equality* on the editorial board, proposed to him by a member of the C.C. Without a settlement of this question by the Executive Committee of the Bolshevik Centre, *no* steps to help Trotsky are *permissible*. Consequently, the Economic Committee is entitled to agree to the printing of *Pravda*[392] at the *Proletary* printing-press only if this will not be help for a *new faction* (for Trotsky is founding a new faction, whereas the Bolshevik C.C. member proposed to him *instead* that he should come into the Party) but a *strictly* commercial deal, for payment, as with any other person, provided the compositors are disengaged, etc. I insist most categorically that the question of the attitude to *Pravda* shall still be decided by the *Executive Committee of the Bolshevik Centre* and that pending this decision not a single step in the way of *help* shall be taken, nor shall we bind ourselves *in any way*.

All the best.

N. Lenin

P.S. Please make a copy of my letter to the Capriotes *in any case*. It may prove necessary for the B.C.

Written August 18, 1909
Sent from Bombon (France)
to Paris

First published in 1933

Printed from
the original

181

TO G. Y. ZINOVIEV[393]

Dear Gr.,

I have received No. 7-8 of *Sotsial-Demokrat*.[394] I object to Trotsky's *signature*; signatures must be omitted. (I have not yet read the articles.)

As regards *Proletary*, I think we should insert in it 1) an article on the elections in St. Petersburg (in connection with the claptrap of *Rech*[395] and Vodovozov, if *Rech* has not misreported him); 2) on the Swedish strike—a summing-up article is essential; 3) ditto on the Spanish events[396]; 4) on the Mensheviks, in connection with their (very vile) polemic with the Geneva (Georgien[397]) anti-liquidator; 5) in the supplement as a special sheet, an answer to the "Open Letter" of Maximov and Co.[398] A proper answer must be given to them so that these scoundrels do not mislead people by their lies.

After three weeks' holiday, I am beginning to come round. I think I could take No. 4 and 5, upon myself, if need be No. 1 as well, but I am still afraid to promise. Write me your opinion and the exact *deadlines*. What else is there for *Proletary*?

No. 2 and 3 can be made up from *Vorwärts*; I shall send it to you, if you will undertake to write.

As regards *Pravda*, have you read Trotsky's letter to Inok? If you have, I hope it has convinced you that Trotsky behaves like a despicable careerist and factionalist of the Ryazanov-and-Co. *type*? Either equality on the editorial board, *subordination* to the C.C. and no one's transfer to Paris except Trotsky's (the scoundrel, he wants to "fix up" the *whole* rascally crew of *Pravda* at our expense!)—

or a break with this swindler and an exposure of him in the C.O. He pays lip-service to the Party and behaves worse than any other of the factionalists.

All the best.
N. Lenin

P.S. I'm afraid we'll have to give Kamenev up as a bad job. An article on *The Social Movement*[399] has been promised six weeks (or six months) ago?

My address is: Mr. Wl. Oulianoff (Chez Madame Lecreux), Bombon (Seine-et-Marne).

Written August 24, 1909
Sent from Bombon (France)
          to Paris

First published in 1933   Printed from
                                                 the original

182
TO A. I. LYUBIMOV

Dear Mark,

I entirely agree, of course, to your making free use of my letter for a report or for publication.* Bear in mind, though, that I am writing an article** for *Proletary* in which I bluntly describe the gang of scoundrels, Maximov and Co., *as canaille*, and call their school nothing but a "Yerogin's hostel".*** And so, *to avoid misunderstanding*: I agree to speak "mildly" only *to workers* who address me *personally* over *their own* signatures.

Maximov and Co., however, are a band of adventurers who have enticed some workers into their Yerogin hostel. To avoid contradictions, *do not circulate* my letter among our people, but *send it exclusively* to organisations with this *reservation* (the reservation had better be published too):

"The appropriate reply to the company of offended writers, unrecognised philosophers and ridiculed god-builders[400] who have hidden away their so-called *"school"* from the Party, will be given in *Proletary*. The present letter, however, is Lenin's personal reply to those workers who have addressed him personally."

I should advise *everyone* either not to go to Bogdanov's lecture—or to answer him in such a way as once and for all to kill the desire to butt in. It is base cowardice to go

---

* The reference is to a letter to students at the Capri Party School (see present edition, Vol. 15, pp. 472-78).—*Ed.*

** If I manage to finish it, I shall send it to you tomorrow express—perhaps it will be in time for the report.

*** See "The Faction of Supporters of Otzovism and God-Building" (present edition, Vol. 16).—*Ed.*

gate-crashing on a faction from which he has already been ejected. There is nothing more harmful now than sentimentalising. A *complete break* and war, *more determined than that against the Mensheviks.* This war will quickly teach the fools who have still "not made things out".

All the best.

N. Lenin

P.S. And *Plekhanov*'s "Dnevnik"![401] *Don't forget I am waiting.*

Written at the beginning
of September 1909
Sent from Bombon (France)
to Paris

First published in 1933   Printed from
                                                            the original

183

TO MAXIM GORKY

November 16, 1909

Dear Alexei Maximovich,

I have been fully convinced all the time that you and Comrade Mikhail were the most hardened factionalists of the new faction, with whom it would be silly of me to try and talk in a friendly way. Today for the first time I met Comrade Mikhail, and had a heart-to-heart chat with him both about affairs and about you, and I perceived that I had been cruelly mistaken. Believe me, the philosopher Hegel was right: life proceeds by contradictions, and living contradictions are so much richer, more varied and deeper in content than they may seem at first sight to a man's mind. I regarded the school as *merely* the centre of a new faction. This has turned out to be wrong—not in the sense that it was not the centre of a new faction (the school was this centre and is so at the present time), but in the sense that this was incomplete, not the whole truth. Subjectively, certain people made such a centre out of the school, objectively, it was such, but in addition the school drew to it real front-rank workers from real working-class life. What happened was that, besides the contradiction between the old and the new faction, a contradiction developed on Capri, between some of the Social-Democratic intellectuals and the workers from Russia, who will bring Social-Democracy on to the true path *at all costs* and whatever happens, and who will do so despite all the squabbling and dissension abroad, despite the "incidents", and so on and so forth. People like Mikhail are a guarantee of it. Moreover, it turned out that a contradiction developed in the school between elements of the Capri Social-Democratic intelligentsia.

I gathered from Mikhail that you are taking things hard, dear A. M. You have seen the working class and Social-Democratic movement from an aspect and in forms and manifestations which already more than once in the history of Russia and Western Europe have led intellectuals of little faith to despair of the workers' movement and Social-Democracy. I am confident that this will not happen in your case, and after my talk with Mikhail I want to shake your hand heartily. With your gifts as an artist you have rendered such a tremendous service to the working-class movement of Russia—and indeed not only of Russia—and will render a still greater service yet, that it is on no account permissible for you to fall a prey to moods of depression evoked by episodes of the struggle abroad. Conditions occur when the course of the working-class movement inevitably gives rise to this struggle abroad, and to splits, dissension and the quarrelling among the circles —but this is not because of the workers' movement being intrinsically weak or Social-Democracy intrinsically erroneous, but because the elements out of which the working class has to forge its Party are too heterogeneous and diverse in calibre. The working class will forge it in any case, it will forge an excellent revolutionary Social-Democratic Party in Russia, and it will do so more speedily than sometimes seems likely from the standpoint of the thrice-accursed emigrant position; it will forge it more surely than might be imagined if one were to judge by some external manifestations and individual episodes. People like Mikhail are a guarantee of that.

All the very best to you and to Maria Fyodorovna. I am now hopeful that we shall meet again and not as enemies.

Yours,
Lenin

Wl. Oulianoff,
4, Rue Marie Rose, 4,
Paris, XIV

Sent from Paris to the Isle
    of Capri (Italy)
First published in 1924

                                        Printed from
                                        the original

184
TO MAXIM GORKY

Dear A. M.,

You are wrong in asking me to come over. Why should I be slanging Maximov, Lunacharsky, etc.? You yourself write about keeping at loggerheads strictly among ourselves and yet you invite us to do the same in public. It's no model. And about repelling the workers, you are wrong there too. If they accept our invitation and call on us, we shall have a chat with them and fight for the views of a certain newspaper,[402] which certain factionalists are abusing (I heard this long ago from Lyadov and others) as being a deadly bore, a semi-literate and useless paper which does not believe in the proletariat or socialism.

As regards a new split, your arguments don't hang together. On the one hand, both are nihilists (and "Slav anarchists"—why, my dear man, the non-Slav Europeans at times like ours fought, cursed and split a hundred times worse than we do!)—and, on the other hand, the split will be not less deep than that between the Bolsheviks and Mensheviks. If it is a question of the "nihilism" of the "loggerheads", of the semi-literacy, etc., of someone who does not believe in what he writes, etc.—then, the split is not deep or it is not a split at all. And if the split is deeper than that between the Bolsheviks and Mensheviks—then it is not a question of nihilism, not a question of writers who do not believe in what they write. It doesn't hold water, really! You are wrong about the present split and justly* say: "I understand people but not their deeds."

What strikes you and Maximov in *Proletary* as insincerity and futility, etc., is due to a totally different viewpoint on the entire present moment (and, of course, on Marxism). We have been marking time for almost two years now, torturing questions which still seem "disput-

---

* An addition "justly": I make a reservation. Without understanding their deeds one cannot understand people either, unless it be ... outwardly. That is to say, it is possible to understand the psychology of one or other participant of a struggle, but not the *meaning* of the struggle, not its party and political *significance*.

able" to Maximov, but which events decided long ago.
And if we were to continue "disputing" about them, we
would still be vainly marking time. But by parting company, we shall show the workers clearly, directly and
definitely, two ways out. The Social-Democratic workers will
make their choice easily and swiftly, for the tactics of
preserving (in storage cans) the revolutionary *words* of
1905-06 instead of applying the revolutionary *method* to
a new, different situation, to a changed epoch, which demands different methods and different forms of organisation—these tactics are dead. The proletariat is moving
towards revolution and will come to it, but *not in the way*
it did prior to 1905. To one who "believes" that the proletariat will make it, but who *does not understand* this "not
in the way"—to him our position is *bound to* seem insin-
cere, futile, tedious, based on lack of faith in the proletariat
and socialism, etc., etc. The divergence resulting from this
is, undoubtedly, deep enough to make a split—at least
abroad—inevitable. But it does not come anywhere near
the split between the Bolsheviks and Mensheviks, if one
is to speak of the depth of the split in the Party, in Social-
Democracy, among Marxists.

You are surprised that I fail to see Mikhail's hysteria,
lack of discipline (it is not for you to say, nor for Mikhail
to listen) and other bad qualities. Well, I have had a little
opportunity of testing him: I thought that nothing would
come of a conversation between you and me, that there
was no sense in writing. Under the impression of my talk
with Mikhail, I wrote at once, in the heat of the moment,
without even reading through the letter, without putting
it off until the next day. The next day I thought: I have
been foolish enough to believe Mikhail. But it turned out
that for all his enthusiasm Mikhail was right *to some extent*,
for we *did* have our talk, you and I—not without hitches,
of course, and not without *Proletary* being annihilated,
but that can't be helped!

All the very best,

N. Lenin

Written not earlier than November 20, 1909
Sent from Paris to the Isle of Capri (Italy)

First published in 1924   Printed from
                                                   the original

185

TO I. I. SKVORTSOV-STEPANOV[403]

Dear friend,

I have received your letter of September 20, 1909, and was extremely glad to hear from you. It is a pity there was no news from you earlier—we are now terribly isolated here; we tried to get in touch with you and Vyach., but failed. These are indeed hellishly difficult years and a possibility of contacts with old friends is ten times more valuable for that reason. I shall answer your letter point by point. You have seen the newspaper up to December 1908. Since then much water has flowed under the bridge.

With the so-called "Lefts" we have a complete split, which was made good in the spring of 1909. If you come across my book on philosophy (I sent it to you immediately it came out, i.e., in the beginning of the summer of 1909) and the newspaper for 1909, you will hardly say that we are making concessions to the silly Lefts. There is a complete and formal split with Maximov and the Maximovites. An out-and-out fight. They may set up their own organ, or they may not. They are stirring things up in St. Petersburg and Odessa, but they cannot become a force; it is the death agony of "otzovism-ultimatumism", in my opinion. The split with Maximov and Co. cost us no little energy and time, but I think it was inevitable and will be useful in the long run. Knowing your views, I think, I am even confident, that we are in agreement here.

As to what you say about it being time to "liquidate the belief in a second coming of the general-democratic onset", I definitely do not agree with you there. You would only be playing into the hands of the otzovists (who are very prone to such "maximalism": the bourgeois revolution is behind us—ahead is the "purely proletarian" one) and the extreme Right-wing Menshevik liquidators. (Incidentally: have you heard about the split among the Mensheviks? Plekhanov has left the editorial board of their newspaper, *Golos Sotsial-Demokrata*, and the editorial board of their collective work: *The Social Movement in Russia in the Twentieth Century*. In August 1909 he published *Dnevnik* No. 9, where he called the Mensheviks the accomplices of the liquidators,[404] and said about Potresov "he is no comrade of mine", and that Potresov had ceased to be a revolutionary, and so on. Things with us are moving towards an alignment with the Plekhanovite Mensheviks with the aim of strengthening the Party.) But the main thing, in my opinion, is that such a view is theoretically wrong. The "German line" is *possible*—without doubt. And we frankly recognised that as early as the beginning of 1908. But this possibility can become a reality only through a number of "general-democratic" onsets (or upsurges, or crises, etc.) just as France came to the end of the "general-democratic" onsets not after 1789-93, but after 1871 (i.e., after 1830, 1848, and 1871), and Germany not in 1849-50, but also after 1871, i.e., after the *Verfassungsstreit** of the sixties. Struve, Guchkov and Stolypin are trying their hardest to "copulate" and produce a Bismarckian Russia—but nothing comes of it. Nothing. They're impotent. All the signs show, and they themselves admit, that nothing comes of it. Stolypin's agrarian policy[405] is correct from the point of view of Bismarckianism. But Stolypin himself "asks" for 20 years to make something "come of it". But twenty years, and even a shorter time, is impossible in Russia without 1830-1848-1871 (if in the French style) and 1863-1865 (if in the German style). It is impossible. And all these dates (both 1830-1848-1871 and 1863-1865) are a "general-democratic onset".

No, we cannot "liquidate" the idea of "a general-democratic onset"—that would be a cardinal mistake. We should recognise the possibility of a "German line", but we should not forget that so far it does *not* exist. It simply

---

* Constitutional conflict.—*Ed.*

does not. We should not link the destinies of the proletarian party with the success or failure of the bourgeois revolution—that is indisputable. We should organise the work so that, whatever the turn events take, it will be a stable, unalienable achievement—that is true. But we are obliged to do our duty as leaders of a democratic, "general-democratic", movement right to the end, until the Russian 1871, until the complete turn of the peasantry to the side of an *Ordnungspartei*.* And such a turn, as far as Russia is concerned, is still a long way off! We cannot deny the possibility of a "German", that is to say, a "rotten", solution of "general-democratic" problems, but we are obliged to do *everything*, we are obliged to work long and hard in order that this solution will be not "rotten", not German, but French, i.e., that of the 1830-1848-1871 type, and not of the 1863-65 type (merely a "constitutional" crisis). There is no guarantee that our 1863-65 will turn out to be "rotten" or successful, but it is our business, the business of the working-class party, to do everything to make the *"rotten"* develop into the *successful*, to make the German *Verfassungsstreit* develop into a real French scrimmage. There are no historical laws to prevent a rotten crisis from turning into a real scrimmage. There are no such laws. Everything depends on the circumstances, on the mass of poor peasants (whom Stolypin has suppressed but not satisfied), on the strength of the workers' party, on the conditions, friction and conflicts between Guchkov and the "spheres", etc., etc. We should see to it that we are stronger (and by the time of our 1863-1865 we shall be stronger than the Germans were then), and that the peasants then do what we tell them, and not what the liberals tell them. Only the struggle will decide how far this will be achieved. We shall demand everything in the sense of a "general-democratic onset": if successful we shall gain *everything*, if unsuccessful—a part; but, in going into battle, we must not confine ourselves to demanding a part. To build in a new way, to organise in a new way, to enter the crisis in a new way— such is the *crucial feature* of the moment, but *all* the old

---

* Party of order.—*Ed.*

slogans, the demand for *"everything"*, must be maintained, developed and strengthened.

All the very, very best. I wish you health and good cheer.

Yours whole-heartedly,

Old Man

Written December 2, 1909
Sent from Paris to St.
Petersburg

First published in 1922   Printed from
                                                the typewritten copy found
                                                      in police record

———

1910

186
DRAFT OF A LETTER TO THE "TRUSTEES"[406]

Letter to the German Trio

To explain the at first glance strange proposal and request which we and the C.C. are addressing to you, we
must clarify the situation in our Party.

To understand this situation, one must have a clear idea,
firstly, of the violent nature of the counter-revolution
and the appalling chaos in the Social-Democratic organisation and Social-Democratic work; and, secondly, of the
basic ideological and political trends in our Party.

On the first question, it is sufficient to note the tremendous decline among the organisations everywhere, almost
their cessation in many localities. The wholesale flight
of the intelligentsia. All that is left are workers' circles
and isolated individuals. The young, inexperienced worker
is making his way forward with difficulty.

On the second question. There were *two* trends among
the Social-Democrats in the revolution (and two factions,
*tatsächlich Spaltung**): the Mensheviks and the Bolsheviks. Stockholm 1906 and London 1907.[407] An opportunist
and a revolutionary wing.

The 1907-08 break-down gave rise (α) among the Mensheviks—to *liquidationism* (definition), (β) among the Bolsheviks—to *otzovizm* (and ultimatumism). Definition.

(α) Beginning with March 1908, the Mensheviks took
absolutely no part in the central work of the Party and
even tried to disrupt it (August 1908). Abroad they predominate (students, immature bourgeois intellectuals, etc.).
A wide-open split abroad (thanks to the Mensheviks) and

---

* An actual split.—*Ed.*

their *complete* non-participation in Party work, plus a struggle against the Party.

The conference of December 1908 brands this.[408]

(β) Otzovism-ultimatumism among the Bolsheviks in 1908-09. The Bolsheviks' resolute struggle against it and *Kaltstellung** of the otzovists and ultimatumists. Removal.

Chaos in Russia increasing.

Plekhanov's statement, August 1909 ("What Can We Do for You?"[409], the liquidationism of *Golos*; liquidationism declared to be petty-bourgeois opportunism; acknowledge-ment of the crisis in the Party [frightful disease]; resig-nation from the editorial board of the *Social Movement* which had taken refuge in a *bürgerlich-liberalen Verlag***).

The significance of Plekhanov's statement = a feeble echo, the confirmation *by a factional enemy of the Bolsheviks* of all their accusations.

The gravitation of the Mensheviks *in Russia* towards the Party (particularly in the case of workers: St. Peters-burg, Moscow).

Experience of *Party* unity on this basis, on the recogni-tion of the struggle on two fronts: against liquidationism and against otzovism-ultimatumism.

Conditions for unity on our part: unconditional recogni-tion of the struggle against liquidationism (half-measure of the C.C.: a personal concession); cessation of factional struggle (=of the split abroad in particular) and *loyal subordination to the majority* of the Party (Bolsheviks+ Poles in particular), which extricated the Party from the 1907-09 crisis and set it on the path of a resolute struggle on two fronts.

Conditions of the Mensheviks: concealment of a clear definition of liquidationism (half-measure in the *unani-mous* resolution) and *equality* on the editorial board of the Central Organ (virtually the leading Party body in view of the extreme weakness and instability of the C.C. in Russia).

In the C.C. an *extremely unstable compromise* is effected 1) a unanimous resolution *deleting* the name liquidation-

---

* Removal.—*Ed.*
** Bourgeois-liberal publishing house.—*Ed.*

ism[410]; 2) three and two in the C.O., in circumstances of the Menshevik declaration about "mechanical suppression", "a state of siege", etc.; 3) refusal of the Mensheviks resolutely, clearly and irrevocably to renounce their factional newspaper and factional organisation, and to recognise *loyal* subordination to the Majority.

Hence our fears. Having dissolved the Bolshevik faction and handed over the money to the C.C. (actually 5 powers in circumstances of an accidental and wavering majority, marred by otzovism-ultimatumism), we fear (have every ground for fearing) a split of the Mensheviks abroad and their dragging in of liquidationism (in the shape of equality on the editorial board).

We are convinced that in view of attempts at a split, organised from abroad by the Mensheviks, the C.C. (i.e., the Bolsheviks+the nationals) will not be strong enough to combat liquidationism, and we will have to *resume* the factional struggle, reply to the split by a split.

The experience of the "truce": the Bolsheviks have disarmed. The experience of the "Party way of life".

The conditions to be put to the Mensheviks: (α) complete disarmament—cessation of the factional newspaper, the factional funds, the factional split abroad; (β) *loyal* implementation of the resolution on the struggle against liquidationism; (γ) *loyal* subordination to the majority in the C.O.; (δ) *loyal* assistance to the C.C. in Russia.

Si non—non!

The flirting of the Mensheviks with the otzovists-ultimatumists. Trotsky's impotence and connivance in regard to the liquidators.

Written in February-early March
1910 in Paris

First published in 1933

Printed from
the original

187

TO N. Y. VILONOV

March 27, 1910

Dear Comrade Mikhail,

How is your health? Are you getting better? Write about this, tell us whether you are putting on weight and how much.

The fog of conciliatory unity among us is beginning to disperse. I am sending you a reprint from No. 12 of *Sotsial-Demokrat*.[411] You will see from it that there has been an all-out fight with the *Golos* group. The question now boils down to whether there are any Plekhanovites in existence, whether there are any *pro-Party* Mensheviks in existence, or whether all the Mensheviks are *Golos* supporters, and Plekhanov is simply an isolated individual.

Intensified agitation has to be carried on for the withdrawal of the Plekhanovites from the *Golos* groups, for the replacement of the *Golos* supporter in the Bureau of the C.C. Abroad by a Plekhanovite and so on—and by means of such agitation to verify *in practice* whether Party unity will result at least in our unity with the Plekhanovites or whether nothing at all will come of it.

The group of Bolsheviks here is about to start such agitation; when it does, you will receive news of it.

The Vperyodists[412] are holding a sort of meeting here; it is said that Bogdanov and Stanislav have arrived. What they intend to do is not known. They are behaving stupidly and the Central Organ will, probably, have to fight them as well, after their first press statement. There was a letter from Russia saying that Alexinsky wrote to the Moscow *Vperyod* group about their plan to organise a school of *their own* for 50 people (they have raised money, then?)

but that the *Vperyod* people in Moscow are said to be inclined towards a general party school.

There is no correspondence with Gorky. It is rumoured
that he has become disillusioned with Bogdanov and has
realised the falsity of the latter's behaviour. Have you
any news from Capri?

There are few forces in Russia. Ah, if only we could send
from here a good Party worker to the C.C. or for convening
a conference! But here everyone is a "has-been".

Keep well and write,

All the best.

Yours,

Lenin

Sent from Paris to Davos
      (Switzerland)

First published in 1930   Printed from
                                                    the original

188

TO G. V. PLEKHANOV

March 29, 1910

My dear comrade,

Fully sharing your idea, stated in *Dnevnik* No. 11, about the need for a close and sincere alignment of all genuinely Social-Democratic elements in the struggle against liquidationism and otzovism, I should very much like to have a talk with you personally about the present state of affairs in the Party. If you, too, find this useful and if your health permits, be so kind as to write me (or wire) a few words as to when you could meet me in San Remo. I am ready to make the journey for that purpose.[413]

With comradely greetings,

N. Lenin

Vl. Oulianoff, 4, Rue Marie Rose, Paris, XIV.

Sent from Paris to San Remo
(Italy)

First published in 1930

Printed from
the original

189

TO N. Y. VILONOV

April 7, 1910

Dear Comrade M.,

I am sending you the resolution of our local Plekhanovites, or, rather, the pro-Party Mensheviks.[414] If it is true that with you in Davos the pro-Party elements preponderate among the Mensheviks, it is extremely important that they should respond immediately, rally together one way or another and come out openly. Obviously, *Bolsheviks* should be very cautious in giving such advice to Mensheviks, for even among the Plekhanovites there is no accusation more terrible, horrible and intolerable than that of "aiding the Bolsheviks" or of working "for the Bolsheviks", etc.

In the present confused situation there are, in my opinion, only two ways out: either back to our own Bolshevik faction, or a *determined fight* together with the Plekhanovites for the Party and against the *Golos* people. The second alternative is the more desirable, but it does not depend on us. So long as it is possible, we shall do all we can for the second way out. Only after trying out *all* possibilities, all means for the second way out, shall we return to the first one.

I am very glad that your acquaintance with pragmatism has begun to turn you away from Machism. In Russia now they are intensively translating all this "latest" philosophical muck: Petzoldt and Co., the pragmatists, etc. This is good: when our people in Russia, especially the Russian workers, see the teachers of our Bogdanov and Co., *au naturel*—they will quickly turn away from both teachers and pupils.

To regard truth as an instrument of cognition means, in effect, to go over to agnosticism, i. e., to abandon materialism. In this and in everything fundamental, the pragmatists, Machists, empirió-monists are birds of a feather.

With warm greetings and wishing you a speedy and lasting recovery.

Yours,

N. Lenin

Sent from Paris to Davos
    (Switzerland)

First published in 1930

Printed from
the original

190

TO MAXIM GORKY

To Al. Max.

April 11, 1910

Dear A. M.,

I did not receive the letter from you and M.F. sent through M. S. Botkina until today. Before I forget: you can write to me at my *private* address (Oulianoff, 4, Rue Marie Rose, 4, Paris, XIV) and at the address of the Party—in which case it is safer to use two envelopes, the inner one marked: for Lenin, private (110, Avenue d'Orléans, Mr. Kotliarenko, Paris, XIV).

I shall try and send you tomorrow the publications you ask for.

Did I criticise you, and where? It must have been in *Diskussionny Listok* No. 1* (published as a supplement to the C.O.).[415] I am sending you a copy. If this is not what your informants had in mind, then I don't remember anything else at the moment. I wrote nothing else during that period.

Now about unity. You ask: is this a fact or an anecdote? I shall have to go back a long way to tell you about this, for there is something both "anecdotal" (rather trivial) about this fact, and something serious, in my view.

There have been deep and serious factors leading to Party unity: in the ideological field—the need to purge Social-Democracy from liquidationism and otzovism; in the practical field—the terribly difficult plight of the Party and of all Social-Democratic work, and the coming to maturity of a new type of Social-Democratic worker.

---

* See "Notes of a Publicist", Section One, "The Platform" of the Adherents and Defenders of Otzovism (present edition, Vol. 16).—*Ed.*

At the C.C. plenum (the "long plenum"—three weeks
of agony, all nerves were on edge, the devil to pay!) to these
serious and deep-lying factors, which were by no means
generally recognised, were added minor, petty factors—
a mood of "conciliation in general" (without any clear idea
with whom, for what, and how); hatred of the Bolshevik
Centre for its implacable ideological struggle; squabbling
on the part of the Mensheviks, who were spoiling for a fight,
and as a result—an infant covered with blisters.

And so we have to suffer. Either—at best—we cut open
the blisters, let out the pus, and cure and rear the infant.

Or, at worst—the infant dies. Then we shall be childless
for a while (that is, we shall re-establish the Bolshevik
faction) and then give birth to a more healthy infant.

Among the Mensheviks, those working for serious unity
are the Plekhanovites (not quite consciously, rather slowly
and waveringly, but they are nevertheless working for it,
and, what is most important, they cannot help working
for it), the *pro-Party*-ists and the workers. The *Golos* people,
however, are fencing, causing confusion and making
mischief. They are building up a strong, legal, opportunist
centre in Russia (Potresov & Co. in the press: see *Nasha
Zarya*[416] No. 2—what a scoundrel this Potresov is!—and
Mikhail, Roman, Yury+the sixteen authors of the "Open
Letter"[417] in No. 19/20 of *Golos*—in practical, organisational work).

The C.C. plenum wanted to unite *everyone*. Now the *Golos*
people *drop out*. This abscess *must* be removed. It cannot be done without squabbling, rows, nervous strain, mud
and "scum".

We are just now in the thick of this squabbling. Either
the C.C. in Russia lops off the *Golos* supporters by removing
them from important bodies (such as the Central Organ,
etc.)—or our faction will have to be re-established.

In No. 11 of *Dnevnik*, Plekhanov has given an appraisal
of the plenum which clearly shows that the sincere and
serious desire to fight opportunism *now* prevails with him
over the minor, petty desire to *utilise* the *Golos* opportunists *against* the Bolsheviks. Here, too, things take a com-
plex and protracted course, but the Mensheviks' legalistic,
liquidationist centre that has been built up in Russia will

inevitably lead to serious Social-Democrats turning away from them.

Now about the Vperyodists. At one time it seemed to me that within this group, too, there were two trends: towards the Party and Marxism, towards renouncing Machism and otzovism, and the opposite. As far as the first trend is concerned, Party unity would enable the patent absurdities of otzovism, etc., to be corrected in a convenient and unembarrassing Party way. But, apparently, the second trend is getting the upper hand among them. Alexinsky (a mere babe-in-arms in politics, but one who has turned angry and is committing one stupidity after another) kicked up a row and resigned from both the editorial board of *Diskussionny Listok* and from the Party's School Committee.[418] They will probably organise a school of *their own*, again a factional one, again on the side. If they do, we shall fight again and win the workers away from them.

And so it works out, that in the matter of unity the "anecdotic" predominates at the present time, is brought into high focus, gives occasion for sniggering and sneering, etc. It is said that the Socialist-Revolutionary Chernov has even written a farce about unity among the Social-Democrats entitled "A Storm in a Tea-cup", and that this farce will be performed here in a day or two before one of the groups of the emigrant colony, who are addicted to sensationalism.

It is sickening to be stuck in the midst of this "anecdotic" situation, this squabbling and row-making, nervous strain and "scum"; to observe all this is also sickening. But one should not allow oneself to succumb to the mood. Life in exile is now a hundred times harder than it was before the revolution. Life in exile and squabbling are inseparable.

But the squabbling will pass away; nine-tenths of it remains abroad; it is an accessory feature. The development of the Party, the development of the Social-Democratic movement goes forward despite all the devilish difficulties of the present situation. The purging of the Social-Democratic Party from *its* dangerous "deviations", from liquidationism and otzovism *goes forward* steadfastly; within the framework of unity it has *progressed considerably farther*

than before. As a matter of fact, we had finished with otzovism ideologically before the plenum. We had not finished with liquidationism at that time; the Mensheviks
succeeded temporarily in *hiding the snake*, but now it has
been dragged out into broad daylight, now everyone sees
it, now we shall kill it!

And this purging is by no means only an "ideological"
task, a labour of armchair workers as that fool (or rogue)
Potresov thinks, who *stands up* for the Machists the way
the Mensheviks at the plenum stood up for the Vperyodists.
No, this purge is inseparably bound up with the mass working-class movement, which learns how to organise Social-
Democratic work in the present difficult period, learns precisely by rejection, finds the right path by rejecting liquidationism and otzovism. Only that windbag Trotsky imagines
that this rejection can be avoided, that it is superfluous, that it does not concern the workers, that the issues
of liquidationism and otzovism have been posed *not* by life
itself, *but* by the wicked polemicists.

I can imagine how distressing the sight of this painful
growth of the new Social-Democratic movement must be
to those who have not seen and lived through its painful
growth in the late eighties and early nineties. At that time
such Social-Democrats were to be counted by the score,
if not in individuals. Now there are hundreds and thousands of them. Hence the crisis and crises. And the Social-
Democratic movement *as a whole* is coping with them openly and will overcome them honestly.

All the very best.

Yours,

Lenin

Sent from Paris to the Isle
    of Capri (Italy)

First published in 1924   Printed from
                                                    the original

191
TO N. A. SEMASHKO[419]

October 4, 1910

Dear N. A.,

We must meet as soon as possible to talk about the *speediest* convocation of a meeting of Bolsheviks (anti-Vperyodists). Yesterday Mark+Lozovsky+Lyova departed with a protest against a factional newspaper.[420] The funny fellows! I am glad that the muddlers are out of it, but we must *speedily* ascertain the attitude of the remaining people. If possible come out as quickly as you can and take steps for an early meeting.

Yours,
Lenin

Sent from Paris to Chatillon
(France)

First published in 1930

Printed from
the original

192

TO JULIAN MARCHLEWSKI[421]

October 7, 1910

Dear Comrade,

I received the letter from you and Wurm and your article late yesterday evening. In accordance with your and Kautsky's request, *lasse ich es bei Ihrem Artikel bewenden.**

I have already written about half of a long article against both Martov and Trotsky.** I shall have to leave it and start on an article against Trotsky. Since you meet Kautsky, please tell him that I am taking care of the reply to Trotsky. If the Germans are so afraid of a polemic, I don't think it matters much whether the reply comes a week earlier or a week later?

What a pity that even Kautsky and Wurm do not see how disgusting and mean such articles as those of Martov and Trotsky are. I shall try to write at least a private letter to Kautsky to clarify the matter. It is really a downright scandal that Martov and Trotsky lie with impunity and write scurrilous lampoons in the guise of "scientific" articles!

By the way, could you help me to clear up two practical questions. First: could a translator from Russian into German be found in Berlin (for articles for *Neue Zeit*)? Or is this unreliable and expensive, so that it would be better to look for someone here? I shall look out for someone here in any case, but I should like to know your opinion, as you have considerable experience in this respect.

---

* I shall confine myself to your article.—*Ed.*
** Reference is to "The Historical Meaning of the Inner-Party Struggle in Russia" (see present edition, Vol. 16).—*Ed.*

Second: what if I were to write a pamphlet (of a size *à la* Cherevanin: *Das Proletariat in der russischen Revolution*) on the subject of the Russian revolution, its lessons, class struggle, etc. Could a German party publisher be found or not? Do the Germans pay for such things, or must payment be looked for only from the Russians, while the Germans are served *nebenbei*?

In connection with the reply to Martov, I have dug into some very interesting strike statistics of 1905-08 and should very much like to analyse them. It is a subject more suitable for a book or pamphlet than for an article.* But the Germans are disgracefully "unconscious" in questions concerning the appraisal of the Russian revolution!

I enclose a brief enumeration of what it is desirable to add against Martov. If you include even a part of it in your article, it would be very good.[422]

Beste Grüsse.

Yours,

Lenin

Here, in my opinion, are the chief (not all, by far) points of Martov's lies and falsehood which it is desirable to point out (if not in full, at least in part):

In saying that Comrade Radek is misquoting, Comrade Martov casts suspicion without giving proof. We, however, have *full* proof that Martov quotes falsely. "So far we have been speaking French" (*Die Neue Zeit*, 1910), Martov quotes Lenin. *The quotation is distorted.* Lenin said: "During the revolution we *learned* to 'speak French'" (*Proletary* No. *46*)**. By distorting the quotation, Martov contrives to conceal the fact that he (like all opportunists) calls on the workers to *unlearn* the methods of revolutionary struggle.

"To speak French"—"*richtiger gesagt*: blanquistisch",*** is Martov's emendation. We thank him for his frankness. To call the participation of the French proletariat in the French revolutions "Blanquism" is precisely the "essence" of the views of Martov and Quessel.[423]

---

* See "Strike Statistics in Russia" (present edition, Vol. 16).— *Ed.*
** See present edition, Vol. 15, p. 458.—*Ed.*
*** "Or rather: in the Blanqui manner".—*Ed.*

"*In ganz Westeuropa,*" writes Martov, "*betrachtet man die Bauernmassen in dem Masse für bündnisfähig, als sie die schweren Folgen der kapitalistischen Umwälzung der Landwirtschaft zu spüren bekommen* ...; *für Russland malte man sich ein Bild aus, wie mit dem Proletariat sich die 100 Millionen Bauern vereinigen* ..., *die noch nicht von der kapitalistischen Bourgeoisie in die Schule genommen worden sind*" (*Neue Zeit,* Seite 909). *Das ist eben russisches Quesseltum!* *

The Russian Quessel *forgot* to mention that in the *agrarian programme* of the Russian Social-Democrats (adopted in Stockholm, 1906, when the Mensheviks had a majority!) it is stated "support for the revolutionary actions of the peasantry to the extent of *confiscation* of the landed estates". Is there anything like this in "Europe", O Russian Quessel? There is not, for in Europe the questions of a *bourgeois* revolution are no longer *revolutionary* issues. The "school of the capitalist bourgeoisie" as far as the Russian peasants are concerned is a school of betrayals and treachery on the part of the liberal bourgeoisie (which has been *betraying* the peasants to the landowners and absolutism), and only extreme opportunists are capable of defending such a *school*.

In scoffing at the "union with the proletariat of 100 million peasants", Martov is scoffing at the whole revolution, which has demonstrated such a union *in practice* both in the arena of the uprising (October, November-December, 1905) and in the arena of *both* Dumas (1906-1907).

Martov vacillates helplessly between the liberals (they are *against* "confiscation of the landed estates", *against* "revolutionary actions of the peasantry") and the Social-Democrats, who so far have by no means withdrawn their support of the peasant *uprising* or their *statement* to this effect contained in their *programme*.

---

* "In the whole of Western Europe the peasant masses are considered suitable for alliance to the extent that they come to experience the painful results of the capitalist revolution in agriculture...; for Russia a picture has been drawn of the union with the proletariat of 100 million peasants... who have not yet been through the school of the capitalist bourgeoisie" (*Neue Zeit,* p. 909). That precisely is Russian Quesselism!—*Ed.*

Martov believes that during the years of revolution (1905-07) it was *not* the question of a republic, *but "die Frage der Unabhängigkeit der Volksvertretung"* (S. 918)* that was on the order of the day. Independence *from* whom? From the monarchy which *had carried out Staatsstreiche?*** The Russian opportunists forget at least the connection between the agrarian and the political revolution (is it possible to fight for the confiscation of the landed estates without fighting for a republic?); they forget that the era of *Staatsstreiche, der Aufstände, der Niederwerfungsstreiks,**** by virtue of its *objective* conditions and not of our will, *puts* the question of a republic on the order of the day. The "republic" as a slogan of the day in 1905 = "romanticism"; "independence" (from the monarchy which carries out *Staatsstreiche* and wages *den Bürgerkrieg*)**** = *Realpolitik*, is not that so, O Russian Quessel?

Apropos. Rosa Luxemburg argued with Kautsky as to whether in Germany the moment *had arrived* for *Niederwerfungsstrategie,****** and Kautsky *plainly and bluntly* stated that he considered this moment was unavoidable and imminent but had not yet arrived. But Martov, "deepening (*verballhornend*[1]) Kautsky, denies the applicability of the *Niederwerfungsstrategie* to the year 1905 in Russia! Martov finds that the uprising in December 1905 was evoked "*künstlich*"[2] (*Neue Zeit*, S. 913). *Die Leute, welche so glauben, können nur* künstlich *zur Sozialdemokratie gerechnet werden.* Natürlich *sind sie Nationalliberale.*[3]

Martov ridicules the view that the proletariat is "*die ausschlaggebende Macht*" (S. 909)[4] in the revolution. So far only the liberals have dared (and not always, at that)

---

* "The question of the independence of the people's representative assembly".—*Ed.*
** Coups d'état.—*Ed.*
*** Coups d'état, uprisings, strikes for political overthrow.—*Ed.*
**** Civil war.—*Ed.*
***** Strategy of overthrow.—*Ed.*
[1] Botching.—*Ed.*
[2] Artificially.—*Ed.*
[3] People who think like that can only *artificially* be reckoned as Social-Democrats. *In effect*, they are National-Liberals.—*Ed.*
[4] "The decisive force" (p. 909).—*Ed.*

to deny the indisputable historical fact that in 1905 the Russian proletariat actually played the part of *"der ausschlaggebenden Macht"*. And when a theory which denies the "hegemony of the proletariat in the Russian revolution" gained the upper hand in the five-volume *Social Movement* (edited by Martov and Potresov), Plekhanov *resigned* from the editorial board and declared the *Social Movement* a work of liquidators. Martov now represents not Menshevism as a whole but only that kind of Menshevism which Plekhanov, who has remained a Menshevik, has repudiated and which he has called opportunism.

Martov contraposes the Russian boycott of 1906 to the anarchists' defence of boycott ("political abstention") *"in ganz Westeuropa"*. We have already spoken about the boycott of 1906 (you have already dealt with this). But speaking of boycott in general, why did Martov *forget* the chief application of a boycott in the Russian revolution, the boycott of the Bulygin Duma (the law of August 6, 1905)? Against this boycott were all the liberals, even those of the *Left* (Osvobozhdeniye League), in favour of it were the Bolshevik Social-Democrats. Is it because *this* boycott was victorious that Martov is silent about it? Is it because *this* boycott was the slogan of a *victorious Niederwerfungsstrategie*?

All the Mensheviks (especially in *Nasha Zarya*, *Vozrozhdeniye* and *Zhizn*[424]) seized on Rosa Luxemburg's dispute with Kautsky in order to declare K. Kautsky a "Menshevik". Martov is trying his hardest, by means of *kleinliche und miserable Diplomatie*, to *deepen* the gulf between Rosa Luxemburg and K. Kautsky. These *elende** devices cannot succeed. Revolutionary Social-Democrats may argue about the *timing* of *Niederwerfungsstrategie* in Germany, but not of its *appropriateness* in Russia *in 1905*. It has never occurred to Kautsky to deny *its* appropriateness for Russia in 1905. Only liberals and German and Russian Quessels can deny that!

Well then, will not the upshot of the question of the mass strike in Magdeburg (the acceptance of Rosa's resolution and her withdrawal of the second part) make for *peace* be-

---

* Pitiful.—*Ed.*

tween her and Kautsky? and the *Vorstand*? Or will it not be soon?[425] ((I wrote to Rosa Luxemburg a couple of weeks ago from Stockholm.))

My address is: Vl. Oulianoff, 4, Rue Marie Rose, 4, Paris, XIV.

Sent to Leipzig
First published in 1925

Printed from
the original

193

TO G. L. SHKLOVSKY[426]

Dear Comrade,

Many thanks for the letter and news of the Plekhanovite agitation. All such information, which gives us an accurate idea of the moods prevailing among the Social-Democrats abroad, is now extremely valuable to us. I too am thinking of going on a lecture tour in Switzerland (Geneva, Lausanne, Berne, Zurich[427]). I don't know whether the journey will be worth it.

Regarding a bloc with Plekhanov, I think you are quite right that we should be in favour of it. Since 1909 I have been *wholly* in favour of a *rapprochement* with the Plekhanovites. And even more so now. We can and should build the Party only with the Plekhanovites—the *Vperyod* and *Golos* people should have been given up as hopeless long ago. It is a mistake to think that the Plekhanovites are weak, mere "ciphers" (as is sometimes said), etc. That is an impression existing abroad. I am deeply convinced that nine-tenths of the Menshevik *workers* in Russia are Plekhanovites. The whole history of Menshevism in the revolution vouches for the fact that Plekhanovism is the best (and therefore the most viable) product of the proletarian stream of Mensheviks.

In Copenhagen, Plekhanov and I talked about publishing a popular newspaper. It is essential. (Trotsky has clearly turned to the liquidators, to support of the *Golos* group, to *disruption* of the Party bloc between the Bolsheviks and Plekhanovites.) Plekhanov and I fully agree that nothing can be done with Trotsky. We shall either establish a popular newspaper under the C.O., *or separately* by the group of Bolsheviks. Plekhanov has promised to contribute. Money will be needed—we have exceedingly little. I am hoping for every assistance from you. We are struggling hard to establish a periodical in Russia (à *la Vozrozhdeniye* or *Zhizn*). We can't get the thing going, there is no secretary, no one through whom to arrange things—our people are continually being arrested, worse luck! Yet a periodical is essential.[428]

All the best.

Yours,

Lenin

Written October 14, 1910
Sent from Paris to Berne

First published (abridged) in 1927
Published in full in 1930

Printed from
the original

194

TO MAXIM GORKY

November 14, 1910

Dear A. M.,

There has been no news from you and M. F. for a very long time. I have been looking forward eagerly to news from Capri. What's wrong? Surely you don't keep count of letters as some people are said to keep count of visits.

Everything here is as of old. A host of trivial affairs and all kinds of trouble connected with the struggle of the various "dominions" inside the Party. Brrr!... It must be nice on Capri....

By way of relaxation from the squabbling we have taken up the old plan of publishing *Rabochaya Gazeta*. With difficulty we raised 400 francs. Yesterday No. 1 came out at last. I am sending you a copy together with a leaflet and a subscription list.[429] Members of the Capri-Neapolitan colony who sympathise with such an enterprise (and with the "rapprochement" between the Bolsheviks and Plekhanov) are invited to afford every assistance. *Rabochaya Gazeta* is necessary, but we can't make a go of it with Trotsky, who is intriguing in favour of the liquidators and the otzovists and *Vperyod* supporters. Already in Copenhagen Plekhanov and I protested vigorously against Trotsky's despicable article in *Vorwärts*. And what a disgusting article he has published in *Neue Zeit*, too, on the historical significance of the struggle among the Russian Social-Democrats[430]! And Lunacharsky's in the Belgian *Le Peuple*—have you seen it?

We are setting up a small legal periodical to combat *Nasha Zarya* and *Zhizn*—this, too, with Plekhanov's participation. We hope to issue No. 1 soon.[431]

And so we jog along. Little by little, hard and slowly we are making headway, extricating ourselves from the squabbles.

What is the news with you? Did you write to Stroyev and what reply did you receive? We wrote a first letter to him to "make contact"; he received it and replied that he did not understand who was writing. We wrote again. Not a word. There's a terrible shortage of the right people, and the old ones have dispersed.

Arrangements were on the point of completion in St. Petersburg for putting out a weekly newspaper together with the Duma group (the Mensheviks there fortunately incline not towards the liquidators, but towards Plekhanov), but the matter has been held up again, the devil knows why.[432]

Write how you are getting on. Is your work going well? Has anything come of the journal we talked about in the summer? How are things with Znaniye?[433]

I have the right to be cross with M. F. She promised to write. Nothing has come. She promised to find out about the Paris library on the history of the Russian revolution. Nothing has come. That's bad.

All the best.

Yours,

Lenin

Tria's report will, probably, be published *after all*. The editorial board of the C.O.[434] decided this. But the squabbling on that editorial board—ye gods!...

Sent from Paris to the Isle
  of Capri (Italy)

First published in 1930   Printed from
                                           the original

195

TO MAXIM GORKY

November 22, 1910

Dear A. M.,

I wrote you a few days ago when sending *Rabochaya Gazeta*, and asked what had come of the journal we talked about in the summer and about which you promised to write to me.

I see in *Rech* today a notice about *Sovremennik*, published "with the closest and *exclusive* [that is what is printed! illiterately, but so much the more pretentiously and significantly] participation of Amfiteatrov" and with you as a regular contributor.[435]

What is this? How does it happen? A "large monthly" journal, with sections on "politics, science, history, social life"—why, this is something quite different from symposia aiming at a concentration of the best forces of *belles-lettres*. Such a journal should either have a perfectly definite, serious and consistent *trend*, or it will inevitably disgrace itself and those taking part in it. *Vestnik Yevropy*[436] has a trend—a poor, watery, worthless trend—but one which serves a definite element, certain sections of the bourgeoisie, and which also unites definite circles of the professorate and officialdom, and the so-called intelligentsia from among the "respectable" (or rather, would-be respectable) liberals. *Russkaya Mysl*[437] has a trend, an odious trend, but one which performs a very good service for the counter-revolutionary liberal bourgeoisie. *Russkoye Bogatstvo*[438] has a trend—a Narodnik, Narodnik-Cadet trend—but one which has kept its line for scores of years, and which serves definite sections of the population. *Sovremenny Mir*[439] has a trend—often Menshevik-Cadet trend (at present with a leaning towards pro-Party Menshevism)—but a trend. A journal without a trend is an absurdity, a ridiculous, scandalous and harmful thing. And what sort of trend can there be with the "exclusive participation" of Amfiteatrov? One cannot expect G. Lopatin to provide a trend, and if the talk (said also to have got into the newspapers) is true about Kachorovsky's participation, then that is a "trend", but a trend of the blockheads, a S.R. trend.

During our talk in the summer when I told you that I had all but written you a disappointed letter about *Confessions* but did not send it because of the split with the Machists which had begun at that time, you replied: "*it's a pity* you did not send it". Then you went on to reproach me for not going to the Capri school,[440] and you said that, if matters had taken a different course, the breakaway of the Machists and otzovists might have cost you less nervous strain, less waste of energy. Recalling these talks, I have now decided to write to you without putting it off and without waiting for any verification, while the impression the news has made is still fresh.

I think that a political and economic monthly with the exclusive participation of Amfiteatrov is something many times worse than a special Machist-otzovist faction. What was and still is bad about this faction is that the *ideological* trend deviated and still deviates from Marxism, from Social-Democracy, without, however, going so far as a break with Marxism, and only creating confusion.

Amfiteatrov's journal (his *Krasnoye Znamya*[441] did well to die when it did!) is a political act, a political enterprise in which there is not even a realisation that a general "leftism" is not enough for a policy, that after 1905 to talk seriously about politics without making clear one's attitude towards Marxism and Social-Democracy is out of the question, impossible, inconceivable.

Things are turning out bad. It's saddening.

Yours,
Lenin

To M.F.—*salut et fraternité.*

Sent from Paris to the Isle
    of Capri (Italy)
First published in 1924   Printed from
                                            the original

196

TO N. G. POLETAYEV[442]

I have received your two letters, which surprised me. What could be easier, it would seem, than to write and tell us simply and clearly what is the matter? We are still in the dark. It should not be difficult to find a person to write sensibly, clearly and frankly at least once a week.

Your attempt to detach the liquidators from liquidationism is unfortunate to a degree. We have never approved this distinction. Only sophists draw it. We earnestly request you not to believe the sophists and not to make this distinction. One can reconcile oneself to anything but the liquidators, and if you do not want the work to be ruined, keep them out of it.

With great difficulty we obtained from a publisher here a further thousand rubles and will send them to you tomorrow. If this publisher approaches you again with questions, advice, conditions, and so on—don't answer at all, or answer as we once advised.

Concerning the little magazine, we have had nothing from anyone.

So we repeat once more our insistent request: we have obtained for you what you require, see that you do not let us down, keep out the liquidators (there is no such thing as liquidationism without liquidators. And who could have played such a cruel joke on you by assuring you of a distinction between liquidationism and the liquidators?) and, further, see to it that we get a sensible, clear, frank and detailed letter every week. Surely these two requests are not difficult, not too much; we cannot manage without it.

Yours....

Written December 7, 1910
Sent from Paris to
St. Petersburg

First published in 1933

Printed from
the typewritten copy found
in police record

1911

197

TO MAXIM GORKY

January 3, 1911

Dear A. M.,

I have long been intending to reply to your letter but intensification of the squabbling* here (a hundred thousand devils take it!) distracted me.

But I should like to have a chat with you.

First of all, before I forget: Tria has been arrested together with Jordania and Ramishvili. It is reported as being true. A pity, for he is a good chap. A revolutionary.

Regarding *Sovremennik*. In *Rech* today I read the contents of the first issue and I am cursing and swearing. Vodovozov on Muromtsev ... Kolosov on Mikhailovsky, Lopatin "Not ours", etc. You can't help swearing. And here are you, teasing as it were: "realism, democracy, activity".

Do you think these are good words? They are *bad* words, used by all the bourgeois tricksters in the world, from the Cadets and S.R.s in our country to Briand or Millerand here, Lloyd George in Britain, etc. The words are bad, turgid, and they carry a S.R.-Cadet message. It's not good.

As regards Tolstoy, I fully share your opinion that hypocrites and rogues will make a saint of him. Plekhanov, too, was infuriated by all the lying and sycophancy around Tolstoy, and in here we see eye to eye. He criticises *Nasha Zarya* for it in the C.O. (the next issue),[443] and I am doing so in *Mysl*** (No. 1 arrived today. Congratulate us on *our own* little journal in Moscow, a Marxist one. This has been a happy day for us). *Zvezda* No. 1 (it appeared on December

---

* That rascal Trotsky is uniting the Golosists and Vperyodists against us. It is war!

** See "Heroes of 'Reservation'" (present edition, Vol. 16).—*Ed.*

16 in St. Petersburg) also contains a good article by Plekhanov with a *trivial* comment, for which we have already
scolded the *editors*. It was probably concocted by that ninny
Yordansky, together with Bonch! But how come *Sovremennik* to combat the "legend about Tolstoy and his religion". Is it Vodovozov with Lopatin? You must be joking.

That they have started hitting out at the students is,
in my opinion, comforting, but Tolstoy must not be allowed
to get away with either "passivism" or anarchism or Narodism or religion.

As regards quixotism in the international policy of Social-Democracy, I think, you are wrong. It is the revisionists who have long been asserting that colonial policy is
progressive, that it implants capitalism and that therefore
it is senseless to "accuse it of greed and cruelty", for "without
these qualities" capitalism is "hamstrung".

It would be quixotism and whining if Social-Democrats
were to tell the workers that there could be salvation somewhere apart from the development of capitalism, not
through the development of capitalism. But we do not say
this. We say: capital devours you, will devour the Per-
sians, will devour everyone and go on devouring until you
overthrow it. That is the truth. And we do not forget to
add: except through the growth of capitalism there is no
guarantee of victory over it.

Marxists do not defend a single reactionary *measure*,
such as banning trusts, restricting trade, etc. But *to each
his own*. Let Khomyakov and Co. build railways across
Persia, let them send Lyakhovs,[444] but the job of the Marxists is to *expose* them to the workers. If it devours, say the
Marxists, if it strangles, fight back.

Resistance to colonial policy and international plunder
by means of organising the proletariat, *by means* of defending freedom for the proletarian struggle, *does not retard*
the development of capitalism but *accelerates* it, forcing
it to resort to more civilised, technically higher methods
of capitalism. There is capitalism and capitalism. There
is Black-Hundred-Octobrist[445] capitalism and *Narodnik*
("realistic, democratic", full of "activity") capitalism.
The more we *expose* capitalism before the workers for its
"greed and cruelty", the more difficult is it for capitalism

of the first order to persist, the more surely is it bound to pass into capitalism of the second order. And this just suits us, this just suits the proletariat.

You think I have fallen into a contradiction? In the beginning of the letter I considered the words "realism, democracy, activity" bad words, and now I find them good? There is no contradiction here; what is bad for the proletariat is good for the bourgeois.

The Germans have an exemplary journal of the opportunists: *Sozialistische Monatshefte*. There gentlemen like Schippel and Bernstein have long been attacking the international policy of the revolutionary Social-Democrats by raising an outcry that this policy resembles the "lamentations of compassionate" people. That, brother, is a trick of opportunist swindlers. Ask for this journal to be sent to you from Naples and have their articles translated if you are interested in international politics. You probably have such opportunists in Italy too, only there are no Marxists in Italy, that's what makes her so nasty.

The international proletariat is pressing capitalism in two ways: by converting Octobrist capitalism into democratic capitalism and, because it drives Octobrist capitalism away *from itself*, by *transplanting* this capitalism to the savages. This, however, enlarges the basis of capitalism and brings its death nearer. There is practically no Octobrist capitalism left in Western Europe; practically all capitalism is democratic. Octobrist capitalism has gone from Britain and France to Russia and Asia. The Russian revolution and the revolutions in Asia=the struggle for ousting Octobrist capitalism and replacing it by democratic capitalism. And democratic capitalism=the last of its kind. It has no next stage to go on to. The next stage is its death.

What do you think of *Zvezda* and *Mysl*? The former is dull, in my opinion. But the latter is *all* ours and I am delighted with it. I'm afraid they'll soon close it down, though.

I was wondering whether you could arrange for my book on the agrarian question to go to Znaniye. Talk it over with Pyatnitsky. I just can't find a publisher, not for love or money.[446]

Reading your postscript: "my hands are shaking and freezing" makes me indignant. What wretched houses you have on Capri! It's a disgrace, really! Even we here have central heating; and your "hands are freezing". You must revolt.

All the very best.

Yours,
Lenin

I have received from Bologna an invitation to come to the school there (20 workers). I have turned it down.[447] I don't want to have anything to do with the Vperyodists. We're trying again to get the workers to come here.

Sent from Paris to the Isle
    of Capri (Italy)
First published in 1924

Printed from
the original

198
TO A. RYKOV

Saturday, February 25, 1911

Dear Vlasov,

I have just received your letter and I hasten to reply at once without waiting for Grigory, who forwarded Samovarov's letter on to you today.

Nadya is writing today to Lyubich. What a pity you didn't think of it before. Now you must write to him not about preparing to leave, but about immediate departure. Write to him again, insisting emphatically on immediate departure, otherwise the enemy will have four (the Bundist + the Lett + two Mensheviks) and we'll have no more than that (three, of whom one is doubtful, + one Pole).

Your letter concerning the declaration grieves me very much, for I see from it how inadequate our agreement still is and hence (to my *extreme regret*) how "precarious" it is.

Among the changes proposed by you, there are some to which no objections can be made. These include: dealing with the question of affairs abroad in a special resolution; adding to the declaration a special paragraph on the significance of the Duma and on the fact that those not assisting in the elections to the Fourth Duma are traitors; *separating* the question of renewing the primary Party cells (although I do not understand why it should be separated and where it should be put. It must be dealt with, however! But where?).

But you propose many more changes that are unacceptable and harmful.

("To recognise that the conference is urgent"? Why try to be cunning? You don't believe in it yourself! To breed hypocrisy and self-deception—there is nothing more harmful than that just now!)

"To express satisfaction that otzovism-ultimatumism has in effect disappeared from the political horizon"....

That is *untrue*. I have seen workers who support *Vperyod*, and *even* Yevgeny in his speeches refutes this untruth.

"To welcome the decision of the *Vperyod* group to take part in the elections"....

There has been *no* such decision so far. And if it does appear tomorrow, it is scandalous "to welcome" the splitters for doing their *duty* and to keep silent about the expro funds.[448]

You write: "I know of no otzovist or ultimatumist statements of *Vperyod after* the plenum"....

You ought to know better. Just look: (1) The leaflet of the *Vperyod* group after the plenum: sheer abuse of the central bodies—not a word about renouncing the otzovist-ultimatumist platform. (2) The symposium No. 1[449]—ditto. *Not a single* guiding article on the *Duma* and Duma activities. (3) Lunacharsky in *Le Peuple* (it is quoted in the C.O.—Lunacharsky was officially delegated by the *Vperyod group* to the Copenhagen Congress). (4) The leaflet of the Geneva *Vperyod* group (it is quoted in part in *Golos S.-D.*), which lines up with Lunacharsky.

Vperyod, after the plenum, was in duty *bound* to issue a new platform, since the *old one* (it came out on December 27, 1909, i.e., *on the eve* of the plenum) is an *otzovist-ultimatumist* platform. *Vperyod* has *not* done this!

Your basic mistake is that you believe *words* and close your eyes to *deeds*. A lot of "good words" have been told you by various people like Domov or Alexinsky and I don't know who else, and you believe them. You write: *Vperyod* "is on the eve of dissolution or is a possible ally of ours", it "is freeing itself from the otzovist-ultimatumist platform".

This is *untrue*. They are the lying words of swindlers who are ready to promise anything so long as they can *disguise* the facts, namely, their own special school, their 85,000 rubles of expro money.

What if Domov does move away from *Vperyod*—Domov is a high school teacher, a philistine, an ignorant old woman, and not a politician. What if Alexinsky has "quarrelled" with Bogdanov and Co.—now, *after returning* from

Bologna, he has quite made it up again and yesterday delivered a lecture *on behalf of* the *Vperyod* group!

You put your trust in *words* and leave *yourself* helpless *in deeds*—which means repeating the *fatal* error of the plenum, an error which has weakened the Party *for a year* at least. If you now, a year after the idiotic conciliatory errors of the plenum, *repeat* these errors, you will completely ruin all prospects of "unity". I say this with the fullest conviction, for I know it thoroughly from experience. Leave it to Samovarov to shout about my having wrecked "unity" (this is the catch-phrase of Trotsky and Yonov!). Samovarov *has* to shout this nonsense (which he *dares not* utter in print and which I have *publicly* dealt with and refuted in No. 2 of *Diskussionny Listok**), for he is *ashamed* to admit the mistake the conciliators made at the plenum. Their mistake was that they almost ruined the prospect of unity with the *pro-Party* Mensheviks, by believing the *words* of the anti-Party Golosists and allowing them to *consolidate themselves in deeds.*

Mind you don't repeat this mistake!

The Vperyodists are very strong. They have a school=a conference=agents. We (and the C.C.) have *not*. They have money—some 80,000 rubles. You think they will give it to you? Are you really so naïve?

And if not, *how* can you regard as "allies" *factionalists* who are keeping a factional fund *against* you!

It is the height of naïveté to write: "I do not want to make it difficult for the *Vperyod* splinter elements to achieve a rapprochement."

They have achieved a rapprochement with the liquidators, they have organised a school against you, they are pulling the wool over your eyes, saying: we are all right, we are not otzovists, and you believe their words *and do not combat their deeds.* It's the limit, really!

You write: "I should not like to have the Vperyodists expelled from the general Party (not factional) organisation abroad."

Either the one or the other: either you *encourage* a special

---

* The reference is to "Notes of a Publicist" (see present edition, Vol. 16).—*Ed.*

faction and let it *keep* its money, in which case we shall
publish our statement to the C.C. (demanding a committee
of enquiry) and say: let the Vperyodists help *such* a C.C.,
we shall not do so.

Or you *condemn* the factionalism of the Vperyodists,
in which case you have to be consistent. *By condemning* in
words only, you make yourself *ridiculous.*

In that case it must be said: *so long as* the Vperyodists
(1) do not publish a *new* platform, (2) do not make pro-
Party statements, (3) do not dissolve their *factional* school,
(4) do not hand over their *factional* funds to the Party—they
remain an anti-Party faction.

If you do not say *this*, you will lose our co-operation *without* gaining that of the Vperyodists. Is that good policy?

As for the splinter elements (*future ones!*), do not worry
about that. If we are *strong*, they will all come to us. If we
are weak, if we believe in words, we shall be laughed at,
that's all. To find the right form is not so difficult: for example, after condemning the Vperyod *faction*, to say that *part*
of the Vperyodist *workers* stand for elections, for legal opportunities, for the Party principle, and that you call on
such workers, such Vperyodists, to come *away from* the
faction and *to* the Party, etc., etc.

In the resolution on unity abroad it should be clearly
specified *who* the disrupters are: the *Golosists* and *Vperyodists must* be named, and it must be explained wherein lies
their "disruption and anti-Partyism": *not* in ideas (argue
and write about this in *Diskussionny Listok*, etc.) *but* in
the special school, in the special school funds, in the special
organ (*Golos*), in the special collections for *Golos*, and in
the special factional groups (which maintain contacts with
Russia *against* the C.C.).

If the Golosists and Vperyodists are not precisely and
clearly named, the whole resolution=0. In that case you
will *compel* us to come out against this *playing* at unity.

If you name them precisely and say *clearly* what their
factionalism is, you will immediately and definitely *win
over the majority* of our people abroad (the Bolsheviks+
the Plekhanovites+pro-Party workers+the bulk of the
groups in the "provinces" and in America, where there are
no *leaders* of Golosism).

If the C.C.'s "struggle" against *factions* consists in its *paying court* to the *anti-Party* factions of *Golos* and *Vperyod*, in hampering *our* work (in a Party spirit) by multi-storey formalities (the Pole, a committee, a collegium of people who are not acquainted with the matter, "invitation" of Vperyodists, quarrel with Alexinsky, etc., etc.), then you can *count us out*.

We have just received a letter from St. Petersburg. Samovarov has proposed to the Social-Democratic Duma group that it issue an electoral platform!

This—to a majority of Mensheviks! (and not a word to us). If Samovarov wants to carry on *in this fashion*, I promise you that I shall begin a series of leaflets *directly* against Samovarov.

If an agreement among us is possible, the *Bolsheviks* must rally into a *trend* and work *harmoniously* (on the basis of the agreement), and not carry on intrigues, nor go over to the Mensheviks.

Write and let me know your opinion as soon as possible.

All the best.

Yours,

Lenin

P.S. Have you seen Nikitich? Has he tried to sell the story of *Vperyod*'s peace-loving nature? He's a great hand at making promises and throwing dust in people's eyes.

Sent from Paris to Berlin

First published in 1931

Printed from
the original

199

TO MAXIM GORKY

May 27, 1911

Dear A. M.,

A few days ago I received a letter from Poletayev. He writes, inter alia: "We have received a letter from Gorky. He is proposing that N. I. should come abroad to work out a plan for unity around some organ, and adds that he has spoken to you about this and to the Menshevik M" (Martov, I assume).

Poletayev adds that N. I. is hardly suitable for this plan and that if somebody must come, it should be somebody else. It is hardly likely that Pokrovsky will make the journey.

Reading this in Poletayev's letter frightened me—no, really.

Our uniting with Mensheviks like Martov is *absolutely* hopeless, as I told you here. If we start arranging a meeting for such a hopeless plan—the result will be nothing but a disgrace (personally I would not go even to a meeting with Martov).

Judging from Poletayev's letter, the participation of the Duma group is planned. Is this necessary? If it is a question of a journal, then the Duma group has nothing to do with it. If it is a question of a newspaper, it should be borne in mind that we have had *plenty* of discord as it is with *Zvezda*: they have no line, they are afraid of going with us, afraid of going with the liquidators, they play hot and cold, they give themselves airs, they vacillate.

Besides, a union of the Plekhanovites+our people+the Duma group threatens to give Plekhanov a *preponderance*, for Mensheviks predominate in the Duma group. Is it desirable and reasonable to give Plekhanov a preponderance?

I *very much* fear that Yordansky is unsuitable for such plans (for he has "*his*" own journal and he will either raise obstacles or try to impose "his" journal, leaving it as *his*, that is, a semi-liberal organ).

To avoid disappointments and hopeless squabbles, I think we should be very careful as regards "unity". Upon my word, we should be not uniting now, but dissociating! If a publisher can be found for a journal or a newspaper, *you* should conclude an agreement with him *off your own bat* (or take money from him without an agreement, if possible), but the arrangement of a meeting will only make a mess. Truly, the result will be a mess.

I am writing to you because I do not want to see *you* of all people wasting your time, nervous energy, etc , on a mess. I *know* from my own bitter experience of 1908-11 that it is impossible to "unite" *now*. In our *Mysl*, for example, Plekhanov more than once behaved temperamentally—he was dissatisfied, for example, with my article on strikes and on Potresov,* saying that I was abusing "him"! We managed to smooth things over and *for the time being* we can and must work with Plekhanov, but *formal* unions and meetings are premature and could spoil everything.

Don't hurry with the meeting!

It is said positively among us that there exists a government circular of Stolypin's for closing down *all* Social-Democratic publications. It sounds like the truth Before the Fourth Duma they will probably put the screw on ten times tighter.

Legal opportunities will evidently diminish in the immediate future. We must push on with illegal work.

M. F. wrote that you have completely withdrawn from Znaniye. That means a complete break with Pyatnitsky and my last letter came too late?

All the best.

Yours,

Lenin

P. S. *Sovremennaya Zhizn*[450] in Baku has also been raided and suppressed!

Sent from Paris to the Isle
    of Capri (Italy)
First published in 1924

Printed from
the original

---

* "Strike Statistics in Russia", "Those Who Would Liquidate Us" (see present edition, Vol. 16, and Vol. 17).—*Ed*

200

TO ANTONÍN NĚMEC[451]

Paris, November 1, 1911

Dear Comrade,

You will be doing me a great service if you can help me with advice and action in the following matter. A number of organisations of our Party intend to call a conference (abroad—of course). The number of members of the conference will be about 20-25. Is there a possibility of organising this conference in Prague (to last about a week)?[452]

The most important thing for us is the possibility of organising it *in extreme secrecy*. No person, no organisation, should know about it. (It is a *Social-Democratic* conference, hence legal according to European laws, but the majority of the delegates *do not have passports* and cannot use their own names.)

I earnestly beg you, dear comrade, if it is at all possible, to help us and tell me as quickly as possible the address of a comrade in Prague who (in the event of an affirmative reply) could make all the practical arrangements. It would be best if this comrade understood Russian—if this is impossible we can also reach agreement with him in German.

I hope, dear comrade, that you will pardon me for troubling you with this request. I send you my thanks in anticipation.

With Party greetings. *N. Lenin*

My address is:
Vl. Oulianoff
4, Rue Marie Rose, 4,
Paris, XIV.

Sent to Prague
First published in 1930
in a Russian translation

Printed from
the original
German text

NOTES

[1] *Axelrod, Pavel Borisovich* (1850-1928)—in the seventies a Narodnik, later a Marxist. In 1883 took part in founding the Emancipation of Labour group. From 1900 a member of the editorial board of *Iskra* and *Zarya*. After the Second Congress of the R.S.D.L.P. (1903), a Menshevik leader.

During the period of reaction (1907-10) one of the leading liquidators. Adopted a hostile attitude towards the October Socialist Revolution. p. 20

[2] This footnote was given by Lenin in view of the fact that the names of towns were ciphered in the letter for purposes of secrecy. p. 20

[3] This refers to the preparations for publishing abroad a non-periodical Miscellany entitled *Rabotnik*. It was published in 1896-99 by the Union of Russian Social-Democrats Abroad and edited by the Emancipation of Labour group. The publication was sponsored by Lenin. In May 1895, during his stay in Switzerland, Lenin made arrangements for its publication with G. V. Plekhanov, P. B. Axelrod and other members of the Emancipation of Labour group. On his return to Russia in September 1895 Lenin developed extensive activities aimed at supplying articles and correspondence from Russia for the Miscellany and organising financial support for the publication. During his trips to Vilna, Moscow and Orekhovo-Zuyevo Lenin made arrangements with the local Social-Democrats for assistance to be rendered this publication.

Altogether 6 issues of *Rabotnik* in three volumes and 10 issues of *Listok Rabotnika* were published. p. 20

[4] This refers to the arrests made among the Social-Democrats in Moscow and Moscow Gubernia. p. 20

[5] *Vorwärts*—a daily, central organ of the German Social-Democratic Party, published in Berlin from 1891. In the late nineties, after the death of Engels, the paper was controlled by the Party's Right wing and systematically published articles of the opportunists. *Vorwärts* tendentiously reported the struggle against opportunism and revisionism within the R.S.D.L.P. and supported the Economists, and later, after the split in the Party, the Mensheviks. p. 21

[6] This refers to the report of the Breslau Congress of the German Social-Democratic Party held in 1895. The correspondence from abroad was sent in the binding of a book.   p. 23

[7] This refers to the illegal printing-press of the young Narodnaya Volya group, organised in January 1895. Lenin negotiated with this group for the purpose of using the press for the publication of literature for the workers. In November 1895 Lenin's pamphlet *Explanation of the Law on Fines Imposed on Factory Workers* (see present edition, Vol. 2) was handed over to this group for printing. This is the fourth thing ("one of ours") which Lenin refers to.   p. 23

[8] This refers to *Rabocheye Dyelo* (Workers' Cause), which was being prepared by the St. Petersburg League of Struggle for the Emancipation of the Working Class. The first number of this newspaper was compiled and edited by Lenin, who also wrote all the main articles: the editorial "To the Russian Workers", "What Are Our Ministers Thinking About? ", "Frederick Engels" (see present edition, Vol. 2). In addition the newspaper contained articles by other members of the St. Petersburg League of Struggle, such as G. M. Krzhizhanovsky, A. A. Vaneyev, P. K. Zaporozhets, L. Martov (Y. O. Tsederbaum) and M. A. Silvin.

In his book *What Is To be Done?* Lenin wrote: "This issue was ready to go to press when it was seized by the gendarmes, on the night of December 8, 1895, in a raid on the house of one of the members of the group, Anatoly Alexeyevich Vaneyev, so that the first edition of *Rabocheye Dyelo* was not destined to see the light of day" (see present edition, Vol. 5, p. 376).   p. 23

[9] While in exile Lenin sent most of his letters to P. B. Axelrod concealed in the inside of book-covers. Passing through several hands, these letters eventually found their way abroad to A. I. Ulyanova-Yelizarova, Lenin's sister, who lived in Berlin at the time, and she forwarded them on to Axelrod. This particular letter was copied out by her and inserted in the middle of the text of her own letter to Axelrod.   p. 24

[10] Meaning Anna Ilyinichna Ulyanova-Yelizarova, Lenin's sister.   p. 24

[11] This refers to the journal *Novoye Slovo* in which two articles of Lenin's were published in 1897: "A Characterisation of Economic Romanticism" and "About a Certain Newspaper Article" (see Vol. 2 of this edition).

Novoye Slovo (New Word)—a scientific, literary and political monthly published in St. Petersburg from 1894 by the liberal Narodniks, and from the spring of 1897 by the "legal Marxists". The journal was closed down by the government in December 1897.   p. 24

[12] *Potresov, Alexander Nikolayevich* (1869-1934)—joined the Marxists in the nineties of the 19th century. For participating in the St. Petersburg League of Struggle for the Emancipation of the Working Class, was exiled. In 1900 went abroad, where he took part in founding *Iskra* and *Zarya*. After the Second Congress of the R.S.D.L.P. (1903) joined the Mensheviks. During the years of reaction (1907-10) was an ideologist of liquidationism; played a leading role in the Menshevik publications *Vozrozhdeniye*, *Nasha Zarya*, and others.

After the October Revolution he emigrated.   p. 25

[13] *Archiv für soziale Gesetzgebung und Statistik* (Archive of Social Legislation and Statistics)—a journal, published from 1888 to 1933 in Berlin—Thüringen—Leipzig.

Lenin here refers to Vol. XII of this journal published in 1898 and containing an article by an anonymous author (probably P. B. Struve) entitled "New Factory Legislation in Russia". p. 25

[14] *Struve, Pyotr Bernhardovich* (1870-1944)—a bourgeois economist and publicist. In the nineties a leading spokesman of "legal Marxism", "supplemented" and criticised the economic and philosophical theories of Marx, and tried to adapt Marxism and the working-class movement to the interests of the bourgeoisie; contributor to and editor of the journals *Novoye Slovo*, *Nachalo* and *Zhizn*. Struve was one of the theoreticians and organisers of the liberal-monarchist Osvobozhdeniye League (1903-05). With the formation of the Cadet Party in 1905—a member of its Central Committee. After the October Revolution—a white émigré. p. 25

[15] *Disciples*—followers of Marx and Engels. This term was used in the nineties as a legal designation for Marxists.   p. 25

[16] *Russkoye Bogatstvo* (Russian Wealth)—a monthly journal published from 1876 to 1918 in St. Petersburg. In the early nineties it passed into the hands of the liberal Narodniks headed by N. K. Mikhailovsky. The journal advocated a conciliatory attitude towards the tsarist government and conducted a bitter fight against Marxism and the Russian Marxists. In 1906 it became the organ of the semi-Cadet Trudovik Popular Socialist Party. p. 25

[17] *Bulgakov, Sergei Nikolayevich* (1871-1944)—bourgeois economist and idealist philosopher. In the nineties a "legal Marxist". Advocated a revision of Marx's doctrine on the agrarian question. After the Revolution of 1905-07 joined the Cadets, preached philosophical mysticism, participated in the counter revolutionary miscellany *Vekhi*.

In 1922 he was deported for counter-revolutionary activities.
                                                                   p. 26

[18] Lenin refers to the polemic between Bulgakov and Struve over the book *Wirtschaft und Recht nach der materialistischen Geschichtsauffassung* by the German Kantian Stammler.   p. 26

[19] Lenin refers to Plekhanov's articles "Bernstein and Materialism" in *Die Neue Zeit* No. 44 (1897-98. Band II) and "Conrad Schmidt against Marx and Engels" in the same journal, issue No. 5 (1898-99. Band I).

Die Neue Zeit—a theoretical journal of the German Social-Democratic Party, published in Stuttgart from 1883 to 1923. Up to October 1917 it was edited by K. Kautsky, and after him by Heinrich Cunow. p. 26

[20] The reference is to Plekhanov's article "The Sixtieth Anniversary of Hegel's Death" in the journal *Die Neue Zeit* Nos. 7, 8, 9 (1891-92. Band I).

Lenin's reference to "the 30th anniversary" is obviously a slip of the pen. p. 26

[21] The reference is to Axelrod's articles "Die historische Berechtigung der russischen Sozialdemokratie" (later issued in Russia as a separate pamphlet under the title *The Historical Position and the Mutual Relations between the Liberal and Socialist Democracy in Russia*), published in the journal *Die Neue Zeit* No. 30 and No. 31 (1897-98. Band II).

Lenin's comments on Axelrod's articles will be found on pp. 29-31 of this volume. p. 26

[22] The reference is to *Economism*, an opportunist trend in Russian Social-Democracy at the end of the nineteenth and beginning of the twentieth centuries. The Economists held that the political struggle against tsarism was mainly the business of the liberal bourgeoisie, while the workers were to confine themselves to an economic struggle for better working conditions, higher wages, etc. They denied the leading role of the party of the working class and the significance of revolutionary theory in the labour movement, and maintained that that movement could only develop spontaneously. Lenin gave a devastating criticism of Economism in his book *What Is To Be Done?* p. 26

[23] *Narodism*—a petty-bourgeois trend in the Russian revolutionary movement, which arose between the 1860s and 1870s. The Narodniks were out to abolish the autocracy and hand over the landowners' land to the peasantry. At the same time they denied the development of capitalist relations in Russia to be a natural tendency, and accordingly regarded the peasantry, and not the proletariat, as the main revolutionary force, and the village commune as the embryo of socialism. With the object of rousing the peasants to the struggle against the autocracy the Narodniks went into the country, "among the people", but gained no support there.

In the eighties and nineties the Narodniks took a conciliatory stand towards tsarism, expressed the interests of the kulaks, and waged a bitter fight against Marxism.

p. 27

[24] Lenin refers to the heated disputes between the Marxists and the Narodniks that raged among the exiles. It was of one such clash in Orlov, Vyatka Gubernia, that Potresov wrote to Lenin about.   p. 27

[25] *Nachalo* (The Beginning)—a scientific literary and political monthly, organ of the "legal Marxists", published in St. Petersburg in the early months of 1899 under the editorship of P. B. Struve, M. I. Tugan-Baranovsky and others. G. V. Plekhanov, V. I. Zasulich and others contributed to it. Lenin wrote a number of book reviews for the journal (see present edition, Vol. 4, pp. 65-73 and 94-103) which also published the first six paragraphs of Chapter III of his book *The Development of Capitalism in Russia* (see Vol. 3 of this edition).   p. 28

[26] The reference is to Lenin's article "The Heritage We Renounce" (see Vol. 2, pp. 491-534, of this edition).
    Skaldin (*Yelenev, Fyodor Pavlovich*) (1828-1902)—a Russian publicist and author; in the sixties of the 19th century a spokesman of bourgeois liberalism, contributed to the journal *Otechestvenniye Zapiski*. Subsequently Skaldin sided with the extreme reactionaries.   p. 28

[27] *Chernyshevsky, Nikolai Gavrilovich* (1828-1889)—great Russian revolutionary democrat, materialist philosopher, author and literary critic, leader of the revolutionary-democratic movement of the sixties in Russia.   p. 28

[28] *Soziale Praxis*—a German monthly, published from 1895 to 1910, after which it came out under another name.   p. 31

[29] Meaning the journal *Nachalo* (see Note 25).   p. 32

[30] *Mir Bozhy* (God's World)—a monthly literary and popular-science journal of a liberal trend, published in St. Petersburg from 1892 to 1906. From 1906 to 1918 it was issued under the name of *Sovremenny Mir* (The Contemporary World).   p. 33

[31] *Nauchnoye Obozreniye* (Scientific Review)—a journal, published in St. Petersburg from 1894 to 1903; accepted contributions from publicists and scientists of all schools and trends; widely used by liberals and "legal Marxists". The journal published occasional articles by Marxists.   p. 33

[32] See Note 11.   p. 33

[33] *Tugan-Baranovsky, Mikhail Ivanovich* (1865-1919)—Russian bourgeois economist, in the nineties a prominent spokesman of "legal Marxism", contributed to the journals *Novoye Slovo, Nachalo*, and others.   p. 34

[34] This refers to Anna Ilyinichna Ulyanova-Yelizarova.   p. 34

[35] This refers to a miscellany of Lenin's, *Economic Studies and Essays*, published in October 1898 (the cover and title-page bore the date 1899).   p. 34

[36] *Frankfurter Zeitung*—a daily newspaper, mouthpiece of the German merchants of Change, published in Frankfurt am Main from 1856 to 1943.   p. 35

[37] *Zhizn* (Life)—a literary, scientific and political journal published in St. Petersburg from 1897 to 1901.

Publication was resumed abroad in April 1902 by the *Zhizn* Social-Democratic group (V. D. Bonch-Bruyevich, V. A. Posse, V. M. Velichkina and others); six issues of the journal, twelve of *Listok Zhizni* and several volumes of the *Zhizn Library* series were published.

The group ceased to exist in December 1902 and the publishing-house was liquidated.   p. 35

[38] Apparently this refers to Plekhanov, with whom Lenin had talks in 1895 during his visit to Switzerland.   p. 35

[39] This refers to the split that took place at the First Conference of the Union of Russian Social-Democrats Abroad held in Zurich (Switzerland) in November 1898.

The *Union of Russian Social-Democrats Abroad* was founded in Geneva in 1894 on the initiative of the Emancipation of Labour group (see Note 58). It had its own press where it printed revolutionary literature and published the non-periodic miscellany *Rabotnik*. At first the Emancipation of Labour group controlled the Union and edited its publications. Eventually control passed to the opportunist elements—the Economists or the so-called "young" group. At the First Conference of the Union held in November 1898 the Emancipation of Labour group announced their refusal to edit the Union publications. The Group finally broke with the Union and left its ranks in April 1900 at the Second Conference of the Union, when the Emancipation of Labour group and its supporters walked out and established their own *Sotsial-Demokrat* organisation.

At the Second Congress of the R.S.D.L.P. held in 1903 the Union's representatives took an extremely opportunist stand and walked out after the Congress declared the League of Russian Revolutionary Social-Democracy Abroad to be the only organisation of the Party abroad. The Second Congress declared the Union dissolved.   p. 36

[40] *Mikhailovsky, Nikolai Konstantinovich* (1842-1904)—a prominent theoretician of liberal Narodism, publicist and literary critic; a representative of the subjective school in sociology; editor of the journals *Otechestvenniye Zapiski* and *Russkoye*

Bogatstvo. Lenin criticised Mikhailovsky's views in his book *What the "Friends of the People" Are and How They Fight the Social-Democrats* (see Vol. 1 of this edition) and other writings.

p. 36

[41] Lenin refers to the miscellany *Material for a Characterisation of Our Economic Development* containing his article (over the pen-name K. Tulin) "The Economic Content of Narodism and the Criticism of It in Mr. Struve's Book. (The Reflection of Marxism in Bourgeois Literature)" directed against legal Marxism (see Vol. 1 of this edition). p. 37

[42] This refers to *Die Neue Zeit* (see Note 19). p. 37

[43] *Gvozdyov (Zimmerman, Roman Emilievich)* (1866-1900)—author, whose short stories and economic articles were published in *Russkoye Bogatstvo*, *Zhizn* and *Nauchnoye Obozreniye*. p. 37

[44] *(N.—on)—Danielson, Nikolai Frantsevich* (1844-1918)—Russian writer and economist, an ideologue of liberal Narodism of the eighties and nineties; in his political activities he reflected the evolution of the Narodniks away from revolutionary action against tsarism towards a conciliatory attitude to it. Completed the translation of Marx's *Capital* into Russian, which was begun by G. A. Lopatin. While working on this translation he carried on a correspondence with Marx and Engels in which he touched on the problems of Russia's economic development. Danielson, however, failed to grasp the essence of Marxism and subsequently came out against it.

Lenin here refers to Danielson's book *Sketches of Our Post-Reform Social Economy* in which its author elaborates Narodnik views on the development of post-reform national economy in Russia. The German edition appeared in 1899 in Munich. The French edition was published in 1902. p. 38

[45] *Russkiye Vedomosti* (Russian Recorder)—a newspaper published in Moscow from 1863 onwards; it expressed the views of the moderate liberal intelligentsia. In 1905 it became the organ of the Right wing of the bourgeois Cadet Party. It was closed down in 1918 together with other counter-revolutionary newspapers.

p. 38

[46] Lenin refers to Plekhanov's article "Konrad Schmidt gegen Karl Marx und Friedrich Engels" published in *Die Neue Zeit* No. 5 for 1898-99. p. 40

[47] Nezhdanov's article mentioned here is entitled "Markets under Capitalist Production (Apropos of Ratner's, Ilyin's and Struve's Articles)". Lenin replied to this in his article "Reply to Mr. P. Nezhdanov" (see Vol. 4 of this edition). p. 41

[48] This refers to the review of A. Bogdanov's book *Fundamentals of the Historic View on Nature*, which came out in St. Petersburg in 1899. The first book by the same author *A Short Course of Economic Science* was reviewed by Lenin in *Mir Bozhy* No. 4 for April 1898 (see Vol. 4 of this edition, pp. 46-54).

Bogdanov, A. (Malinovsky, Alexander Alexandrovich) (1873-1928)—philosopher, sociologist and economist, by education a physician. During the nineties took part in the work of the Social-Democratic circles. After the Second Congress of the R.S.D.L.P. (1903) joined the Bolsheviks. During the years of reaction (1907-10) he became the leader of the otzovists and of the Vperyod group, which came out against Lenin and the Party. In questions of philosophy he attempted to set up a system of his own, known as "empirio-monism", a species of subjective-idealist Machian philosophy, which was sharply criticised by Lenin in his book *Materialism and Empirio-criticism* (1909) (see Vol. 14 of this edition).   p. 41

[49] The remarks referring to the end of Lenin's article "Capitalism in Agriculture" were taken into consideration by Lenin when publishing the article (see Vol. 4 of this edition).   p. 43

[50] *Krupskaya, Nadezhda Konstantinovna* (1869-1939)—a professional revolutionary and outstanding member of the Communist Party and the Soviet Government; the wife of V. I. Lenin. Joined the revolutionary movement in 1890. In 1895 was one of the organisers of the St. Petersburg League of Struggle for the Emancipation of the Working Class. In 1901 emigrated and worked as secretary of the *Iskra* editorial board. Took an active part in preparing the Second Congress of the R.S.D.L.P which she attended as a non-voting delegate. After the Congress she was secretary of the editorial boards of the Bolshevik newspapers *Vperyod* and *Proletary*. During the first Russian revolution (1905-07) worked as secretary to the Central Committee of the Party in Russia. Took an active part in preparing and carrying out the October Socialist Revolution.   p. 44

[51] Apparently this refers to A. N. Potresov.   p. 44

[52] This refers to the announcement concerning the resumption of publications by the Emancipation of Labour group issued at the end of 1899. The date given by Lenin is a slip of the pen.
                                                                       p. 46

[53] *(V. I—n) Ivanshin, Vladimir Pavlovich* (1869-1904)—one of the editors of the journal *Rabocheye Dyelo*, organ of the Union of Russian Social-Democrats Abroad; maintained close contact also with *Rabochaya Mysl*, the newspaper of the St. Petersburg Economists. In his articles he drew a line between the immediate economic interests of the workers and the political tasks of Social-Democracy.

After the Second Congress of the R.S.D.L.P. (1903) he joined the Mensheviks.   p. 46

[54] On September 6 Lenin left Nuremberg for Munich, which was chosen as the residence for the members of the editorial board of the all-Russia illegal Marxist newspaper *Iskra*.   p. 48

[55] This refers to the group consisting of V. I. Lenin, Y. O. Martov and A. N. Potresov formed on Lenin's initiative upon his return from exile at the beginning of 1900 with the object of setting up abroad an all-Russia illegal Marxist newspaper.   p. 48

[56] This refers to the Union of Russian Social-Democrats Abroad (see Note 39).   p. 48

[57] Here and elsewhere the reference is to Lenin's talks with Ts. Kopelson ("Grishin"), a member of the Union of Russian Social-Democrats Abroad.   p. 48

[58] This refers to the Emancipation of Labour group, the first Russian Marxist group, founded by Plekhanov in Geneva in 1883. Other members of the group were P. B. Axelrod, L. G. Deutsch, V. I. Zasulich and V. N. Ignatov. The E. L. group did a great deal to disseminate Marxism in Russia. It translated into Russian, published abroad and distributed in Russia the works of the founders of Marxism: *Manifesto of the Communist Party* by Marx and Engels; *Wage-Labour and Capital* by Marx; *Socialism: Utopian and Scientific* by Engels and other works. Plekhanov and his group dealt a severe blow to Narodism. The two drafts of a programme for Russian Social-Democrats written by Plekhanov in 1883 and 1885 and published by the E. L. group were an important step towards preparing the ground for and establishing a Social-Democratic Party in Russia. An important part in spreading Marxist views in Russia was played by Plekhanov's essays: *Socialism and the Political Struggle* (1883), *Our Differences* (1885) and *The Development of the Monist View of History* (1895). The E. L. group, however, committed serious errors; they clung to remnants of the Narodnik views, underestimated the revolutionary capacity of the peasantry and overestimated the role of the liberal bourgeoisie. These errors were the embryo of the future Menshevik views held by Plekhanov and other members of the group.

Lenin pointed out that the E.L. group "only laid the theoretical foundations for the Social-Democratic movement and took the first step towards the working-class movement" (see Vol. 20, p. 278 of this edition).

At the Second Congress of the R.S.D.L.P. in August 1903 the E.L. group announced that it had ceased its activities as a group.   p. 48

[59] The rumour refers to the forthcoming publication of the newspaper *Iskra*.

Iskra (The Spark) was the first all-Russia illegal Marxist newspaper; it was founded by Lenin in 1900 and played an important role in building the Marxist revolutionary party of the working class in Russia.

As it was impossible to publish a revolutionary newspaper in Russia on account of police persecution, Lenin, while still in exile in Siberia, evolved a detailed plan for its publication abroad. When his exile ended (in January 1900) Lenin immediately set about putting his plan into effect.

The first issue of Lenin's *Iskra* was published in Leipzig in December 1900; later issues were published in Munich; from July 1902 the paper was published in London, and from the spring of 1903 in Geneva. Considerable help in getting the newspaper going (the organisation of secret printing-presses, the acquisition of Russian type, etc.) was rendered by the German Social-Democrats Clara Zetkin, Adolf Braun and others, as well as by Julian Marchlewski, a Polish revolutionary residing at Munich at the time, and by Harry Quelch, one of the leaders of the English Social-Democratic Federation.

The editorial board of *Iskra* consisted of V. I. Lenin, G. V. Plekhanov, Y. O. Martov, P.B. Axelrod, A.N. Potresov and V. I. Zasulich. The first secretary of the board was I. G. Smidovich-Leman; in the spring of 1901 this post was taken over by N. K. Krupskaya, who also conducted the correspondence between *Iskra* and the Social-Democratic organisations in Russia. Lenin was virtually Editor-in-Chief and the leading figure in *Iskra*, in which he published his articles on all fundamental issues of Party organisation and the class struggle of the proletariat in Russia, and dealt with the most important international events.

Iskra became the centre for the unification of Party forces, for the gathering and training of Party cadres. R.S.D.L.P. groups and committees of a Leninist *Iskra* trend were set up in a number of Russian cities (St. Petersburg, Moscow, Samara and others). Iskrist organisations sprang up and worked under the direct leadership of Lenin's disciples and associates N. E. Bauman, I. V. Babushkin, S. I. Gusev, M. I. Kalinin, P. A. Krasikov, G. M. Krzhizhanovsky, F. V. Lengnik, P. N. Lepeshinsky, I. I. Radchenko, and others.

On the initiative and with the direct participation of Lenin the *Iskra* editorial board drew up a draft programme of the Party (published in *Iskra* No. 21), and prepared the Second Congress of the R.S.D.L.P., which was held in July-August 1903. By the time the Congress was convened most of the local Social-Democratic organisations in Russia had adopted the *Iskra* position, approved its tactics, programme and plan of organisation, and recognised the newspaper as their leading organ. A special resolution of the Congress noted *Iskra*'s exceptional role in the struggle to build the Party and adopted the newspaper as the Central Organ of the R.S.D.L.P. The Second Congress approved an editorial board consisting of Lenin, Plekhanov and Martov. Despite the Congress decision Martov refused to participate, and issues Nos. 46-51 of *Iskra* were edited by Lenin and Plekhanov. Later Plekhanov adopted a Menshevik stand and demanded that all the old Menshevik editors be included in the editorial board of *Iskra*, although they had been rejected by the Congress. Lenin could

not agree to this, and on October 19 (November 1), 1903, he re-
signed from the *Iskra* editorial board. He was co-opted to the
Central Committee, from where he conducted a struggle against the
Menshevik opportunists. Issue 52 was edited by Plekhanov alone.
On November 13 (26), 1903, Plekhanov, on his own initiative and
in defiance of the will of the Congress, co-opted all the old Men-
shevik editors to the editorial board. Beginning with issue 52 the
Mensheviks turned *Iskra* into their own organ.   p. 48

⁶⁰ Meaning the newspaper *Iskra*.   p. 49

⁶¹ In August 1899, upon receiving from A. I. Ulyanova-Yelizarova
in St. Petersburg the manifesto of the Economists which she
called "the Credo of the 'young' group", Lenin wrote his Anti-
Credo—"A Protest by Russian Social-Democrats" (see Vol. 4,
pp. 167-82 of this edition). The author of the *Credo* was Y. D. Kus-
kova, then a member of the Union of Russian Social-Democrats
Abroad. The manifesto of the Economists was not intended for
the press, and, as Lenin pointed out, was published "without
the consent and perhaps even against the will of its authors",
because the Economists feared public criticism of their opportunist views (see Vol. 5, p. 364 of this edition).   p. 50

⁶² *Vademecum for the Editors of Rabocheye Dyelo. A Collection
of Material Published by the Emancipation of Labour Group,
with a Preface by G. V. Plekhanov* (Geneva, February 1900) was
directed against opportunism in the ranks of the R.S.D.L.P.,
chiefly against Economism of the Union of Russian Social-Democrats Abroad and of its organ, the journal *Rabocheye Dyelo*. p. 50

⁶³ *Rabocheye Dyelo* (Workers' Cause)—a journal, organ of the Union
of Russian Social-Democrats Abroad, published in Geneva from
April 1899 to February 1902. Twelve numbers (nine books) were
issued in all. The editorial board of *Rabocheye Dyelo* was the
centre of the Economists abroad. *Rabocheye Dyelo* supported
Bernstein's slogan of "freedom of criticism" of Marxism, and took
an opportunist stand on questions of the tactics and organisational tasks of the Russian Social-Democrats. Its supporters
propagated opportunist ideas making the proletariat's political
struggle subservient to the economic struggle; they exalted spon-
taneity in the working-class movement and denied the leading
role of the Party. V. P. Ivanshin, one of the journal's editors,
also took part in editing *Rabochaya Mysl*, organ of the outspoken
Economists, which *Rabocheye Dyelo* supported. At the Second
Congress of the R.S.D.L.P. the *Rabocheye Dyelo* group represented the extreme Right, opportunist wing of the Party. p. 50

⁶⁴ *Yakubova, Apollinaria Alexandrovna* (1870-1917)—a participant
in the Social-Democratic movement from 1893, prominent expo-
nent of Economism. A member of the St. Petersburg League of
Struggle for the Emancipation of the Working Class; in 1897-

98 was one of the organisers of the St. Petersburg publication of the Economists' newspaper *Rabochaya Mysl*. In 1898 was exiled to Siberia for a term of four years and emigrated in the summer of 1899. Assisted in the organisation of the Second Congress of the R.S.D.L.P. which she attended as a non-voting delegate. After the split in the Party, she sympathised with the Mensheviks. Retired from political activities after 1905.   p. 51

[65] The reference is to Plekhanov.   p. 51

[66] The reference is to Lenin's reply to Plekhanov, who asked Lenin's advice concerning the Economists' invitation to contribute to their newspaper *Rabochaya Mysl*.   p. 51

[67] *Rabochaya Mysl* (Workers' Thought)—a newspaper, organ of the Economists, published from October 1897 to December 1902. Sixteen issues were published (St. Petersburg—Berlin—Warsaw—Geneva). Edited by K. M. Takhtarev and others. A criticism of *Rabochaya Mysl* views, described as the Russian variety of international opportunism, was given by Lenin in his article "A Retrograde Trend in Russian Social-Democracy" (see Vol. 4 of this edition) and in articles published in *Iskra* and in his book *What Is To Be Done?* (see Vol. 5 of this edition).   p. 52

[68] This apparently refers to Y. O. Martov.   p. 52

[69] *Bernsteinism*—an opportunist anti-Marxist trend in the international Social-Democratic movement, which originated in Germany at the end of the nineteenth century and was named after Eduard Bernstein, the German Social-Democrat. Bernstein tried to revise Marx's revolutionary doctrine in the spirit of bourgeois liberalism and to turn the Social-Democratic Party into a petty-bourgeois party of social reform. In Russia this trend found support among the "legal Marxists" and the Economists.   p. 53

[70] *Plekhanov, Georgi Valentinovich* (1856-1918)—an outstanding leader of the Russian and international labour movement, the first propagandist of Marxism in Russia, founder of the first Russian Marxist group, the Emancipation of Labour group (Geneva 1883). At the beginning of the twentieth century Plekhanov, together with Lenin, edited the newspaper *Iskra* and the journal *Zarya*, took part in drafting the Party Programme and preparing the Second Congress of the R.S.D.L.P. After this Congress he stood for a conciliatory attitude towards opportunism and eventually joined the Mensheviks. In 1908-12 Plekhanov came out against the liquidators and headed the pro-Party Mensheviks. During the First World War (1914-18) he adopted a social-chauvinist stand. His attitude to the October Socialist Revolution was hostile, but he took no part in anti-Soviet activities.

Lenin thought highly of Plekhanov's philosophical works and his role in disseminating Marxism in Russia; at the same time he sharply criticised Plekhanov for his deviations from Marxism and the serious mistakes in his political activities. p. 55

[71] This refers to the negotiations between the editorial board of *Iskra* and the liberals concerning the publication of a supplement *Sovremennoye Obozreniye* to the journal *Zarya*. The talks, in which Lenin, Zasulich, Potresov, and Struve took part, started on December 29, 1900, and continued through January 1901. Struve rejected Point 7 of the draft agreement proposed by the *Iskra* and *Zarya* group concerning full freedom for the editors of *Iskra* to use all the political material received by *Sovremennoye Obozreniye*. Statements concerning the issue of *Sovremennoye Obozreniye* were written by Plekhanov on behalf of *Iskra* and *Zarya* and by Struve on behalf of the "democratic opposition" group. The publication, however, did not materialise in view of Dietz's refusal to publish the statements, which did not fulfil censorship requirements. The talks between *Iskra* representatives and Struve were broken off and not resumed. p. 55

[72] *Zarya* (Dawn)—a Marxist scientific and political journal, published in Stuttgart in 1901-02 by the *Iskra* editorial board. Only four numbers (three books) were issued. *Zarya* criticised international and Russian revisionism, came out in defence of the theoretical premises of Marxism; it published the following writings of Lenin dealing with this question: "The Persecutors of the Zemstvo and the Hannibals of Liberalism" (see Vol. 5, pp. 31-80, of this edition), the first four chapters of "The Agrarian Question and the 'Critics of Marx'" (see Vol. 5 of this edition) and "The Agrarian Programme of Russian Social-Democracy" (see present edition, Vol. 6, pp. 107-50), as well as Plekhanov's "Criticism of Our Critics. Part 1. Mr. Struve as Critic of Marx's Theory of Social Development", "Cant versus Kant, or Herr Bernstein's Spiritual Testament" and others. p. 56

[73] The reference is to Dobrogeanu-Gherea (Kats, K. A.) (1855-1920) —leader of the opportunist wing of the Rumanian Social-Democrats. p. 58

[74] *Rittmeyer*, *G.*—a Munich Social-Democrat at whose place Lenin lived in 1900-01 under the name of Meyer. Letters to Lenin were sent to his address from December 1900 to the end of July 1901. p. 58

[75] *Dietz*—owner of a Stuttgart printing-house at which *Zarya*, the Marxist scientific and political journal, was printed.
G.m.b.H.—Gesellschaft mit beschränkter Haftung. p. 58

[76] This refers to an article of Axelrod's intended as an editorial for the first issue of *Zarya*. In the phrase that was to appear on the cover of the journal "Published in close co-operation with G. V. Plekhanov, V. I. Zasulich, P. B. Axelrod and several Russian Social-Democrats", Dietz crossed out the last five words. p. 58

[77] This refers to D. Zhukovsky, a publisher of books on philosophy.
                                                                        p. 58

[78] The secret memorandum of tsarist minister S. Y. Witte under
the heading "The Autocracy and the Zemstvo", with a preface
by P. B. Struve (using the pseudonym R.N.S.), was published
illegally by *Zarya* in 1901. Both the memorandum and the preface were sharply criticised by Lenin in his article "The Persecutors of the Zemstvo and the Hannibals of Liberalism" (see Vol. 5
of this edition).   p. 59

[79] Referring to Maria Ulyanova and M. T. Yelizarov.   p. 59

[80] This refers to Y. O. Martov.   p. 59

[81] The pseudonym of *Blumenfeld, Yosif Solomonovich* (born 1865)—
a Social-Democrat, active member of the Emancipation of Labour
group, later a member of the *Iskra* organisation, by trade a com-
positor. In the E. L. group and *Iskra* was in charge of printing
and shipping arrangements. In March 1902 was arrested with
a parcel of *Iskra* publications and imprisoned in a Kiev jail,
whence he escaped abroad in August 1902. After the split at the
Second Congress of the R.S.D.L.P. he joined the Mensheviks.
In December 1903 became secretary of the editorial board of the
Menshevik *Iskra* and subsequently worked in the Menshevik
organisations in Russia and abroad.   p. 59

[82] This refers to the *Iskra* leaflet "First of May" issued in April
1901.   p. 59

[83] *Parisians*—the *Borba* (Struggle) literary group abroad who considered themselves affiliated to the R.S.D.L.P. The group was
dissolved by decision of the Second Congress of the Party (see
Note 93).
    Zurichers—Lettish Social-Democrat students living in Zurich
who handled the shipment of illegal publications to Russia.
                                                                        p. 60

[84] This refers to the Union of Russian Social-Democrats Abroad
(see Note 39).   p. 60

[85] The author of "Comments" was D. Ryazanov.
    Ryazanov, David Borisovich (1870-1938)—participant in the
Social-Democratic movement of the nineties. In 1900 went abroad
and was one of the organisers of the *Borba* literary group, which
opposed the Party programme worked out by *Iskra* and Lenin's
principles of Party organisation. The Second Congress of the
R.S.D.L.P. declared against the participation of the *Borba* group
in the Congress proceedings and rejected a motion inviting Ryazanov to the Congress in the capacity of its representative.
    In 1909 he was lecturer at the Capri school of the *Vperyod*
faction.   p. 60

[86] *Listok Rabochevo Dyela* (Rabocheye Dyelo Supplement)—a non-periodic publication of the Union of Russian Social-Democrats Abroad; appeared in Geneva in 1900-01.   p. 60

[87] This refers to members of the *Iskra* promotion group in Berlin.   p. 61

[88] See Note 57.   p. 61

[89] The revolutionary organisation *Sotsial-Demokrat* was formed by members of the Emancipation of Labour group and their followers in May 1900 after the split in the Union of Russian Social-Democrats Abroad which took place at its Second Conference. In October 1901 *Sotsial-Demokrat*, on Lenin's proposal, united with the foreign section of the *Iskra* organisation into the League of Russian Revolutionary Social-Democracy Abroad. p. 61

[90] Lenin's plan was carried out in October 1901, when the League of Russian Revolutionary Social-Democracy Abroad was founded. Affiliated to the League were the foreign section of the *Iskra* organisation, and the *Sotsial-Demokrat* organisation. The task of the League was to disseminate the ideas of revolutionary Social-Democracy and promote the building up of a militant Social-Democratic organisation. The League was the representative abroad of the *Iskra* organisation. It issued several bulletins and pamphlets, including Lenin's *To the Rural Poor* (see Vol. 6 of this edition).

The R.S.D.L.P.'s Second Congress endorsed the League as the only Party organisation abroad having the status of a committee and working under the guidance and control of the Central Committee of the R.S.D.L.P. After the Second Congress the Mensheviks entrenched themselves in the League and launched a struggle against the Bolsheviks. At the League's second congress in October 1903 the Mensheviks slandered the Bolsheviks, upon which Lenin and his followers walked out. The Mensheviks got new Rules adopted, directed against the Party Rules approved by the Second Congress of the R.S.D.L.P. From then on the League became a stronghold of Menshevism. It existed until 1905. p. 61

[91] *Bauman. Nikolai Ernestovich* (1873-1905)—a professional revolutionary, prominent leader of the Bolshevik Party. Began his revolutionary activities in the early nineties. In 1900 was one of the founders of the *Iskra* organisation and worked in Moscow as its agent in 1901-02. At the Second Congress of the R.S.D.L.P. joined the Bolsheviks.   p. 65

[92] The pseudonym "Leopold" has not been deciphered. Apparently it was the code name given to the shipping group associated with N. E. Bauman.   p. 66

[93] The *Borba* group was formed in Paris in the summer of 1900 and consisted of D. B. Ryazanov, Y. M. Steklov and E. L. Gurevich.

The name *Borba* (Struggle) was adopted by the group in May 1901. In an attempt to reconcile the revolutionary and opportunist trends in Russian Social-Democracy, the *Borba* group took the initiative in convening (in June 1901) the Geneva conference of representatives of the Social-Democratic organisations abroad— the *Iskra* and *Zarya* editorial board, the *Sotsial-Demokrat* organisation, the Foreign Committee of the Bund and the Union of Russian Social-Democrats Abroad—and took part in the "unity" conference of the R.S.D.L.P.'s organisations abroad at Zurich (September 21-22 [October 4-5], 1901). In November 1901 the group issued a programmatic "Advertisement of the Publications of the Social-Democratic *Borba* Group". In its publications the group distorted the revolutionary theory of Marxism, interpreted it in a doctrinaire scholastic spirit and was hostile to Lenin's organisational principles for building up the Party. Owing to its deviations from Social-Democratic views and tactics, its disruptive activities and lack of contact with the Social-Democratic organisations in Russia, the group was refused admission to the Second Congress, by whose decision it was dissolved. p. 67

[94] *The Bund*—the General Jewish Workers' Union of Lithuania, Poland and Russia—was organised at an inaugural congress of Jewish Social-Democratic groups held in Vilna in 1897; it united mostly semi-proletarian elements of the Jewish artisans in the Western regions of Russia. At the First Congress of the R.S.D.L.P. (1898) the Bund joined the Party "as an autonomous organisation, independent only as far as questions affecting the Jewish proletariat are concerned" (*K.P.S.S. v rezolutsiyakh i resheniyakh syezdov, konferentsii i plenumov TsK* [*The C.P.S.U. in the Resolutions and Decisions of Its Congresses, Conferences and Plenums of the Central Committee*], Part I, 1954, p. 14).

The Bund brought nationalism and separatism into the Russian working-class movement and took an opportunist stand on the most important issues of the Social-Democratic movement. After the Second Congress of the R.S.D.L.P. rejected the Bund's demand that it be recognised as the sole representative of the Jewish proletariat, the Bund left the Party, rejoining it in 1906 on the basis of a decision of the Fourth (Unity) Congress.

Within the R.S.D.L.P. the Bundists constantly supported its opportunist wing (the Economists, Mensheviks and liquidators) and waged a struggle against the Bolsheviks and Bolshevism. To the Bolshevik programme's demand for the right of nations to self-determination the Bund opposed the demand for autonomy of the national culture. During the years of reaction (1907-10) the Bund adopted a liquidators' stand and took an active part in forming the anti-Party August bloc. During the First World War (1914-18) the Bundists took a social-chauvinist stand. In 1917 the Bund supported the counter-revolutionary Provisional Government and fought on the side of the enemies of the October Socialist Revolution, its leaders joining forces with the counter-revolution during the years of foreign military intervention and civil war. At the same time a swing towards co-operation with the Soviet government was to be observed among the Bund's rank and file. In March 1921 the Bund dissolved itself.   p. 67

[95] This letter is a postscript to N. K. Krupskaya's letter.

Knipovich, Lydia Mikhailovna (1856-1920)—a professional revolutionary, started her revolutionary activities in the seventies, carried on extensive cultural and educational work among the workers and played a prominent part in establishing *Iskra*'s contacts with the local organisations in Russia. After the Second Congress of the R.S.D.L.P. adhered to the Bolsheviks.   p. 70

[96] Lenin proposed setting up *Iskra* abroad, having a matrix made from the type-setting and the matrix sent to Russia to be stereotyped and printed.   p. 70

[97] This letter is a postscript to that of N. K. Krupskaya.   p. 71

[98] *Galperin, L. Y.* (1872-1951)—a Social-Democrat, joined the revolutionary movement in 1898. While in exile, in Astrakhan Gubernia, he established contact with the *Iskra* organisation and was sent to Baku as its agent in the spring of 1901, where he worked at setting up the Baku Committee of the R.S.D.L.P., and an illegal printing-press, and at organising the transportation of illegal literature from abroad and its distribution in Russia.

After the Second Congress of the R.S.D.L.P. he joined the Bolsheviks and for a time represented the editorial board of the Party's Central Organ on the Party Council and was afterwards co-opted to the Central Committee. Adopted a conciliatory attitude towards Menshevism and was against convening the Third Congress of the Party. Retired from active political work in 1906.   p. 72

[99] Lenin refers to his visit to the Moscow Art Theatre with I. Lalayants, of which he wrote to his mother M. A. Ulyanova in his letter dated February 20, 1901.   p. 72

[100] *Berdayev, Nikolai Alexandrovich* (1874-1948)—a reactionary idealist philosopher and publicist.

The reference here is to his article "The Fight for Idealism", published in the journal *Mir Bozhy* No. 6, for 1901.   p. 74

[101] *Struvefreundliche Partei*—the name by which Potresov and Zasulich were jokingly called among the editorial staff of *Iskra*.   p. 74

[102] The reference is to the books: N. Shakhovskoi, *Agricultural Outside Employments*, Moscow, 1896; N. I. Tezyakov, *Agricultural Workers and the Organisation of Sanitary Supervision Over Them in Kherson Gubernia,* Kherson, 1896.   p. 74

[103] The preface to Witte's "memorandum" was written by P. B. Struve. Lenin "trounced" Struve's preface in Chapter V of his article "The Persecutors of the Zemstvo and the Hannibals of Liberalism" (see Vol. 5 of this edition).   p. 75

[104] This refers to Nevzorov's (Y. M. Steklov's) article "And So, Where Do We Begin?" directed against Lenin's article "Where To Begin" (see Vol. 5 of this edition).   p. 75

[105] *Tsederbaum, Sergei Osipovich* (1879-1939)—joined the Social-Democratic movement in 1898. Worked on the organisation of transport facilities for *Iskra* publications. After the Second Congress of the R.S.D.L.P. became an active Menshevik. After the October Socialist Revolution retired from political activities. p. 76

[106] *Yuzhny Rabochy* (Southern Worker)—a Social-Democratic illegal newspaper, published from January 1900 to April 1903 by a group of this name. At the Second Congress of the R.S.D.L.P. the group's delegates adopted a "Centre" position (that of "middling opportunists", as Lenin called the representatives of the Centre). The Second Congress decided to dissolve the *Yuzhny Rabochy* group as well as all separate Social-Democratic groups and organisations.   p. 76

[107] The *Sotsialist* group was organised in St. Petersburg in the summer of 1900. It was one of the groups that were dissatisfied with the Economist tendency of the St. Petersburg League of Struggle, and gave prominence to the political struggle. In January 1901 it amalgamated with the *Rabocheye Znamya* group. The group broke up after the arrests in the spring of 1901.   p. 79

[108] The *Rabocheye Znamya* group (Workers' Banner) came into being during the second half of 1897. It disapproved of Economism and set itself the aim of conducting political propaganda among the workers. It published the newspaper *Rabocheye Znamya* (three issues were put out) and several pamphlets and leaflets. In January 1901 the St. Petersburg *Rabocheye Znamya* group amalgamated with the *Sotsialist* group, but in the course of January-April the members of the united group who were in Russia were arrested. Most of the members of the St. Petersburg *Rabocheye Znamya* group joined the *Iskra* organisation.   p. 79

[109] *Volnoye Slovo* (Free Word)—a weekly, and from issue No. 37 a fortnightly publication which appeared in Geneva from 1881 to 1883; altogether 62 issues were put out. Founded for provocative purposes with the knowledge of the Russian secret political police by members of the Svyashchennaya Druzhina (Holy Squad)—a secret organisation of the landed gentry and tsarist dignitaries headed by Prince P. Shuvalov. Edited by the police agent A. P. Malshinsky.   p. 81

[110] The reference is to *Der Sozialdemokrat*, Central Organ of the German Social-Democrats, published illegally in Zurich and London from 1879 to 1890. p. 82

[111] *Die Neue Rheinische Zeitung*—a daily, published in Cologne from July 1, 1848, to May 19, 1849, edited by K. Marx. "No German newspaper, before or since," wrote Engels, "has ever had the same power and influence or been able to electrify the proletarian masses as effectively as the *Neue Reinische Zeitung*" (Marx and Engels, *Selected Works*, Vol. II, Moscow, 1962, pp. 336-37). In his article "Karl Marx" Lenin called this newspaper "the finest and unsurpassed organ of the revolutionary proletariat" (see present edition, Vol. 21, p. 81). p. 82

[112] This is a reply to Axelrod's remarks on Lenin's article "The Persecutors of the Zemstvo and the Hannibals of Liberalism" (see Vol. 5 of this edition). p. 83

[113] See Note 102. p. 85

[114] This refers to Kalmykova's bookstore in St. Petersburg, which was used as a secret rendezvous by Social-Democrats. p. 85

[115] This refers to V. Kuleman's book *The Trade Union Movement, an Essay on the Trade Union Organisation of the Workers and Associations of Employers in All Countries*, St. P., 1901. p. 85

[116] *Dragomanov, Mikhail Petrovich* (1841-1895)—Ukrainian historian, ethnographer and publicist, a bourgeois liberal. He was assistant professor at Kiev University; contributed to liberal journals. p. 85

[117] The reference is to Engels's article "Zur Kritik des sozialdemokratischen Programmentwurfes 1891". p. 87

[118] Lenin refers to his trip to Zurich to attend the "unity" conference of the R.S.D.L.P.'s organisations abroad: *Iskra-Zarya, Sotsial-Demokrat* (including the Emancipation of Labour group), the Union of Russian Social-Democrats Abroad, the Bund and the *Borba* group. The conference was held on September 21-22 (October 4-5), 1901. p. 87

[119] The articles referred to were: F. Engels "Zur Kritik des sozialdemokratischen Programmentwurfes 1891" (*Die Neue Zeit* No. 1 for October 2, 1901); K. Kautsky "Die Revision des Programms der Sozialdemocratie in Oesterreich" (*Die Neue Zeit* No. 3 for October 16, 1901). p. 88

[120] This refers to the review of the book *Aus dem literarischen Nachlass von Karl Marx, Friedrich Engels und Ferdinand Lassalle. Herausgegeben von Franz Mehring. I. Gesammelte Schriften von Karl*

Marx und Friedrich Engels. Von März 1841 bis März 1844. Stuttgart, Verlag von I.H.W. Dietz Nachfolger 1902. p. 88

[121] See Note 162. p. 88

[122] The five points indicate where this letter was to be sent. Point 4 refers to the Tver Social-Democratic organisation, the letter for which was forwarded to the address of A. Bakunin. Point 5, given in quotes, is the title of a letter received from an *Iskra* representative in Russia. This letter was published by Lenin in full in his article "A Talk with Defenders of Economism" (see Vol. 5 of this edition). Under this point Lenin meant the *Iskra* representative from whom the letter had been received. p. 90

[123] By the "conflict abroad" Lenin meant the incident at the "unity" conference of R.S.D.L.P.'s organisations abroad, when the members of *Iskra, Zarya* and *Sotsial-Demokrat* walked out. p. 90

[124] *Smidovich, Inna Germogenovna*—a Social-Democrat. From the first day of *Iskra*'s organisation until the arrival of N. K. Krupskaya in Geneva in April 1901 she discharged the duties of secretary of the Editorial board, and afterwards handled literature shipments across the frontier. p. 92

[125] *Vperyod*—a newspaper of an Economist trend, published in Kiev in 1896-1900. p. 92

[126] *Goldman, L. I.* (1877-1939)—joined the revolutionary movement in 1893. In 1900 went abroad, where he joined the *Iskra* organisation. In May 1901 organised an illegal printing-press in Kishinev, where *Iskra* and other Social-Democratic publications were printed. Was arrested in 1902 and escaped from exile in 1905; was secretary of the Menshevik *Iskra* editorial board.

After the October Socialist Revolution he worked as business executive and engaged in publishing activities. p. 93

[127] An *Iskra* illegal printing-press, organised at Kishinev, printed various issues of the newspaper for distribution in Russia. Lenin's letter refers to the report about the Kishinev press having printed issue No. 10 of *Iskra*. p. 93

[128] This apparently refers to I. B. Basovsky, who organised a dispatch office in Kiev in August 1901 to handle *Iskra* literature arriving from abroad; this office also distributed all the literature printed in Kishinev. p. 93

[129] *Iskra* No. 13 for December 20, 1901, featured Lenin's article "Demonstrations Have Begun" (see Vol. 5 of this edition). p. 93

[130] See Marx and Engels, *Selected Works*, Vol. II, Moscow, 1962, p. 35. p. 94

[131] *Conrad's Jahrbücher—Jahrbücher für Nationalökonomie und Statistik*—a periodical published in Jena from 1863 by the bourgeois economist J. Conrad. p. 94

[132] *Torgovo-Promyshlennaya Gazeta* (Commercial Industrial Gazette)— a daily supplement to *Vestnik Finansov, Promyshlennosti i Torgovli* (Finance, Industry and Trade Herald); published in St. Petersburg from 1893 to 1918. From 1894 onward was issued as an independent publication. p. 94

[133] *Erfurt programme*—the programme of the German Social-Democratic Party adopted at the Congress in Erfurt in October 1891. See Engels's article, Note 117. p. 96

[134] The text of the commission's draft programme was the result of the work of the co-ordinating commission appointed by the *Iskra* editorial board to draw up a unified draft programme of the R.S.D.L.P. on the basis of Lenin's and Plekhanov's previous drafts. The members of the *Iskra* editorial board were to give their comments on the commission's draft, and the co-ordinating commission was to draw up a final draft programme. The commission's draft was endorsed by the members of the *Iskra* editorial board in Zurich on April 14, 1902, in Lenin's absence. p. 98

[135] Lenin here refers to *Iskra*'s removal from Munich to London. p. 100

[136] *Pridneprovsky Krai* (Dnieper Region)—a scientific, literary, political and economic daily, published in Ekaterinoslav from 1901. p. 100

[137] *Krzhizhanovsky, Gleb Maximilianovich* (1872-1959)—veteran leading member of the Communist Party, well-known Soviet scientist, power engineer, joined the revolutionary movement in 1893. In December 1895 he was arrested and exiled to Siberia for three years. Upon his return in 1901 he settled in Samara, where he helped to organise an *Iskra* centre. In the autumn of 1902 he was elected to the Organising Committee for convening the Second Congress of the R.S.D.L.P. At the Congress, in his absence, he was elected to the Central Committee. Took an active part in the revolution of 1905-07. p. 101

[138] *Sasha*—name used to denote the Conference of R.S.D.L.P. Committees held at Byelostok on March 23-28 (April 5-10), 1902. The Conference set up an Organising Committee for convening the Second Congress of the Party. p. 101

[139] Lenin refers to the preparations for the Second Congress of the Party. p. 102

[140] Lenin refers to the beginning of the disagreements in connection with the drafting of the Party programme, the first discussion

of which took place at a meeting of the *Iskra* editorial board in Munich on January 21, 1902. At this meeting Lenin sharply criticised the first draft of the programme drawn up by Plekhanov and submitted his own amendments and proposals.   p. 104

[141] *Socialist-Revolutionaries* (S.R.s)—a petty-bourgeois party in Russia, formed at the end of 1901 and beginning of 1902 through the amalgamation of various Narodnik groups and circles. The S.R.s saw no class distinctions between the proletariat and the peasantry, glossed over the class differentiation and antagonism within the peasantry and denied the leading role of the proletariat in the revolution. The tactics of individual terrorism which the S.R.s advocated as the principal method of fighting the autocracy caused great harm to the revolutionary movement and made it difficult to organise the masses for revolutionary struggle.

The agrarian programme of the S.R.s envisaged the abolition of private ownership of the land and its transfer to the village communes on the basis of equalised tenure, as well as the development of all forms of co-operation. There was nothing socialistic in this programme, which the S.R.s sought to present as a programme for "socialising the land", since abolition of private ownership of the land alone, as Lenin pointed out, cannot abolish the domination of capital and the poverty of the masses.

The Bolsheviks exposed the S.R.s' attempts to pose as socialists, fought hard with them for influence over the peasantry and showed how harmful their tactics of individual terrorism were to the working-class movement. At the same time, they were prepared, on certain conditions, to make temporary agreements with the S.R.s in the struggle against tsarism.

The absence of class homogeneousness among the peasantry was responsible for the political and ideological instability and the organisational confusion in the S.R. party, and for its constant vacillation between the liberal bourgeoisie and the proletariat. There had been a split in the Socialist-Revolutionary Party during the first Russian revolution, its Right wing forming the legal Trudovik Popular Socialist Party, which held views close to those of the Cadets, and the Left wing taking shape as the semi-anarchist league of Maximalists. During the years of reaction (1907-10) the S.R. party suffered a complete ideological and organisational break-down, and the First World War found most of the S.R.s taking a social-chauvinist stand.

After the victory of the February bourgeois-democratic revolution in 1917 the S.R.s, together with the Mensheviks and Cadets, were the mainstay of the counter-revolutionary Provisional Government of the bourgeoisie and landowners (the party's leaders Kerensky, Avksentyev and Chernov were members of that government). The Left wing of the S.R.s founded an independent party of Left Socialist-Revolutionaries at the end of November 1917. In an effort to maintain their influence among the peasant masses, the Left S.R.s formally recognised the Soviet power and entered into an agreement with the Bolsheviks, but shortly afterwards turned against the Soviet power.

During the foreign military intervention and civil war the S.R.s carried on subversive counter-revolutionary activities, strongly supported the interventionists and whiteguards, took part in counter-revolutionary plots, and organised terrorist acts against leaders of the Soviet state and the Communist Party. After the civil war, the S.R.s continued their hostile activity against the Soviet state.   p. 105

[142] Lenin met his mother in France, and not in Germany. From the second half of June to July 25, 1902, Lenin lived at Loguivy (Northern coast of France) with his mother and his sister A. I. Ulyanova-Yelizarova.   p. 105

[143] *Leiteisen, Gavriil Davidovich* (1874-1919)—a Social-Democrat, contributor to *Iskra* and *Zarya*. Started revolutionary activities in the nineties; at the beginning of the twentieth century emigrated abroad, where he joined the Emancipation of Labour group and then became a member of the Union of Russian Social-Democrats Abroad. After the Second Congress of the R.S.D.L.P. joined the Bolsheviks, and contributed to the newspapers *Vperyod*, *Proletary* and other Bolshevik organs.   p. 106

[144] *Smidovich, Pyotr Germogenovich* (1874-1935)—Social-Democrat, Iskrist; after the Second Congress of the R.S.D.L.P.—a Bolshevik. By profession an electrical engineer. Started his revolutionary activities in St. Petersburg in the late nineties; at first was inclined towards Economism, and then joined *Iskra*. At the end of 1900 was arrested and in 1901 deported abroad; was a member of the League of Russian Revolutionary Social-Democracy Abroad. In 1905 worked in the Moscow District Committee of the Party. After the October Socialist Revolution occupied important administrative and business posts.   p. 108

[145] *Noskov, Vladimir Alexandrovich* (1878-1913)—a Social-Democrat. In the late nineties joined the St. Petersburg League of Struggle for the Emancipation of the Working Class. In April 1902 attended the Zurich meeting of the *Iskra* editorial board where the Party's draft programme was discussed. In 1902-03 organised the transportation of illegal Social-Democratic literature to Russia and took part in organising the Second Congress of the R.S.D.L.P. At the Second Congress joined the Bolsheviks and was elected to the Central Committee; after the Congress adopted a conciliatory attitude towards the Mensheviks; came out against the convocation of the Third Congress.   p. 110

[146] *Osvobozhdeniye* (Emancipation)—a fortnightly, published abroad from June 18 (July 1), 1902 to October 5 (18), 1905, edited by P. B. Struve. The journal was the organ of the Russian liberal bourgeoisie and expounded the ideas of moderate-monarchist

liberalism. In 1903 the *Osvobozhdeniye* League formed around the journal (officially it came into existence in January 1904). The League existed up till October 1905. p. 112

[147] Lenin here refers to the members of the *Borba* group (see Note 93). p. 112

[148] *Semyon Semyonovich*—a code name for the Northern League of the R.S.D.L.P. (or the Northern Labour League), which arose in 1900-01. The League united the Social-Democratic organisations of the Vladimir, Yaroslavl and Kostroma gubernias. From the outset the Northern League was linked with *Iskra* and supported the latter's political line and plan of organisation.

After the Second Congress of the R.S.D.L P. the Northern Labour League was reconstituted as the Northern Committee of the R.S.D.L.P., the local committees becoming groups of the Northern Committee. At the conference of Northern organisations of the R.S.D.L.P. held in Kostroma in July 1905 the Northern Committee was liquidated and separate committees were formed in Ivanovo-Voznesensk, Yaroslavl and Kostroma. p. 113

[149] *Levin, E. Y.* (born 1873)—a Social-Democrat, one of the leaders of the *Yuzhny Rabochy* group, a member of *Yuzhny Rabochy* editorial board. At the Pskov meeting of the Organising Committee for convening the Second Congress of the R.S.D.L.P. (November 1902) was elected a member of the O.C. At the Second Congress adopted a centrist stand; after the Congress joined the Mensheviks. In September 1903 he was arrested and subsequently retired from political activity. p. 114

[150] This refers to the members of the group and editorial board of the newspaper *Yuzhny Rabochy* who remained at large after the mass arrests in the spring of 1902. In August 1902 they entered into negotiations with the editorial board of *Iskra* for joint work to restore the unity of Russian Social-Democracy. The declaration of solidarity with *Iskra* by members of the *Yuzhny Rabochy* group (published in *Iskra* No. 27, for November 1, 1902 and in *Yuzhny Rabochy* No. 10, for December 1902) was of great importance in consolidating the ranks of Social-Democracy in Russia. In November 1902 the *Yuzhny Rabochy* group, together with the *Iskra* organisation in Russia, the St. Petersburg Committee of the R.S.D.L.P. and the Northern League of the R.S.D.L.P., took part in setting up the Organising Committee for convening the Second Congress of the R.S.D.L.P. and participated in its activities. p. 114

[151] *Chernyshev, I. V.*—a Social-Democrat, wavering between the Economists and Iskrists, member of the *Yuzhny Rabochy* group. In August 1902 he went abroad, where he negotiated with the *Iskra* editorial board for joint work in uniting the Party. In April 1903 joined the Economists and declared himself an adherent of the Union of Russian Social-Democrats Abroad. p. 114

[152] *The League of Southern Committees and Organisations of the R.S.D.L.P.* was formed in December 1901 at a conference of representatives of the Social-Democratic committees and organisations in the South of Russia (Ekaterinoslav, Nikolayev, Odessa, Kharkov and Kishinev) on the initiative of the *Yuzhny Rabochy* group. The conference elected a Central Committee of the League and declared the newspaper *Yuzhny Rabochy* to be its central organ. The group's attempt (in opposition to the *Iskra* plan of creating in Russia a centralised Marxist party with the aid of an all-Russia political newspaper) to restore the R.S.D.L.P. by setting up regional Social-Democratic associations proved impracticable, and after the mass police raids in the spring of 1902 the League disintegrated. p. 114

[153] *Krasnukha, V. P.* (1868-1913)—a Social-Democrat, an Iskrist; since 1899 worked in the St. Petersburg Social-Democratic organisation; at the beginning of April 1902 represented the St. Petersburg League of Struggle at the Byelostok Conference. In November 1902 attended the Pskov meeting of the Organising Committee for convening the Second Congress of the R.S.D.L.P. at which he was elected a member.

Stasova, Yelena Dmitrievna (born 1873)—veteran of the revolutionary movement, member of the Bolshevik Party since 1898. In 1902-03 a member of the St. Petersburg Committee. From August 1905 to January 1906 carried out Party assignments in Geneva. p. 116

[154] Bouncer (*Vyshibalo*)—pseudonym of Tokarev, leader of the St. Petersburg Economists. As a member of the St. Petersburg League of Struggle, Tokarev protested against the July declaration of the St. Petersburg Committee recognising *Iskra* and *Zarya* as the leading organs of Russian Social-Democracy. He also demanded that the representative of the *Iskra* organisation be expelled from the committee of the St. Petersburg League of Struggle. p. 116

[155] This refers to the July declaration of the R.S.D.L.P.'s St. Petersburg Committee announcing solidarity with the newspaper *Iskra* and the journal *Zarya* and recognising them as the leading organs of Russian Social-Democracy. This declaration was issued in July 1902 in the form of a separate leaflet and subsequently printed in *Iskra* No. 26 for October 15, 1902. p. 117

[156] *Krasikov, Pyotr Ananievich* (1870-1939)—professional revolutionary, Bolshevik. Started his revolutionary activities in 1892 and joined the *Iskra* organisation in 1900. At the Pskov meeting of the Organising Committee for convening the Second Congress of the R.S.D.L.P. (November 1902) he was elected a member of the O.C. At the Second Congress (1903) joined the Bolsheviks. After the Congress took an active part in the fight against the Mensheviks. In August 1904 attended the meeting of the 22 Bolsheviks in Geneva. Took an active part in the revolution of 1905-07. p. 118

[157] This refers to the meeting of the *Iskra* editorial board with representatives of the St. Petersburg Committee of the R.S.D.L.P., the *Iskra* organisation in Russia and the Northern League of the R.S.D.L.P. held on August 15, 1902. At this meeting an Iskrist nucleus of the Organising Committee for convening the Second Congress of the Party was set up.   p. 118

[158] Meaning Krasnukha and Krasikov.   p. 118

[159] The *Organising Committee* (O.C.) for convening the Second Congress of the R.S.D.L.P. was set up on Lenin's initiative at a meeting of S.D. committees in Pskov on November 2-3, 1902. The Iskrists formed a preponderant majority on the new committee. P. A. Krasikov, F. V. Lengnik, P. N. Lepeshinsky and G. M. Krzhizhanovsky were co-opted to the O.C. on behalf of the *Iskra* organisation in Russia, and A. M. Stopani on behalf of the Northern League of the R.S.D.L.P.   p. 118

[160] *Fyokla*—secret code name for the *Iskra* editorial board.   p. 120

[161] Meaning the Bund (see Note 94).   p. 120

[162] The *Svoboda* group, calling themselves the "revolutionary-socialist" group, was founded by E. O. Zelensky (Nadezhdin) in May 1901. Lenin described this group as one of those "small and rootless groups" which "had no stable or serious principles, programme, tactics, organisation, and no roots among the masses" (see Vol. 20, pp. 356 and 357, of this edition). The group published a journal *Svoboda* (Freedom) in Switzerland (two numbers were issued: No. 1 in 1901 and No. 2 in 1902). The *Svoboda* group advocated the ideas of terrorism and Economism, and in a bloc with the St. Petersburg Economists came out against *Iskra* and the St. Petersburg Committee of the R.S.D.L.P. The group ceased to exist in 1903.   p. 121

[163] This refers to the Amsterdam Congress of the Second International planned to be held in 1903. It was held in August 1904.   p. 121

[164] This refers to Plekhanov's article against the article by K. Tarasov (pseudonym of N. S. Rusanov, a Narodnik publicist) published in the Socialist-Revolutionary journal *Vestnik Russkoi Revolutsii*.   p. 123

[165] *Revolutsionnaya Rossiya* (Revolutionary Russia)—an illegal newspaper of the Socialist-Revolutionaries, published in Russia from the end of 1900. From January 1902 to December 1905 it came out abroad (Geneva) as the official organ of the S. R. party.
p. 124

[166] This refers to the forthcoming meeting of the International Socialist Bureau, which was held in Brussels on December 29, 1902. Plekhanov did not attend the meeting.   p. 124

[167] Lenin probably refers to his London lecture of November 29, 1902, on the subject of S.R. programme and tactics.   p. 124

[168] *Zhiznites* members of the *Zhizn* Social-Democratic group (see Note 37).   p. 124

[169] *Krasnoye Znamya* (Red Banner)—a journal, organ of the Economists, published in Geneva by the Union of Russian Social-Democrats Abroad from November 1902 to January 1903 in place of *Rabocheye Dyelo*. Three numbers of the journal were published.   p. 124

[170] *Lavrov, V. I.*—a Social-Democrat, Iskrist; from November 1902 was stand-in to Y. D. Stasova on the St. Petersburg Committee in case of her arrest. In 1903 was in charge of technical arrangements for the St. Petersburg Committee; conducted correspondence with *Iskra*.
Re: Stasova, see Note 153.   p. 126

[171] This refers to the St. Petersburg League of Struggle for the Emancipation of the Working Class organised by Lenin in the autumn of 1895. In December 1895 the tsarist government dealt the League a severe blow by arresting a considerable number of its leading members, Lenin included. The long absence of the League's founders, who were exiled to Siberia, facilitated the prosecution of an opportunist policy on the part of the "young" members and the Economists, who, from 1897, through the newspaper *Rabochaya Mysl*, implanted on Russian soil the ideas of trade-unionism and Bernsteinism. In the second half of 1898 control of the League passed to the most outspoken of the Economists—the *Rabochaya Mysl* adherents. The old surviving members of the League took part in preparing and holding the First Congress of the R.S.D.L.P. In the autumn of 1900 the League of Struggle amalgamated with the St. Petersburg Workers' Organisation, and was recognised as the St. Petersburg Committee of the R.S.D.L.P. The struggle between the Iskrists and Economists in the St. Petersburg Organisation ended in the summer of 1902 with the St. Petersburg Committee of the R.S.D.L.P. adopting an *Iskra* stand.   p. 126

[172] *Workers' Organisation*—an organisation of supporters of Economism, which arose in St. Petersburg in the summer of 1900. In the autumn of the same year it amalgamated with the League of Struggle for the Emancipation of the Working Class, and the St. Petersburg Committee of the R.S.D.L.P. was formed, consisting of two parts: the Committee proper, and the Committee of the Workers' Organisation. With the *Iskra* trend gaining the ascendancy in the St. Petersburg Social-Democratic organisation (1902) the group of Economist-minded Social-Democrats broke away from the St. Petersburg Committee and again set up an independent Workers' Organisation, which existed until the beginning of 1904.   p. 126

[173] *Lengnik, Friedrich Wilhelmovich* (1873-1936)—a professional revolutionary, Bolshevik, joined the Social-Democratic movement in 1893. In 1896 was arrested in connection with the activities of the St. Petersburg League of Struggle for the Emancipation of the Working Class and exiled to Eastern Siberia. On his return from exile joined the *Iskra* organisation; at the Pskov meeting of the Organising Committee for convening the Second Congress of the R.S.D.L.P. (November 1902) was elected a member of the O.C. At the Congress was elected, in his absence, to the Central Committee and Council of the Party. In 1903-04 took an active part in the fight against the Mensheviks abroad.   p. 128

[174] *Babushkin, Ivan Vasilyevich* (1873-1906)—a professional revolutionary, started revolutionary activities in 1893. An active member of the St. Petersburg and Ekaterinoslav Leagues of Struggle for the Emancipation of the Working Class. Took an active part in organising the Leninist newspaper *Iskra* (1900). An active participant in the revolution of 1905-07.   p. 129

[175] Lenin received a letter from Babushkin asking him to make out a question paper for "examining" members of the propagandist group, that is, to ascertain their position in regard to *Iskra* principles.   p. 129

[176] *Zubatov organisation* pursued a policy of "police socialism" initiated by S. V. Zubatov, a Colonel of the Gendarmes and Chief of the Moscow Secret Political Police, under which legal workers' organisations were set up during 1901-03 for the purpose of diverting the workers from the political struggle against the autocracy.   p. 129

[177] Lenin refers to the two leaflets (that of September and October) of the Workers' Organisation Committee quoted in the article "The St. Petersburg Split" published in *Iskra* No. 30, for December 15, 1902.
    The September leaflet was previously published in the "Supplement" to *Otkliki* (Comments) No. 1, December 1902, issued by the *Svoboda* group in Geneva.   p. 131

[178] Krasnukha V. P., the St. Petersburg member of the O.C., was arrested in November 1902.   p. 132

[179] The reference is to the pamphlet *Listok Rabochikh Kass* (Issue 2, published by the organised workers of Kharkov) and the hectographed journal *Kharkovsky Proletary* published in October 1901.   p. 134

[180] Issue No. 16 of *Rabochaya Mysl* for November-December 1902 contained "A Protest of the Workers' Organisation Committee" against the statement of the St. Petersburg Committee of the R.S.D.L.P. recognising the newspaper *Iskra* and the journal

Zarya as the leading organs of the Party. The same issue published a letter of the Workers' Organisation Committee to the *Svoboda* group and the *Otkliki* editorial board expressing gratitude for their sympathy and readiness to give support. The *Rabochaya Mysl Listki* were issued by the Iskrist St. Petersburg Committee in December 1902 and January 1903 in place of the newspaper *Rabochaya Mysl.* Listok No. 1 was destroyed by decision of the Committee in view of its unhappy wording.   p. 135

[181] The secret code name for *Iskra*'s Baku group.   p. 137

[182] Meaning N. K. Krupskaya.   p. 137

[183] This refers to the Bureau of the Organising Committee for convening the Second Congress of the Party.   p. 138

[184] Simultaneously with this letter Lenin wrote the "Draft Appeal of the Russian Organising Committee to the League of Russian Revolutionary Social-Democracy, the Union of Russian Social-Democrats Abroad and the Foreign Committee of the Bund" (see Vol. 6 of this edition) and sent it on February 5 to Martov in Paris to be discussed with the members of the Russian Organising Committee P. A. Krasikov and V. A. Noskov, who had arrived there (see p. 141 of this volume).   p. 139

[185] *Martov, L.*—pseudonym of Tsederbaum, Y. O. (1873-1923)— joined the Social-Democratic movement in the nineties. In 1895 took part in organising the St. Petersburg League of Struggle for the Emancipation of the Working Class. In 1900 helped to prepare the publication of *Iskra* as a member of its editorial board. At the Second Congress of the R.S.D.L.P. (1903) became minority (Menshevik) leader, and from then on was one of the leaders of the Mensheviks' central bodies and an editor of their publications. After the October Socialist Revolution opposed the Soviet power. Emigrated to Germany in 1920.   p. 141

[186] The *Foreign Section of the Organising Committee* consisted of L. G. Deutsch, representing the *Iskra* editorial board, A. I. Kremer representing the Bund, and N. N. Lokhov (Olkhin) representing the Union of Russian Social-Democrats Abroad.   p. 141

[187] Meaning the *Yuzhny Rabochy* group. (See Note 106.)   p. 142

[188] The Nizhni-Novgorod Committee decided not to appeal against the sentence passed on the workers of Sormovo and Nizhni-Novgorod in connection with the May Day demonstration of 1902.
                                                                      p. 144

[189] The leaflet "To All Nizhni-Novgorodians issued by the Nizhni-Novgorod Committee of the R.S.D.L.P. was disseminated in the city two days before the trial of the workers, which was held on October 29-31, 1902.   p. 145

[190] Lenin refers to the dispute following his lecture in Paris on March 3-6, 1903, on the agrarian programme of the Socialist-Revolutionaries and the Russian Social-Democrats. Nevzorov (Y. M. Steklov) was one of Lenin's opponents in this dispute.   p. 147

[191] This refers to P. Maslov's book *The Agrarian Question in Russia*, Vol. I, the first edition of which appeared in 1903.   p. 150

[192] Lenin is referring to his lectures at the Russian School of Social Sciences and at the meeting of Russian political emigrants, which he read in Paris in February 1903.   p. 150

[193] This refers to the book *Sozialismus und Landwirtschaft* by E. David. The reference to Kautsky concerns his article "Sozialismus und Landwirthschaft" (*Die Neue Zeit* Nos. 22-26 for February and March 1903) in which he examines this book.   p. 150

[194] The Polish Social-Democrats' statement of solidarity with the R.S.D.L.P. did not appear in *Iskra*. Representatives of the Polish Social-Democratic Party attended the Second Congress as non-voting delegates.   p. 152

[195] The Bund's attack on the Ekaterinoslav Committee of the R.S.D.L.P. is fully dealt with in Lenin's article "Does the Jewish Proletariat Need an 'Independent Political Party'?" (see Vol. 6 of this edition).   p. 153

[196] See Note 186.   p. 154

[197] *Alexandrova, Yekaterina Mikhailovna* (1864-1943)—joined the revolutionary movement in 1890. In 1902, during her residence abroad, joined the *Iskra* organisation, then worked as its agent in Russia. At the Orel meeting of the O.C. for convening the Second Congress of the R.S.D.L.P. (February 1903) was elected to the O.C.; at the Congress she joined the Mensheviks; after the Congress became an active Menshevik. After the October Socialist Revolution worked in cultural and educational institutions.   p. 156

[198] The "den" was the common room in the London flat shared by V. I. Zasulich, Y. O. Martov and I. S. Blumenfeld, so called on account of its constantly disorderly state.   p. 156

[199] Meaning the *Yuzhny Rabochy* group. (See Note 106.)   p. 156

[200] *P.P.S. (Polska Partia Socjalistyczna)*—the Polish Socialist Party, a reformist nationalist party founded in 1892.   p. 156

[201] *Kalmykova, Alexandra Mikhailovna* (1849-1926)—a progressive public worker; ran a bookstore in 1889-1902, which served as a rendezvous for Social-Democrats; rendered financial aid to *Iskra*

and *Zarya*. In 1902 she was deported abroad for three years; after the split in the Party she gave financial aid to the Bolsheviks. p. 160

[202] By "Californian" sources Lenin is apparently referring to the financial aid which *Iskra* had been regularly receiving. These sources have not been ascertained. p. 163

[203] This refers to the financial aid for *Iskra*. p. 163

[204] Meaning the Second Congress of the R.S.D.L.P. held on July 17(30)-August 10 (23), 1903, first in Brussels, then in London. p. 164

[205] This refers to P. B. Axelrod. p. 165

[206] *Yegors, Yegor's countries*—Martov's followers, Mensheviks living in Geneva. p. 167

[207] This refers to the appointment of two representatives of the Central Committee to the Party Council, in accordance with the Rules adopted at the Second Congress of the R.S.D.L.P. p. 167

[208] The law on factory stewards was passed on June 10, 1903. Lenin dealt in detail with this law in his article "An Era of Reforms" (see Vol. 6 of this edition). p. 171

[209] *Manifesto of Rabochaya Volya*—a declaration by the Odessa Social-Democratic Union *Rabochaya Volya* recognising the correctness of *Iskra* views and tactics, announcing adherence to the Odessa Committee of the R.S.D.L.P. and closing the Union as a result of it. The Manifesto was published in *Iskra* No. 50 for October 15, 1903. p. 172

[210] This letter was sent also to P. B. Axelrod, V. I. Zasulich, A. N. Potresov (Old Believer) and L. D. Trotsky with the omission of the second and sixth (last) paragraphs.
Lenin wrote on the envelope "Very important. Copy of my and Plekhanov's letter to Martov & Co. dated October 6, 1903 and Martov's reply". p. 174

[211] The state of affairs in the Caucasus in connection with the behaviour of the Tiflis delegate Topuridze (Isari), who deserted to the Mensheviks after the Second Congress, is fully dealt within Lenin's letter to the Caucasian Union Committee (see pp. 179-80 of this volume). p. 177

[212] This refers to the Central Committee's announcement (report) concerning the Party's Second Congress which had been held; the draft announcement had been sent to Russia. p. 178

²¹³ The three persons mentioned here by their pseudonyms were delegates of the Caucasian union committees at the Second Congress of the R.S.D.L.P.: B. M. Knunyants, representing the Baku Committee, A. G. Zurabov, representing the Batum Committee, and Topuridze, representing the Tiflis Committee. The first two adhered to the Majority (Bolsheviks) at the Congress and after it, while the latter wavered at the Congress and afterwards supported the Minority (Mensheviks). p. 179

²¹⁴ This refers to the resolution adopted by the Don Committee on the results of the Party's Second Congress. p. 181

²¹⁵ This refers to the resolution adopted by the Committee of the Mining and Metallurgical Workers' Union on the results of the Party's Second Congress. p. 182

²¹⁶ See Note 90. p. 186

²¹⁷ This refers to Lenin's statement of resignation from the Party Council and from the editorial board of the Central Organ (see Vol. 7 of this edition, p. 91). p. 189

²¹⁸ This refers to the report concerning the Second Congress of the Party. See Note 212. p. 190

²¹⁹ *Lyadov, Martyn Nikolayevich* (1872-1947)—professional revolutionary. Began revolutionary activities in 1891. At the Second Congress of the R.S.D.L.P.—a Bolshevik, afterwards carried on an active struggle against the Mensheviks in Russia and abroad. Took an active part in the revolution of 1905-07. p. 193

²²⁰ This refers to I. I. and L. I. Axelrod. p. 195

²²¹ *Schweitzer J. B.* (1833-1875)—leader of the Lassalleans in the German labour movement in the sixties; dictatorially ruled the General German Workers' Union and strongly opposed the Eisenachers, headed by Bebel and Liebknecht. p. 200

²²² Lenin wrote this letter for F. V. Lengnik, the representative of the Central Committee abroad. p. 202

²²³ This refers to the C.C.'s negotiations with the Mensheviks concerning the situation which arose within the Party after the Second Congress. p. 202

²²⁴ *Moskovskiye Vedomosti* (Moscow Recorder)—one of the oldest Russian newspapers, originally issued (in 1756) as a small sheet by Moscow University. In 1863 it became a monarcho-nationalist mouthpiece reflecting the views of the most reactionary sections of the landowners and the clergy. From 1905 onwards was one of the leading organs of the Black Hundreds. Continued to appear until the October Socialist Revolution in 1917. p. 202

225 The reference is to the Central Committee's ultimatum presented to the Mensheviks on November 25, 1903, the chief points of which were set forth by Lenin in his letter to the C.C. dated November 4, 1903 (see p. 187 of this volume). With strong support from Plekhanov, who, the very next day after the ultimatum, co-opted all the old editors to the editorial board of the Central Organ, the Mensheviks rejected the C.C.'s ultimatum and declared open war against the Majority of the Party.

An appraisal of the C.C.'s ultimatum was given by Lenin in his book *One Step Forward, Two Steps Back* (see Vol. 7 of this edition). p. 202

226 The C.C.'s Executive Committee was set up in the second half of October 1903 and consisted of three C.C. members—G. M. Krzhizhanovsky, L. B. Krasin and F. V. Gusarov. p. 204

227 This refers to the publication of material concerning the C.C.'s negotiations with the Menshevik (Geneva) opposition abroad. p. 205

228 *Vilonov, Nikifor Yefremovich* (1883-1910)—professional revolutionary. Began his revolutionary activities in 1901. In 1902 joined the Kiev Social-Democratic organisation, became a supporter of *Iskra*. After the Second Congress of the R.S.D.L.P. (1903)—a Bolshevik. Took an active part in the revolution of 1905-07. p. 207

229 Vilonov's letter, slightly abridged, was published by Lenin in his "Postscript to the Pamphlet *A Letter to a Comrade on Our Organisational Tasks*" (see Vol. 7 of this edition). p. 207

230 The three persons were G. M. Krzhizhanovsky, F. V. Lengnik and V. A. Noskov. p. 209

231 On Krzhizhanovsky's return from abroad and on the basis of his report concerning the results of the negotiations with the Mensheviks, the C.C. circulated a letter to the local committees which played down the acute Party struggle and advocated a conciliatory policy towards the Mensheviks. p. 211

232 Lenin wrote this letter for Lengnik, the C.C.'s representative abroad. p. 213

233 This refers to the resolution passed by the editorial board of the new, Menshevik, *Iskra* concerning the publication as a separate sheet of Lenin's letter "Why I Resigned from the *Iskra* Editorial Board" (see Vol. 7 of this edition). p. 213

234 This letter is a postscript to the previous letter of December 30, 1903, both being dispatched on January 5, 1904. p. 218

235 This refers to Axelrod's article "The Unity of Russian Social-Democracy and Its Tasks", published in *Iskra* Nos. 55 and 57.

Lenin here refers to the first part of this article published in issue No. 55 under the sub-heading "Liquidation of Primitivism Summed Up". p. 218

[236] Meaning the publication of material concerning the C.C.'s negotiations with the Menshevik (Geneva) opposition. p. 222

[237] This letter was an insertion to the rough copy of Lengnik's letter sent in reply to that of Y. O. Martov. p. 223

[238] This and the next letter were written for Lengnik, the C.C.'s representative abroad. p. 224

[239] This letter is an addition to the letter of N. K. Krupskaya on the subject of Stake's (Lengnik's) non-withdrawal from the C.C. p. 237

[240] This refers to Lenin's agreement with Noskov, who had arrived in the capacity of the C.C.'s representative abroad and its second member on the Party Council to replace Lengnik, who had returned to Russia; the agreement covered joint action by Noskov and Lenin abroad on behalf of the C. C. and was signed on May 13 (26) in the presence of a third member of the C.C., M. M. Essen, who was abroad at the time (see Vol. 7, pp. 430-31, of this edition). p. 238

[241] *Krasin, Leonid Borisovich* (1870-1926)—prominent Soviet statesman, joined the Social-Democratic movement in the nineties. After the Second Congress of the R.S.D.L.P. (1903)—a Bolshevik; co-opted to the C.C. of the Party, where he adopted a conciliatory attitude towards the Mensheviks and helped to co-optate three of their representatives on to the C.C. Shortly afterwards, however, he broke with the Mensheviks. An active participant in the first Russian revolution. p. 240

[242] The reference is to D. S. Postolovsky, Russian Social-Democrat, agent of the C.C. of the R.S.D.L.P. from the spring of 1904. A conciliator. p. 240

[243] *Soft members*—C.C. members, conciliators: V. A. Noskov, L. Y. Galperin and L. B. Krasin. p. 242

[244] This refers to the Party Council's decision of May 31 (June 13), 1904, concerning representation at the forthcoming Amsterdam Congress of the Second International. p. 244

[245] *Vladimirov, Miron Konstantinovich* (1879-1925)—Social-Democrat, Bolshevik, joined the R.S.D.L.P. in 1903. Carried on Party work in St. Petersburg, Gomel, Odessa, Lugansk and Ekaterinoslav. Delegate to the Third Congress of the R.S.D.L.P. Participant in the revolution of 1905-07. After the October Socialist Revolution occupied various important posts. p. 245

[246] This refers to the decision adopted in July 1904 on behalf of the
C.C. by C.C. conciliator members Krasin, Noskov and Galperin.
In this decision the conciliators recognised the validity of the
Iskra Menshevik editorial board co-opted by Plekhanov. They
co-opted three more conciliators on to the C.C. The conciliators
were against convening the Third Congress of the Party and adopted a decision dissolving the Southern Bureau of the C.C. which
agitated for the convocation of this Congress. They deprived
Lenin of the right to represent the C.C. abroad and attempted
to ban publication of his writings which did not have the permission of the C.C.'s collegium.

The adoption of the "July Declaration" was a complete betrayal
of the decisions of the Second Congress of the R.S.D.L.P. on the
part of the conciliator members of the C.C. who openly sided
with the Mensheviks.   p. 248

[247] V. A. Noskov informed Lenin of the C.C.'s decision to co-optate
three new members on to the C.C., namely, L. Y. Karpov,
A. I. Lyubimov, and I. F. Dubrovinsky, and asked Lenin to give
his vote for or against the nominated candidates within a week.
                                                          p. 251

[248] Lenin did not attend the Amsterdam Congress and transferred
his mandate to M. N. Lyadov and P. A. Krasikov, who were included in the delegation of the R.S.D.L.P. to the Congress. p. 256

[249] Three conferences of local Bolshevik committees—the Southern,
Caucasian and Northern conferences—were held in September-
December 1904. (1) The Southern Regional Conference (three
committees: those of Odessa, Ekaterinoslav and Nikolayev) was
held in September 1904. The conference declared in favour of
convening the Third Congress of the Party and proposed that an
Organising Committee for convening the congress be set up, con-
sisting of R. S. Zemlyachka, M. N. Lyadov and A. Bogdanov.
The conference instructed Lenin to constitute the full Organising
Committee.

(2) The Regional Conference of the Caucasian Union Committee
(four committees: those of Baku, Batum, Tiflis and Imeretia and
Mingrelia) was held in November 1904 in Tiflis. The conference
declared in favour of immediately convening the Third Congress
of the Party and elected a bureau to make preparations for the
congress.

(3) The Northern Regional Conference (six committees: those
of St. Petersburg, Moscow, Tver, Riga, Northern and Nizhni-
Novgorod) was held in December 1904. The conference passed
a vote of non-confidence in the Party's central bodies seized by
the Mensheviks, declared strongly in favour of convening the
Third Congress of the Party, and set up a special bureau for organising the congress.   p. 257

[250] This refers to the meeting held in the neighbourhood of Geneva
on Lenin's initiative during the early part of August 1904. The

meeting was attended by 19 members of the R.S.D.L.P., including Lenin, Krupskaya, Olminsky, Lyadov, and Lepeshinsky. The initial variant of the appeal "To the Party", written by Lenin, was adopted (see Vol. 7 of this edition). Shortly afterwards three more Bolsheviks added their votes to the decisions of this meeting, and the appeal "To the Party" was issued on behalf of 22 Bolsheviks.

The appeal became the Bolsheviks' programme of struggle for convening the Third Congress of the Party.   p. 257

251 *The Bonch-Bruyevich and Lenin publishing house of Social-Democratic party literature* was set up by the Bolsheviks after the Menshevik editorial board of *Iskra* refused to publish the statements of organisations and Party members supporting the decisions of the Second Congress and demanding the convocation of the Third Congress of the Party.   p. 258

252 The decisions of the Council of the R.S.D.L.P. were published in a separate supplements to Nos. 73 and 74 of *Iskra*. The first of these decisions dealing with the procedure for ·convening the Third Congress listed a number of measures aimed at obstructing agitation in favour of the congress and preventing its being convened in the immediate future.   p. 258

253 This refers to the pamphlet *To the Party*, in which the appeal under the same heading written by Lenin was published (see Vol. 7 of this edition), and N. Shakhov's pamphlet *The Fight for a Congress*, to which Lenin wrote a preface (see Vol. 7, p. 490, of this edition).   p. 261

254 *The question of representation at the Amsterdam Congress* was this: The Party Council, in its September decision, accused Lenin, Lyadov and Krasikov of a breach of Party discipline, expressed in their applying directly to the International Socialist Bureau on the question of Lenin transferring his mandate to the Congress. The Council further maintained that Lenin demanded for himself, as a representative of the C.C., the right to attend the Congress "at a time when he was already in antagonism with the Central Committee". Actually, Lenin sent representatives to the Congress early in August, that is, before his conflict with the conciliator section of the C.C., which took place towards the end of August.   p. 261

255 This refers to the *Report of the Delegation of the Russian Social-Democratic Labour Party to the Amsterdam International Socialist Congress (August 14-20, 1904)*, Geneva, 1904.   p. 261

256 *The Caucasian S.D. Union* united the working-class organisations of the Caucasus (Tiflis, Baku, Batum, Kutais, Guria, etc.). At the first Congress of the Caucasian Union held in March 1903 a leading Party organ was set up—the Caucasian Union Committee of the R.S.D.L.P.

Lenin and the Caucasian Union Committee were in constant and close contact. In September 1904 the C.U.C. supported the resolution of the meeting of the "22" and started agitation in favour of the immediate convocation of the Party's Third Congress.

p. 262

[257] *Stopani, Alexander Mitrofanovich* (1871-1932)—professional revolutionary, joined the revolutionary movement in 1892. At the Second Congress of the R.S.D.L.P. (1903) and after it—a Bolshevik. After the Congress, on the instructions of the C.C., he worked in Yaroslavl, where he organised an illegal printing-plant; left for Baku in the summer of 1904 after the plant was raided by the police; was one of the organisers of the Baku Bolshevik Committee. After the October Socialist Revolution occupied leading Party posts.

p. 264

[258] The manuscript contains Lenin's note: "(quote in full)" followed by dots and special marks indicating that the text of the corresponding resolution of the Conference of the Southern Committees was to be quoted here. The text of the resolution was not quoted in the letter, nor was the reply of the "22" (see p. 257 of this volume).

p. 265

[259] Lenin speaks of the need for creating the illegal Bolshevik newspaper *Vperyod*, the first issue of which came out on January 4, 1905 (December 22, 1904)

p. 267

[260] Meaning the statement of the Caucasian Union Committee and the Caucasian representative of the C.C. protesting against the decisions of the Party Council published in a supplement to Nos. 73 and 74 of *Iskra*.

p. 268

[261] Lenin was on a lecture tour (on the subject of the situation within the Party) in Paris (up to December 5), Zurich (December 6-7) and Berne (December 8).

p. 269

[262] *Zemlyachka, Rozalia Samoilovna* (1876-1947)—a leading member of the Communist Party and the Soviet Government. Joined the revolutionary movement in 1893; upon her return from abroad in 1896 became a member of the Kiev Committee of the R.S.D.L.P. From 1901 an agent of *Iskra*, carried on work in Odessa and Ekaterinoslav. At the Second Congress of the R.S.D.L.P. (1903) an Iskrist of the Majority. After the Congress she was co-opted on to the Central Committee from the Bolsheviks, took an active part in the fight against the Mensheviks. In August 1904 participated in the meeting of the 22 Bolsheviks in Geneva, was elected to the Bureau of the Majority Committees. Worked as secretary of the St. Petersburg Party organisation and was its delegate to the Third Congress of the Party.

Litvinov, Maxim Maximovich (1876-1951)—prominent Party member and statesman, distinguished Soviet diplomat. Started revolutionary work in 1898 as a propagandist in workers' circles. In 1900 worked in the Kiev Committee; in 1901 was arrested, in prison joined the Iskrists. In August 1902 escaped from prison with ten other Iskrists and emigrated. Took an active part in disseminating *Iskra*, was a delegate at the Second Congress of the League.   p. 271

263 Lenin intended to enlist the services of A. Bogdanov (Rakhmetov) for work on the newspaper *Vperyod*, the mouthpiece of the Bolsheviks, which was being organised (see Note 265).   p. 273

264 This refers to the resolutions of the Regional Conference of the Caucasian Union Committee held in Tiflis in November 1904. On the basis of the previous resolutions of the Caucasian committees giving support to the resolution of the "22" and to the idea of convening an emergency congress of the Party the Conference adopted a resolution calling for the organisation of broad agitation and struggle for the Third Congress, for which purpose it elected a special bureau with instructions to contact the Bolshevik group of "22". In the postscript to this letter Lenin wishes to be informed as to what organisational forms of relationship existed between the Bureau of the Majority Committees and the bureau set up by the Conference of the Caucasian committees, and asks them to send a delegate.   p. 280

265 *Vperyod* (Forward)—an illegal Bolshevik newspaper published in Geneva from December 22, 1904 (January 4, 1905) to May 5 (18), 1905. Eighteen issues were put out. Lenin was the newspaper's organiser, manager and ideological guide. Other members of the editorial board were V. V. Vorovsky, M. S. Olminsky, and A. V. Lunacharsky. The outstanding role which the newspaper played in combating Menshevism and highlighting the tactical issues posed by the revolutionary movement was acknowledged in a special resolution of the Third Party Congress (1905), which recorded a vote of thanks to the editorial board.   p. 280

266 *Borba Proletariata* (Struggle of the Proletariat)—an illegal Bolshevik newspaper, organ of the Caucasian Union of the R.S.D.L.P., founded by decision of the First Congress of the Caucasian Union of the R.S.D.L.P. Published from April-May 1903 to October 1905; 12 numbers were issued. The newspaper was published in three languages—Georgian, Armenian and Russian. The editors maintained close contact with Lenin and the Bolshevik centre abroad.   p. 281

267 *Essen, Maria Moiseyevna* (1872-1956)—a Social-Democrat. Joined the revolutionary movement in the early nineties. After the Second Congress of the R.S.D.L.P. a Bolshevik; was co-opted on to the Central Committee at the end of 1903. In 1906 a member of the Moscow Committee. During the period of reaction (1907-10) retired from active political life.   p. 282

[268] *The Northern Regional Conference* (six committees: St. Petersburg, Moscow, Tver, Riga, Northern and Nizhni-Novgorod) was held in December 1904 (see Note 249).   p. 283

[269] This refers to the committees, at the conferences of which the Bureau of the Majority Committees was elected.   p. 284

[270] *Yeramasov, A. I.* (died 1927)—a Social-Democrat, Iskrist. From the time of *Iskra* up to the October Socialist Revolution gave financial assistance to the Bolshevik Party.   p. 285

[271] This refers to the second Mensheviks' "Letter to Party Organisations" published in leaflet form in December 1904 over the signature of the *Iskra* editorial board. A critical analysis of *Iskra*'s first letter mentioned by Lenin lower down was given by him in the pamphlet *The Zemstvo Campaign and Iskra's Plan* (see Vol. 7 of this edition) Lenin also deals with these letters in his article "Two Tactics" (see Vol. 8 of this edition).   p. 287

[272] The editorial "Democrats at the Parting of the Ways" in No. 77 of the Menshevik *Iskra* was criticised by Lenin in his article "Working-Class and Bourgeois Democracy" published in *Vperyod* No. 3, for January 24 (11), 1905 (see Vol. 8 of this edition).   p. 288

[273] On January 6, 1905 (December 24, 1904), Lenin read a lecture on working-class and bourgeois democracy to an audience of political emigrants in Geneva.   p. 290

[274] Issue No. 1 of *Vperyod* was dated January 4, 1905 (December 22, 1904).   p. 290

[275] This refers to the three conferences of the Bolshevik local committees (the Southern, the Caucasian and the Northern) held in September-December 1904, which went on record for the immediate convocation of the Third Congress of the R.S.D.L.P. (see Note 249).   p. 291

[276] This refers to *Fyodorova-Shtremer, N. I.*—secretary of the St. Petersburg Committee. In December 1904 she adopted a conciliatory stand in regard to the Mensheviks.   p. 291

[277] This refers to the election of the Bureau of the Majority Committees for convening the Third Congress of the R.S.D.L.P. p. 292

[278] See Note 146.   p. 293

[279] *Gapon, Georgi Apollonovich* (1870-1906)—a priest, *agent provocateur* in the service of the tsarist secret political police. On the eve of the revolution of 1905-07, acting on the instructions of the Department of the Police, he organised the Association of Russian Factory Workers of St. Petersburg, which was subsidised

by the Department of the Police and the St. Petersburg secret political police. Provoked the procession of St. Petersburg workers to present a petition to the tsar on the Ninth of January, 1905 (see Note 281). Escaped abroad, where he had close ties with the Socialist-Revolutionaries. He returned to Russia and resumed contact with the secret political police. Exposed as an *agent provocateur*, Gapon was killed in accordance with a sentence passed on him by the Socialist-Revolutionary Party.   p. 293

280 The tables of correspondence with Russia were compiled by N. K. Krupskaya, who kept a record of all the correspondence.
                                                                    p. 293

281 *The Ninth of January 1905*—"Bloody Sunday", the day on which, by order of the tsar, a peaceful procession of St. Petersburg workers was shot down. The workers, led by the priest Gapon, were marching to the Winter Palace to present a petition to the tsar. This cold-blooded massacre of unarmed workers started a wave of mass political strikes and demonstrations all over Russia under the slogan of "Down with the autocracy!" The events of January 9th precipitated the revolution of 1905-07.   p. 293

282 The reference is to the Third Congress of the R.S.D.L.P., preparations for which were in hand.   p. 293

283 In his letter of February 3, 1905, August Bebel notified Lenin that in order to liquidate the split in the R.S.D.L.P. the Executive Committee of the German Social-Democratic Party had instructed him to preside at a court of arbitration in which representatives of the Bolsheviks (*Vperyod*) and the Mensheviks (*Iskra*) were to be included. Bebel asked the Bolsheviks to confirm their readiness, in the event of their agreeing to a court of arbitration and election of their representatives to such a court, to accept the court's award. It was stipulated that the Mensheviks and the Bolsheviks were to cease all polemics from the moment they submitted to the court.   p. 295

284 Bebel's proposal was reported in *Vperyod* No. 8, for February 28 (15), 1905, in a note to the editors' comment following the text of the announcement of the Bureau of the Majority Committees concerning the convocation of the Third Congress of the Party (see Vol. 8, p. 178, of this edition).   p. 295

285 *Gusev, Sergei Ivanovich* (1874-1933)—Social-Democrat, Bolshevik. From December 1904 to May 1905 secretary of the Bureau of the Majority Committees and the St. Petersburg Committee of the Party, then a leader of the Bolshevik organisation in Odessa. From January 1906 a member of the Moscow Committee of the R.S.D.L.P. During the years of reaction (1907-10), came out against liquidationism and otzovism.
   After the October Socialist Revolution, held positions of trust.
                                                                    p. 296

[286] A paragraph from Moscow reporting that a representative of the Central Committee had made a statement at a meeting to the effect that all the members of the C. C. agreed to the convening of the Third Congress was published in *Vperyod* No. 8, for February 28 (15), 1905. It was accompanied by an afterword "From the Editors" written by M. S. Olminsky. The afterword stated that the C.C. for some months had resisted a congress and dismissed the committees that had declared for it, and that now that its tactics had failed it was declaring its agreement to have a congress convened immediately, obviously with the intention of wrecking it. Lenin added to Olminsky's text the following words: "We hope that neither the Bureau nor the local committees will let themselves be deceived by the subterfuges of the Party's 'Shidlovsky Commission'." p. 298

[287] *The Shidlovsky Commission*—a special government commission set up by royal Ukase of January 29 (February 11), 1905, "to enquire into the causes of the discontent among the workers of the city of St. Petersburg and its environs" in connection with the mounting strike movement following the events of Bloody Sunday (January 9). The Commission, headed by Senator Shidlovsky, was made up of government officials, managers of state factories and manufacturers. The Commission was to include representatives of the workers elected by two-stage elections. The Bolsheviks launched a campaign in connection with these elections, exposing the true designs of tsarism, which had organised this Commission in order to draw the workers away from the revolutionary struggle. When the electors presented their demands to the government, namely, freedom of speech, of the press, and of assembly, etc., Shidlovsky stated on February 18 (March 3), 1905 that these demands could not be granted. After this the majority of the electors withdrew from the elections and appealed to the workers of St. Petersburg, who supported them by going on strike. The Commission was dismissed on February 20 (March 5), 1905, without having started work. p. 299

[288] The leaflets of the Bureau of the Majority Committees: the first, "Vital Issues" (concerning the uprising), was published in the newspaper *Vperyod* No. 9, for March 8 (February 23), 1905; the second, "The Attitude of the Russian Social-Democratic Labour Party to the Liberals", in Issue No. 10 for March 15 (2), 1905. p. 300

[289] A quotation from Virgil's *Aeneid* "I fear the Danaans, though their hands proffer gifts". p. 302

[290] In regard to the conference of socialist organisations of Russia see Lenin's article "A Militant Agreement for the Uprising" (Vol. 8, pp. 158-66, of this editon) and "Speech on an Agreement with the Socialist-Revolutionaries" delivered on April 23 (May 6), 1905, at the Third Congress of the R.S.D.L.P. (Vol. 8, pp. 416-21). p. 303

291 *Icons abroad*—an ironical name for the Menshevik leaders.   p. 303

292 This   refers to a conference of representatives of the C.C. of the R.S.D.L.P., the Bund, the Lettish S.D.L.P., and the Revolutionary Ukrainian Party held abroad in January 1905. It was convened on the initiative of the Bund with the object of uniting all the Social-Democratic organisations. The conference adopted a resolution on agreements with the liberal and democratic parties and on a "bloc" of the revolutionary and opposition organisations in Russia.   p. 303

293 *Posledniye Izvestia*—the bulletin of the Bund Committee Abroad, published in London and Geneva in 1901-06.   p. 303

294 In reply to this letter, Lydia Knipovich, a member of the Odessa Committee of the R.S.D.L.P., informed Lenin that the mandate to the congress previously issued to V. V. Vorovsky in the name of the Odessa Committee was being transferred to Lenin and that Vorovsky would receive his mandate from the Nikolayev Committee.   p. 307

295 This refers to the agreement between the C.C. of the R.S.D.L.P. and the Bureau of the Majority Committees concluded on March 12 (25), 1905, on the question of setting up an Organising Committee for convening the Third Congress of the Party.   p. 309

296 *Vinogradova, Olga* (1881-1913)—joined the revolutionary movement in 1901. In 1903 carried on propaganda and agitation in Nizhni-Novgorod. In 1903-04—a member of the Bolshevik group in Berlin. In the spring of 1905 worked in the Odessa organisation. Was a correspondent of the newspapers *Vperyod* and *Proletary*. In 1905-07 worked in St. Petersburg, was a member of the agitators' collegium under the St. Petersburg Committee. Afterwards worked in Saratov.   p. 310

297 This letter was a reply to that of Olga Vinogradova dated February 18, 1905, from Odessa; in which she wrote to Lenin: "In your letter to Comrade T. you mention my promise to write about Nizhni-Novgorod."   p. 310

298 This refers to the *Geneva Conference of the Mensheviks* held simultaneously with the Third Congress of the R.S.D.L.P. in April 1905.   p. 312

299 *The Third Congress of the R.S.D.L.P.* was held in London from April 12 to 27 (April 25-May 10), 1905, and was attended by 24 voting delegates and 14 delegates with a consultative voice. It was the first Bolshevik congress.

All the Congress proceedings were guided by Lenin. He wrote the drafts of all the basic resolutions adopted by the Congress and spoke on the question of the armed uprising, on the participation of Social-Democrats in the provisional revolutionary government, on the attitude towards the peasant movement, on the Party Rules and on a number of other questions. The Minutes of the Congress record over a hundred speeches and motions made by Lenin.

The Congress condemned the actions of the Mensheviks, their opportunism in organisational and tactical questions; it laid down the tactical line of the Bolsheviks aimed at the complete victory of the bourgeois-democratic revolution and its development into a socialist revolution. The resolutions of the Congress outlined the tasks of the proletariat as the leader of the revolution and the strategic plan of the Party in the bourgeois-democratic revolution, namely, the proletariat, in alliance with the peasantry, and with the liberal bourgeoisie isolated, was to fight for the victory of the revolution.

The Congress amended the Party Rules: a) it adopted Lenin's wording of Clause One; 2) it defined precisely the rights of the Central Committee and its relations with the local committees; c) it modified the organisational structure of the Party's central bodies: in place of the two centres (the Central Committee, the Central Organ) the Congress established a single competent Party centre—the Central Committee.   p. 312

300 *Proletary* (The Proletarian)—underground Bolshevik weekly, Central Organ of the R.S.D.L.P., founded in accordance with a resolution of the Third Party Congress. By a decision of the plenary meeting of the Party C. C. of April 27 (May 10), 1905, Lenin was appointed Editor-in-Chief.

Proletary was published in Geneva from May 14 (27) to November 12 (25), 1905. Twenty-six numbers were put out. The newspaper carried on the line of the old, Leninist, *Iskra*, and maintained complete continuity with the Bolshevik newspaper *Vperyod*. Lenin wrote over sixty articles and paragraphs for the newspaper. His articles were reprinted in the local Bolshevik periodicals and published in leaflet form.   p. 312

301 The question of the R.S.D.L.P.'s representation in the International Socialist Bureau was discussed in the C.C. of the R.S.D.L.P. on May 7 (20), 1905. Plekhanov's appointment as representative of the R.S.D.L.P. in the I.S.B. was signed by Krasin, Lenin and Postolovsky with a reservation to the effect that Lenin was instructed to implement this decision in the event of a satisfactory conclusion of the negotiations started with Plekhanov. Lenin considered recognition of the validity of the Third Congress, membership of the Party and acceptance of its decisions to be obligatory on the part of Plekhanov.

The Mensheviks nominated Plekhanov to the I.S.B. at their conference. On June 16, 1905, Plekhanov notified the I.S.B. that he had been authorised to represent the Party by both splinter

groups and gave a tendentious account of the split in which he denied the necessity and validity of the Party's Third Congress.
p. 313

[302] The Report on the Third Congress and the major resolutions were published in *Proletary* No. 1, for May 14 (27), 1905. p. 315

[303] Lenin is here referring to the decision of the plenary meeting of the C.C. of the R.S.D.L.P. (the first plenum after the Third Congress), held on April 27 (May 10), 1905, concerning the next plenary meeting to be held in Geneva on September 1 (14). This decision was not carried out.   p. 315

[304] Bebel's offer to mediate in uniting the Bolsheviks and Mensheviks was addressed to the International Socialist Bureau after he had received a negative reply to a similar proposal addressed directly to Lenin on January 21 (February 3), 1905. (See Lenin's reply, p. 295 of this volume).   p. 318

[305] The Report on the Third Congress of the R.S.D.L.P. and the resolutions of the Congress were published in the pamphlet *Bericht über den III Parteitag der S.D.A.P.R.*, München. K. Kautsky wrote an article "Die Spaltung der russischen Sozialdemokratie" ("The Split in Russian Social-Democracy") in *Leipziger Volkszeitung*, the mouthpiece of the German Left Social-Democrats (No. 135 for June 15,1905), against the circulation of this pamphlet. In reply to Kautsky's article Lenin wrote his "Open Letter to the Editorial Board of the *Leipziger Volkszeitung*" (see Vol. 8 of this edition), which the editors did not publish.   p. 318

[306] *The Open Letter* of the C.C. to the Organisation Committee of the Mensheviks, written by A. A. Bogdanov, was published in *Proletary* on August 9 (July 27), 1905, issue No. 11.
     The C.C. of the R.S.D.L.P. proposed to the Menshevik centre—the Organisation Committee—to enter into negotiations for unity on the following terms, with the Bolsheviks and the Mensheviks preserving ideological independence:
     (1) the local committees unite on the basis outlined by the Third Congress of the R.S.D.L.P.;
     (2) the central bodies come to an arrangement for joint activities aimed at re-establishing unity;
     (3) the parallel existence of the Party organs to be preserved.
     This plan was criticised by Lenin in his letter to the C.C. of the R.S.D.L.P. dated August 14, 1905 (see pp. 326-27 of this volume).   p. 319

[307] In the "Open Letter" the tactical differences between the Bolsheviks and the Mensheviks were recognised as "insignificant". The pamphlet here referred to by Lenin is *Two Tactics of Social-Democracy in the Democratic Revolution*, on which he worked in the course of June-July 1905 (see Vol. 9 of this edition). p. 319

[308] The decision appointing Plekhanov Editor-in-Chief of the Party's scientific organ was adopted by the C.C. of the R.S.D.L.P. on May 7 (20), 1905; Lenin was instructed to implement this decision in the event of the negotiations with Plekhanov being satisfactorily concluded.   p. 321

[309] The Social-Democratic Federation, founded in 1884, included within its ranks representatives of reformism (Hyndman and others), anarchists, and Marxists representing the Left wing of the British socialist movement. In 1907 it was renamed the Social-Democratic Party; in 1911 this Party and the Left elements of the Independent Labour Party formed the British Socialist Party, which, in 1920, together with the Socialist Unity group, played the chief role in establishing the Communist Party of Great Britain.   p. 321

[310] A secret resolution of the Third Congress on the question of "preparing the terms of unification with the Mensheviks" stated that the Congress "instructs the C.C. to take steps towards preparing and working out the terms of unification with the breakaway section of the R.S.D.L.P., which terms are to be submitted for final endorsement to a new Party congress" (see *The C.P.S.U. in the Resolutions and Decisions of Its Congresses, Conferences and Plenums of the Central Committee*, Part I, 1954, p. 90).   p. 321

[311] *Lunacharsky, Anatoly Vasilievich* (1875-1933)—joined the revolutionary movement in the early nineties. After the Second Congress of the R.S.D.L.P. (1903) a Bolshevik. Member of the editorial boards of the Bolshevik newspapers *Vperyod, Proletary* and later *Novaya Zhizn*. During the reaction deviated from Marxism and participated in the anti-Party *Vperyod* group. Advocated the combination of Marxism with religion. Lenin sharply criticised Lunacharsky's views in his book *Materialism and Empiriocriticism* (1909). In 1917 Lunacharsky was enrolled in the Party at the Sixth Congress.

After the October Socialist Revolution a prominent Soviet statesman.   p. 323

[312] Meaning the participants in the mutiny aboard the armoured cruiser *Potemkin*.   p. 324

[313] The Menshevik *Iskra* published the minutes of the meeting between the C.C. of the R.S.D.L.P. and the Mensheviks' centre—the Organisation Committee—held on July 12, 1905, to discuss unification of the Party. The Mensheviks proposed a plan, which, considering the impossibility of convening a congress, called for unification of the Party "by means of sufficient mutual concessions by both sections of the Party". The plan set forth in the minutes provided for the organisation of a Central Committee consisting of representatives of both sections of the Party, and for retaining *Iskra* and *Proletary* as the official organs of the Party. The

representatives of the C.C. of the R.S.D.L.P. found the point concerning the formation of a Central Committee consisting of representatives of both sections of the Party acceptable; the question of the functioning of two organs was postponed pending clarification of the attitude towards this on the part of the editorial boards concerned; as to the terms in general, the representatives of the C. C. of the R.S.D.L.P. considered that, although they did not conflict with the basic principles of the Party Rules, not all of them were practicable.   p. 326

[314] This refers to the agreement concluded by member of the C.C. of the R.S.D.L.P. Leonid Krasin and the Social-Democrat V. L. Kopp (Frockcoat) arranging for illegal transportation to and from Russia. On the basis of this agreement V. L. Kopp attempted not only to monopolise the business of illegal communication with Russia, but to seize some of the property and literature belonging to the Bolsheviks.   p. 327

[315] This refers to the publication of the minutes of the Third Congress of the R.S.D.L.P.   p. 327

[316] The Orel-Bryansk Committee, having heard the report on the Third Congress of the R.S.D.L.P., did not "consider it possible to take one or another stand" and recommended the Minority, not represented at the Third Congress, "to amalgamate with the Party", declaring that "in the area of its revolutionary work it would make no distinction between the comrades of the Minority and those of the Majority, both of which it considered members of a single Russian Social-Democratic Labour Party".   p. 327

[317] "Black-Hundred Literature"—articles of Kostrov (N. Jordania) published first in *Sotsial-Demokrat* (organ of the Georgian Mensheviks), Nos. 1-3, and subsequently in pamphlet form under the title *Majority or Minority?*   p. 328

[318] *Dnevnik Sotsial-Demokrata* (Diary of a Social-Democrat) No. 2 for August 1905 published Plekhanov's article "Selected Passages From Correspondence With Friends (A Letter to the Editors of *Proletary*)" in which the author answered Lenin's article "On the Provisional Revolutionary Government. Article One. Plekhanov's Reference to History" (see Vol. 8 of this edition), and accused Lenin and the Bolsheviks of Blanquism.   p. 329

[319] A plan of the pamphlet *The Working Class and Revolution* was drawn up by Lenin (see Vol. 9 of this edition), but the pamphlet on this subject was not written.   p. 329

[320] The manifesto concerning the Bulygin Duma was published on August 6 (19), 1905. On August 29 (16) *Proletary* published an article of Lenin's on this subject entitled "Oneness of the Tsar and the People, and of the People and the Tsar" (Vol. 9, pp. 191-99, of this edition).   p. 329

[321] *Lepeshinsky, Panteleimon Nikolayevich* (1868-1944)—a prominent member of the Communist Party. Joined the Social-Democratic movement in the early nineties. In 1900 he took an active part in organising the promulgation of *Iskra*. In 1903 he emigrated to Switzerland; took part in preparing the Third Congress of the R.S.D.L.P. During the revolution of 1905-07 carried on revolutionary work in Ekaterinoslav and St. Petersburg.   p. 330

[322] This letter of Lenin's (*Decision* of the C. C. representative abroad) was written in connection with the conflict that had arisen between various members of the Bolshevik Geneva group.   p. 330

[323] The Conference of Social-Democratic Organisations in Russia was held in Riga on September 7-9 (20-22), 1905. It was attended by representatives of the C.C. of the R.S.D.L.P., of the Organisation Committee of the Mensheviks, of the Bund, of the Lettish Social-Democrats, of the Social-Democrats of Poland and Lithuania and the Revolutionary Ukrainian Party. The Conference approved the Bolshevik tactics of active boycott of the Bulygin Duma. The Conference decisions were assessed by Lenin in his articles "The First Results of the Political Alignment" and "The Hysterics of the Defeated" (see Vol. 9 of this edition). The Mensheviks refused to sign the resolutions of the Conference. p. 336

[324] *The Armenian Social-Democratic Federation*—a nationalist organisation formed in 1903, shortly after the Second Congress of the R.S.D.L.P., which proclaimed itself the sole representative of the Armenian proletariat; like the Bundists, it recognised only the federative principle of party organisation.   p. 337

[325] *Letuchie Listki* (Leaflets) of the Central Committee of the R.S.D.L.P.—a non-periodical publication dealing with current tactical and organisational questions in keeping with the decisions of the Third Congress of the Party. Altogether four numbers were put out. *Listok* No. 1 was printed in June 1905 at the print-shop of the St. Petersburg Committee of the Party and reprinted in abridged form in July by the Moscow Committee of the Party.

Rabochy (The Worker)—an illegal popular Social-Democratic newspaper, published in pursuance of the decision of the Third Congress of the Party by the Central Committee of the R.S.D.L.P. in Moscow in August-October 1905. The de facto editor of the paper was A. A. Bogdanov.   p. 338

[326] "Financier"—L. B. Krasin (see Note 241).   p. 338

[327] The report of the Menshevik *Iskra* published in the French socialist newspaper *Le Socialiste* No. 11, dealt with the attitude of the local Party organisations to the Third Congress of the R.S.D.L.P. *Iskra* declared that the Congress was recognised as lawful by only eight organisations of the R.S.D.L.P. (Tver, Tula, Ivanovo-Voznesensk, Yaroslavl, Kostroma, Orel, Kursk and Minsk) uniting 2,000,000-2,500,000 workers; 25 organisations,

according to *Iskra*, did not recognise the Congress; in four organisations the Congress was recognised by a minority, and the attitude to the Congress on the part of nine organisations was unascertained. Since this false information was not given by *Iskra* to the press in Russia, Lenin published in *Proletary* No. 9, for July 26 (13), 1905, under the heading "Our Khlestakovs" a full translation of the article printed in *Le Socialiste* with his introductory and concluding comments. The statistics concerning the committees of the R.S.D.L.P. which allegedly "refused to recognise" the Third Congress of the Party were also dealt with by Lenin in his article "Keeping International Social-Democracy Informed of Our Party Affairs" published in *Proletary* No. 15, for September 5 (August 23), 1905 (see Vol. 9 of this edition).   p. 339

[328] Issue No. 5 of the Marxist journal *Zarya* was being prepared for the press but did not appear.   p. 341

[329] S. I. Gusev, who worked as secretary of the Odessa Committee of the R.S.D.L.P. during the latter half of 1905, wrote to Lenin about the tactics of the Bolsheviks in the revolution of 1905, reported what educative work the Odessa Committee was doing among the masses, and criticised the resolutions of the Geneva Conference of the Mensheviks. Excerpts from Gusev's letter were published in *Proletary* No. 20, for October 10 (September 27), 1905, with an editor's preface written by Lenin (see Vol. 9, p. 335, of this edition).   p. 342

[330] A. A. Bogdanov's article "Fundamentals of Party Organisation" was not published in *Proletary*.   p. 344

[331] This refers to Lenin's trip to Finland to attend a meeting of the C.C. of the R.S.D.L.P. In a letter dated October 17 (30) he was given the address for a rendezvous in Stockholm.   p. 345

[332] This refers to representation in the I.S.B. By a decision of the C.C. of the R.S.D.L.P. Lenin was appointed representative.
                                                                        p. 345

[333] *Malykh, Maria*—publisher of legal Social-Democratic literature in 1905.   p. 345

[334] *The Fourth (Unity) Congress of the R.S.D.L.P.* was held in Stockholm on April 10-25 (April 23-May 8), 1906.
    It was attended by 112 voting delegates representing 57 local organisations and 22 delegates with a consultative voice. There were, in addition, three representatives each from the Social-Democratic Party of Poland and Lithuania, the Bund, and the Lettish S.D.L.P. and one each from the Ukrainian S.D.L.P. and the Labour Party of Finland, and a representative of the Bulgarian Social-Democratic Labour Party. The Bolshevik delegates included, among others, V. I. Lenin, F. A. Artyom (Sergeyev), M. V. Frunze, M. I. Kalinin, S. G. Shahumyan, and V. V. Vorov-

sky. The principal items on the agenda were the agrarian question, the current situation, the class tasks of the proletariat, the attitude to the Duma, and organisational questions. On all issues a sharp struggle was waged between the Bolsheviks and the Mensheviks. Lenin made reports and speeches on the agrarian question, the current situation, on the question of tactics in regard to the Duma elections, on the armed uprising and other questions.

The Mensheviks' numerical preponderance at the Congress, though slight, determined the character of the Congress decisions. On a number of questions the Congress adopted Menshevik resolutions (the agrarian programme, the attitude towards the Duma, etc.). The Congress adopted Lenin's formulation of Clause One of the Party Rules concerning membership of the Party. The Congress admitted into the R.S.D.L.P. the non-Russian Social-Democratic organisations of Poland and Lithuania and the Lettish Social-Democratic Labour Party, and made arrangements for the Bund to join the R.S.D.L.P.

The Central Committee elected at the Congress consisted of three Bolsheviks and seven Mensheviks. Only Mensheviks were elected to the editorial board of the Central Organ.

An analysis of the Congress is given in Lenin's pamphlet *Report on the Unity Congress of the R.S.D.L.P.* (see Vol. 10 of this edition).   p. 346

[335] The steamship *John Grafton* carrying weapons for revolutionary purposes ran aground off the coast of Finland on August 26 (September 8), 1905. Some of the weapons were put ashore, after which the vessel was blown up by its crew.   p. 348

[336] *The South-Russian Inaugural Conference of the Mensheviks* was held in Kiev in August 1905. It was attended by twelve delegates from Menshevik groups and committees. The Conference adopted resolutions on the following   questions: amalgamation of both sections of the Party; the Duma; the composition of *Iskra* editorial board; representation of the R.S.D.L.P. in the International Socialist Bureau; the Articles of Association, and others.

Lenin sharply criticised the decisions of the Conference in his articles "A New Menshevik Conference" and "The Latest in *Iskra* Tactics, or Mock Elections as a New Incentive to an Uprising" (see Vol. 9 of this edition).   p. 350

[337] The reference is to Lunacharsky's article published, apparently, after Lenin's suggested revision, under the heading "Parliament and Its Significance" in *Proletary* No. 25, for November 16 (3), 1905.   p. 352

[338] *Leipziger Volkszeitung*—organ of the Left wing of German Social-Democracy. The newspaper was published daily from 1894 to 1933; for a number of years it was edited by Franz Mehring and Rosa Luxemburg. From 1917 to 1922 the paper was the mouthpiece of the German "Independents". After 1922 it was the organ of the Right Social-Democrats.   p. 352

[339] Lenin is referring to Rudolph Hilferding's article "Parlamenta-
rismus und Massenstreik" published in *Die Neue Zeit* No. 51,
for September 13, 1905.   p. 352

[340] *The Moscow events*—the strikes and demonstrations started by
the Moscow workers, which Lenin dealt with in his articles "The
Political Strike and the Street Fighting in Moscow" and "The
Lessons of the Moscow Events" (see Vol. 9 of this edition). The
strike movement spread to St. Petersburg and was followed by a
general political strike all over the country (see Lenin's article
"The All-Russia Political Strike", Vol. 9 of this edition). p. 352

[341] *Cadets*—abbreviated name for members of the Constitutional-
Democratic Party, the chief party of the liberal-monarchist bourgeoisie in Russia. Founded in October 1905, its membership was
made up of representatives of the bourgeoisie, Zemstvo leaders
of the landowning class and bourgeois intellectuals. The Cadets
called themselves the "party of people's freedom". Actually they
strove towards a deal with the autocracy in order to preserve
tsarism in the form of a constitutional monarchy. Their watchword
from the beginning of the imperialist war was "war to a victorious finish". After the February revolution of 1917, as a result
of a deal with the S.R. and Menshevik leaders of the Petrograd
Soviet, they occupied key positions in the bourgeois Provisional
Government and pursued a counter-revolutionary policy opposed
to the interests of the people.

After the victory of the October Revolution the Cadets came
out as implacable enemies of the Soviet power. They took part
in all the counter-revolutionary armed actions and campaigns
of the interventionists. Living abroad as émigrés after the defeat
of the interventionists and whiteguards, the Cadets did not
cease their anti-Soviet activities.   p. 352

[342] Karl Marx, "The Class Struggles in France, 1848 to 1850" (see
Marx and Engels, *Selected Works*, Vol. 1, Moscow 1962, pp. 139-
242).   p. 353

[343] Lenin refers to his translation of the preface to the pamphlet *The
Peasant War in Germany* quoted in his book *What Is To Be Done?*
(see Vol. 5, pp 371-72, of this edition).   p. 356

[344] *Novaya Zhizn* (New Life)—the first legal Bolshevik daily published in St. Petersburg from October 27 (November 9) to December 3(16), 1905. Lenin took over the editorship upon his return
to Russia early in November 1905. *Novaya Zhizn* was, in effect,
the Central Organ of the R.S.D.L.P. Closely associated with the
paper were V. V. Vorovsky, M. S. Olminsky and A. V. Lunacharsky. Maxim Gorky contributed articles and gave the paper financial aid. The paper's circulation reached 80,000.

Novaya Zhizn was constantly persecuted. Fifteen of its twenty-seven issues were confiscated and destroyed. It was banned after the publication of No. 27. The last issue No. 28 came out illegally.

p. 362

[345] *The events of the last few days* apply to the general political strike in Russia in October 1905.

p. 363

[346] The three persons were A. Bogdanov, V. Bazarov and A. Lunacharsky.

p. 364

[347] In a note from the editorial board published in *Proletary* No. 20, for October 10 (September 27), 1905, Lenin wrote about the necessity of convening "two congresses", that of the Majority and the Minority, "at the same time and in the same place" (see "On the Question of Party Unity", Vol. 9, pp. 327-28, of this edition).

p. 368

[348] Lenin and Meshkovsky (I. P. Goldenberg) were delegates to the International Socialist Congress in Stuttgart (August 18-24, 1907). This letter was apparently written in Berlin.

p. 369

[349] Gorky did not attend the Stuttgart Congress.

p. 369

[350] Maria Fyodorovna Andreyeva, the well-known Russian actress and public figure, was the wife and assistant of A. M. Gorky.

p. 369

[351] This refers to the pamphlet by A. V. Lunacharsky (Voinov) on the attitude of the Party towards the trade unions, which was written in connection with the discussion of this question at the Seventh, Stuttgart, Congress of the Second International. Lunacharsky attended the Congress as a member of the Russian delegation and a representative of the Bolsheviks. He was elected to the committee that drafted a resolution on the question of "the relations between political parties and the trade unions".

Lunacharsky's pamphlet was not published owing to the tightening of the censorship in 1908. See Lenin's preface to the pamphlet in Vol. 13 of this edition.

p. 370

[352] This refers to the Essen Congress of the German Social-Democratic Party, held on September 21-23, 1907, at which Bebel came out against Karl Liebknecht, who had criticised Noske's chauvinist stand and the whole behaviour of the German delegation at the Stuttgart Congress. Bebel also came out against Rosa Luxemburg and all the German Left wingers for the "methods" (i.e., for their bloc with the Bolsheviks) which they adopted at the Congress in their struggle against the social-chauvinists and social-imperialists.

p. 371

[353] *Proletary*—a Bolshevik illegal newspaper, edited by Lenin, published from August 21 (September 3), 1906 to November 28 (December 11), 1909. Altogether 50 issues were put out. *Proletary,*

in effect, was the Central Organ of the Bolsheviks. The paper devoted a good deal of space to tactical and general political questions, and published reports on the activities of the C.C. of the R.S.D.L.P., the decisions of conferences and C.C. plenary meetings, C.C. letters on various questions of Party activity, and a number of other documents. The paper was in close touch with the local Party organisations.

During the years of the Stolypin reaction *Proletary* played an important role in preserving and strengthening the Bolshevik organisations and combating the liquidators, otzovists, ultimatumists and god-builders.

By a decision of the plenary meeting of the Party's C.C. of January 1910 the paper was closed down.

Zarnitsy (Summer Lightning)—a Bolshevik legal symposium, published in St. Petersburg in 1907.   p. 371

[354] Gorky toured Italy in October-December 1907 and met Lunacharsky in Florence.   p. 372

[355] This refers to the first volume of Lenin's writings entitled *Twelve Years* published in St. Petersburg in November 1907 (the cover bore the date 1908). See Lenin's "Preface to the Collection *Twelve Years*", Vol. 13 of this edition.   p. 372

[356] Arrangements for delivering *Proletary* to Russia through Gorky and Andreyeva were made in the early months of 1908, but hitches occurred owing to police interference. In a letter to Morgari, socialist M. P., editor of *Avanti!*, Gorky wrote at the beginning of May 1908 that two parcels containing the newspaper *Proletary* had been sequestered in Genoa and asked for an explanation of this "strange misunderstanding". Gorky's letter was published in *Avanti!* on May 5 (18), and on May 25 the newspaper reported that the ban on *Proletary* had been lifted.   p. 374

[357] *Rothstein, Theodore Aronovich* (1871-1953)—a Social-Democrat. In 1890 he was compelled to emigrate from Russia. Settled in England, joined the English Social-Democratic Federation where he adhered to its Left wing. Joined the R.S.D.L.P. in 1901. Contributed to the Russian and foreign socialist press. Took part in founding the Communist Party of Great Britain. Returned home in 1920. From 1921 to 1930 engaged in diplomatic work, afterwards Director of the Institute of World Economy and World Politics. From 1939 an Academician.   p. 375

[358] During the Fifth (London) Congress of the R.S.D.L.P. (April 30-May 19 [May 13-June 1], 1907), owing to the Party's extremely difficult financial position, a loan was raised with the help of Maxim Gorky and George Lansbury, the money being advanced by an English soap manufacturer and was to be repaid by January 1, 1908. The loan not being repaid in time, the lender wrote to Theodore Rothstein, reminding him about it,

and the latter, then a member of the English Social-Democratic Party, wrote to Lenin about it.

After the October Revolution the Soviet Government, through L. B. Krasin, repaid the debt to the lender's heirs who returned the letter acknowledging the debt signed by all the participants of the Congress.   p. 375

[359] N. A. Semashko was arrested in Geneva at the end of January 1908. Lenin's statement was published in the newspaper *Berner Tagwacht* No. 29, for February 5, 1908.   p. 377

[360] The announcement concerning the resumption of *Proletary* abroad was issued as a separate leaflet, stating that the publication had been transferred from Russia to Geneva and giving publication dates, the names of contributors and subscription rates.   p. 377

[361] Gorky's *Notes on Philistinism* were published in the legal Bolshevik newspaper *Novaya Zhizn* in October-November 1905.
                                                              p. 378

[362] *Berner Tagwacht*—a daily, organ of the Swiss Social-Democratic Party, founded in Berne in 1893. At the beginning of World War I the paper published articles by Karl Liebknecht, Franz Mehring and other Left Social-Democrats. From 1917 the paper openly supported the social-chauvinists.   p. 378

[363] This refers to Gorky's statement for the press in connection with the arrest of Semashko.   p. 379

[364] The article "On Cynicism" was written by Gorky for the French magazine *Les Documents du Progrès* and was first published in the symposium *Literaturny Raspad* (Zerno Publishers, St. Petersburg, which appeared in 1908) and afterwards in the March issue of the French magazine. The article contained erroneous ideas of a god-building nature.   p. 379

[365] Gorky's letter of January 30, 1908, to Henryk Sienkiewicz was an answer to the opinion poll organised by the latter on the attitude to the seizure of the Poznan landowners' estates by the Prussian government.

Gorky's letter was an accusatory document directed against Sienkiewicz's defence of big private landownership in Poznan. Gorky wrote to Sienkiewicz that, while he appreciated his gift as an artist, he protested against Sienkiewicz appealing to Wilhelm II with such arguments as the "peaceful" behaviour of the Poles, who were "not kindling the fire of revolution", were punctually paying their taxes and providing soldiers for the Prussian army. "These words give me reason to doubt the strength of your love for the Polish people," Gorky wrote in conclusion.

The 252 replies to Sienkiewicz's questionnaire were published by him in book form in Paris, but Gorky's reply was left out.
                                                              p. 379

366 Lenin was engaged in the work of issuing the newspaper *Proletary*, publication of which had been transferred from Finland to Geneva at the end of 1907.   p. 379

367 *Kwakalla*—a jocular name for the village Kuokkala, in Finland, where Lenin lived during May-November 1907.   p. 380

368 The Bolshevik symposia were published after the coup of June 3rd when the legal newspapers and periodicals were obliged to close down owing to censorship persecution. The year 1907 and beginning of 1908 saw the publication of the symposia *Golos Zhizni* (The Voice of Life), *Zarnitsy* (Summer Lightning), *Kalendar dlya vsekh* (Popular Calendar) *for 1908*, *Tyemi Dnya* (Topics of the Day), *Tekushchaya Zhizn* (Current Life), *O Veyaniakh Vremeni* (Spirit of the Times).   p. 380

369 This refers to the refusal of E. Ferri, leader of the centrist majority of the Italian Socialist Party, to edit the Party's Central Organ *Avanti!*. Lunacharsky's article "The Crisis in the Italian Workers' Party" was published in *Proletary* No. 23, for March 11 (February 27), 1908.   p. 384

370 The reference is to a meeting on Capri, sponsored by Gorky, which was to have been attended by Lenin, Bogdanov, Bazarov, Lunacharsky and Skvortsov-Stepanov to discuss questions of publishing activities and theoretical questions. The meeting took place in April 1908 (Skvortsov-Stepanov did not attend; he came to Geneva for a week to meet Lenin). Lenin mentions it in his "A Letter to Students at the Capri Party School" dated August 30, 1909 (see Vol. 15 of this edition).   p. 384

371 *The Fifth Congress of the R.S.D.L.P.* was held in London on April 30-May 19 (May 13-June 1), 1907. It was attended by 336 delegates, of whom 105 were Bolsheviks, 97 Mensheviks, 57 Bundists, 44 Polish Social-Democrats, 29 Lettish Social-Democrats and 4 non-factionalists. The Poles and Letts supported the Bolsheviks, who had a solid majority at the Congress. One of the main questions discussed was that of the attitude to the bourgeois parties. Lenin delivered the report on this question. On all fundamental issues the Congress adopted Bolshevik resolutions. A Central Committee was elected consisting of 5 Bolsheviks, 4 Mensheviks, 2 Polish and 1 Lettish Social-Democrats. Among the alternate members elected to the C.C. were 10 Bolsheviks, 7 Mensheviks, 3 Polish and 2 Lettish Social-Democrats.

The Fifth Congress of the R.S.D.L.P. marked the victory of Bolshevism in the Russian working-class movement. The decisions of the Congress summed up the struggle of the Bolsheviks against the opportunist, Menshevik wing of the Party in the period of the bourgeois-democratic revolution. The Bolsheviks' tactics were approved by the Congress and accepted as the tactics of the whole Party.   p. 386

[372] *Golos Sotsial-Demokrata* (Voice of a Social-Democrat)—a newspaper, the organ of the Mensheviks, published from February 1908 to December 1911, first in Geneva, then in Paris. The newspaper coming out in open support of the liquidators, Plekhanov resigned from the editorial board in May 1909, after which the paper took definite shape as the ideological centre of the liquidators. p. 386

[373] Lenin is referring to the group of empirio-critics and empiriomonists, adherents of the reactionary idealist philosophy of Mach and Avenarius, namely, Bogdanov, Bazarov and Lunacharsky. p. 386

[374] This refers to an invitation to Lenin to attend the meeting of the International Socialist Bureau. p. 387

[375] A journal which was to have been published by Gorky. The plan for its publication did not materialise. p. 389

[376] Gorky's article on Tolstoy did not appear in *Proletary*. Asked in 1927 whether he had written such an article, Gorky answered: "I wrote something about Tolstoy for *Proletary*. I don't remember what the title was. Possibly, 'A Great Man'." p. 391

[377] "*Notebooks*"—"Notes of an Ordinary Marxist on Philosophy"—was written by Lenin in 1906 in connection with Bogdanov's book *Empirio-monism* (Issue III). Lenin deals with these "Notes" in greater detail in his letter to Gorky dated February 25, 1908 (see Vol. 13 of this edition). p. 393

[378] *The Bolshevik Centre* was elected by the Bolshevik group of the Fifth (London) Congress of the R.S.D.L.P. in 1907. p. 393

[379] Lenin is referring to his article "Marxism and Revisionism" published in the symposium *Karl Marx—1818-1883*, in which he stated for the first time in print that he would shortly write a number of articles or a separate book against the neo-Humist and neo-Berkeleyan revisionists—Bogdanov, Bazarov and others (see Vol. 15, pp. 29-39, of this edition). p. 393

[380] This letter has not been found. p. 394

[381] *Vorovsky, Vatslav Vatslavovich* (1871-1923)—a prominent member of the Bolshevik Party, journalist and literary critic. Joined the revolutionary movement in 1890. In 1902 he emigrated abroad and became a contributor to Lenin's *Iskra*. In 1905 co-editor with Lenin on the newspapers *Vperyod* and *Proletary*, delegate to the Third Congress of the R.S.D.L.P. From the end of 1905 worked in the St. Petersburg organisation of the Bolsheviks and on the Bolshevik newspaper *Novaya Zhizn*. In 1906 a delegate to the Fourth (Unity) Congress of the R.S.D.L.P. In 1907 headed

the Bolshevik organisation in Odessa. Was arrested and exiled
for his revolutionary activities.

After the October Revolution held leading diplomatic posts.
p. 395

382 Lenin is referring to his book *Materialism and Empirio-criticism.
Critical Comments on a Reactionary Philosophy* (see Vol. 14 of
this edition).   p. 395

383 This letter was written in reply to that of the Menshevik Machist
Yushkevich offering Lenin to contribute to literary-philosophical
symposia.   p. 396

384 *Luxemburg, Rosa* (1871-1919)—a prominent member of the international labour movement, one of the leaders of the Left wing of
the Second International. Started revolutionary activities in the
late eighties, was one of the founders and leaders of the Social-
Democratic Party of Poland. From 1897 took an active part in
the German Social-Democratic movement.

After the revolution of November 1918 in Germany took a leading part in the Inaugural Congress of the Communist Party of
Germany. In January 1919 she was arrested and killed by order
of the Scheidemann government.

Lenin, who thought highly of Rosa Luxemburg, often criticised
her mistakes, thus helping her to adopt a correct stand.   p. 397

385 Lenin and Krupskaya visited Rosa Luxemburg early in January
1908 when they stopped over in Berlin on their way to Geneva
from Stockholm.   p. 397

386 The notice (note) concerning the appearance of Lenin's book *Materialism and Empirio-Criticism* was published in the journal
Die Neue Zeit, I. Band, No. 2, October 8, 1909.   p. 397

387 *Otzovists* (from the Russian word *otozvat*—recall)—the name giv-
en to some of the Bolsheviks (Bogdanov, Pokrovsky, Lunacharsky, Bubnov and others) who demanded that the Social-Democratic deputies in the Third Duma should be recalled and that
work in the legal organisations should be stopped. In 1908 the otzovists formed a group of their own and waged a struggle against
Lenin. They emphatically refused to sit in the Duma or work in
the trade unions, co-operative societies and other mass legal
and semi-legal organisations of the workers. They strove to shut
themselves up within the framework of the illegal organisation:
to tear the Party away from the non-party masses and expose it
to the attacks of reaction. Lenin called the otzovists "liquidators
of a new type" and "Mensheviks inside out".

A variety of otzovism was ultimatumism. The ultimatumists
differed from the otzovists only in form. They proposed that an ultimatum should first be presented to the Social-Democratic group
in the Duma and if it was not complied with, the Social-Democratic
deputies should be recalled from the Duma.

Ultimatumism was virtually otzovism in disguise. Lenin called the ultimatumists "bashful otzovists".

In the spring of 1909 the otzovists, ultimatumists and god-builders formed a promotion group to organise an anti-Party school on the Isle of Capri (Bogdanov, Alexinsky, Lunacharsky and others). This group, in effect, was the centre of the anti-Party faction of otzovists, ultimatumists, and god-builders.

A meeting of the extended editorial board of *Proletary* held in June 1909 adopted a decision that "Bolshevism, as a definite tendency in the R.S.D.L.P. has nothing in common with otzovism or ultimatumism" and called upon the Bolsheviks to resolutely combat this defection from revolutionary Marxism. Bogdanov (Maximov), the guiding spirit of otzovism, was expelled from the ranks of the Bolsheviks.

Later, in his book *"Left-Wing" Communism—an Infantile Disorder*, Lenin wrote that the Bolsheviks were able to make an orderly retreat and preserve their forces after the failure of the revolution because "they ruthlessly exposed and expelled the revolutionary phrase-mongers, those who did not wish to understand that one had to retreat, that one had to know how to retreat, and that one had absolutely to learn how to work legally in the most reactionary of parliaments, in the most reactionary of trade unions, co-operative and insurance societies and similar organisations" (see Vol. 31, p. 28, of this edition). p. 397

[388] The article referred to was "Revolutionary Hangover" published in *Proletary* No. 44, April 8 (21), 1909. p. 397

[389] The reference is to Kautsky's stand at the meeting of the International Socialist Bureau on October 11, 1908 on the question of the British Labour Party's membership of the Second International. This is dealt with in Lenin's article "Meeting of the International Socialist Bureau" (see Vol. 15 of this edition). p. 397

[390] *Lyubimov, A. I.* (1879-1919)—a Social-Democrat, joined the revolutionary movement in 1898. Repeatedly persecuted by the tsarist government. In 1904 was co-opted on to the C.C. of the R.S.D.L.P. Delegate of the Party's Council to the Third Congress of the R.S.D.L.P. Adopted a conciliatory stand towards the Mensheviks both after the Second Congress of the Party and during the years of reaction. p. 398

[391] See Lenin's "A Letter to the Organisers of the Party School on Capri" (Vol. 15 of this edition).

The *Capri school* was organised in 1909 on Capri (Italy) by the otzovists, ultimatumists and god builders. The meeting of the extended editorial board of *Proletary* exposed the factional anti-Bolshevik nature of the school, which was condemned and qualified as "a new centre being formed for a faction breaking away from the Bolsheviks" (see Vol. 15, p. 450, of this edition).

The school began to function in August, lectures being read by

Bogdanov, Alexinsky, Lunacharsky, Gorky, Lyadov, Pokrovsky and Desnitsky. Lenin declined the organisers' invitation that he come to Capri as a lecturer. In his letter to the school's students, who insisted on his reading a cycle of lectures to them, Lenin explained that he could not do it inasmuch as it was "a school *deliberately hidden away from the Party*" in "a remote foreign spot" and bearing a factional character. Lenin proposed to the students that they should come to Paris where they would learn real Social-Democracy instead of the "*separatist* factional '*science*'" of the otzovists and god-builders (see Vol. 15, pp. 472-78, of this edition). p. 398

[392] This refers to the Mensheviks' liquidator newspaper *Pravda*, Trotsky's factional mouthpiece, published in 1908-12. The first issues appeared in Lvov, and from No. 4 onward the paper came out in Vienna. p. 398

[393] *Zinoviev, Grigory Yevseyevich* (1883-1936)—joined the R.S.D.L.P. in 1901. From 1908 to April 1917 was an emigrant abroad, member of the editorial board of the Party's Central Organ *Sotsial-Demokrat* and of the Bolshevik newspaper *Proletary*. During the years of reaction (1907-10) and the new revolutionary upsurge he adopted a conciliatory attitude towards the liquidators, otzovists and Trotskyists. In the period of preparation and conduct of the October Revolution he wavered and was opposed to an armed uprising.

In November 1927 he was expelled from the Party for factional activities, was twice reinstated and expelled again for anti-Party activities. p. 399

[394] *Sotsial-Demokrat*—Central Organ of the R.S.D.L.P., an illegal newspaper published from February 1908 to January 1917. The editorial board, by decision of the C.C. elected at the Fifth (London) Congress of the R.S.D.L.P., was composed of representatives of the Bolsheviks, Mensheviks and Polish Social-Democrats. The paper was virtually run by Lenin. p. 399

[395] *Rech* (Speech)—a daily newspaper, Central Organ of the Cadet Party, published in St. Petersburg from February 1906. Closed down by the Military Revolutionary Committee on October 26 (November 8), 1917. p. 399

[396] The reference is to the general strike in Sweden, which broke out on August 4, 1909, following the lockout of 83,000 workers in various branches of industry, and to the revolt in Catalonia. Articles on these subjects were published in *Proletary* No. 47-48 under the headings: "Lessons of the Class Struggle (the General Strike in Sweden)", a leading article and "Colonial Robbery and Revolution". p. 399

[397] The polemic Lenin intended writing about was carried on in June and August-September 1909 in *Golos Sotsial-Demokrata*, Nos.

15 and 16-17, in connection with an article by a Geneva anti-liquidator Menshevik, apparently Victor Tevzaya (Georgien), entitled "A Word on a Topical Subject", in which he defended the idea of an illegal party and urged that the Menshevik organisations clear their ranks of the liquidator legalists. In leading articles headed "Concerning the Article of a Geneva Comrade" and "On the Organisational Discussion" the *Golos* people denied that they "winked at" liquidationism and accused the author of sectarianism. In his reply ("On the Same Subject") Georgien quoted a number of documents reflecting the activities of the liquidators in the organisations in Russia. No special article on this polemic appeared in *Proletary*. Reference to a promised analysis and evaluation of liquidator ideas "piled up" in issue No. 15 of *Golos Sotsial-Demokrata* is contained in a footnote to Lenin's article "The Liquidation of Liquidationism" (see Vol. 15, p. 460, of this edition). p. 399

[398] This refers to the contents of the current issue, No. 47-48, of *Proletary*, which published the following articles by Lenin: "The Liquidators Exposed", "On the Open Letter of the Executive Committee of the Moscow Regional Committee", and "The Elections in St. Petersburg", and to the supplement to this issue containing the article "The Faction of Supporters of Otzovism and God-Building" (see Vol. 16 of this edition) p. 399

[399] L. B. Kamenev's article on the Menshevik five-volume publication *The Social Movement in Russia at the Beginning of the Twentieth Century* edited by L. Martov, P. Maslov and A. Potresov, was published in *Proletary*, Nos. 47-48 and 49, September 5 (18) and October 3 (16), 1909. p. 400

[400] *God-builders*—adherents of a religious-philosophical trend, hostile to Marxism, which in the period of reaction (1907-10) arose among a section of the Party intellectuals who had moved away from Marxism after the defeat of the revolution of 1905-07. The god-builders advocated the creation of a new "socialist" religion and tried to reconcile Marxism with religion. An extended meeting of the editorial board of *Proletary* held on June 8-17 (21-30), 1909 condemned god-building and declared in a special resolution that the Bolshevik section of the Party had nothing in common with "such a distortion of scientific socialism". (See *the C.P.S.U. in the Resolutions and Decisions of Its Congresses, Conferences and Plenums of the Central Committee*, Part I, 1954, p. 222.)

The reactionary nature of god-building was exposed by Lenin in his book *Materialism and Empirio-criticism* (see Vol. 14 of this edition). p. 401

[401] *Dnevnik Sotsial-Demokrata* (Diary of a Social-Democrat)—a non-periodical organ published by Plekhanov in Geneva from 1905 to 1912. The last issue appeared in Petrograd in 1916. p. 402

[402] The newspaper referred to was *Proletary* (see Note 353).   p. 405

[403] *Skvortsov-Stepanov, Ivan Ivanovich* (1870-1928)—one of the oldest participants in the Russian revolutionary movement, a Marxist writer. Joined the revolutionary movement in 1892; from
the close of 1904 a Bolshevik. In 1906 a delegate to the Fourth
(Unity) Congress of the R.S.D.L.P., at which he adopted a Leninist stand. In the period of reaction (1907-10) adopted a conciliatory attitude towards the *Vperyod* faction, but under the influence
of Lenin he rectified these errors. He was repeatedly arrested and
exiled for his revolutionary activities.

   After the October Socialist Revolution he occupied important
government and Party posts.   p. 407

[404] *Liquidators*—adherents of an opportunist trend dominant among the
Mensheviks during the period of reaction following the defeat of
the first Russian revolution of 1905-07. They demanded the liquidation of the revolutionary illegal party of the proletariat and
the creation in its stead of an opportunist party operating legally
within the framework of the tsarist regime. Lenin and other Bolsheviks untiringly denounced the liquidators, who were betraying
the cause of the revolution. The Prague Conference of the R.S.D.L.P.
(January 1912) expelled the liquidators from the Party.   p. 408

[405] Meaning Stolypin's agrarian reform aimed at using the kulaks as
a bulwark of the regime in the countryside. The tsarist government issued a Ukase on November 9 (22), 1906, regulating the peasants' withdrawal from the communes and the establishment of
their proprietary rights on the allotment lands. Under this Stolypin law (which got its name from P. A. Stolypin, Chairman of the
Council of Ministers) the peasant was free to withdraw from the village commune, take possession of his allotment on a proprietor-
ship basis, and sell it. The rural community was obliged to give the
peasants who withdrew from the commune an allotment of land
in one place (an *otrub*, homestead). The Stolypin reform speeded
up the development of capitalism in the countryside and the proc-
ess of differentiation among the peasantry, and sharpened the
class struggle in the village. The Stolypin reform is characterised
and evaluated in a number of works by Lenin, notably in his
*The Agrarian Programme of Social-Democracy in the First Russian
Revolution, 1905-1907* (see Vol. 13 of this edition).   p. 408

[406] This document is the draft of a letter of Lenin's to Karl Kautsky,
Franz Mehring and Clara Zetkin, the "trustees", to whom the
funds of the Bolshevik section of the Party were handed over in
accordance with the decision of the January 1910 Plenum of the
C C. of the R.S.D.L.P. Details of this will be found in Lenin's
article "The Results of the Arbitration of the 'Trustees'" (see Vol.
17, pp. 365-67, of this edition).   p. 411

[407] Lenin is referring to the Fourth (Unity) Congress of the R.S.D.L.P.

held in Stockholm on April 10-25 (April 23-May 8), 1906, and the
Fifth (London) Congress held on April 30-May 19 (May 13-June 1),
1907.   p. 411

⁴⁰⁸ Lenin refers to the Fifth (All-Russia) Conference of the R.S.D.L.P.
which condemned liquidationism.   p. 412

⁴⁰⁹ A phrase used by Plekhanov and addressed to the newspaper of
the Menshevik liquidators *Golos Sotsial-Demokrata* (Voice of a
Social-Democrat).   p. 412

⁴¹⁰ Lenin here refers to the resolution "The State of Affairs in the
Party" adopted by the Plenum of the C.C. of the R.S.D.L.P. in
January 1910. A critical analysis of this resolution is given by
Lenin in his article "Notes of a Publicist" (see Vol. 16 of this
edition).   p. 412

⁴¹¹ The reprint from No. 12 of *Sotsial-Demokrat* for March 23 (April 5),
1910 contained Lenin's article *"Golos* (Voice) of the Liquidators
Against the Party (Reply to *Golos Sotsial-Demokrata*)" (see Vol. 16
of this edition).   p. 414

⁴¹² *Vperyodists*—adherents of the *Vperyod* anti-Party group, consisting of otzovists, ultimatumists, god-builders and empirio-monists;
organised in December 1909 on the initiative of Bogdanov and
Alexinsky; the group had its press organ of the same name. In
1912 together with the Menshevik liquidators they joined the general anti-Party bloc (the August bloc) against the Bolsheviks,
which was organised by Trotsky. Lacking support among the workers, the group virtually fell to pieces in 1913. It disintegrated
completely in 1917, after the February revolution.   p. 414

⁴¹³ In answer to this letter Plekhanov wrote on April 2, 1910: "I,
too, think, that the only way of coping with the crisis our Party
is now living through is by a close alignment among the Menshevik Marxists and the Bolshevik Marxists, and I believe that you
and I should talk this over." Plekhanov, however, wrote that this
meeting should be held later. During the Copenhagen Congress of
the Second International, at which Plekhanov and Lenin wrote
to the Executive Committee of the Social-Democratic Party of
Germany protesting against the publication in *Vorwärts* of an
anonymous and libellous article by Trotsky, an agreement was
reached between Lenin and Plekhanov for a joint struggle for the
Party and the Party principle against liquidationism and the
liquidators, and for Plekhanov's contribution to *Rabochaya
Gazeta*.   p. 416

⁴¹⁴ *Pro-Party Mensheviks*—a small group of Mensheviks headed by
Plekhanov, who broke away from the Menshevik liquidators
and came out against liquidationism in 1908-12. The resolution
here referred to was adopted by the pro-Party Mensheviks

(in Paris) on April 4, 1910, concerning the necessity of closing down the liquidator newspaper *Golos Sotsial-Demokrata* in accordance with the decision of the January 1910 Plenum of the C.C. of the R.S.D.L.P.   p. 417

[415] *Diskussionny Listok* (Discussion Bulletin) was started by decision of the January 1910 ("Unity") Plenum of the C.C. Its editorial board was composed of representatives of all the existing trends and national organisations in the Party. It appeared as a supplement to the Central Organ *Sotsial-Demokrat* in Paris from March 6 (19), 1910, to April 29 (May 12), 1911. Three issues were put out.   p. 419

[416] *Nasha Zarya* (Our Dawn)—a monthly legal journal of the Menshevik liquidators, published in St. Petersburg from 1910 to 1914. It became the centre of the liquidators in Russia.   p. 420

[417] The "Open Letter" was by a group of prominent Mensheviks, who proposed liquidating the Party.   p. 420

[418] The Party's School Committee was organised in accordance with a decision of the January 1910 ("Unity") Plenum of the C. C. of the R.S.D.L.P. and was made up of Bolsheviks, Mensheviks, Vperyodists (2 representatives each) and one representative each from the Bund, the Social-Democrats of Poland and Lithuania and the Lettish Social-Democrats. The C.C.'s Bureau Abroad was instructed "to take all steps to induce Comrade Maximov (Bogdanov) and others to give up the idea of organising a separate school and to join the organisation of the school under the C. C., in which they should be guaranteed full opportunity of applying their teaching and lecturing talents" (see *The C.P.S.U. in the Resolutions and Decisions of Its Congresses, Conferences and Plenums of the Central Committee*, Part I, 1954, p. 240).   p. 421

[419] *Semashko, Nikolai Alexandrovich* (1874-1949)—prominent Soviet statesman. Member of the Bolshevik Party since 1893. Took an active part in the revolution of 1905-07. Was arrested in 1907 by the Swiss authorities; on his release from prison he moved to Paris, where he was secretary of the Bureau Abroad of the Central Committee of the Bolshevik Party.   p. 423

[420] Here and lower down (see pp. 430-31 and 432) the reference is to arrangements for publishing abroad the Bolshevik newspaper *Rabochaya Gazeta*.   p. 423

[421] *Marchlewski, Julian* (1866-1925)—prominent member of the revolutionary movement in Poland, Germany and Russia. Was one of the organisers and leaders of the Social-Democratic Party of Poland and Lithuania. Took an active part in the revolution of 1905-07. At the Fifth (London) Congress of the R.S.D.L.P. was elected alternate member of the Central Committee. From 1909 worked chiefly in the German Social-Democratic Party. p. 424

[422] The article against Martov by Marchlewski (Karsky) was published in the journal *Die Neue Zeit* (I. Band, No. 4, October 28, 1910) under the heading: "Ein Mißverständnis" (A Misunderstanding). This article dealt with Martov's distortion of the quotation from Lenin's article and his application to the Russian revolution of 1905-07 of Kautsky's idea to the effect that "the strategy of overthrow" was inapplicable to Germany. p. 425

[423] *Quessel, L.*—German Social-Democrat, ultra-opportunist, who gave an opportunist appraisal of the revolution of 1905. p. 425

[424] *Nasha Zarya*, see Note 416.
Vozrozhdeniye (Renascence)—a legal journal of the Menshevik liquidators, published in Moscow from December 1908 to July 1910.
Zhizn (Life)—a legal socio-political journal, organ of the Menshevik liquidators, published in Moscow; two issues were put out (in August and September 1910). p. 428

[425] This refers to the controversy between Rosa Luxemburg and Karl Kautsky in the German Social-Democratic press on the question of the general political strike. The Magdeburg Congress of the German Social-Democratic Party held on September 18-24, 1910, adopted the first part of a resolution proposed by Rosa Luxemburg recognising the general political strike as a method of struggle for an electoral reform in Prussia; the part of the resolution Lenin refers to deals with the question of propaganda of the idea of a general strike. p. 429

[426] *Shklovsky, G. L.* (1875-1937)—member of the R.S.D.L.P. since 1898, carried on Party work in the towns of Byelorussia and abroad. From 1909 a political emigrant. Returned to Russia after the February bourgeois-democratic revolution of 1917; worked in Nizhni-Novgorod and Moscow.
After the October Socialist Revolution worked in Party and government institutions. p. 430

[427] Lenin's lecture tour in Switzerland evidently did not take place. p. 430

[428] In this and his next letter Lenin writes about arrangements for publishing the Bolshevik legal journal *Mysl*. p. 431

[429] Lenin's "Announcement on the Publication of *Rabochaya Gazeta*" (see Vol. 16 of this edition). *Rabochaya Gazeta* (Workers' Gazette)—an illegal popular organ of the Bolsheviks, published in Paris in 1910-12. p. 432

[430] During the International Socialist Congress in Copenhagen (August 28-September 3, 1910) Lenin and Plekhanov submitted a joint protest to the Executive of the German Social-Democratic

Party against the publication in *Vorwärts*, the Central Organ of the German Social-Democrats, of an anonymous and slanderous article penned by Trotsky concerning the state of affairs in the Russian Social-Democratic Party.

Lenin came out against this slander of Trotsky's in his article "How Certain Social-Democrats Inform the International About the State of Affairs in the R.S.D.L.P." published in the newspaper *Sotsial-Demokrat* No. 17, for September 25 (October 8), 1910, and in his article "The Historical Meaning of the Inner-Party Struggle in Russia" published in *Diskussionny Listok* No. 3, for April 29 (May 12), 1911 (see Vol. 16 of this edition).   p. 432

[431] Lenin has in mind preparations for the publication of the Bolshevik legal monthly *Mysl* (Thought), the first issue of which appeared in Moscow in December 1910. The journal was published up till April 1911, altogether five numbers being issued.

The journal was founded on Lenin's initiative to step up the fight against the liquidators' legal organs and to educate the advanced workers and intellectuals in the spirit of Marxism. Lenin directed the journal from abroad and carried on a regular correspondence with the editors.   p. 432

[432] This refers to the publication of the Bolshevik legal newspaper *Zvezda* (Star). It appeared from December 16 (29), 1910 to April 22 (May 5), 1912. Up till the autumn of 1911 the pro-Party Mensheviks (the Plekhanovites) contributed to *Zvezda*. Ideological guidance of the newspaper was effected by Lenin from abroad.   p. 433

[433] *Znaniye* (Knowledge)—a book-publishing house, founded in St. Petersburg in 1898 by a group of writers; later Maxim Gorky was closely associated with it.   p. 433

[434] *The Central Organ of the R.S.D.L.P.*, the illegal newspaper *Sotsial-Demokrat*, was published from February 1908 to January 1917 (see Note 394).   p. 433

[435] *Sovremennik* (The Contemporary)—a monthly literary and political journal, published in St. Petersburg in 1911-15. Grouped around it were Menshevik liquidators, Socialist-Revolutionaries, "Popular Socialists" and Left liberals. The journal had no ties whatever with the working-class masses. A leading role in the journal at the beginning of its existence was played by A. V. Amfiteatrov.

As a result of Lenin's letter, Gorky demanded that the words in the announcement describing him as "a regular contributor" should be deleted (see V. I. Lenin and A. M. Gorky, *Letters, Reminiscences, Documents*, Second Russ. ed., Moscow, 1961, p. 59). Gorky broke with *Sovremennik* in August 1911, but resumed his contributions in 1912 when Amfiteatrov resigned from the editorial staff.   p. 434

[436] *Vestnik Yevropy* (European Messenger)—a monthly magazine devoted to politics, history and literature, bourgeois-liberal in trend, published in St. Petersburg from 1866 to 1918.   p. 434

[437] *Russkaya Mysl* (Russian Thought)—a monthly literary and political journal published in Moscow from 1880 to 1918. Up to 1905 it was of a liberal-Narodnik trend. In the nineties it sometimes published articles of the Marxists. After the revolution of 1905 it became the organ of the Right wing of the Cadet Party. The editor was P. B. Struve.   p. 434

[438] *Russkoye Bogatstvo*. See Note 16.   p. 434

[439] *Sovremenny Mir* (The Modern World)—a monthly literary, scientific and political journal, appeared in St. Petersburg from 1906 to 1918.   p. 434

[440] See Note 391.   p. 435

[441] *Krasnoye Znamya* (Red Banner)—a bourgeois political and literary journal founded by A. V. Amfiteatrov. Published in Paris from 1906.   p. 435

[442] *Poletayev, Nikolai Gurievich* (1872-1930)—Social-Democrat, Bolshevik, a turner by trade. Took part in the workers' circles in the 1890s. Repeatedly sentenced to imprisonment. Deputy to the Third Duma from St. Petersburg Gubernia, member of the parliamentary Social-Democratic Party. Closely associated with the publication of the Bolshevik newspapers *Zvezda* and *Pravda*. After the October Socialist Revolution—a business executive.   p. 436

[443] This refers to Plekhanov's article "Karl Marx and Leo Tolstoy" published in the newspaper *Sotsial-Demokrat* No. 19-20, for January 13 (26), 1911.   p. 437

[444] *Lyakhov, V.*—a tsarist army colonel, commanded the Russian troops who suppressed the revolutionary movement in Persia in 1908.   p. 438

[445] The *Black-Hundreds* were monarchist gangs of pogromists organised by the tsarist police to fight the revolutionary movement.
Octobrists—members of the Octobrist party (or Union of October Seventeenth), a counter-revolutionary party of the big industrial bourgeoisie and landowners who engaged in capitalist farming. It was founded in November 1905. While paying lip service to the Manifesto of October 17, in which the tsar, frightened by the revolution, promised the people "civil liberties" and a constitution, the Octobrists unreservedly supported the home and foreign policies of the tsarist government. The leaders of the Octobrists were the well-known industrialist A. Guchkov and the owner of vast estates M. Rodzyanko.   p. 438

[446] Lenin is apparently referring to his book *The Agrarian Question in Russia Towards the Close of the Nineteenth Century* written in 1908 for the Granat Bros. Encyclopaedia. It was not published there for censorship reasons, and Lenin intended, as his letter indicates, to have it published by the Znaniye book publishers. However, it was first published in Moscow in 1918 as a separate booklet by the Zhizn i Znaniye Publishing House (see Vol. 15 of this edition).   p. 439

[447] The anti-Party school in Bologna (November 1910-March 1911) was a continuation of the Capri school. Lecturers at this school were Bogdanov, Lunacharsky, Trotsky, Lyadov, Maslov, Sokolov and others. An invitation to read lectures there was turned down by Lenin in view of the anti-Party tendency and splitting activities of the school's organisers. Lenin invited the students to Paris, where he promised to read them a number of lectures on the questions of tactics, the situation within the Party and the agrarian question. The lectures in Paris did not take place.   p. 440

[448] Meaning the funds on which the second Vperyodist school existed; these funds were received mainly from the Ural Party people, who carried out the Miass expropriation.   p. 442

[449] This refers to the symposium *Vperyod*, organ of the anti-Party *Vperyod* group, published in Geneva in 1910-11.   p. 442

[450] *Sovremennaya Zhizn* (Modern Life)—a Bolshevik legal journal, appeared in Baku in March-April 1911.   p. 447

[451] *Němec, Antonín* (1858-1926)—a Right Social-Democrat. From 1897 virtual leader of the Czech Social-Democrats, whom he represented in the Second International. In 1906-18 Social-Democratic deputy to the Vienna Imperial Council; in 1918-25 deputy to the National Assembly of the Czechoslovak Republic.   p. 448

[452] This refers to arrangements for the Sixth All-Russia Conference of the R.S.D.L.P., which was held in Prague on January 5-17 (18-30), 1912.
  The Czech Social-Democrats rendered great help in organising this Conference. They not only gave the premises for the Conference, but provided accommodation for the delegates in the homes of Czech workers and generally took care of the delegates. The building in which the Prague Conference was held (7, Gibern St.) is now a Lenin Museum.   p. 448

IDENTIFICATION OF PSEUDONYMS, NICKNAMES AND INITIALS USED IN THE TEXT

A. A., Al. Al.—Bogdanov A. A.
Absolute—Stasova Yelena
Akim—Goldman L. I.
Akim's Brother—Gorev-Goldman B. I.
Alexander—Kremer A. I.
Alexandrov—Postolovsky D. S.
Alexei—Martov Y. O.
A. M., Al. M.—Gorky A. M.
A. N.—Potresov A. N.
An. Al.—Lunacharskaya Anna
Andreyevsky—Ulyanov D. I.
A. P.—Potresov A. N.
Arseniev—Potresov A. N.
Auntie (*Tyotka*)—Zasulich Vera (p. 58)
Auntie—Kalmykova Alexandra (p. 164)
A. Vas., An. Vas., Anat. Vas.—Lunacharsky A. V.

B.—Andropov S. V.
Balalaikin—Trotsky L. D.
Baron—Essen E. E.
Barsov—Tskhakaya M. G.
Bear (*Medved*)—Ulyanova Maria
Beard (*Boroda*)—Desnitsky V. A.
Beast, Beastie (*Zver, Zverev, Zverushka*)—Essen Maria
Beggar (*Nishchy*)—Vinogradova Olga
Beltov—Plekhanov G. V.
Berg—Martov Y. O.
B. N.—Noskov V. A.
Bogdan—Babushkin I. V.
Bonch—Bonch-Bruyevich V. D.
Bookseller (*Knigoprodavets*)—Potresov A. N.
Boris, Boris Nikolayevich—Noskov V. A.
Bouncer (*Vyshibalo*)—Tokarev A. S.

Brodyagin—Silvin M. A.
Bruskov—Andropov S. V.
Brutus—Krzhizhanovsky G. M.
Bundist—Portnoi K.
Bychkov—Lepeshinsky P. N.

Calf (*Telyonok*)—Struve P. B.
Ch.—Smidovich P. G.
Claire—Krzhizhanovsky G. M.
Cook (*Povar*)—Shchekoldin F. I.

Danevich—Gurevich E. L.
Danila—Novomirsky D. I.
Deer (*Lan*) — Krzhizhanovsky G. M.
Delta—Stasova Yelena
Dementiev—Basovsky I. B.
Demon—Zemlyachka Rozalia
Destroyer (*Minonosets*)— Lunacharsky A. V.
Doe(*Lanikha*)—Krzhizhanovskaya Zinaida
Doctor—Gusarov F. V.
Domov—Pokrovsky M. N.
Dubois—Postolovsky D. S.
Dvinskaya — Ettinger-Davidson E. S.
Dyadin—Knipovich Lydia
Elder Sister (*Starshaya Sestra*)—Zasulich Vera

Embryon—Baramzin Y. V.
Ernest—Rollau E.

Falcon (*Sokol*)—Essen Maria
Feld—Blumenfeld I. S.
Felix—Litvinov M. M.
Fred—Vladimirov M. K.
Frey—Lenin V. I.
Frockcoat (*Syurtuk*)—Kopp V.L.

G.—Kopelson T.
Galyorka—Olminsky M. S.
Genosse—Yermansky O. A.
George—Plekhanov G. V.
Glebov—Noskov V. A.
Grigory—Zinoviev G.
Grishin—Kopelson T.
G. V.—Plekhanov G. V.
Gvozdyov—Zimmerman R. E.
Gurvich—Dan F. I.

Hairpin (*Shpilka*)—Krasikov P.A.
Handsome (*Krasavets*)—Krokhmal V. N.
Hans—Krzhizhanovsky G. M.
Heron (*Tsaplya*)—Stasova Yelena
Horse (*Loshad*)—Krasin L. B.

Ignat—Krasikov P. A.
Igor—Gorev-Goldman B. I.
Ilyin—Lenin V. I.
Inok, Innokenty— Dubrovinsky I. F.
Insarov—Lalayants I. K.
Isari—Topuridze D.

Jacques—Alexandrova Yekaterina
Josephine—Vorovsky V. V.
Judas—Struve P. B.
Julius, Yuli Osipovich—Martov Y. O.

Kamensky—Plekhanov G. V.
Karelin—Zasulich Vera
Kasyan—Radchenko I. I.
Khariton—Gusev S. I.
Kiroff—Zasulich Vera
Koltsov—Ginsburg B. A.
Konyaga, Konyagin—Galperin L. Y.
Kostrov—Jordania N.
Kurtz—Lengnik F. V.

Lebedev—Gusev S. I.
L. Gr.—Deutsch L. G.
Lidin—Lyadov M. N.
Lightmind (*Legkomyslenny*)—Lunacharsky A. V.
L. M.—Martov Y. O.
Lyova—Vladimirov M. K.
Lyubich—Sammer I. A.

M.—Vilonov N. Y.
Maria Fyodorovna—Andreyeva Maria
Mark—Lyubimov A. I.
Martyn, Martyn Nikolayevich—Lyadov M. N. (pp. 257, 269, 271, 272)
Martyn—Rozanov V.N. (pp. 200, 203, 221)
Matryona—Smidovich P. G.
Maximov—Bogdanov A. A.
Mermaid (*Rusalka*)—Lyadov M.N.
Meshkovsky—Goldenberg I. P.
Meyer—Lenin V. I.
M. F.—Andreyeva Maria
Mikhail—Vilonov N. Y. (pp. 403, 404, 406, 414)
Mikhail—Isuv I. A. (p. 420)
Mitrofan, Mitrofanov—Gusarov F. V.
Monist—Plekhanov G. V.
Monk (*Monakh*)—Yeramasov A.I.
Motya—Belopolsky I. I.
Mouse (*Mysh*)—Kulyabko P. I.
Myamlin—Essen A. M.

Nadezha—Dan F. I.
Nadya—Krupskaya Nadezhda
Natalya Ivanovna—Alexandrova Yekaterina
Nation (*Natsia*)—Gusev S. I.
Nevzorov—Steklov Y. M.
N. G.—Zhitlovsky H. I.
N. I.—Yordansky N. I. (p. 446)
N. I.—Fyodorova-Shtremer N.I. (p. 291)
Nikitich—Krasin L. B.
Nikolai—Rollau E.
Nik. Iv.—Lalayants I. Kh.
Nil—Noskov V. A.
Nina Lvovna—Essen Maria
N.—on—Danielson N. F.
Novitskaya—Babushkin I. V.
Novobrantsev—Peshekhonov A.V.

Old Believer (*Starover*)—Potresov A. N.
Old Man (*Starik*)—Lenin V. I.
Olin—Lepeshinsky P. N.
Orlovsky—Vorovsky V. V.
Orsha—Radchenko L. N.
Orthodox—Axelrod L. I.

Osip—Levitsky K. O.
Osipov—Zemlyachka Rozalia

P.—Nogin V. P.
P. A , P. Andr.—Krasikov P. A.
Pakhomy—Martov Y. O.
Pakhomy's Brother—Tsederbaum
S. O.
Pankrat—Krasikov P. A.
Papasha—Litvinov M. M.
Pavlovich—Krasikov P. A.
P. B.—Axelrod P. B. (pp. 55,
74, 81, 86, 96)
P. B.—Struve P. B. (pp. 33,
34, 35, 36, 41)
Pen (Pero)—Trotsky L. D.
Petrov, Petroff—Lenin V. I.
Poletayev—Bauman N. E.
"Praktik"—Dubrovinsky I. F.
Private (Ryadovot)—Bogdanov
A. A.
Puttman—Potresov A. N.

Rakhmetov—Bogdanov A. A.
Rakhmetova—Bogdanova Natalia
Rashid-Bek—Zurabov A. G.
Raznotsvetov—Blumenfeld I. S.
Reinert—Bogdanov A. A.
R. N. S.—Struve P. B.
Roman—Yermolayev K. M.
Rook (Grach)—Bauman N. E.
Rosa—Zemlyachka Rozalia
(p. 250)
Rosa—Luxemburg Rosa
Ru—Galperin L. Y.
Ruben—Knunyants B. M.

Samovarov—Nogin V. P.
Schmidt—Rumyantsev P. P.
Schwarz—Vorovsky V. V.
Serafima—Afanasieva Sophia
Sergei Petrovich—Krasikov P. A.
She—Gorev-Goldman B. I.
Simonov—Gutovsky V. A.
Skaldin—Yelenev F. P.
Smith—Krzhizhanovsky G. M.
Sokolovsky—Makhlin L. D.
Sommer—Lyubimov A. I.
Stake (Kol)—Lengnik F. V.
Stanislav—Sokolov A. V.
Stroyev—Desnitsky V. A.
Sysoika—Bogdanov A. A.

Teacher of Life (Uchitel Zhizni)—
Sponti Y. I.
Tick (Kleshch)—Bibikov I. I.
Travinsky—Krzhizhanovsky G.M.
Tria—Mgeladze V. D.
Tsvetov—Blumenfeld I. S.
Tu—ra—Stopani A. M.
2a3b—Lepeshinsky P. N.

Uncle—Knipovich Lydia

Vadim—Noskov V. A.
Valentin—Galperin L. Y.
Vanya—Krasnukha V. P.
Varvara Ivanovna—Stasova Yele-
na
Vasiliev—Lengnik F. V.
Vas. Vas., Vasily Vasilievich—
Olminsky M. S.
Velika, Velika Dmitrievna—Za-
sulich Vera
V. I. V. Iv.—Zasulich Vera
V. I—n—Ivanshin V. P.
Vlas—Rerikh A. F.
Voinov—Lunacharsky A. V.
Volgin—Plekhanov G. V.
V. U.—Lenin V. I.
Vyach—Rozhkov N. A.

Werner—Bogdanov A. A.
Winter—Krasin L. B.
Wolf—Lengnik F. V.
Wood (Derevo)—Dan F. I.

X.—Knipovich Lydia

Yablochkov—Nogin V. P.
Yakov—Tsederbaum S. O.

Yegor—Martov Y. O.
Yeryoma—Shneerson A. A.
Yevgeny—Vulpe I. K.
Y. O.—Martov Y. O.
Yurdanov—Yordansky N. I.
Yuri—Bronstein P. A.
Yuriev—Vecheslov M. G.
Zarin—Lengnik F. V.
Zernova—Essen Maria
Zverev—Essen Maria
ZZ—Lalayants I. Kh.

ъ/з—Galperin L.Y.

В. И. ЛЕНИН
СОЧИНЕНИЯ
Том 34

На английском языке

Printed in the Union of Soviet Socialist Republics